THE TRUTH ABOUT YOUR FUTURE

THE MONEY GUIDE

YOU NEED NOW, LATER, AND MUCH LATER

Advance Praise for
The Truth About Your Future

"Brilliant! As Singularity University's Founding Track Chair of Finance and Economics, I am blown away by how completely Ric Edelman has nailed the essential lessons of Singularity University and applied them directly to everyday life. Filled with facts, but written in a breezy, conversational style, *The Truth About Your Future* is without question the best introduction yet written to the thundering changes that are right ahead of us. It's the first book to put exponential technological change into the context of today's life. If you want to understand why the world seems to be changing all around you—and wonder how this will affect you in the next year, decade and century—look no further than this monumentally important guide. *The Truth About Your Future* should be mandatory reading for everyone who plans to live longer than . . . tomorrow. An absolute "must read"—it is an indispensable guide for living in the 21st century. *The Truth About Your Future* is more than just truth; it is gospel. Ric Edelman's *The Truth About Your Future* is a monumentally important book that should be read and reread by anyone who wants to know what the world of tomorrow will be like! You owe it to yourself, your spouse and your children to read this book cover to cover . . . and then read it again."

David S. Rose, *New York Times* bestselling author of *Angel Investing* and *The Startup Checklist* and Founding Track Chair for Finance, Entrepreneurship & Economics at Singularity University

"In his highly approachable book, Ric Edelman provides deep insights into exponential technologies and the disruptions they cause as the exponential reaches the knee of the curve, which is now happening in one field after another. He provides outstanding, specific and actionable advice to be the beneficiary of our transformed future, and in particular in an era of ever faster change."

Ray Kurzweil, Inventor, author and futurist

"Baby Boomers are facing a future no prior generation ever contemplated. Yesterday's model of retirement is being replaced with new opportunities and many new challenges. You can expect to live longer and healthier than you ever expected, with important implications for your finances. In Ric Edelman's profound new book, you not only get a glimpse of what the future holds, you get the insights you need to help you thrive in the 21st century. This visionary book is an essential aid to help you prepare for every aspect of your personal finances."

Ken Dychtwald, Ph.D., CEO of Age Wave, psychologist, gerontologist and author of *Age Wave; A New Purpose: Redefining Money, Family, Work, Retirement and Success, Healthy Aging;* and *Gideon's Dream: A Tale of New Beginnings**

"If you're interested in taking control of your financial future, this book is a must-read. In his signature style, Ric Edelman expertly demystifies the unfamiliar topic of Exponential Technologies and the impact that advances in computing, big data and biotechnology will have on our lives. Ric sees a future where we live longer and heathier lives that break from the traditional path of college, career, marriage, kids and retirement. This book is a powerful tool to help you achieve the financial agility needed to navigate our ever-evolving world. Your future self will thank you."

Tom Nally, President, TD Ameritrade Institutional

"Ric Edelman's breakthrough thinking in *The Truth About Your Future: The Money Guide You Need Now, Later, and Much Later* gives us the gift of exploring how technology is changing the landscape of personal finance."

Bernie Clark, Executive Vice President, Schwab Advisor Services

"At last, a financial guide to the singularity! This is the first book to explain how exponential technologies are dramatically changing our understanding of the future, and how to survive and thrive in this new era. Ric Edelman cuts through the technobabble and gives unique advice relevant to the future as it will actually be. He gives example after example of how the world is changing exponentially. Then he tells us the best strategies to take advantage of the coming changes. Unique, comprehensive, practical, and fun to read!"

Robert A. Freitas Jr., winner of the 2009 Feynman Prize in Nanotechnology for Theory, Senior Research Fellow, Institute for Molecular Manufacturing, and author of *Nanomedicine*

"*The Truth About Your Future* gives you the specific, practical advice you need to put into place right now. This book is a must-read book. A true eye-opener!"

"Ric's new book is spot-on both in terms of timing and topic. From all the possible impact XT is gaining there is one that we're all going to benefit from: health(care). As the ongoing enrollment of XTt is delocalizing, democratizing, digitizing health(care) and will be more and more about dollars (hence my 4D approach) as it is a growing 'market' for many. At this very moment we see pre-paradigmshift signals coming up by the day, and Ric's books touches many of them. A guide into society of the future!"

"Self-driving cars, 3D printing, genome engineering and other exponential technologies are rapidly changing the rules of transportation, manufacturing, medicine—even finance! Planning your financial investments without consideration for these seismic shifts is like navigating an unfamiliar metropolis without GPS. Ric Edelman's *The Truth About Your Future* dares to drink from the firehose of data on these technologies and distill it into understandable and actionable personal finance insights. It's an essential and timely read."

"This is not only Ric Edelman's best book yet, it's the most important book he's ever written. Everyone needs to read it—not just consumers, for whom he wrote this book, but the entire financial planning profession and financial services industry, as well as Washington policymakers. In *The Truth About Your Future*, Ric makes a convincing case for the importance of thinking about financial planning in a completely new way—all due to rapidly changing technological advances that few outside of Silicon Valley are aware of. Ric's book is certain to start a national dialogue. And consumers who read this book now get a head start, helping them with their own situation. Indeed, Ric has created a new path that many would be wise to follow."

"Exponential technologies will dramatically impact every facet of our society, perhaps none more so than the world of finance. Ric Edelman's latest book serves as the people's financial sherpa guiding them on how 21st-century technologies will impact both their wallets and their families. Ric does an outstanding job of translating complex scientific topics into simple language we can all understand. *The Truth About Your Future* is an indispensable guide for those who want to know how rapidly emerging technologies will impact the global economy and personal finance. Read it today—the future will be here quicker than you think."

> **Marc Goodman**, founder, Future Crimes Institute, is a global strategist and consultant on cybercrime, cyberterrorism and information warfare, former Senior Advisor to INTERPOL, and former Senior Researcher for the United Nations Counter-Terrorism Task Force

"A good financial advisor must be steeped in asset allocation, risk management, and goal setting, but for that advice to be truly useful, it must be tailored not only to the individual, but to the world that they will inhabit. In short, great financial advisors must be futurists, analyzing changes in technology, health care, and society in order to anticipate clients' future needs. To that end, Ric Edelman's new guide will open many eyes to both the future's opportunities and its potential dark side."

> **Don Phillips**, Managing Director, Morningstar

"In his signature provocative style Edelman here lays out for readers the unforeseen—and in some cases unwelcome—implications of exponential technologies' inevitable incursion into everyday life. With thoughtful depth he examines how both savvy consumers and the financial services industry in general will have to adapt. It is a stimulating, enlightening, valuable read—Bravo!"

> **Sterling Shea**, Associate Publisher, head of Advisory Programs, *Barron's*

"Ric Edelman's book takes personal finance into the real world of today, by focusing on how people must prepare for the likelihood that the won't just change jobs, but will change careers; how they must be prepared for living longer than any past generation; and how they should evaluate the growing number of options that exist for retirement living. This is a must-read book for everyone who hopes one day to enjoy retirement."

> **Don Farish**, President, Roger Williams University

"Ric Edelman has presented an extremely thoughtful analysis of exponential technologies, and their wide ranging implications on personal finance. This book will help you assess the future through a new lens."

> **Jeffrey Goldstein**, Ph.D., Managing Director, Hellman & Friedman, former Under Secretary of the Treasury and former Chief Financial Officer of the World Bank.
> Dr. Goldstein serves on the Edelman Financial Services board of directors.

"Ric explores how tech and social factors converge to shape our lives in strange and powerful ways, in this indispensable guide to your financial future."

> **Nell Watson**, Associate Faculty, Artificial Intelligence Department, Singularity University, and Senior Advisor to The Future Society at Harvard University

"The world is changing faster than most people realize, and the idea of a traditional 20th-century retirement is over. In this book, Ric Edelman explains in detail how exponential technologies are disrupting the status quo and how you can adapt your life to benefit from it."

> **Evan Simonoff**, Editorial Director, *Financial Advisor* magazine

"Exponential technologies impact all of us and Ric redefines how we plan for our financial futures. Concise, easy to read and gives you the information you need to make solid, long-term financial decisions."

> **R.J. Shook**, President & Founder, SHOOK Research

"One of the major challenges for investors today is planning for longer retirements. Ric looks at the technologies and trends that may begin to shape how investors plan for lifetime income needs that are far different from those of past generations."

> **David Booth**, Chairman and Co-CEO, Dimensional Fund Advisors

"Ric Edelman's new book, *The Truth About Your Future*, brings important financial planning insights to the masses in a way that is remarkably refreshing and simple to understand and use. This book is a must-read for those concerned about their future finances."

> **Dr. Ali A. Houshmand**, President, Rowan University

"People are living and working longer, making it more important than ever to plan, as Ric says, "for now, later and much later." What sets this book apart is Ric's description of how exponential technologies will impact you. This book can help you (and your future self) manage the evolving landscape."

Don M. Blandin, President and CEO, Investor Protection Trust

"Exponentially changing technologies are fundamentally transforming all aspects of society. Ric Edelman expertly analyses the implications for finance in general, and your pocketbook in particular. Short, medium, and long-term financial planning cannot be based on business-as-usual; it must be based on business-as-exponential and anticipate new opportunities and threats in the radically different world of the future."

Nicholas Haan, Ph.D. Faculty Chair, Global Grand Challenges Singularity University

Also by Ric Edelman

The Truth About Retirement Plans and IRAs

Rescue Your Money

The Lies About Money

What You Need to Do Now

Discover the Wealth Within You

Ordinary People, Extraordinary Wealth

The New Rules of Money

The Truth About Money

THE TRUTH ABOUT
YOUR
FUTURE

THE MONEY GUIDE
YOU NEED NOW,
LATER, AND MUCH LATER

Ric Edelman

Simon & Schuster

New York   London   Toronto   Sydney   New Delhi

Simon & Schuster
1230 Avenue of the Americas
New York, NY 10020

First Simon & Schuster hardcover edition February 2017

SIMON & SCHUSTER and colophon are registered trademarks of Simon & Schuster, Inc.

For information about special discounts for bulk purchases, please contact Simon & Schuster Special Sales at 1-866-506-1949 or business@simonandschuster.com.

The Simon & Schuster Speakers Bureau can bring authors to your live event. For more information or to book an event contact the Simon & Schuster Speakers Bureau at 1-866-248-3049 or visit our website at www.simonspeakers.com.

Interior design by Ric Edelman, Andrew Makowski and Christine Janaske

Manufactured in the United States of America

10 9 8 7 6 5 4 3 2 1

Library of Congress Cataloging-in-Publication Data has been applied for.

ISBN 978-1-5011-6380-7
ISBN 978-1-5011-6382-1 (ebook)

To those supporting STEAM education,
and to our nation's students who are planning on
careers in science, technology, engineering,
the arts and mathematics.

You represent the future, and
the future is everything.

CONTENTS

CONTENTS

Acknowledgments

Writing is regarded as a solo activity, but the following list demonstrates how dependent I have been on others in my efforts to produce this book. I am grateful for the extensive support and assistance I received from everyone named below. And it never ceases to amaze me how many people it takes to publish a book!

Dozens of staff members of Edelman Financial Services read the initial manuscript; their collective comments led me to almost completely rewrite the book—demonstrating the importance of asking for (and receiving) honest critiques. Those who read the initial manuscript were Aaron Rowe, Bill Hayes, Brett Conlon, Catherine Caceres, Christine Janaske, Cristina Lipson, Eraine Parker, James Mendelsohn, John Cobb, Joe Bottazzi, Kala Payne, Liz Dougherty, Maribeth Bluyus, Matt Coughlin, Michael Newhouse, Mike Attiliis, Mike Gifford, Nate Jencks, Niambi Winter, Rene Chaze, Rosa Wray and Tom Begley.

They weren't the only ones who read the first draft; dozens of my firm's financial planners also studied the manuscript—and as you might expect, their redlines appeared on almost every page. These colleagues are Alan Wheedleton, Ashley Zephir, Beth London, Bob Andreola, Brad Hartzel, Brian Amper, Brian Lipps, Brian McGuire, Brian Mueller, Cathy Jones, Christine Wessinger, Clay Ernst, Corbin Dunn, Corey Fast, David Balestriere, David Heinemann, David Lubitz, David Morgan, Douglas Ulrich, Erich Hoffman, Gary Riederman, George Dougherty, Greg Grasso, James Selu, Jason Fang, Jay Mendela, JB Liebstein, Jeanne Baldwin, Jennifer Sevier, Jeremy Albrecht, Jesse Wilson, John McCafferty, John Sperger, Karen Morse, Ken Murray, Kevin Colleran, Kevin Yorkey, Lakeisha Hill, Linda Campbell, Loran Coffman, Lori Bensing, Mary Ellen Nicola, Matt Cuiffo, Matt Duskey, Michael Horne, Michael Krowe, Michelle Muhammed, Noah French, Peter Holliday, Rachel Vivian, Rey Roy, Rick Mueller, Ruth Sully, Sal Marino, Scott Butera, Sean Wintz, Seth Kelly, Steve Bermack, Surendra Dave, Tom Wood, Troy Wyman and Yolanda Waters.

ACKNOWLEDGMENTS

(In case you haven't noticed, we list ourselves by first names in our staff directories!)

Because my revision was so extensive—rearranging massive portions of the text, altering key passages, adding chapters and more—I needed volunteers to read it *again*. Lots of people stepped up, meaning they read the manuscript twice! Those folks were Anna Dawson, Aric Jacobson, Brad Parker, Christine Cataldo, Dave Eelman, Denise Zuchelli, Ed Moore, Ed Schweitzer, Keith Spengel, Lesley Roberts, Mike Lewis and Ryan Parker. Lots of our financial planners did likewise, including Adam Karron, Alan Facey, Alexis McComb, Alfonso Burgos, Anderson Wozny, Andrew Coyne, Andrew Massaro, Ann Crehan, Aura Carmi, Bill Hoffman, Brandon Corso, Brendan McGillick, Caitlin Chen, Carl Sanger, Carlos Rodriguez, Charlie Nardiello, Chris Davidson, Daniel Lennon, David Sheehan, David Skolnik, Diane Jensen, Doug Rabil, Edward Hungler, Edward Swikart, Eric Lasso, Fahima Shaw, Fearghal O'Riain, Frances Martin-Falanga, Jack London, Jan Kowal, Jason Cowans, Joanna Cecilia-Fleming, John M. Davis, Jonathan Saxon, Kevin Garvey, Kevin Maguire, Lisa Eitzel, Marcelle Belisle, Mariah DeHaven, Mark Palmer, Mary Caruso, Mary Davis, Matt Hickes, Nick Friedman, Patrick Day, Rick Fletcher, Rob Steczkowski, Robert Sisti, Ron Sisk, Ryan Poirier, Stuart Berrin, Todd Hillstead and Valentino Taddei.

As you'll see, most sentences contain facts—data I've been collecting for more than seven years. That means a lot of my information was outdated, necessitating a massive hunt for current information. Many of those data points were researched by Mitch York and Eric Olsen, while other members of my team verified every fact and statistic. This highly detailed effort was performed by Craig Engel, Emily Peters, Julia Mazina, Kristin Oakley, Kristin Rafferty, Mark Guarino, Shateela Winters, Terence Downie and Tracy Cigarski. And because I ended up rewriting the book, the team had to endure a second round of this effort, and it was performed by Emily Peters, Julia Mazina, Liz Dougherty, Mark Guarino and Tracy Cigarski.

The layout, based on my design, was completed by Christine Janaske and Andrew Makowski. Julia Mazina and Tracy Cigarski obtained all image permissions, and Rob Steczkowski trekked the streets of New York for a photo I couldn't find elsewhere (sorry, Rob, but I ended up finding it in the Caribbean islands).

I also wish to thank Paul Blumstein, a longtime client who dutifully collects cartoons for me. You'll find many of his discoveries throughout these pages.

Perhaps the most difficult element of this project was coordinating everyone's activities, and getting everyone's contributions within our tight production deadlines. Production management and coordination was masterfully performed by the director of my office, Liz Dougherty (who also read the manuscript and participated in the fact-checking effort), ably assisted by her assistant, Tracy Cigarski, and Rosa Wray.

I'm also thankful to my longtime agent, Gail Ross, and to the team led by Executive Editor Ben Loehnen at Simon & Schuster, which included Assistant Editor Amar Deol, Managing Editor Kristen Lemire, Assistant Managing Editor Amanda Mulholland, Senior Production Manager Beth Maglione, Copyediting Manager Jonathan Evans and Director of Copyediting Navorn Johnson.

I'm also grateful to the folks at exponential technologies' "ground zero"—Singularity University—and in particular Cofounder and Chancellor Ray Kurzweil (who introduced me to the field), Founding Executive Director and Global Ambassador Salim Ismail and CEO Rob Nail. I'm also grateful to faculty members Dan Barry (former NASA astronaut), Marc Goodman (chair, Policy, Law & Ethics), Nicholas Haan (chair, Global Grand Challenges), Neil Jacobstein (chair, Artificial Intelligence & Robotics), Dan Kraft (chair, Medicine & Neuroscience), Gregg Maryniak (cochair, Energy & Environmental Systems and Space), Raymond McCauley (chair, Digital Biology), Avi Reichental (3D Manufacturing), Kathryn Myronuk (chair emeritus, Finance and Economics), Ramez Naam (cochair, Energy & Environmental Systems), Brad Templeton (chair, Networks & Computing Systems) and Andrew Hessel (Medicine).

My biggest thanks go to my wife, Jean, who (for the ninth time) put up with me as I sequestered myself to write (and rewrite) the book. Her love and support are responsible for everything I do. She completely transcends for me anything that any technology might ever deliver.

Finally, a shout-out to Lucas B., age 14, who noticed that my cousins, Jill and Jenna (then ages 12 and 10), got their names in the acknowledgment of *The Lies About Money* by each paying me a dollar. Wanting to replicate their feat but determined to outdo them, Lucas paid me two dollars. That's good enough to get his last initial published.

Foreword

By Peter H. Diamandis

There is no question that we live in exciting, but tumultuous times.

But rather than believing the future is bleak, I am convinced that the future will be filled with increasing abundance.

It will also be unlike anything you expect it to be. And that's why I'm so excited about the book that's in your hands.

Let me explain. I've devoted my career and professional life to helping make the world a better place. The XPRIZE Foundation that I founded in 1994 resulted less than a decade later in the first private manned space flight in history, and SpaceShipOne now resides in the Smithsonian Institution alongside Charles Lindbergh's *Spirit of St. Louis*. Other XPRIZES produced the first car capable of exceeding 100 MPG-equivalent and a device that cleans oil spills 600 percent better than before, and future XPRIZEs will create global solutions in health care, environmental protection, education and more.

Along the way, I've met and nurtured hundreds of entrepreneurs and technologists who are changing the world for the better. Singularity University (SU), which Ray Kurzweil and I co-founded in 2008 at the NASA AMES Research Park in Silicon Valley, has become a "ground zero" of sorts for the study of exponential technologies and their impact.

It's there that I first met Ric Edelman. He graduated from SU's Executive Program in 2012, and Ray and I were so impressed that we invited Ric to become an investor in SU and to join us as a guest lecturer—something we've offered rarely to our graduates.

Since then, Ric helped us bring a new program, Exponential Finance, to New York, to introduce exponential technologies to executives in the brokerage, investment, banking, insurance and credit-card industries. Ric and I appeared together at the inaugural event in 2014, and he has spoken at each event ever since.

The reason I'm so enthused about this book—and the reason I'm excited that you're reading it—is because Ric offers information and a perspective I've not found elsewhere within the study of exponential technologies. While I and others have written extensively about accelerating technologies, Ric's book takes a different approach: It distills the broad landscape of technology to reveal its impact on you and your life, helping you to understand the implications of exponential technologies on your personal finances.

Where my best-selling book *Abundance: The Future Is Better Than You Think* shows why the world is getting better, Ric—using his expertise in personal finance—reveals his conclusions about how the coming changes are going to impact your life. Within these pages, you'll discover why the emerging importance of lifelong learning and career planning; how your strategies for housing and home ownership, estate planning, long-term care, insurance, and investment management all need to be modified and updated to adjust for the fact that you are likely to live far longer—and far healthier—than you ever imagined.

Indeed, Ric makes a compelling case that traditional financial planning advice is outdated, and why you should build not one but three financial plans—for now, for later and for much later—to help you achieve and sustain the lifestyle you want for yourself and your family. Ric shares his wisdom so you can consider how social, political, economic and environmental changes might affect your job, your home, your relationships, your health—and of course, your wealth.

If you're new to the notion of exponential technologies, you'll find this book eye-opening. And as you read it, you can be sure that what you're reading is indeed *The Truth About Your Future.*

Abundantly yours,

Peter H. Diamandis, MD
Founder & Exec. Chairman, XPRIZE Foundation
Founder & Exec. Chairman, Singularity University
Cofounder, Human Longevity Inc. (HLI)
Author of the *New York Times* best sellers *Abundance* and *BOLD*

Preface

I have written eight books on financial planning, offering advice on virtually every aspect of your personal finances. Why write another one?

For just one reason: to tell you that your efforts to prepare yourself and your family for the future could fail if you don't alter your personal finance strategies.

I realize this is a bold statement. But my research of the past seven years has convinced me that you must adopt a completely new perspective.

Here's the problem: If you're like most people, you assume you'll remain in your current occupation until you retire in your sixties or seventies and that you'll live until your eighties or nineties. Along the way, you will send your children to college and possibly incur long-term care costs before passing your assets to your surviving spouse and children. Life has been this way for generations, so most people believe it will be this way for them, too.

But for a great many people—probably including you—this scenario is wrong.

The reason? My research has convinced me that the world will be completely different in the future.

This requires a radical change in thinking. Consider your mother when she was age 50 versus when she was 70. Big changes in her health, occupation and income during those 20 years, right? But the world she lived in probably didn't change much at all. She shopped the same way, enjoyed leisure the same way, traveled the same way, got medical care the same way and so on.

But you won't have the same experience. Your world will be vastly different 20 years from now—and that's why I'm writing this book. I'm going to show you the future.

More precisely, I'm going to show you your future and that of your kids and grandkids. As a result, you'll find advice within these pages that no financial planner has ever offered you.

A lot of what you're about to read will therefore be shocking, completely contradictory to your current thinking. But much of what you're about to discover will also make you excited, even joyful. Some parts might upset or worry you—and you'll flatly dispute some of the statements you're about to read. But rest assured: Any disdain or skepticism will eventually give way to acceptance. And through it all, this book will be fascinating to read.

Anyway, that emotional experience has been my journey over the past seven years. In addition to operating my growing financial planning firm—now one of the nation's largest—I've devoted a substantial amount of time since 2010 to studying the future. In addition to reading pretty much every book I can find on the topic and interviewing dozens of experts in the field (many of whom have been guests on my radio and television shows), I graduated from Singularity University's Executive Program in 2012 (and subsequently accepted its invitation to become a guest lecturer and investor).

Unlike others, my interest in the future has been focused on one question: Is the financial planning and investment management advice my colleagues and I give our clients still valid, and if not, how must our advice change?

This is a pretty important question. And now, after more than seven years of study, I present the answers to you in this book.

In the pages that follow, you'll learn why you and your children should not spend—and shouldn't even plan on spending—hundreds of thousands of dollars on a college education. You'll discover that your job is likely to disappear and learn how to prepare for your next career—and the one after that. You'll understand why you probably shouldn't pay for long-term care insurance and why you won't need auto insurance. You'll see how longer life spans will end retirement as you know it, cause people to marry later in life and more often (creating complications for estate planning) and introduce new concepts of leisure and recreation. And perhaps most important, you'll realize a fundamental mistake you're making with your investments—and how to fix it so your portfolio will be designed to meet your needs in the future that you're going to live in.

As you read this book, please keep one important fact in mind: I am a financial planner and investment advisor. What I mean is, I am not a scientist. So if you are a scientist, please excuse me if some of the text isn't as descriptive or detailed as you might like. This is a book for everyday people, not a journal for scholars.

Just tryin' to set expectations.

Predict Your Future

Your future consists, probably, of working in your current field until you retire.	☐ True	☐ False	☐ n/a
You'll probably retire in your 60s or early 70s.	☐ True	☐ False	☐ n/a
In retirement, all or almost all of your income will probably come from some combination of Social Security, a pension, investments and savings.	☐ True	☐ False	☐ n/a
You'll probably live until your 80s or 90s.	☐ True	☐ False	☐ n/a
As you age, chronic health issues will probably develop or worsen.	☐ True	☐ False	☐ n/a
If you'd like to travel during retirement, you probably need to do so during the earlier part of your retirement, rather than the latter part, for reasons of stamina and health—either yours or your spouse/partner's.	☐ True	☐ False	☐ n/a
At some point in the future, either for your needs or those of your spouse/partner, you'll probably need to sell your house and move to an independent living community, assisted care facility or nursing home.	☐ True	☐ False	☐ n/a
When you pass, your death will probably be due to heart disease or stroke; cancer; respiratory disease, influenza or pneumonia; Alzheimer's disease; or diabetes, as these illnesses account for 65% of all deaths in the United States.	☐ True	☐ False	☐ n/a

Did you answer "true" to many of the above statements? If so, get ready for a shock, because the answer to all the above is probably false. Indeed, for reasons this book will reveal, you are not likely to ever retire—but you probably won't keep working in your current field, either. That means you'll need more education and training. You can also expect that you'll live well into your 100s—120 is not unrealistic—and that your health will improve as you age, meaning you'll probably be as healthy and fit at age 95 as at 55. You can probably forget about living in a nursing home, therefore, and it's highly unlikely that you'll die from today's leading causes of death. Instead, accidents will be the most common cause of death (already ranked #4, according to the Centers for Disease Control and Prevention). Yes, bad luck and stupidity will be among the leading causes of death.

Surprised to hear all this? So is everyone else. That's why you need to read this book—so you can learn *The Truth About Your Future*.

Come, and discover: what the future holds for your career, how to get the education you'll need to earn an income, where you'll live, how you'll manage your investments, whether you need long-term care insurance, and how to design an estate plan that meets your and your family's changing dynamics.

In short, as baseball great Yogi Berra said, "The future ain't what it used to be."

Prologue:
Why Yogi Berra Was Right

Financial planning is all about anticipating and preparing for the future. So to understand what your future will be like, you need to understand why it's going to be so radically different from what you've been assuming.

The reason is technology. And not just ordinary technology but exponential technologies—innovations that are advancing at rates of exponential growth. These include artificial intelligence, machine learning, nanotechnology and materials science, augmented and virtual reality, robotics, 3D printing, bionics, bioinformatics, medicine and neuroscience, energy and environmental systems, big data, education technology, leisure and recreation and financial technology.

And what an impact they will have. They'll affect virtually every aspect of your life— your education, occupation, residence, income, expenses, marital status, health, avocations and life expectancy. Therefore, to improve your strategies for college planning, retirement planning and estate planning, as well as your decisions about insurance and investment management, you need to understand exponential technologies.

So although this book is ostensibly about financial planning, it begins as an exploration of exponential technologies. Our tour will explain them and reveal their implications for you and your personal finances—implications that will affect you, your spouse, your children and your grandchildren *now*, *later* and *much later*.

The Two Laws of Exponential Technologies

To frame our conversation, let's explore Moore's Law and Dator's Law. You're probably familiar with the first, created by Intel cofounder Gordon Moore in 1966: A computer's speed doubles and its price drops by one-half every 24 months.[1] The result, as you can see in Figure P.1, is that transistors have been steadily shrinking in size—boosting computer processing speeds and collapsing the cost.

Incidentally

IBM's first PC, launched in 1981, contained a computer chip of 29,000 transistors—compared to 12 billion transistors found on the Titan X chip released by Nvidia in 2016.

Although Moore's Law is well known, its implications are not. Based on the reactions I've gotten from the thousands of people who have attended my presentations on this subject at seminars and conferences around the country, it's safe to say you're going to be astonished by what you're about to read. In fact, your initial response to much of this information may be *"Ridiculous!"*

Which brings us to Dator's Law.

Created by Jim Dator, Director of the Hawaii Research Center for Future Studies at the University of Hawaii at Manoa, Dator's Law states, "Any useful statement about the future should appear to be ridiculous."[2]

For example, wanna see a glow-in-the-dark cat?

Yeah, that's a ridiculous question. Except it isn't. There are such cats[3]—they were created by scientists in South Korea. Researchers were trying to understand how the AIDS virus had jumped from primates to humans, so they implanted into a cat's embryo the gene that lets a jellyfish produce phosphorescence—and, voilà, you get a glow-in-the-dark cat. This research was instrumental in helping scientists convert AIDS from a fatal disease into a chronic illness.

---

[1] It's since been updated to reflect actual results over the past 50-plus years: doubling occurs every 18 months, not 24, and prices drop about 30% every year, not 50% every two years. In other words, the rate of acceleration has been accelerating.

[2] Unlike Kepler's laws of planetary motion, Newton's laws of gravity and Einstein's theory of general relativity, neither Moore's nor Dator's law is an actual physical law. Moore and Dator are talking about commerce and consumer behavior, not physics. In other words, they're making a point—not describing immutable fact.

[3] I would display a photo of one here, but presenting the photo in black and white wouldn't do the image justice. Google it.

TRANSISTORS ARE SHRINKING

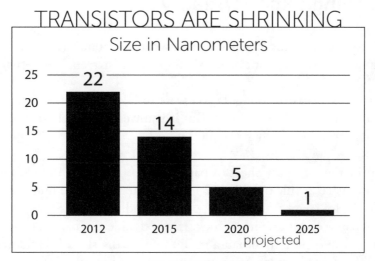

FIGURE P.1

COMPUTER SPEED IS RISING

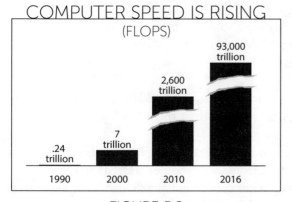

FIGURE P.2

COMPUTER COST IS COLLAPSING

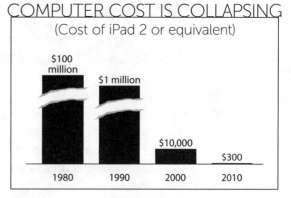

FIGURE P.3

By the way, glow-in-the-dark cats are soooo 2007. Yep, the technology that produced them is more than 10 years old! Wait 'til you see what researchers in this field are doing now (more on that in chapter 6).

Keep Dator's Law in mind as you read (I'll give you an occasional helpful reminder), because you are almost certain to wake the person sleeping next to you with periodic exclamations of "That's ridiculous!"

Understanding Exponentiality

You're used to counting linearly—one, two, three, four, five, six. But when counting exponentially, we count one, two, four, eight, sixteen, thirty-two.

The difference is astonishing. If you were to take 30 linear steps, you would travel a distance of about 80 feet. But if you were to travel 30 exponential steps, you would travel more than 665,000 miles!

Or consider an ordinary sheet of paper. It's 0.003606 inch thick. Two pieces of paper are twice as thick: 0.007212 inch. If you double the number of pages 9 times (two, four, eight, sixteen, 32, 64, 128, ending with 256 pages) you'll have a stack of paper about one inch thick. If you double the pages 20 times, you'll have so many—more than half a million—that the stack laid sideways on a football field would reach from one goal post to the other. If you double the number of pages 39 times, your stack would encircle the globe with plenty left over, and if you double number of pages just 51 times you'd have a pile of paper so high you could reach from the earth to the sun—and come halfway back again! A mere tripling of the doublings[4] takes you from a football field to the sun! That's the power of exponentiality.

This is not just theoretical. Exponential growth is how the 2016 iPad Mini was able to have 50,000 times more computing power than the 1986 space shuttle.

As Moore's Law dictates, computers are not only getting exponentially faster, they're getting exponentially cheaper, too. Consider Google's 3D LIDAR Sensor, the technology behind its self-driving cars. That sensor cost $75,000 in 2007. By 2016, the cost had dropped to $250, and Velodyne, a manufacturer, expects the price to be $100 by 2020—and that might prove to be too conservative an estimate. That's because MIT researchers in 2016 created a LIDAR system that fits on a dime and has no moving parts. They say it can be mass-produced for $10 apiece.

Or consider the digital camera. In 1976, it weighed four pounds, shot photos of only 0.01 megapixel and cost $10,000. Today, digital cameras weigh less than a quarter of a pound, feature 10-plus megapixels and cost under $10. Resolution, weight and price is each 1,000 times as good—and still improving. That's how you're able to have a camera inside your phone.

---

[4]You following this?

If exponentiality doesn't roll off the tongue, let's change to *the power of compound growth.*

"'A penny saved is a penny earned'? What are you, some kind of nut?"
© 2010; reprinted courtesy of Bunny Hoest

Ah, now, *that's* familiar. Sure, you know that a penny saved is a penny earned—Ben Franklin said so. So let's apply compound growth (exponentiality) to Ben's penny. If we double its value every day for seven days, the penny grows to 64 cents, as Figure P.4 shows. After 14 days, the penny is worth about $80. After three weeks, it's worth more than $10,000, and after 31 days it's worth $10 million!

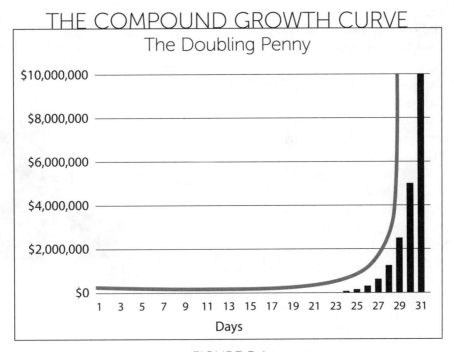

FIGURE P.4

Of course, you can't actually convert a penny into $10 million in just 31 days. So how is it possible to double our computer capabilities every 24 months?

The answer is information. Unlike commerce, information feeds on itself. To see what I mean, think about putting gas in your car. Before you arrive, the fuel is in the pump; when you leave, the fuel is in your car's tank. Either the gas station owner possesses the fuel or you do; you can't both possess the gasoline simultaneously.

But that's not how information works.

If I know that 1 + 1 = 2 and I convey that information to you, we now both possess that knowledge. Whereas one person knew this before, two people now know. And if both of us each tells one other person, four people will know it. And if each of us shares this knowledge with one other person, eight people will know that 1 + 1 = 2. Soon, 16 people, then 32, then 64, then 128 people will have this knowledge. Eventually, every person on the planet—7 billion people— can have this information.

Thus, *knowledge grows exponentially.* And once knowledge starts doubling, it never stops.

Today, knowledge is spreading faster than ever—thanks to the Internet. Although only 23% of the global population had Internet access in 2010, according to futuretimeline .net, it's estimated that 5 billion people will have access by 2020 (92% of American toddlers already do, according to Internet security firm AVG). Knowledge will spread further and faster than ever before!

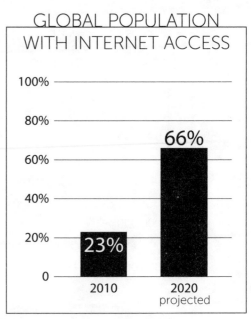

GLOBAL POPULATION WITH INTERNET ACCESS

FIGURE P.5

The Compound Growth Curve

Our lesson about exponentiality isn't over just yet. That's because it's not enough to know that a penny doubles to $10 million in 31 days; you also need to understand the nature of the growth curve.

So take a look at Figure P.6. It shows the progression of the penny's doubling over those 31 days. The growth is imperceptible until day 23—and at that point, it appears to blast off like a rocket ship. This point—where the line appears to go from horizontal to vertical—is called "the knee of the curve."

Exponentiality explains why the future will arrive fast—and why you don't realize it. You've been watching that penny every day for three weeks, and nothing much has happened. So you assume the fourth week will be the same. Only it won't be.

Likewise, technologically speaking, our entire world is at the knee of the curve. As a result, amazing things are about to happen.

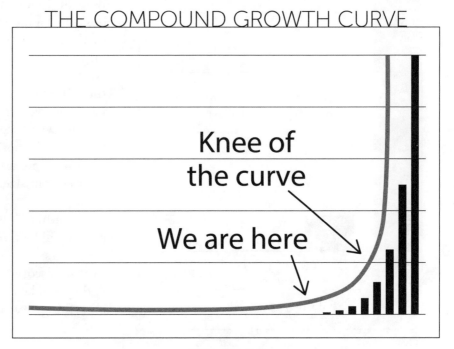

THE COMPOUND GROWTH CURVE

Knee of
the curve

We are here

FIGURE P.6

But you're skeptical.[5]

Overcome your skepticism. To help, consider man-made light. In his excellent book *Abundance*, Peter Diamandis showed that one had to work 50 hours in 1750 B.C. to earn enough money to purchase sesame oil that could power a lamp. By A.D. 1800, a candle cost the equivalent of six hours of work. Eighty years later, a kerosene lamp required 15 minutes of work.

Follow that timeline: we hadn't made much progress after 3,500 years. No one in the 1880s would have guessed that man-made light would soon require only a half second of work, as it does now.

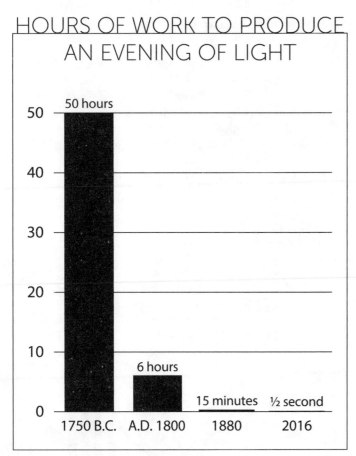

HOURS OF WORK TO PRODUCE AN EVENING OF LIGHT

FIGURE P.7

You might be making this very mistake. For example, you know that in the 1950s an entire building was needed to house a single computer and that by the 1970s a computer could fit into a room. You also know that the 1980s gave us desktop computers and that by the 2000s computers sat on your lap. And you certainly are aware that today they fit on your wrist. But have you ever stopped to wonder what's next? Clearly we're not done; computers are not stuck at their current size.

Thus within 20 years, computers will be no bigger than a grain of sand, and, as we will discover in chapter 4, they will be embedded in everything—certainly your

---

[5]Cue Dator's Law.

©Glasbergen / glasbergen.com

GLASBERGEN

**"The computer says I need to upgrade my brain
to be compatible with its new software."**

clothing, definitely your appliances, probably your skin and possibly even your brain.[6]

Exponentiality isn't just affecting size; it's also impacting speed. In 2020, for example, the 5G phone will be released. It will be 50 times faster than 4G phones; you'll be able to download 33 high-definition films in one second.

No wonder computer scientists anticipate that by the mid-2020s, personal computers will match the speed of the human brain. By 2030, they say, PC processing power will approach the speed of light—that's 3 million times as fast as the human brain. And those computers are expected to retail for just $1,000.

The journal *Science Advances* reported in 2015 that scientists at the University of California, San Diego, have built the first brainlike computer prototype that bypasses the limits of modern electronics. Called the *memcomputer*, it's the first computer that can simultaneously process and store information.

To appreciate how much faster the memcomputer is than currently available devices, scientists offer this challenge: Ask a computer to find out, from a list of 10 million numbers, how many add up to 10. It would take an ordinary 300,000 years to complete the task, but a memcomputer could figure it out in just 116 days.

Computers are not only getting faster, smaller and cheaper, they're getting smarter, thanks to artificial intelligence and machine learning. AI refers to a computer that is aware of its surroundings and acts in a way that maximizes the likelihood it will complete its task. In other words, it does what you would do.

---

[6]Dator! Get me Dator!

Thus, AI researchers are trying to improve the ability of a computer to communicate, learn, perceive, plan, reason and move.[7] AI therefore involves linguistics, mathematics, neuroscience, philosophy and psychology.

Although AI gets all the attention when the media cover computers, machine learning ought to as well. It's one thing for a human to program a computer to do something well—such as beat humans at chess—but it's far more impressive when a computer teaches itself how to do so. That's why building machines that can learn on their own is the most exciting area of computational research today.

A robot built at the University of Bremen in Germany taught itself to make pizza by reading Wikihow.

When computers can think and learn on their own, and do it at the speed of light, software intelligence will be indistinguishable from biological intelligence. This is known as "The Singularity"—the point in time where technology and biology merge. In his profound 2005 book *The Singularity Is Near*, the futurist Ray Kurzweil predicted that this will occur in 2029. Because of exponentiality, he says, if his estimates are off by a factor of 1,000, singularity will be delayed only eight years. If his estimates are off by a factor of 1 million, singularity will be delayed 15 years, and if he's wrong by a factor of a billion, singularity will be delayed just 21 years.

In other words, somewhere between 2029 and 2050, life is going to change in ways that are hard to imagine or comprehend.

But we're going to try, by taking you on a tour of exponential technologies. This will help you appreciate coming changes that will affect virtually every aspect of life on our planet. With that information in hand, you'll be able to tackle the key question: What does all this mean for you and your personal finances?

By the time you've finished reading this book, you'll echo Yogi's sentiment: The future ain't what it used to be.

---

[7] A computer that moves? Yep—it's called a robot. We'll get into robotics in chapter 3.

PERSONAL FINANCE IMPLICATIONS

1. You'll derive benefits from compound growth only if you earn sufficient rates of return. Growing money at the rate of inflation won't produce material gains—ever. Thus, it is important to seek higher returns if you want to accumulate greater wealth.

2. It's vital that you start today. As shown by the knee of the curve, if you wait 20 years, you will be too late. *Today* is the precise moment in time that you must apply this information about exponential technologies to your personal finances.

PART ONE

A Tour of Exponential Technologies

Chapter One: Connecting with Each Other

I couldn't wait until I got my driver's license! Having a car (or, rather, borrowing my mom's) meant I was able to get to the mall, to my friend Peter's house, to anywhere my friends would be hanging out. Having a car meant being connected, and being connected was vital for a teenager.

It still is. But it no longer takes an automobile to do it. Today we connect online, and physical proximity is no longer relevant. It's no surprise, therefore, that today's youths are less dependent on automobiles. According to the University of Michigan Transportation Research Institute, nearly half of 18- to 24-year-olds say they would choose having Internet access over owning a car.

Connectivity turns even the mundane into a marvel. Consider pizza, one of the world's most popular foods. It's also one of its oldest and to a large extent is still made the way it's been made for centuries. But the way it's *sold* is changing

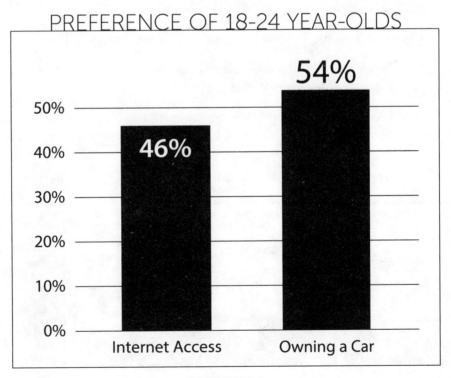

FIGURE 1.1

Incidentally

rapidly. Domino's, for example, lets you order a pizza via voice command while driving a Ford Fiesta. Using GPS technology, the store knows where you are and can calculate how long it will take you to get home—so the pizza arrives when you do.

Not to be outdone, Pizza Hut lets gamers order pizzas while playing with an Xbox—no need to interrupt the game merely to manage your munchies. Both companies say half their orders arrive digitally, and both say their IT departments are the fastest-growing divisions in their businesses.

Thanks to online connectivity:

- Facebook was able to become huge. That's where people are for two minutes out of every seven that they're online.

- 30 billion messages were sent using WhatsApp in 2015.

- YouTube's 1 billion users view 4 billion videos every day and upload 300 hours of video every minute.

- Google generates more revenue than all newspapers and magazines combined. YouTube, iTunes and Netflix each generates more revenue than the AMC cable network.

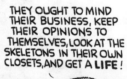

And much of this connectivity is being done via mobile devices. Nine in 10 Americans have a mobile phone, and there are now more mobile devices connected to the Internet than desktop computers. In fact, according to the Mobile Marketing Association, there are now more mobile phones on the planet than there are toothbrushes—and, unlike toothbrushes, more than 90% of smartphone users keep their phones within arm's reach 24/7.

Lots of people are already using their phones to make purchases—and I don't just mean by ordering products using Amazon's mobile app. At Cheesecake Factory and other restaurants, your order appears on an app, and you can pay the bill whenever you want—even splitting it with others dining with you—without having to wait for the server to bring the check. The Sweetgreen restaurant chain won't even let you pay with cash; you must use an electronic form of payment. Android Pay is accepted at more than 1 million stores, Samsung Pay can be used at swipe-only terminals, and Apple Pay can be used with credit cards from 1,300 card issuers. Chase, Capital One, and Walmart are among those launching ways to make it easier for you to pay your bills. In 2015, 45% of all online purchases made in the United States were done via a mobile device, according to Demandware.

Soon, though, it won't be our telephones that connect us to the Internet—it'll be our clothing. Researchers are developing clothes that kill bacteria, trap toxic gases, conduct electricity, block ultraviolet rays, measure our heart rate, analyze our sweat, monitor brain signals, heat or cool our skin—and let us talk to each other.

Levi's has partnered with Google to create conductive fabrics, while Ralph Lauren sells a shirt that detects your breathing, heart rate, stress level and calorie burn—sending the data to a smartphone app that creates a custom workout program for you. The shirt, which features an accelerometer and gyroscope to capture movement and direction, sells for $295. (Expect the price to come down.)

> **Soon you won't even need clothing to help you track your fitness. Companies are creating "tech tats," high-tech tattoos made of conductive paint that collect, store, send and receive data. Known as "biowearables," this technology will do more than serve as a fitness tracker. It could monitor vital signs after surgery, let you pay a bill with the swipe of your hand or, as in the case of wearable electronic tattoos being developed by Motorola and MC10, provide password authentication.**

WEARABLES
Annual Sales

billions

$40 billion

- $40
- $30
- $20
- $10
- $0

$11 billion

2014 2019 projected

FIGURE 1.2

Sales of connected wearables were $11 billion in 2014 and are projected to be $40 billion by 2019, according to IHS Markit.

It's one thing to connect people to the Internet; it's quite another to connect the *things* people use. And that's a problem, because the Internet is running out of capacity. Today's platform can handle only 4.9 billion devices. Considering that 3 billion people are already connected to the Internet (many with more than one device—the number of mobile devices is about to outpace the number of people on the planet), it's obvious that we're running out of room.

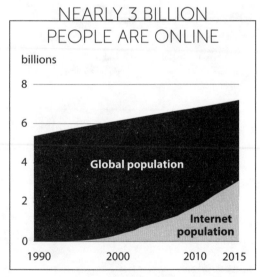

NEARLY 3 BILLION PEOPLE ARE ONLINE

FIGURE 1.3

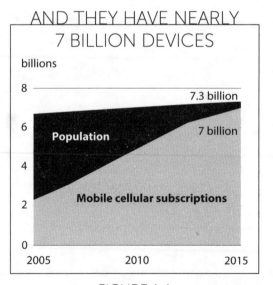

AND THEY HAVE NEARLY 7 BILLION DEVICES

FIGURE 1.4

That's why a new platform is being launched in 2020. It will have the capacity to handle 78 octillion devices—that's 78 billion billion billion devices. In other words, every grain of sand on earth could have 1 trillion IP addresses.

The Internet of Things

That will move us to the next phase of connectivity, to what is being called IoT—the Internet of Things. Everything that operates with electricity will be connected to the Internet, as will a great many things that don't use electricity, such as food.

"I moved to the Internet to be closer to my children."
Drew Dernavich/The New Yorker Collection/The Cartoon Bank

This is already under way. You can install thermostats that let you alter room temperatures without being in your house; the devices can also detect when people enter the room and adjust the temperature accordingly. Samsonite, Trunkster, Hontus, LugLoc and LEV Technology offer luggage that features Wi-Fi hot spots, USB chargers, digital locks, built-in scales, Bluetooth speakers and cellular-enabled tracking systems so you always know where your bag is. Refrigerators can tell you when the milk has gone sour or that the carton is low. (Soon the refrigerator will place the order for you, and the milk will be delivered to your home without your taking any action—probably by a drone.)

In 2015, only 8 billion devices were connected to the Internet. By 2020, there will be 50 billion, and by 2030 there will be 1 trillion. We're just 1% of the way there.

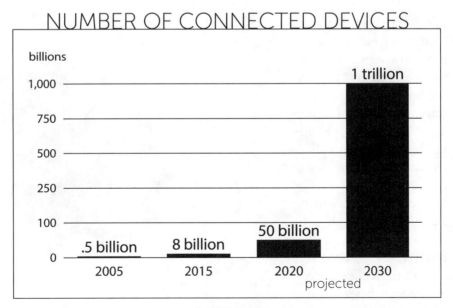

NUMBER OF CONNECTED DEVICES

billions

1,000	1 trillion
750	
500	
250	
100	50 billion
0	.5 billion · 8 billion

2005 · 2015 · 2020 · 2030
projected

FIGURE 1.5

Virtual Reality and Augmented Reality

As exciting as mobile connectivity is, that's nothing compared to two other emerging exponential technologies: virtual reality and augmented reality.

VR goggles cover your eyes, making you feel as though you're immersed in a different universe. You can explore maps of the brain's neurons, check out your favorite retailer's latest products or roam forests where you can fight dragons with virtual weapons.

By 2020, according to *Fortune* magazine, virtual reality devices will let car buyers test-drive vehicles, doctors practice surgical procedures, military procurement officers evaluate defense system capabilities, cruise ships let you see what a vacation experience would be, hotels let travelers visit their properties without actually having to go there and architects take you on tours of buildings before they are constructed.

Those who've used VR complain that the goggles are bulky. And when you're using them, you can see only the alternative reality being displayed; you're unaware of your actual surroundings. That limits the devices' practicality. These problems are solved by an even more fascinating technology, called augmented reality.

AR doesn't require you to wear headgear; instead you just aim your smartphone or tablet's camera (and, in the future, your eyewear) toward an object. Instantly a display pops up, providing you with details about whatever you're looking at.

While watching a ball game, point your phone's camera at anyone on the field—and it will reveal the player's name, key performance statistics and video

"See how virtual reality makes it feel like you're actually falling."
Ken Krimstein/The New Yorker Collection/The Cartoon Bank

highlights. Tourists will be able to point their phone at a famous landmark and instantly receive information about the site. Surgeons will be able to use the devices to see arteries invisible to the naked eye.

In 2017, 2.5 billion AR apps will be downloaded onto smartphones worldwide. The most famous so far was launched in 2016: the game Pokémon Go. You simply look at the image shown by your phone's camera; while doing so, Pokémon characters appear on your screen as though they really exist. The goal of the game is to capture as many characters as possible. But first you have to find them—and that means walking around, not just in your house but through-out your neighborhood, even traveling to other cities. Parents who lament that their video game–playing kids get no exercise are relieved that this game requires outdoor physical activity.

A Case Study in Exponential Technologies

Because Pokémon Go was the first widely available consumer AR application, it's worth taking a closer look at it. There are 7 billion people in the world, and few gave any thought to augmented reality until July 6, 2016, when the game was released. Within weeks, more than 75 million people worldwide were play-ing it—making it the most downloaded app in history.

Financially speaking, the immediate beneficiaries were Nintendo, Niantic (the game's creator) and Apple (which gets 30% of the revenue collected by the game through its App Store). The investment banking firm Needham & Company estimated that Pokémon Go could generate $3 billion in revenue for Apple alone by 2018.

PEARLS BEFORE SWINE ©2016 Stephan Pastis. Reprinted by permission of UNIVERSAL UCLICK. All rights reserved.

Businesses and entrepreneurs raced to exploit the game's popularity. Bars, restaurants, retail stores and businesses of all kinds quickly encountered Pokémon-searching consumers looking for the creatures. L'inizio Pizza Bar in Queens, New York, set itself up as a place where Pokémon could be found and told Bloomberg News that its food and drink sales had risen 30% thanks to increased customer traffic. In Iceland, a tour bus company offered Pokémon Go hunting trips. A French furniture store offered a Pokémon Go promotion at 200 stores, while the yogurt retailer Stonyfield Farm placed ads near 10,000 Pokéstops to promote its brand.

Incidentally

Pokémon Go has inspired baby names. Babycenter.com says names such as Eevee, Onyx and Ash—all names of characters—rose after the game was introduced. It says half of the moms visiting its site say they play the game.

Major companies got involved, too. Sberbank, the biggest bank in Russia, arranged for its branches to attract Pokémon players. In Japan, McDonald's converted 400 outlets into Pokémon "gyms" so users could battle one another on their smartphones. The Jacksonville Jaguars professional football team staged a Pokémon Go promotion that attracted 15,000 people. And on the 2016 campaign trail, both political parties staged Pokémon Go events to register people to vote.

The game produced some negative side effects, however. Player enthusiasm led many to violate codes of social behavior. The Arlington National Cemetery released a statement asking players to stay away. "We do not consider playing 'Pokémon Go' to be appropriate decorum on the grounds of ANC," cemetery officials said. The U.S. Holocaust Museum asked to have itself removed as a game site, as did the Auschwitz Museum in Poland, a cemetery in Edmonton, and many churches, mosques and synagogues worldwide.

Federal, state and local officials also fretted over traffic congestion and accidents caused by or involving the game's players. The City of Canada Bay said it had to pay for extra security and waste disposal due to increased park visitors. Various legislation to combat the risk to public safety and user privacy was introduced, while the Japanese government's National Center of Incident Readiness and Strategy for Cybersecurity warned users of safety hazards. New York now requires sex offenders, as a condition of their release from prison, to agree "not to download, access or otherwise engage" in Pokémon Go. (Lawmakers said the game is "a virtual road map to children" because its "lure" feature has "the potential to be abused by perpetrators.")

The source of those concerns? In just the first few weeks of the game's release:

- A 28-year-old in New York crashed his car into a tree while playing the game.

- A 15-year-old in Pennsylvania playing the game was hit by a car after walking into traffic.

- San Diego firefighters had to rescue two men who walked off a cliff while trying to catch Pokémon characters.

- A search-and-rescue team found a group of teenagers in the United Kingdom who got lost in a cave.

- Two Canadian teens unwittingly crossed the border and were detained by the U.S. Border Patrol.

- A man trying to sneak into the Stockholm Olympic Stadium to catch a Pokémon impaled himself on a metal fence.

- A Baltimore driver crashed into a police car while playing Pokémon Go while driving.

- A woman in Japan was struck and killed by a car whose driver told police that he hadn't been watching the road because he was playing Pokémon Go.

There are thousands more stories of errant, rude and just plain stupid behavior by some of the game's players.

PEARLS BEFORE SWINE ©2016 Stephan Pastis. Reprinted by permission of UNIVERSAL UCLICK. All rights reserved.

Prior to Pokémon Go, few consumers had ever heard of augmented reality, fewer understood it and virtually none had ever seen it. But within a very short time, more than 100 million people took a major step forward with a leading technology, whose rate of growth and market penetration can only be called . . . exponential.

Coming next? Holograms.

Jimmy Kimmel has already had performers appear on his television show in digital format (holograms), and the comedians Redd Foxx and Andy Kaufman toured in 2016 the same way—even though they're both dead. You can expect the innovations to continue—including 3D avatars performing in your living room, where your perspective on the movie you're watching will depend on where in the room you're sitting or standing.

And this is just the beginning. All told, a 2013 report by Cisco predicts that the Internet of Things will add $14 trillion to the global economy by 2025.

No wonder Scott Cook, a cofounder of Intuit, says, "We're still in the first minutes of the first day of the Internet revolution."

PERSONAL FINANCE IMPLICATIONS

1. Increased use of mobile devices to make purchases increases the importance of selecting the right credit and debit cards (since you can't use cash or checks online). Comparative shopping for cards has never been more important.

2. Massive growth in wearables, connectivity and the Internet of Things will create huge investment opportunities. We'll learn more about this in chapter 17.

3. AR, VR and holograms could eliminate the need for business travel. It would save you and your employer money—but have huge implications for the travel and hospitality industries.

4. AI will improve the analytical tools we use in financial planning. Better modeling capabilities will let us produce more accurate financial planning projections and better portfolio management systems.

5. The constant flow of new devices and applications into the marketplace makes it difficult to stay up to date. This can put non-tech-savvy consumers at a disadvantage when making financial decisions.

6. Increased connectivity could result in more volatility in the financial markets, as more and more people get the ability to trade their accounts with just a few taps on their phones. Be prepared for even greater volatility in your portfolio—and don't let it scare you into buying or selling frantically.

Chapter Two: Big Data

My goodness, you certainly take a lot of photographs. You send a ton of emails, and you type a whole bunch of texts.

So does everyone else.

Every day in 2015, we collectively sent 205 billion emails, ran 3.5 billion Google searches, tweeted 500 million times, downloaded 200 million apps, and uploaded so many videos it would take you 49 years to watch them all.

> And increasingly, those data are being produced by and viewed on mobile devices: In 2015, mobile devices accounted for 32% of all Internet traffic. And though we produced less than 1 exabyte (a million million bits) of mobile data in 2000, according to Cisco, that figure jumped to 44.2 exabytes by 2015—and is projected to be 300 exabytes by 2019. Three-quarters of it will be video.[8]

It's an incredible amount of information. The federal government alone offers almost 200,000 databases at data.gov. The real estate site Zillow and GPS app Garmin both rely on it, as do many other companies. (Want to know where to open a coffee shop? Data.gov can show you the streets that have the most pedestrians and neighborhoods that have lots of young residents.)

This is the field of Big Data. It involves collecting, storing, accessing and analyzing data. It's a big business.

Data Creation

It's not just big, it's new: In just the past two years, says IBM, we created 90% of all the data that exist in the world. Put another way, we've created nine times as much data in the last two years as we created in the entire history of humanity before that. And we keep creating more, at the rate of 2.5 quintillion bytes a day.

By 2020, according to IDC, we will have created 42 zetabytes of data—that's 42 bits of data followed by 21 zeros (42,000,000,000,000,000,000,000).

---

[8]Schools in 41 states no longer teach cursive writing. Will students stop typing, too?

And our ability to create even more data is constantly growing. Every week during NFL season, football fans upload and download twice as much data as exist in the Library of Congress. And when the Square Kilometre Array (SKA) telescope goes online in the next decade, it will generate as much data *every week*—5 exabytes—as humans produced *in total* from the dawn of time to 2003. All by itself.

That's *a lot* of data.

Data Storage

The data we produce are never thrown away. Fortunately, it's gotten cheap to store it; a 6-terabyte hard drive can store all the music ever recorded yet costs under $230. Samsung sells a storage device that holds 512 GB of data—and it's smaller than a postage stamp and weighs less than a dime.

But scientists say the ultimate archival storage system will be made up of DNA. Separate experiments by researchers at the University of Washington, the University of Illinois and the European Bioinformatics Institute have shown that a single gram of DNA can hold as much data as 1 million compact discs; all of the world's digital information could fit into a space equivalent to six bottles of wine. And if stored in a cold, dry and dark storage facility, the data will remain intact for tens of thousands of years.

And because being able to produce and store data cheaply just encourages us to produce even more,[9] our need for storage will continue to grow.

Data Usage

Once you collect all this data, how do you make it useful? After all, if you're looking for a new planet, you can't sort through the 5 exabytes of data that the SKA telescope will produce every week. (You have enough trouble finding that certain photo you want to show your friend. Where *is* that?)

---

[9]Remember when your camera had only enough film to take 12 pictures? You chose your shots very carefully. But now your phone's seemingly unlimited data capacity lets you take thousands of photos without worry.

The solution to searching databases: create an algorithm. These computer programs are designed to sort through massive amounts of data in order to solve complex problems.

Consider UPS. The company has 55,000 routes in its U.S. fleet, delivering 16 million packages per day. Its drivers average 120 stops daily. UPS executives asked themselves a simple question: What are the most efficient routes for our drivers?

The question is simple, but the answer is highly complex. UPS engineers recognized that, combined, there are hundreds of thousands of trillions of alternative routes. So they created an algorithm. The program identified efficient routes, cutting 85 million miles a year and saving UPS $300 million a year.

Algorithms like that are used by every industry. They help Wall Street firms make investment decisions, law enforcement officials track terrorists, lenders calculate credit scores and online dating sites find mates for people.

Facebook's DeepFace program, for example, can recognize human faces with the same level of accuracy as the average human, while Microsoft's Cortana can tell the difference between a Cardigan Welsh Corgi and a Pembroke Welsh Corgi. Such programs could let retailers scan the faces of people entering stores to identify preferred customers—and known shoplifters. Hilton Hotels, for example, uses facial recognition software to scan the faces of guests, so employees can greet visitors by name.

FIGURE 2.1

Algorithms created by Quill are used to write articles in everyday language; the software is used by such companies as *Forbes*, T. Rowe Price and USAA; the Associated Press uses a competing product called Wordsmith.

Read the following and decide which were written by algorithm versus a human. The answers are on page 20.

A. "We are raising our rating on KSU from Neutral to Buy based on our view that the challenges of 2014 and 2015 have already been reflected in the stock and KSU's long-term volume growth story is differentiated from the broader rail group."

B. "Despite an upper single-digit sales CAGR through 2025, limited margin leverage mutes earnings momentum. Intuitive has the highest OEM/GM ratio in devices even following recent softer top-line growth pressuring operating margin profits through 2015."

C. "Things looked bleak for the Angels when they trailed by two runs in the ninth inning, but Los Angeles recovered thanks to a key single from Vladimir Guerrero to pull out a 7–6 victory over the Boston Red Sox at Fenway Park on Sunday."

Algorithms created by the Filene Research Institute's Jumiya Project found that people who exercise, eat well and consume little alcohol are more likely to pay their bills and invest, that runners are six times as likely to pay their bills on time as the average American and that heavy drinkers are five times as likely to file for bankruptcy as the average American. These data can be used to evaluate creditworthiness.

BlitzD uses massive amounts of information about past games to predict with 78% accuracy whether the next play in a professional football game will be a run or a pass and whether the play will go to the left, to the right or up the middle. (The NFL is evaluating the fairness of using this technology during games.)

Data Brokerage

A lot of data are available free at sites such as Wikipedia and data.gov. But far more is available if you're willing to pay for it. And lots of companies are. Thus, data brokerage has become a huge industry—valued at $156 billion, or twice as much as the U.S. government's intelligence budget.

Data brokers have collected an astonishing amount of information about you. They know your birth date, occupation, education level, marital status, race and gender. They also know your height, weight, health status and even whether you are left- or right-handed.

And that's not all. Data brokers know your telephone number, your home's address and its square footage, your automobile's make, model and year, the number of children you have, the number of people who live with you and the number of pets you have—as well as their breeds.

There's more. Data brokers are also aware of the recent purchases you've made, your religious and political views, even the size of your investment portfolio. All this might be highly personal information to you, but to them it's just data—and they're willing to sell it to anyone who wants to buy it.

The Ultimate Data Center: Your Body

If you're looking for a target-rich environment from which to pull data, look no further than your own body. Indeed, bioinformatics is one of the fastest-growing fields of all of Big Data.

Your doctor typically tracks your health by examining your temperature, blood pressure and pulse. That happens only when you go

Incidentally

A photo posted on Craigslist can reveal your home's address.

Allstate has patented steering wheel sensors that can evaluate a driver's physiology. The company can sell the data to lenders, health insurers, employers, landlords, credit rating firms and marketers.

Your mobile phone's GPS tracks the roads you travel. AT&T collects that data and sells it to Clear Channel Outdoor Americas, which owns tens of thousands of billboards throughout the country. This lets Clear Channel tell advertisers which of its billboards they should advertise on if they want you to see it.

for a visit—something that for many of us occurs once a year or so. But the human body has 30 trillion cells; imagine if we could measure each—and not with just three metrics but with a hundred. And not just once a year but nonstop.

It's happening. People are wearing devices (or have had them inserted into their bodies) that provide data to health care professionals in real time. And 300,000 more patients receive wireless implantable medical devices every year.

Incidentally

Most urine tests measure only a handful of chemicals. But researchers at the University of Alberta can detect more than 3,000 chemicals in urine, revealing key information about a person's health, as well as what food, drink and drugs the person has been consuming and what pollutants he or she has been exposed to. This will allow the creation of fast, cheap and painless medical tests using urine instead of blood or tissue biopsies, including tests for colon and prostate cancer, celiac disease, ulcerative colitis, pneumonia and organ transplant rejection.

Health care professionals, researchers and others use bioinformatics software provided by Los Alamos National Laboratory to identify DNA from viruses and all parts of the Tree of Life (a representation of the genetic divergence of modern species from a common ancestor). The software helps identify pathogen-caused diseases, select cancer treatments and optimize crop yields, to name a few examples—and it does it 250,000 times as fast as conventional methods.

Meanwhile, thousands of scientists use the Molecular Evolutionary Genetics Analysis. MEGA is free bioinformatics software that aids in examining health and disease coded within the genome. MEGA has been downloaded more than 1 million times by scientists in 184 countries and is cited in more than 10,000 publications every year, making it one of the most widely used tools by scientists worldwide.

ResearchKit, developed by Apple, lets medical researchers collect data from millions of people around the world, while Stanford has a free app that more than 50,000 people have downloaded to participate in a cardiovascular study that, every three months, tracks them taking a walk. (It's become one of the largest cardiovascular research trials ever conducted.)

Answers: **A.** Human **B.** Human **C.** Computer

Meanwhile, India is creating the largest government-sponsored biometric identity database in the world. Its goal: to obtain data on every one of its 1.2 billion citizens. The project is more than halfway done.

Managing Medical Information

No field can produce more data than the health care industry. But it's difficult enough for your physician to analyze the data available about yourself. Imagine trying to aggregate and analyze the data accumulated on billions of people!

The only way to do it is with computing systems. One of the most advanced is IBM's Watson. Watson can process 500 gigabytes, the equivalent of a million books, per second. Its sources of information include journals, encyclopedias, dictionaries, thesauri, newswire articles and literary works, as well as databases, taxonomies and ontologies.

Watson became famous when IBM pitted it against the greatest *Jeopardy!* champions—Ken Jennings, who had won the most games, and Brad Rutter, who had won the most money. Watson easily defeated them both using its accumulation of 200 million pages of data, which it could access at the rate of 80 trillion operations per second. That enabled it to provide the correct answer to such rhyming riddles as "a long tiresome speech delivered by a pie filling."[10]

Incidentally

Continuous monitoring of your health can help doctors identify diseases at stage zero—before they begin to develop. So expect to wear a device that's programmed with your gender, height, weight and age; it will continuously analyze your blood pressure, heart rhythm and other functions, determine when something's amiss and alert your doctor via a smartphone app—even if you don't have symptoms. Similar devices installed in toilets will analyze body waste and transmit data directly to your physician. EKG monitors attached to your smartphone will send data directly to your doctor.

These technologies will be of particular help to people in Third World countries where doctors and hospitals are far away. This is partly why the World Economic Forum says the world's poorest countries will be the first to benefit from major technological innovations. It cites such examples as nationwide drone delivery services in Rwanda, vaccination campaigns targeting areas selected by satellite-based geographic data systems and genetic sequencing used to curb Africa's Ebola epidemic.

---

[10]What is a meringue harangue?

Defeating the *Jeopardy!* champions was just IBM's way of making a point. Getting serious, IBM sent Watson to Memorial Sloan Kettering Cancer Center so doctors could teach it how to help them make better decisions regarding cancer diagnosis and treatment. Watson now helps physicians identify the treatments that are most likely to succeed by comparing a patient's individual data to databases around the world. Watson also tells physicians how confident it is (using a scoring system) about its recommendations. Watson is now being used by more than a dozen hospitals, including Cleveland Clinic, Duke Cancer Institute and Yale Cancer Center. (At a Japanese hospital in 2016, Watson compared a cancer patient's genetic data against a database of 20 million oncological studies. In just 10 minutes, it made the correct diagnosis, which had stumped doctors, allowing treatment to start that saved the patient's life.)

"WOULD YOU MIND IF I ASK SIRI FOR A SECOND OPINION?"

Cartoon by Harley Schwadron

Watson is also in Hollywood. In 2016, Watson helped 20th Century Fox create a trailer for its thriller *Morgan*. Watson "watched" dozens of horror movie trailers to understand what makes a scene scary to humans—and then decided which scenes of *Morgan* to include in the trailer. A human editor patched the scenes together, and the entire trailer was produced in less than a day. Most trailers take a month to complete.

When Watson defeated the *Jeopardy!* champions in 2011, the computer was the size of a large bedroom. Today it is the size of three stacked pizza boxes. It's also 2,300% faster. Moore's Law says that by 2050 Watson will be the size of a grain of sand and 1 billion times faster than today.

Watson's ability to manage data relieves physicians from information overload. This, in turn, is leading to huge advances in the field of medicine. More on that in chapter 6. For now, all I'll say is that by 2020 Watson will be in your smartphone, and *Star Trek*'s tricorder[11] will be real.

Privacy in the Information Age

The more information you have, the better your decisions. That's the good news about data. But privacy advocates find the availability of so much information very disturbing. To them I say: You've already lost the war.

Seven of 10 human resource professionals surveyed say they have rejected job candidates based on information they found online. Eight in 10 divorce attorneys search social media on behalf of their clients, according to the American Academy of Matrimonial Lawyers, and a third of divorce filings feature the word "Facebook." Lenders have found that people who make phone calls at night are better credit risks, as are gamblers. They've also learned that the faster you drain your cell phone battery and the less frequently you travel, the less likely you are to repay loans. Some even base the interest rate they charge you on whom you've friended on Facebook.

How did all this information about you get online?

You put a lot of it there.

As I said, many of the battles privacy rights advocates have lost are self-inflicted. Whenever you respond to a poll, complete a survey, fill out a warranty card, visit a website, buy a product or post a review, you're asked to state your income, the amount of money you have invested and your age, gender and marital status. You freely tell strangers how long you've lived at your current address, what you do for a living and the name of your employer. You also post huge amounts of personal information on social media. College yearbooks reveal the year you graduated, your major and your club memberships.

---

[11]In the 1960s TV series, Dr. Leonard McCoy was able to diagnose his patients by waving a handheld device at them.

According to a survey by Visa, of those using social networks:

- Nearly 50% have shared their birth date.

- 14% have posted their mother's maiden name.

- 29% have provided their telephone number.

- 20% have revealed their address.

- 15% have disclosed their upcoming travel plans.

- 7% have shared their Social Security number!

It's bad enough if you give this information to friends. But according to a creditdonkey.com survey, 25% of social media users accept friend requests from people they don't know—meaning you're giving information about yourself to strangers.

Your local government posts lots of data about you, too. Public records, for example, reveal when you bought your home, the amount you paid for it, the name of your lender and the size of your mortgage.

Data brokers collect the information you and others provide for free—and sell it.

So the privacy war is over. All you can do now is to recognize that we live in a brave new world and you must therefore learn how to minimize the risk that your data will be used in nefarious ways.

PERSONAL FINANCE IMPLICATIONS

1. The days of anonymity are over. It's important that you learn how to safeguard your privacy. We'll cover those strategies in chapter 16.

2. Data brokerage is big business, and that means investment opportunities. We'll explore those in chapter 17.

3. By applying big data to portfolio theory and behavioral finance, investment decision making can be dramatically improved.

Chapter Three: Robotics

Robotics is the fastest-growing industry in the world and will become the world's largest in the 2020s, according to the Littler Workplace Policy Institute. Microsoft says it will be a $37 billion industry by 2018.

Currently, 1.1 million robots work in companies around the world. In automobile manufacturing, robots do 80% of the work, according to the International Federation of Robotics. Consider:

- Amazon has 10,000 robots that move items from shelves to shipping.

- Baxter, an industrial robot that costs less than $25,000, can be programmed within minutes by employees who don't need to know computer coding. And unlike other industrial robots, humans can work alongside Baxter in complete safety.

- The PR2 robot can open doors, fold laundry, clean houses—and even fetch beer and play pool. (Not to be outdone, MIT built a bot that plays ping pong, while one from Japanese researchers beats humans in rock-paper-scissors.[12])

- TUG works in 150 hospitals, delivering medicine, patients' meals and laundry.

- The da Vinci robot performs half a million surgical procedures annually worldwide, with 80% fewer complications and faster recovery times, while telepresence robots let doctors appear at patient bedsides remotely. Another robot kills viruses in five minutes using ultraviolet rays that are 25,000 times as bright as fluorescent lights, cutting hospital infection rates by 60%.

- PaPeRo can read to your children and lets you speak with them and send them texts.

- Pepper can serve as a companion for the elderly, an elementary school teacher, a retail sales clerk or office aide. It's able to read emotions and facial expressions and respond appropriately, yet costs only $1,600. It sold out within minutes when first made available in Japan in 2015.[13]

---

[12]There's a point to creating robots that play games: It's an effective way to learn how to make robots that can interact with humans. The rock-paper-scissors bot, for example, uses a high-speed camera to identify the shape of the opponent's hand, and the robot's superfast reflexes let it respond with the corresponding move to win.
[13]Don't worry—they're making more.

If you go to Japan to buy Pepper, you might want to stay in the Henn-na Hotel near Nagasaki. The property features android receptionists, waiters, cleaning staff and cloakroom attendants. They speak Japanese, Chinese, Korean and English. Although most of the receptionists look like humans, one is a velociraptor—the dinosaur featured in the *Jurassic Park* movies.[14] Because Henn-na is staffed almost entirely by robots, the hotel's payroll is very low. As a result, rooms cost only $60 per night.

Hilton Hotels is moving in this direction, too. Its lobbies are starting to offer robot concierges named Connie (for founder Conrad Hilton), using IBM's Watson. Connie tells guests about tourist attractions, dining recommendations and hotel amenities.

Meanwhile, robotic shopping assistants help patrons at Lowe's, the home improvement store chain. The bots escort customers to items they're seeking; hold the item in front of a bot's 3D scanner, and it will tell you what the item is, how it works, how to use it, what it costs and other details.

DILBERT ©2015 Scott Adams. Used By permission of UNIVERSAL UCLICK. All rights reserved.

It's no surprise that robots have virtually unlimited military applications, including these:

- The unmanned MQ-9 Reaper has capabilities similar to those of the F-22 fighter jet but costs 90% less.

---

[14] I mean, why not?

- The Air Force's Global Hawk has a wingspan of 130 feet and can cruise at 60,000 feet for two days; its camera can track all the ground movements of a medium-sized city.

- PackBot can detect and destroy bombs.

- TALON is light enough to be carried by soldiers, has treads like a tank and can be armed with machine guns, .50-caliber rifles, grenade launchers or antitank rockets.

- The U.S. Navy protects ships using USVs (unmanned surface vehicles), which can autonomously "swarm" hostile vessels.

- BEAR can lift and carry an injured soldier off the battlefield.

- BigDog can carry 400 pounds of gear and weapons over rugged terrain.

In 2011, the Army had one robot in Afghanistan for every 50 soldiers; by 2023, the Defense Department expects it to have one soldier for every 10 robots.

Commercial applications for robots are under development, too:

- Cheetah can run 30 mph.

- SandFlea weighs only 11 pounds but can jump 30 feet high.[15]

- RiSE can climb walls.

- PrecisionHawk can find disaster victims.

- SAM can lay 1,200 bricks per day, equal to the productivity of four human masons.

- Volvo is developing remote-controlled bots for garbage trucks; they'll pick up heavy bins so sanitation workers can avoid injury.

Incidentally

In 2016, a Golf Laboratories robot named LDRIC sank a hole in one at the 163-yard 16th hole at TPC Scottsdale in Arizona—20 years after Tiger Woods did it there. The robot then repeated the feat five swings later. Imagine playing a round with your friends and a robot coach or watching an all-robot golf tournament. It's one of many ways technology could change the sports world. (More on that in chapter 9.)

[15] Yep, it can leap a tall building in a single bound.

- And a six-foot-tall humanoid bot developed at Virginia Polytechnic Institute can detect and extinguish fires, using thermal imaging to detect heat and see through smoke.

It's easy to understand why military and commercial enterprises like robots: bots don't get sick, don't make mistakes, never have a bad attitude, don't harass employees or create hostile work environments and are capable of working 24/7.

Currently, most robots handle repetitive, dull and dangerous tasks that don't require skill. That means the end of ditch digging for humans and no more sweatshops. Later, they will do far more. Ultimately, any physical thing a human wants done will not require a human to do it.

Incidentally

The European Union has proposed that robot workers be classified as "electronic persons." Their owners would be required to pay social security taxes on every bot they use.

There are two reasons reason robots aren't ubiquitous yet: They have limited capabilities, and they're expensive. But consistent with Moore's Law, improvements are occurring rapidly. AI and sensor technologies are improving at exponential rates, and so are prices (an industrial robot that cost $500,000 in 2008 was 95% cheaper in 2016). By 2025, robots will be so good at what they do and so affordable that everyone will be able to have one—and you'll probably own several.[16]

Of course, you won't call it a robot—just as your daughter or granddaughter doesn't call her Barbie a robot. But that's essentially what Hello Barbie is. Launched in 2015, Hello Barbie uses artificial intelligence to have natural-language conversations with children. She retails for about $75.

You'll use robots to handle basic chores in your household: dusting, laundry, grocery shopping, running errands, answering the door, preparing meals, even babysitting. Because robots are always present, patient and reliable (unlike teenagers), they'll make great companions. Soft, furry, friendly-faced robots have proven to be very popular in nursing homes. Loneliness disappears.

What happens when people prefer robots over human interaction? You might want to skip this paragraph because it's about to get icky. The futurologist Ian

---

[16]Yeah, I know: Ridiculous. Reread Dator's Law.

Pearson says the most common use of domestic robots by 2050 will be . . . sex. Already, his research shows, more than 25% of Internet searches are related to pornography, and the sex toy market has been growing by 6% a year. Hey, I *told* you to skip this paragraph.

Flying Robots

The cost of drones has been collapsing at an exponential rate. In 2007, a drone cost $100,000; today you can buy one for less than $500. That helps explain why the commercial use of drones jumped 84% in 2016, according to Juniper Research. The two biggest industries for drone use: video (movies and news) and agriculture.

Consumer use of drones is growing even faster, according to the FAA. More than 2.5 million drones were sold to hobbyists in 2016, and the FAA expects 7 million drones to be purchased annually by 2020.

Amazon wants to deliver your order by drone; Domino's wants to bring your pizza to you the same way. The Remote Area Medical volunteer corps already delivers prescriptions to patients in rural areas who lack access to pharmacies.

Drones come in all sizes, from smaller than a penny to larger than a 747. They can work individually or in groups. And they can be operated spontaneously or programmed to follow carefully choreographed flight patterns.

This flexibility offers a wide range of uses. Drones are being used in photography and cinematography by film producers, sports broadcasters and journalists. They assist in disaster recovery—their small size lets rescuers get close-up views of areas planes and helicopters can't reach. And drones with thermal sensors can find lost people, even at night. Drones can also deliver walkie-talkies, medical supplies and water to stranded victims until rescue crews arrive.

Drones can also reach dangerous or difficult-to-access locations such as volcanos, flooded areas, eroded coastlines and mountaintops. They can produce high-resolution 3D maps and help companies inspect power lines, oil and gas pipelines, transmission towers, buildings and bridges, wind turbines and rotor blades.

Drones are also revolutionizing agriculture. They can be used to monitor crops, improving yields while reducing the use of water and pesticides. It's difficult to grow crops on steep hillsides, but drones solve that problem.[17]

Law enforcement officials use drones to help with crowd surveillance and public safety, monitor criminal activity, examine crime scenes and conduct investigations. Border patrols use drones to detect smuggling activities. Drones also deter poachers and illegal loggers and will help researchers monitor wildlife and learn about animal behavior.

Construction companies use drones to check on progress. Storm forecasters and trackers send drones into hurricanes and tornadoes—places where aircraft with human pilots can't safely go.

With all these uses—and with flying drones so much fun—no wonder the drone market is expected to be $89 billion by 2023.

Autonomous Robots

Perhaps the most impactful robot is the SDV—the self-driving vehicle. This particular robot is so important, and will affect your life in so many ways, that it's worth a closer look.

Let's start with this: There are 5.3 million automobile crashes in the United States every year. Auto accidents are responsible for 2.5 million visits to hospital emergency rooms annually, forcing more than 200,000 people to spend a total of 1 million days in the hospital. And 33,000 people are killed.

Auto accidents are the number one killer of children ages 5 to 14 and the number two killer of adults ages 25 to 64. And of all U.S. workers killed on the job, one in three is a trucker, according to the Department of Labor, making that occupation the most dangerous in the United States.

In fatal crashes, 84% of drivers never braked; they were distracted or drunk (41% of accidents involve alcohol). This doesn't even begin to consider the huge

---

[17]They can till fields and harvest crops from the air.

"I was reading the anti-texting billboard."

Pat Byrnes/The New Yorker Collection/The Cartoon Bank

economic losses due to property damage, lost wages, lost household production, medical costs, physical and vocational rehabilitation costs, workplace costs due to lost productivity and the inevitable legal expenses.

Indeed, the RAND Corporation calculates that auto crashes cost the United States $800 billion every year. That's 2.2% of our nation's GDP. This is why automobile insurance is so important and why Americans collectively pay $157 billion annually for coverage. That's another 1.5% of our GDP. Thus the total economic cost of automobile crashes is 4.9% of GDP—more than what we spend annually to operate the Treasury, Justice, Housing and Urban Development, Transportation, Education, Veterans Affairs and Homeland Security departments combined.

Fortunately there is a solution: SDVs.

McKinsey estimates that self-driving vehicles will eliminate 90% of all car accidents[18]—and allow drivers to cut the time they spend in cars an average of 50 minutes per day!

---

[18]At the moment, SDVs are involved in five times as many crashes as regular vehicles, and their passengers are four times as likely to be injured, according to the University of Michigan's Transportation Research Institute. This suggests that SDVs are more, not less, dangerous than human-controlled cars. But analysis of every accident involving SDVs found that all but one were the fault of human drivers. (For example, SDVs are rear-ended 50% more often than other cars.) This illustrates the challenges of transitioning to new technologies; often we take a few steps back while we strive to take major leaps forward.

Getting to your destination faster means burning less fuel; McKinsey says greenhouse gas emissions from passenger cars, SUVs, pickup trucks and minivans would drop by 16%. At the same time, road capacity would triple and infrastructure costs would fall.

> **No more drivers would also mean no more standing in line at the Department of Motor Vehicles! Wahoo!**

The advent of self-driving vehicles can vastly improve the lives of millions of people currently forced to the sidelines of society. Children, the elderly, people with disabilities, those with medical conditions that restrict their ability to drive, religious observants whose faiths prevent them from driving, women living in countries where they're not allowed to drive and others whose beliefs, attitudes or abilities restrict their ability to drive—all would suddenly enjoy newfound freedom, social interaction and economic opportunity.

SDVs are not far into the future—in fact, they're already here. Many vehicles on the road have such features as self-parking, lane keeping, auto cruise control, pedestrian collision warning, slow autopilot and temporary autopilot.

Completely autonomous driving already occurs in restricted environments such as mining and farming, cutting labor costs up to 90% and reducing carbon dioxide emissions up to 60%.

Fully autonomous cars are also found on today's highways. The most famous are the Google cars, which have driven more than 2 million miles through 2016. SDVs are approved for use in California, Florida, Michigan, Nevada and Washington, DC, and the National Highway Traffic Safety Administration says that autonomous cars are considered "drivers" under the law.

Tesla's automobiles are capable of self-driving 90% of the time, while Audi's autonomous RS7 set a speed record at Germany's Hockenheim Raceway. General Motors sells automobiles that control steering, acceleration and braking both in stop-and-go traffic and at highway speeds of 70 mph. Volvo and Renault both say they will introduce self-driving by 2020.

R&D budgets are exploding; major automobile manufacturers are collectively spending more than $43 billion on SDV technology every year. And they're not alone: Google has spent $60 million so far, and venture capitalists invested more than $400 million in 2015 alone—154% more than the year before.

Mcity, a joint venture of Ford, Toyota, GM and Honda in partnership with the Michigan Department of Transportation and Xerox, opened in 2015. It's a 32-acre simulated town containing miles of roads, roundabouts, crosswalks and other obstacles—a proving ground for self-driving vehicles.

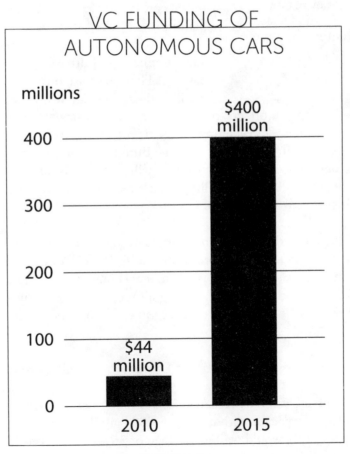

FIGURE 3.1

Incidentally

In 2016, a Tesla saved the life of Joshua Neally of Branson, Missouri.

During his commute to work one morning, Joshua had piercing chest and stomach pains. He programmed the nearest hospital into his GPS and placed the car into autopilot mode. It drove him to within a few blocks of the emergency room. Joshua took over, arrived at the hospital and was treated for a pulmonary embolism.

There are many people who believe fully autonomous SDVs will never exist (we'll meet some of them in chapter 12). But all the money being invested strongly suggests otherwise.

Interestingly, SDVs' biggest impact might not be on driving at all. Instead, their biggest impact might be on *parking*. After all, there are 245 million cars in the United States, and most are parked 95% of the time. The RAND Corporation says that 31% of city space is devoted to parking, and 30% of city traffic consists of drivers who are merely *looking* for parking.

The elimination of drivers means the elimination of parking. That's because once you get where you're going, self-driving cars won't park there; instead they will drop you off, go to a remote location (or stay busy ferrying others) and return when needed. By eliminating street parking, two new lanes of capacity will be created in existing city streets. Bumper-to-bumper traffic will become nonexistent. Parking lots and garages will become obsolete, creating redevelopment opportunities for 61 billion square feet of prime real estate, according to McKinsey.

Simultaneously, the number of vehicles on the road will drop by 99%—from 245 million vehicles to 2.4 million, according to PWC. All this will occur as we shift from owning cars to merely using them, via on-demand and car-sharing services such as Uber and car2go. Destroying all those cars and converting all that real estate will launch an era of immense job creation, generating $1 trillion in new income.

Already, surveys show that 60% of U.S. adults are willing to ride in an autonomous car, and 32% say they will stop driving once SDVs are available. A study by Columbia University researchers says that Uber could replace New York City's 13,237 taxicabs with a fleet of 9,000 autonomous cars—a reduction of 32%; passengers would wait an average of 36 seconds for a ride that would cost $.50 per mile.

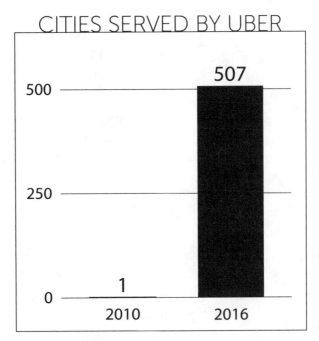

CITIES SERVED BY UBER

FIGURE 3.2

If the notion of self-driving cars freaks you out, just wait for self-driving cars that can *fly*.[19]

At least half a dozen companies are engaged in the development of flying cars. These include:

- Aviation Industry Corporation of China, which unveiled a concept vehicle in 2015.

- Carplane, a German manufacturer.

- Terrafugia, headquartered in Massachusetts. Its prototype has also already flown (the vehicle comes equipped with a parachute, just in case), and it plans to begin selling its flying cars in 2026. The four-seater will retail for $120,000, which is cheaper than . . .

---

[19]Admit it. You think that's ridiculous.

Incidentally

In 2016, Adrian Flux became the world's first insurance company to offer product liability insurance to cover SDV technology. Based in the United Kingdom, the policy covers drivers who use such autonomous features as self-parking and cruise control. The policy will pay for loss or damage:

- **due to satellite failure or outages affecting navigation systems**
- **caused by the vehicle's operating system**
- **if the driver fails to manually override the system to prevent an accident should the system fail**
- **if the car gets hacked**

Incidentally

Self-driving cars never exhibit anger, aggression or road rage—unlike 80% of human drivers, according to the AAA Foundation for Traffic Safety. If there's only one reason we need to get humans out of the driver's seat, it's this one: In 2014, 5.7 million drivers deliberately bumped or rammed another vehicle in anger. That's 3% of all drivers. In addition:

- **51% of all drivers admit that they purposefully tailgate.**
- **47% yell at other drivers.**
- **45% honk to display annoyance or anger.**
- **33% make angry gestures.**
- **24% try to block other vehicles from changing lanes.**
- **12% cut off other vehicles on purpose.**
- **4% get out of their vehicle to confront other drivers.**

Two in 3 drivers believe that aggressive driving is a bigger problem than it was in 2013 and is getting worse, and 9 in 10 believe that aggressive drivers are a serious threat to safety.

SDVs solve all these problems.

- . . . the $280,000 two-seat Volocopter, made by e-volo. It looks like a helicopter but has 18 propellers and reportedly is far quieter, and it is cheaper than . . .

- . . . Slovakia-based AeroMobil 3.0, which first flew in 2012. It seats four, fits in a standard parking space and runs on gasoline and costs $400,000. Orders are being taken.

- Joby Aviation, which started flying prototypes in 2016.

- Pal-V One, from a company based in the Netherlands. A prototype flew in 2012.

- Lilium Aviation, which is working on the first all-electric plane, is funded by the European Union. Its launch date is 2018.

- Moller International's Skycar, which will cost $500,000 to $1 million and seat four, with a maximum range of 805 miles and top speed of 308 mph—far farther and faster than any of its competitors.

- Zee.Aero, which is building a one-seat aircraft funded by Google cofounder Larry Page.

Wondering how people will be able to safely fly a car? No worries, because they won't. Instead, the vehicles will fly themselves, just as drones do today. All you'll do is enter your destination into the car's GPS (as you do now); the car's computer will use data from onboard magnetometers, accelerometers and gyroscopes to control the rotors or propellers. You'll just be along for the ride.

> But perhaps you'll be more comfortable with the more traditional type of aircraft: the blimp.
>
> Meet Worldwide Aeros Corporation's ML86X, an airship that, when completed in the 2020s, will be 920 feet long, 215 feet high and 355 feet wide. That's nearly the length of three football fields, the height of the Tower of Pisa and the width of two Boeing 747s. It's supposed to be able to carry 500 tons of cargo, equivalent to about 150 elephants.
>
> The company says that more than half the world's population has no access to paved roads. Airships able to take off and land without runways could deliver entire warehouses of equipment and other materials cheaply, quietly and safely.

And why stop with cars and planes? If they can become driverless, so can ships. Rolls-Royce thinks unmanned ships could operate 22% cheaper than today's vessels, according to *The Wall Street Journal*—mostly by saving payroll costs. It expects unmanned cargo ships to be sailing the seas by 2030.

Bionics

If you get queasy thinking about machines controlling cars, I hesitate to have you ponder machines controlling . . . your legs.

That's the field of bionics, the science of constructing artificial systems that mimic living systems. Yeah, we're talking about Steve Austin.[20] Imagine having eye, ear and brain implants that let you:

- See in the dark

- Hear any conversation, even in noisy restaurants, rock concerts or sporting events

- Recall everything you ever read

- Search the Web merely by thinking about a subject[21]

---

[20]You remember the 1970s TV show *The Six Million Dollar Man*, don't you? If you don't, ask your parents or grandparents—or Google or Alexa.
[21]Ridiculous? Neuroprosthetics have been helping those with hearing impairments or Parkinson's disease since the 1990s.

But bionics isn't just about mimicking human abilities; the field is equally interested in replicating animal and plant systems, too. Scientists have actually been doing this for centuries: Leonardo da Vinci sketched designs for flying machines based on his observation of birds in flight. The Wright Brothers got the idea for their plane's wingwarping mechanism by watching buzzards. And Velcro—widely considered one of the most practical bionics developments in history—was invented by the Swiss engineer George de Mestral in 1941 after he noticed that burrs from a burdock plant got stuck in his dog's fur. (He discovered that the burrs are covered in small hooks that catch onto anything with a loop, such as clothing and animal fur, and turned it into a useful product.)

Today, bionics is used in many fields, including engineering, medicine, computer science, chemistry, materials science, electronics, molecular genetics and more. Boat hulls are being made to imitate the thick skin of dolphins. Sonar, radar and medical ultrasound imaging imitate the echolocation of bats. And house paints repel dirt and water by copying traits found in lotus leaves.

Spiders produce silk that can stretch 40% beyond its original length, is stronger than steel and twice as elastic as nylon and can withstand temperatures to 570 degrees Fahrenheit. A spiderweb with strands as thick as a pencil could catch a jumbo jet in flight as if it were a butterfly, experts say. So imagine if we could create spider silk artificially—and use it industrially.

Well, apparently we can. The Japanese firm, Spiber, combines bacteria with recombinant DNA to produce spider-thread proteins, converts the proteins into powder and then into thread. One gram of the protein produces more than 5 miles of artificial spider silk. It joined with North Face in 2016 to produce a prototype parka designed to withstand freezing temperatures at the South Pole. The company says its silk will also be used to make lighter and stronger aircraft fuselages, automotive parts, surgical materials (including artificial blood vessels), bulletproof vests and space suits.

Other examples of bionic engineering include:

- A jacket that acts as a GPS system. Using haptic technology (which mimics the sense of touch through vibration), sensors embedded in clothing made by Wearable Experiments will tap your shoulder to let you know which way to turn.

- Robotic tentacles thinner than a human hair, created by scientists at Iowa State University, have been used to pick up an ant without damaging it. The innovation could be used in microscopic surgery.

- Swimsuits that give swimmers greater speed. Speedo has created a swimsuit with tiny scales similar to a golf ball's indentations. Based on the skin of sharks, the indentations help reduce drag so athletes can swim faster.

- A building that's ventilated and cooled like termite mounds on the savannah. Simple air exchange give the mounds constant humidity and temperature regardless of outside conditions, and the building, constructed in Zimbabwe, does the same by using materials that have a high heat capacity.

But what really captures our imagination is artificial systems that can be implanted into humans. Some noteworthy advances are:

- A bionic lens that would give humans perfect vision—almost three times 20/20—ending the need for glasses and contact lenses. The artificial lenses would eliminate cataracts by replacing natural lenses when they decay with age.

- A wireless implant called WiSE (wireless stimulation of the endocardium) for heart patients who don't respond well to pacemakers or CRT devices. It uses an electrode smaller than a grain of rice that hooks into the inner wall of the left ventricle. It's available in Europe; U.S. clinical trials are under way.

- A prosthetic hand that uses electrodes implanted in the forearm to allow amputees to regain the sense of touch.

- A "bionic spine," 3 centimeters long and a few millimeters wide, that should enable paralyzed patients to walk by giving them control over bionic limbs with the power of thought.

- Lab-grown skin that has all three layers of tissue found in human skin, thus enabling it to hold hair follicles and sweat glands. It would revolutionize treatment for burn victims and those with skin diseases.

- Cures for ailments using electricity instead of chemicals. By regarding the human body as an electrical system instead of a chemical one, therapies could be developed that would alter the electrical pulses that run through the body's nerves. Researchers are working on electric medicine treatments for such disorders as chronic pain, post-traumatic stress disorder and inflammatory bowel disease.

- A lightweight exoskeleton whose countermovements cancel the tremors associated with Parkinson's disease.

We're already creating prosthetics that enable people who are paralyzed to regain motion and provide functioning limbs to people who don't have them. You've seen hundreds of such stories already, including that of Amy Purdy, who became a medal-winning snowboarder after losing both of her legs below the knee, and Danny Letain, a Paralympic skier who says he can "feel" the tips of his prosthetic limb's fingers.

There are so many people with disabilities using robotic technology that they have their own sporting events; the first Cyborg Olympics were held in 2016 in Zurich, Switzerland.

The field of robotics is so diverse—cars, planes, ships, drones, bionics—and has so many applications—military, commercial and personal—that it's easy to see why this will be the world's biggest industry in the next decade and beyond. It will also be one of the most impactful of the exponential technologies.

It will be used for fun, too, driven to a large degree by our devotion to sports (covered in chapter 9). Forget all the noise you hear these days about illegal use of performance-enhancing drugs by athletes. In the future, every athlete will be legally enhanced. And it won't just be improved uniforms or a specific forum such as the Cyborg Olympics; tomorrow's athletes will be optimized through CRISPR and other yet-to-be-introduced gene-editing technologies.

And, yes, drugs will be used. They will be safe, detectable—and permitted—to improve players' psychological and physiological abilities. We already know which genes help produce great athletes:

- EpoR increases oxygen delivery as much as 50%.

- ACE lets you climb 8,000-meter peaks without oxygen tanks.

- SCN9A lets athletes play through pain.

- MSTN, when deactivated, lets the body double its muscle mass.

- PEPCK burns fatty acid for energy, with no lactic acid, so athletes can run at top speed 60% longer.

- TNC & COL5A1 determine whether the body is susceptible to tendon and ligament injury.

- LRP5 creates "unbreakable" bones by increasing skeletal density.

Performance enhancement won't be limited to athletes; these innovations will make their way to everyday people as well. A drug or gene therapy that improves muscles or strengthens bones will be prescribed for people with osteoporosis, for example. Just as technologies created for NASA and the military eventually make their way into the consumer marketplace, so will enhancements created for athletes.

By 2025, the Future of Sports report predicts, genetic alteration of athletes will be permitted for injury prevention. That will lead to acceptance of therapies for performance enhancement, and all restrictions (within safety limits) will soon thereafter be eliminated. By 2040, leagues will be divided into three types: natural athletes, performance-enhanced athletes (including bionics, not just gene therapy and drugs) and robotic athletes. And the best of each will compete in championships, to see who is truly best.

PERSONAL FINANCE IMPLICATIONS

1. Millions of jobs will be lost to robots; decide now if yours might be one of them, and if so, begin now to develop skills and abilities you can use in a new career. More on this in chapter 14.

2. Automobiles are fast becoming like smartphones: New technology (including, most importantly, safety systems) will cause you to replace them long before they wear out. Used-car values will fall faster than they used to, so think twice before buying a new car. In fact, you might even consider never buying a car again and just leasing instead.[22]

3. Plan on canceling your automobile insurance in coming years.

4. Don't buy municipal bonds. Local governments that can't generate revenue from driving infractions could find it difficult to repay investors. Their credit ratings could drop and interest rates could rise—reducing the value of existing muni bonds.

5. Many of the nation's largest companies might suffer declines or go out of business as robotics renders their products obsolete. This has implications for your investment portfolio. More on that in chapter 17.

---

[22]For more on car leasing, read chapter 50 of *The Truth About Money*.

Chapter Four: Nanotechnology and Materials Science

Some of the biggest changes we're going to experience are coming from the tiniest of innovations.

And I mean tiny. We're talking *nanometer* here—that's one-*billionth* of a meter. For perspective, a human hair and a sheet of paper are both about 100,000 nanometers thick. But nanotechnology involves dimensions of less than 100 nanometers! Indeed, nanotech often involves manipulation of individual atoms and molecules.

The technology is about to change everything. The American Society of Mechanical Engineers says that nanotechnology "will leave virtually no aspect of life untouched and is expected to be in widespread use by 2020."

As we saw in the introduction, computers have been shrinking ever since they were invented. We're already building transistors that are only 14 nm wide; by 2020 transistors will be only 5 nm across—and by 2025 they will be a single nanometer in width.

Incidentally

Stanford University researchers are using 3D printers to create computer chips made of carbon nanotubes. The chips, they say, could hit processing speeds 1,000 times as fast as the best existing chips.

Those individual atoms make a big difference. After all, the difference between sand and silicon chips is how the atoms are arranged. The same is true of coal and gold—and compared to an old, infirm patient and a young, healthy adult.

Sound confusing? Consider that all the words in the English language use only 26 letters—we simply decide which letters to use and in what order. Rearrange a couple, and dog becomes god. The implications are profound.

Advances in nanotechnology are already reaching the marketplace. Today you can buy tennis racquets, spill-proof pants and cosmetics manufactured with nanotech features. By 2018, smartphones will project holographic images that hover above the phone, using projectors the size of a Tic Tac.

The advances will be startling—ultra high-yield agriculture, environmental remediation, zero-pollution manufacturing and even personal spacecraft.[23]

But perhaps the most exciting advances will come in the field of medical nanorobotics. Artificial blood cells will travel the body, seeking out and destroying invading diseases and viruses. Tiny robots will repair torn ligaments and clogged arteries, perform glaucoma surgery and gastric bypass operations and even make dental repairs—often through quick and painless treatments that require no incisions or risk of infection and are 90% cheaper than current techniques.

The possibilities of nanotechnology are virtually endless—as, it seems, is the funding. Venture capital investments in nanotechnology have skyrocketed, from $4 billion in 2005 to more than $1 trillion in 2015, according to the National Science Foundation. With all that funding, it won't be long before some truly remarkable innovations are brought to the marketplace.

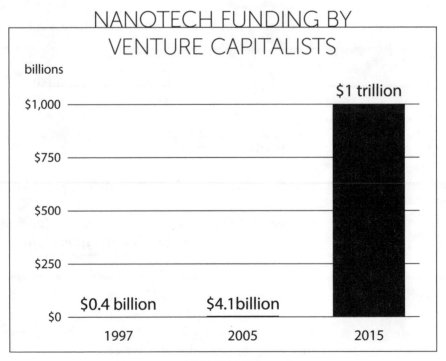

NANOTECH FUNDING BY VENTURE CAPITALISTS

FIGURE 4.1

---

[23]Dr. Dator! Paging Dr. Dator!

One of the most impressive results of nanotechnology is the invention of completely new materials that have an astonishing array of features never before seen.

To illustrate, let's consider graphene, the world's first two-dimensional material. It is the thinnest material known—just one atom tall.

Graphene is made from one of the most abundant minerals on earth: graphite, the material in your no. 2 pencil.[24] For a rough idea of how graphene is made, imagine using your pencil to draw a line across a sheet of paper. The graphite that's now on the page has a considerable height to it—at least in nanoscale terms. Imagine taking a pair of tweezers and peeling away the graphite's top layer. Do it again and again, slowly peeling away layer after layer, until the only thing remaining is a single layer of graphite. You now have a material that's a single atom in height; that, dear reader, is *graphene*.

Graphene is the strongest material ever measured—200 times as strong as steel, yet as pliable as rubber (it can stretch to 120% of its size). It's almost completely transparent, transmitting 97.7% of light. And it's highly conductive—150 times as much as silicon. It's the only substance known that's completely impermeable to liquids and gas, yet it weighs almost nothing.

Graphene has been theorized by scientists for decades and was first isolated in a laboratory in 2004. Today more than 25,000 patents exist using the product.

Half of those patents have been filed by Chinese companies, according to the United Kingdom's National Physical Laboratory. No surprise there: China is home to 70% of the world's known graphite, and the country's current Five-Year Plan (for the period 2016–2020) calls graphene "strategically important."

---

[24]That's right: your lead pencil contains graphite, not lead. And we drive on parkways but park on driveways. I don't know why.

Incidentally

Potential uses of graphene include:

COMPUTERS: Ultra-long-life batteries and photovoltaic cells that could power everything from mobile devices to your home; computers that are 100 times faster than today's fastest machines; touch screens, liquid crystal displays and organic LEDs for smartphones, tablets and televisions that would be superthin and bendable yet unbreakable.

ENVIRONMENT: Products made with graphene could eliminate radioactive waste and toxic spills; be deployed in water filtration systems for desalinization; create biofuels and improved solar cells.

AVIATION: Graphene-infused conductive paint could remove ice from aircraft; weight-saving inflatable slides and rafts could be installed on aircraft.

INDUSTRY: Graphene generates electricity when stressed; absorbs radio waves; acts as a sound transducer; generates faster chemical reactions than other materials; can be used in thermal management and the creation of structural materials; and can be used as a lubricant.

MILITARY: Body armor made of graphene can be produced for military personnel and vehicles.

HEALTH CARE: Graphene "scaffolds" can be used to repair spinal cord injuries; detect and diagnose microbes; monitor glucose, hemoglobin, cholesterol and DNA sequencing; measure the performance of implants as well as patients' breathing, heart rate and movement; conduct medical imaging; and deliver cancer therapies. Graphene could also be used for tissue regeneration and used in bionic devices that are implanted into living tissues connected directly to neurons, giving people who are paralyzed the ability to move.

During years of research for this book, my colleagues and I collected hundreds of announcements about nanotech innovations made by companies, governments and universities and in various academic journals. I'll spare you the details here[25] but thought you'd like to see a quick bullet list of what's coming. So:

---

[25]If you really want to see our entire 400-plus-page collection, give us a call.

Nanotechnology will enable us to:

- prevent, detect, treat and cure:
  - acne
  - aging
  - Alzheimer's disease
  - autoimmune diseases
  - baldness
  - blindness
  - brain injuries
  - cancer
  - diabetes
  - heart disease
  - HIV
  - infections
  - infertility
  - memory problems
  - nicotine dependence
  - osteoporosis
  - Parkinson's disease
  - tooth decay
  - vision problems
- grow real diamonds in two weeks in a lab
- create the world's fastest computers
- detect toxic gases and gas pollutants
- fight fires with a foam that gets stronger when temperatures increase
- repair oil and gas pipelines
- cover floors with antibacterial, antistatic and antiabrasion properties
- create a superglue tougher than the natural adhesives used by mussels and barnacles
- produce cotton clothing that:
  - alerts you if harmful bacteria are nearby
  - captures harmful gas
  - changes color
  - collects energy from our body as we move and uses it to power our electronic devices
  - communicates with computer networks
  - conducts electricity
  - converts sound and light into electrical signals that can be understood by a computer
  - detects explosives
  - kills bacteria
  - monitors your health
  - never stains
  - shields you from radiation
  - wards off malaria
  - warms or cools you
  - weaves transistors into shirts and dresses
- print extremely bright colors without using ink
- keep phone and tablet screens scratch-free, smudge-free and water-resistant
- detect gases emitted by rotting meat so we don't eat food that isn't safe to eat
- clean up oil spills
- detect avian flu outbreaks on farms
- charge a battery in 60 seconds
- use keyboards that can identify users by the way they type
- write on paper that:
  - can be erased and written on more than 20 times
  - is virtually indestructible, doesn't use trees, is 24 times stronger than ordinary paper, waterproof, dirt-proof, tear-proof, unsinkable and fire-resistant, yet lets you write notes and highlight passages
- kill mosquitos and other insects
- convert 90 percent of captured light into heat
- repel and attract objects with a tractor beam
- hide objects by applying an illusion coating that makes them invisible or appear to be something entirely different
- find bombs by detecting smells better than dogs
- apply paint that:
  - changes color when exposed to high temperatures, so we won't touch products that are hot
  - makes audible sound waves, turning painted surfaces into speakers
- conduct genetic tests in minutes and inexpensively
- protect stored grain from insects
- combat counterfeit goods
- store nuclear fuel
- conduct blood tests in minutes
- construct buildings that block 90% or more of the sun's energy when it is hot, cutting heating and cooling costs
- produce artificial skin that senses touch, humidity and temperature

PERSONAL FINANCE IMPLICATIONS

1. Expect to spend a lot of money replacing, upgrading and acquiring products boasting nanotech features. You'll want new clothes, furniture and carpets, freshly painted walls and much more. Be sure to factor this into your projections of how much income you'll need.

2. Anticipate improvements in health care as a result of new medical products and treatment options. This could cause you to spend more money—for both medical care and leisure (since being healthier could enable you to be more active).

Chapter Five: 3D Printing

Few innovative technologies have captured our imagination as much as 3D printing.

3D printing is actually quite simple: You stack tiny bits of material on top of one another until the desired product is complete. 3D printers can create physical objects from any digital model. And products can be made from thousands of materials, including metal, plastic, wax, rubber, composites, nylon, concrete— even food.

Using 3D printers reduces research, development and production costs, produces virtually no waste and allows for extreme personalization (it's how BMW offers buyers 10,000 options). And as with so many aspects of technological innovation, the cost is falling fast. In 2007, a 3D printer cost $40,000; today you can buy one for as little as $150—one four-hundredth as expensive in just nine years.

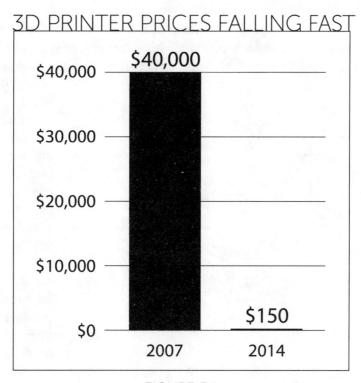

FIGURE 5.1

As is often the case, the military and NASA are leading the development of the technology. The Marines' F-35 fighter jet has more than 900 3D-printed parts; NASA is funding the development of a 3D food printer so astronauts can survive long-distance journeys.

> Expect 3D printers to become a standard kitchen appliance; families could print their dinner using cartridges of powders and oils that contain all the nutrients needed for a healthy and delicious diet.[26]

We're well beyond just government applications. Harvard's Materials Research Science and Engineering Center has printed electronic circuits on a 3D printer that costs less than $10,000, while the FDA has approved Spritam, a 3D-printed drug that treats epileptic seizures. (It delivers a higher dosage and dissolves more quickly than pills of comparable size that are manufactured using more traditional means.)

One of the most important benefits of 3D printing is the ability to produce structures of incredible complexity with extreme precision. Doctors at the University of Michigan have used a 3D printer to create tiny splints for a child born with a defective windpipe. Other physicians are using 3D printers that cost just $5,000 and require materials that cost as little as $20 per use to create replacement ears, vertebrae, ribs and prosthetics for children who are missing fingers.

At Oxford University, scientists can print material half the width of a human hair to deliver medicine or replace tissue. Germany's Max

"I wish I'd never bought Harold that 3-D printer."
Shannon Wheeler/The New Yorker Collection/The Cartoon Bank

---

[26]Interested in buying a plane ticket to Hawaii to visit Dr. Dator?

Planck Institute has printed a robot that can travel through the bloodstream to deliver medicine to a single spot or to provide missing substances, such as cartilage, while engineers at the University of Stuttgart in Germany have developed a 3D-printed, three-lens camera small enough to fit inside a syringe. Its lenses could be used to explore the human body, aiding in disease diagnostics and treatment.

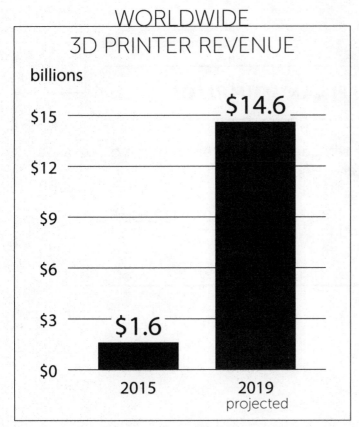

FIGURE 5.2

For consumers, the exciting element of 3D printing is the ability to customize all one's possessions. Unique jewelry, art and clothing can all be made using 3D printers. Nike manufactures the world's lightest running shoe, the Flyknit, using 3D printers. At Disney World, little girls can watch as their image is transformed into a statuette of their favorite Disney princess, featuring exact replicas of their faces.

No wonder 3D printer revenue, which was $1.6 billion in 2015, is projected to reach $14.6 billion by 2019, according to Gartner. That's an 815% growth rate. And if all this isn't exciting enough for you, just wait for 4D and 5D printing.

4D printers would create products that are deployed only when needed—upon a change in time, light, sound, temperature, humidity or some other environmental occurrence. For example, a pipe might need insulation only if it leaks. Or beach umbrellas might open only when the sun is shining.

5D printing would take this a step further: after deployment, the product would revert back to its original state when no longer needed. Think George Jetson's briefcase.[27]

There are few technologies as exciting—and fun—as 3D printing. I'm not sure we'll be installing *Star Trek*-like replicators in our homes anytime soon, but 3D printers will get us awfully close.

PERSONAL FINANCE IMPLICATIONS

1. If you're planning to remodel your kitchen or home office, allot space for a 3D printer.

2. Investment opportunities in companies developing and using 3D technologies abound. We'll learn more about these in chapter 17.

[27] Yes, George Jetson. Ask Dad.

Chapter Six: Medicine and Neuroscience

Imagine never getting old.

It's quite possible, because scientists have discovered that aging is not an inherent part of life. Rather, they say, aging is merely a disease—and, like other diseases, it can be treated, cured and ultimately prevented.

You're probably aware of many people of advanced age who are living and behaving like people decades younger than themselves. Consider Nola Ochs, who obtained a master's degree at age 98; Ruth Flowers, a professional DJ at age 82; Armand Gendreau, a skydiver at age 101; Johanna Quas, a gymnast at age 87; Dan Pellman, who set five world records at the Senior Olympics—at age 100; and Shirley Claire, who belted out Sinatra's hit "The Best Is Yet to Come" on the TV show *America's Got Talent* at age 87.

And then there's Ed Zarowin. After being fired as the head coach of the men's and women's cross-country and track-and-field teams at Hunter College in 2015, he filed an age discrimination suit—at the age of 88.

Although we can currently count the number of centenarians who are as healthy as 60-year-olds, they'll soon be so plentiful that their exploits won't be worth writing about. It's another case of our being at the knee of the curve.[28]

Consider that the average life expectancy in 1900 was 47 years. Today, according to the Society of Actuaries, it's 86.6 years for the average American male and 88.8 years for the average American female. And just as Watson will shrink to the size of a grain of sand, average life spans are extending. In fact, we're adding three months to our life expectancies every year, according to the National Institute on Aging; it estimates that by 2036, we'll be adding more than a year to our life expectancies annually—meaning the longer you live, the longer you're going to live.

So you might want to think about living for a really long time. Way more than 100 years.

---

[28]Recall the exponential growth curve from page xxxvii: this is the inflection point.

Incidentally

Why are life expectancies growing so dramatically? First, thank improvements in public health. Better hygiene, clean water and superior nutrition helped us prevent disease and improve our ability to recover when infected. That was followed by advances in medical technology—everything from anesthetics and antibiotics to X-rays and CAT scans—which allow doctors to diagnose and treat us with greater effectiveness and results than ever before.

How far will coming advances in medicine and neuroscience take us? Well, Ray Kurzweil thinks you might live forever. Before you dismiss this notion as entirely crazy—something so ridiculous that even Jim Dator can't mollify you—be aware that, in 2016, *Time* magazine called Ray "one of the 7 smartest people in the world." He's the director of engineering at Google, a member of the faculty of Harvard University, a cofounder of Singularity University,[29] a world-renowned scientist, and a recipient of the National Medal of Technology and Innovation. He's received 20 honorary doctorates, awards from three U.S. presidents and is the author of numerous bestselling books. So when Ray says you might live forever, you might want to ponder that statement instead of dismissing it.

I'm not going to delve into Ray's rationale, which you can read in his books.[30] Instead, I'll simply say this: When I interviewed Ray on my television show,[31] I observed that life expectancies have more than doubled in the past 100 years and asked if longevity is now about as far as it can go. His response was blunt. He asked, "What makes you think we're going to stop here?"

---

[29]It was Ray who introduced me to SU after he appeared on my television show.
[30]My suggested reading list is in the back.
[31]You can watch the interview at ricedelman.com.

This explains why, in 2015, *Time* conjectured that today's babies will live more than 140 years, while *Bloomberg Businessweek* suggested that we all just might live forever.

Rapid advances in medicine, neuroscience and synthetic biology are underneath all this. Scientists now understand that DNA is software, a four-letter code arranged in a specific order. They are learning how to rearrange that code and introduce new elements into it.

Their efforts began with sequencing the human genome, and the story of its success is itself an excellent illustration of the power of exponentiality. When the Human Genome Project was launched in 1990, it was expected to take 15 years and cost $6 billion. After seven years, only 1% of the genome had been sequenced; at that rate, it would take another 700 years to finish the project. But what many people failed to realize is that the sequencing rate was doubling every year. As a result, the project was completed just four years later—two years ahead of schedule. And the cost was $2.7 billion, less than half the projected budget.

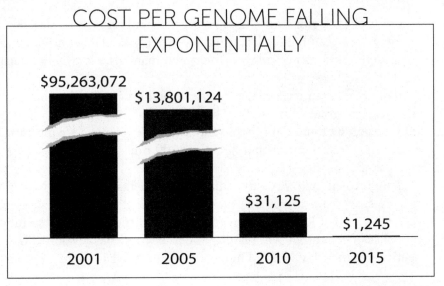

COST PER GENOME FALLING EXPONENTIALLY

$95,263,072 — 2001
$13,801,124 — 2005
$31,125 — 2010
$1,245 — 2015

FIGURE 6.1

And we didn't stop there. It now costs less than $1,000 to have your genome sequenced, and the results are available in a day. By 2020, it will cost less than a penny, and the results will be delivered almost instantaneously to your smartphone.

It's estimated that by 2020, all cancers will be renamed for their genomes; there will be no more "liver" or "lung" cancers. We already refer to the BRCA1 and BRCA2 genes in evaluating whether a woman is at risk for breast or ovarian cancer, and we will do this for virtually all other cancers as well. Such extreme accuracy will be of profound value in our pursuit of improved health care.

You can glimpse the future by studying the case of Nicholas Volker, the first child whose disease was cured through genetic manipulation. At age four, he was dying of an undiagnosed disease. Doctors evaluated more than 16,000 genetic variances and found a pathogenic gene. A blood transplant replaced the mutated gene with a healthy one—and cured the boy. That was in 2011.

Such advances are changing the very nature of medicine. Indeed, a new field has emerged: regenerative medicine. It involves the use of stem cells to replace cells damaged by age, disease or trauma. The Los Alamos National Laboratory has produced software that identifies virus DNA in just hours—250,000 times as fast as prior methods. The mChip cuts HIV testing from weeks to minutes, requires only a drop of blood instead of a vial as older methods do and costs only a dollar.

Biotechnology is not confined to medical schools and research laboratories. Today, anyone can build a lab, using tools freely available on the Internet. Virus construction kits, complete with their own manuals, are widely available online.

Autodesk, for example, offers a synthetic biology interface so high school students can program DNA online. Jack Andraka, a 14-year-old ninth grader, used information he found on Google and YouTube to create a pancreatic cancer early-stage detection test that he says is 100 times as sensitive, 28 times as fast and 1 26,000th the cost (it costs only three cents) as current testing technology. Although it will take years to confirm whether his invention lives up to its promises, everyone agrees that Jack's achievement heralds a new age for medical research and development. There seems to be little question that future high school science projects will feature students who have developed new pharmaceuticals in their high school biology labs and the basements of their homes.

The most exciting biotech activity involves the CRISPR/Cas9 system, named "Breakthrough of the Year" by *Science* magazine in 2015 and twice named one of 10 breakthrough technologies by *MIT Technology Review.*

In 2016, an advisory committee of the National Institutes of Health approved the technology as a cancer treatment; human trials to cure lung cancer are already under way in China. CRISPR/Cas9 is also being tested as a treatment for autism, schizophrenia, Alzheimer's disease and bipolar disorder. Scientists have also figured out how to remove HIV from human cells (so far, only in a lab).

Indeed, thousands of research papers have been published mentioning CRISPR[32]—by the time you read this, hundreds, perhaps thousands, of additional innovations will be under way. That's because the technology isn't limited to humans; CRISPR exists in every animal and plant species in the world. So yeasts are being modified to make biofuels. Crops are being altered so they can resist disease, need less water and produce higher yields. Biologists are creating mushrooms that don't brown, mosquitoes that can't spread malaria, cows that produce more milk, tomatoes that taste better, and bacteria that eat plastic waste. Scientists are even trying to bring back extinct species.[33]

Some people get worried about the idea of modifying crops. But we've been doing that for thousands of years—we're simply now able to manipulate plants at the molecular level. And we're getting really good at it, too: the first plant genome was sequenced in 2000 after seven years of effort (and at a cost of $70 million); today it takes less than three minutes (and costs under $100). The result are such achievements as the Arctic Apple, approved by the FDA in 2015: it doesn't turn brown within a day or two of being sliced open as ordinary apples do.

Also, we've been using genetically engineered seeds for more than 30 years; 93% of all the cotton planted in the United States is genetically engineered. So are 94% of all the soybeans and 92% of the corn. Collectively, more than 1 trillion genetically engineered meals have been served worldwide. These crops don't need as much water or pesticides, don't require plowing, don't cause as much soil erosion—yet produce more food per acre of farming, providing more income for

---

[32]Clustered Regularly Interspaced Short Palindromic Repeats. Happy now?
[33]Did I say scientists? Try teenagers. You can buy your own CRISPR kit online for about a hundred bucks. High school science fairs will never be the same.

farmers and more food for people. In a world where one-seventh of the population doesn't have enough to eat and 5 million children die annually from malnutrition, these advances are extremely valuable.

And we're not just genetically modifying plants. In vitro meat that's less vulnerable to disease and contamination will be grown in laboratories from stem cells. Essentially, a single cow—or rather, the DNA from it—will feed the world.

Don't bother calling Dr. Dator, because this is already happening. The first such beef was grown in a Dutch lab in 2013. It took researchers years to create a hamburger patty of approximately one-third of a pound, and it cost about $400,000. Three years later, another lab—this one in San Francisco—created a meatball from the cells of cows, chickens and pigs. It cost just $18,000—a price cut that exceeds the pace suggested by Moore's Law. The firm that created that meatball, Memphis Meats, says it will get the process cheap enough to let it sell the product by 2021. So it won't take long before you can order burgers made of lab-grown beef at your local fast-food joint![34]

Producing meat in a lab means we won't need to raise livestock. If all the grain we grow in the United States to feed cows, chickens and hogs were instead consumed by people, we could feed 840 million people worldwide, according to David Pimentel, an ecology professor at Cornell University's College of Agriculture and Life Sciences. 17% of the world's population currently suffers from hunger, but that figure will fall to just 6% by 2026, according to the U.S. Department of Agriculture. New technologies will help make that happen.

Supporters of this research include People for the Ethical Treatment of Animals. PETA believes this innovation could end animal cruelty on a global scale.

We're also genetically modifying insects. By creating mosquitoes that can't reproduce, scientists hope to eliminate dengue and chikungunya, and eventually, malaria and Zika. More than 70 million of these mosquitoes have been released so far in the Cayman Islands, Malaysia, Brazil, Panama and Florida, reducing infection rates as much as 90%.

---

[34]Okay, you can call Dr. Dator now.

Advances such as these are not merely going to help us live longer; they're also going to help us get healthier, feel better and act younger as we age. Yep, you will likely have the body of a 55-year-old when you are age 95.

All this means we are entering what some are calling "P4 Medicine": Medicine is becoming personalized, predictive, preventive and participatory.

In fact, the biggest boom in medicine right now is cosmetic enhancement. In 2014, there were 8 million procedures and surgeries in the United States. That's twice as many as in 2000. Today, more than half of American adults are considering cosmetic treatments. The number of Americans undergoing cosmetic procedures is up by 38% for Caucasians over the past 10 years, 72% for African Americans, 77% for Hispanic Americans, and 146% for Asian Americans.

The United States is not alone in this trend. In South Korea, one in five women has had cosmetic surgery. Iranian women lead the world in rhinoplasty. In Brazil, cosmetic surgery is tax-deductible.

Scientists at MIT and Harvard, for example, are working on an invisible film made of common, nontoxic ingredients that could be "painted" onto your face to make under-eye bags and wrinkles disappear. During a test of 170 subjects, no one reported allergic reactions. But the researchers say the technology isn't intended only as a beauty enhancement; they see it also as a breakthrough treatment for skin conditions such as psoriasis and eczema.

Incidentally

The 22nd Century Group, a plant biotechnology company, has developed tobacco with very low amounts of nicotine; the USDA has approved its export. Will smoking become acceptable again?

Incidentally

The website RealSelf had 51 million visitors in 2014. It offers detailed information on and physician referrals for such treatments as:

- Botox
- breast lift or reduction
- butt lift
- cellulite treatment
- chemical peel
- chin implant
- dental implants
- eyelid surgery
- facelift
- hair removal or transplant
- lip augmentation
- liposuction
- porcelain veneers
- rhinoplasty
- skin lightening
- tattoo removal
- teeth whitening

It's not just vanity that makes people want to improve their appearance; many studies have demonstrated that self-esteem rises with physical improvements to the face and body, and as it does, so do one's personal finances. According to the economist Daniel Hamermesh, people with above-average looks earn $230,000 more in the course of their careers than people with below-average looks.

We're already capable of changing ourselves cosmetically, and with advances in biotechnology, we'll soon be able to change ourselves physiologically as well, thanks to manipulation of our DNA. Therefore, it's easy to anticipate the day when we will alter the genes of our unborn children.

That's beginning to happen, too: 20% of the couples who visit the HRC Fertility Clinics in California don't have problems getting pregnant; they're hiring the clinic so they can choose the sex of their baby. The clinic uses in vitro fertilization and preimplantation genetic diagnosis to allow parents to choose which embryos to impregnate. The cost is $20,000 (not covered by insurance—yet).

If we can currently select the sex of our baby, how long will it be before we are also able to choose our baby's height, weight, left- or right-handedness, hair color, athleticism, intelligence and sexual orientation?

©Glasbergen
glasbergen.com

I won't attempt to answer that question. Instead, I'll merely say that advances such as those described in this chapter mean you must rethink your concept of aging—and consider what living 30 or 50 years longer than you always assumed will mean for you and your family.

"Your baby is developing very nicely. Would you like to send him an e-mail?"

PERSONAL FINANCE IMPLICATIONS

1. You must rethink your assumptions about retirement, career, income and leisure.

2. Depending on your age, health and life expectancy, you might need to make major changes to your financial plan; living decades longer will have a profound impact on your strategies for retirement, investments and insurance. We'll cover all this for you in the coming chapters.

Chapter Seven: Energy and Environmental Systems

We have certainly made a mess of our planet. Unbridled growth of cities without regard to environmental impact has placed Earth in a precarious position. Fortunately, innovations from exponential technologies may not only stop further deterioration of our environment but actually bring about remediation.

As we've seen, everything consists of atoms. So if toxic sludge is made up of atoms, let's rearrange them so the sludge becomes a harmless material.

Amazing efforts are under way, such as the Smog Free Project, launched in Rotterdam in 2015. It features the largest air purifier in the world, a tower 23 feet tall. It not only removes pollutants from the air, it compresses them into tiny cubes and fashions jewelry out of them. Its principals plan to build more towers in cities worldwide.

Energy

Everyone knows the problem with energy: Most of our natural resources are difficult to obtain, dangerous to produce, expensive to buy, hazardous to our health and environmentally damaging to use. Many relatively benign energy sources, such as wind, cost too much or are politically unpopular. (It's gotten so bad that the acronym NIMBY[35] has been replaced by BANANA.[36])

Fortunately, the solution is right in front of us. More accurately, it's right above us.

It's the sun.

The sun provides 10,000 times as much energy as we need; a square kilometer of desert can collect as much energy from the sun as we'd get from 1.5 million barrels of oil or 300 tons of coal. The deserts of North Africa alone could generate enough solar power to supply 40 times as much energy as the whole world needs.

---

[35]Not In My Back Yard.
[36]Build Absolutely Nothing Anywhere Near Anybody.

So what's stopping us from using solar energy more extensively?

Cost. Current technology is simply too expensive.

Fortunately, the situation is improving: in 1984, it cost $30 to produce a kilowatt-hour of energy via solar technology; today, it costs less than 16 cents—a 200-times improvement. And the cost is still dropping—by half every 24 months. If this rate of price improvement continues, solar energy could provide 100% of the world's needs by 2040.[37]

Of course, you might be wondering why we'd bother producing more energy than we need. The reason we want more energy is the same reason you want a bigger closet: Greater energy production creates greater capacity, and greater capacity enables us to do more than before. It's a virtuous cycle rather than a vicious one.

The technological challenge doesn't stop at producing solar energy cheaply. We also have to figure out how to store and distribute it. That's because the sun doesn't shine at night or on cloudy and rainy days. And most of the world's population doesn't live in sun-drenched deserts. So we have to grab the sun's energy where and when we can, store it for later use and transport it to places that can't collect enough sunshine on their own.

In other words, we need to dramatically improve battery technology. Batteries of the future will be built with cheap, abundant elements such as sodium and water instead of lithium, will release energy evenly (avoiding surges that can break electronics), won't corrode and will be so safe you could eat them without risk. They'll be quiet, too, require no maintenance and produce no environmentally damaging greenhouse gases.

Sound ridiculous? MIT and Samsung have already developed what they say is "an almost perfect battery" that's rechargeable, never wears out, is 30% smaller than current batteries and can't overheat. Dongxu Optoelectronic Technology has produced a graphene battery that can be charged in just 15 minutes—20 times as fast as a standard lithium-ion battery—and can be recharged every day

---

[37]As Ray Kurzweil might say, don't stop there: If the price continues to fall by 50% every two years, solar energy could provide 200% of the world's needs in 2042, 400% of the world's needs by 2044, 800% by 2046, and so on. Dontcha just love exponentiality?

for 10 years before it wears out. A Ukrainian start-up has created a device that fits inside an iPhone and can wirelessly charge the battery; it simply needs to be within 16 feet of a power source. Other companies are making similar advances.

Imagine a world where solar panels on your roof produce cheap energy, which batteries in your basement store until needed. If your solar panels start producing more energy than you need, what will you do with the excess?

Many state and local governments require power companies to buy the energy produced by such home owners. In Brooklyn, New York, TransActive Grid lets home owners sell their excess solar energy to neighbors. It started in 2016 on a street involving 15 houses—and that's obviously just the beginning.

This technology threatens the nation's utilities—and they know it. The Edison Electric Institute released a report stating that power companies face the risk of "declining retail sales," "loss of customers" and "potential obsolescence."

Water, Electricity and Heat

> *"Water, water, every where,*
> *Nor any drop to drink."*

That's from Samuel Taylor Coleridge's famous poem, published in 1798. It accurately describes not only the fate of the mariner in his tale but that of hundreds of millions of people around the world today.

Indeed, 780 million people, half of whom live in sub-Saharan Africa, lack access to clean, drinkable water, according to the United Nations. Also, according to the United Nations, the typical toilet bowl in an American home contains purer water than the murky, disease-infested water all these people drink every day.

This explains why diarrhea is one of the world's leading causes of death for children under five. It kills 800,000 children each year.

The lack of clean water is a big reason why there's so much poverty: Women and girls living in poor villages spend up to six hours a day fetching water, preventing them from going to school or earning an income. Indeed, studies show that reducing the time spent fetching water by just 30 minutes a day would increase school attendance by 12%.

Even those in school aren't necessarily receiving the freshwater they need; the United Nations says that a third of the world's schools don't have freshwater or sufficient sanitation to prevent disease, resulting in 443 million lost school days due to water-related illnesses that compromise students' ability to learn.

And water isn't the only thing children spend their day fetching. They also devote hours to looking for animal dung. Three billion people rely on it for fuel, according to the World Health Organization.

Women burn the dung in their huts for warmth and light and as a fuel for cooking. But the material is extremely unhealthy: The resulting household air pollution, WHO says, not only contributes to climate change, it causes pneumonia; stroke; heart disease; chronic obstructive pulmonary disease; lung, nasopharyngeal and laryngeal cancers; low birth weight; tuberculosis; cataracts; burns; and other diseases.

All told, the toxic fumes kill 4.3 million people a year. Four times as many people in sub-Saharan Africa die of the fumes as of AIDS, and the soot is responsible for more than half the deaths among children under age 5 (who die of pneumonia after inhaling it).

How can we solve these problems? By fixing the toilet.

Yes, the ordinary, humble toilet operates largely the same as it has for more than 150 years. But that is about to change. With funding from the Bill & Melinda Gates Foundation, the "Reinvent the Toilet Challenge" aims to not only revolutionize how we deal with this basic bodily function but dramatically improve the lives of billions of people around the world—and the environment as well.

Sounds grandiose, because those of us living in the developed world think nothing of using the toilet. We flush, and the bowl's contents . . . simply go away.[38] The plumbing and sewer systems required to manage this flow are engineering marvels, produced at massive cost and labor over hundreds of years.

---

[38] When was the last time you wondered *where* it goes?

But billions of people live in villages that don't have enough money—or water—to create, let alone sustain, the elaborate systems enjoyed by those living in the United States and other developed nations. And the Gates Foundation is convinced that the toilet can solve all three problems of water, heat and electricity.

It envisions a self-contained system that requires no infrastructure, pipes, septic system or sewers. The system would burn feces and flash-evaporate urine, making everything sterile simultaneously. It would return fertilizer, table salt, freshwater and electricity—enough to power your home. The total cost: just 5 cents per day.

And by eliminating the need to hunt for fuel, children could go to school and their parents could go to work, creating vast new opportunities for economic growth and giving people the chance to raise themselves out of abject poverty and enter the middle class.

It's not just the Third World that can benefit from a new toilet. It could be of tremendous value to developed nations as well. In many cities, centuries-old sewer systems are crumbling, wasting massive amounts of water and creating environmental damage. This new system could provide an economical alternative to replacing millions of miles of pipes while generating free electricity to help power our homes.

The lowly toilet. Who would've thought that improving this age-old tool could create such vast opportunities in the 21st century?[39]

That's not the only innovation aimed at solving the dirty-water problem. Another example comes from Carnegie Mellon, where researchers have created a "drinkable book." Each page is a filter: Simply tear one out, pour contaminated water through it and out comes pure, drinkable water! The filter kills 99.9% of bacteria—equal in safety to U.S. tap water. Each page lasts a month with daily use; a single book meets one person's drinking water needs for four years. And the pages cost just pennies to produce.

---

[39]Well, duh. Bill and Melinda Gates did.

Bottling the Ocean

Another key solution to our water problem is desalination. The world's most abundant resources of water—our oceans and seas—are of little use to us because of their high salt content. In fact, according to the World Business Council for Sustainable Development, we access only one-half of 1% of Earth's water. But new technologies are allowing us to remove salt from seawater with greater efficiency and effectiveness than ever.

For example, Israel opened the world's largest desalination plant in 2013; when fully operational in 2020, it will deliver 20% of all the country's water needs.

Incidentally

Researchers at the University of Southampton have created a device that turns water into ultrasound waves. Tap water could thus clean anything—from your kitchen counter to biological contaminants on surgical steel.

But it's worth noting that we don't drink most of the water we use. Instead, we use 80% of it on agriculture. Indeed, it takes 237 gallons of water to produce a pound of wheat and 147 gallons for a pound of corn, according to a study from professors at Colorado State University. The irony is that we don't grow all those crops so we can eat them. Instead, we use the crops to feed our animals (mostly cattle, chickens and pigs). And we eat *them*—not the crops themselves.

Research by David Pimentel show that it takes 12,000 gallons of water to produce one pound of beef. The inefficiency is astonishing: For every ton of animals that humans consume, the animals we eat consume 6 tons of plants.

In chapter 6, we saw how the grains currently eaten by livestock could feed 840 million people. Pimentel says that if those grains were exported, the annual U.S. trade balance would improve by $80 billion.

Eliminating the need to feed all those animals would also free up vast areas of land, which we could use for other purposes or allow to revert to its natural state. According to the Department of Agriculture, the area of the United States is 2.3 billion acres; slightly more than half, or 1.2 million acres, is devoted to agriculture. And three-quarters of that is used for raising livestock. Imagine what real estate developers could do with three-quarters of a billion acres of land.

Until we get to the point where we no longer need to raise animals on farms, we'll have to continue feeding them. That means we need to figure out how to grow the crops they—and we—need, without requiring so much water or land.

Hydroponics and Aeroponics

Enter two new sciences. Hydroponic farmhouses allow plants to grow in a nutrient solution without soil; water usage efficiency is increased by 70%. Aeroponic factories, which grow plants in midair, are even better than hydroponic ones; water use is cut by an astonishing 98%. These processes are so efficient that a single 30-story building in New York City could feed 50,000 people per year. One acre in a skyscraper is equivalent to as many as 20 traditional soil-based acres.

It's estimated that 150 vertical farms could feed everyone in New York City. These facilities would be immune to weather, produce crops year-round, generate no agricultural runoff, reduce the need for fossil fuels and allow us to reforest old farmland or put that acreage to other uses.

This is not merely conjecture; such projects are under way. In Newark, New Jersey, an old steel factory is now the world's largest vertical farm. Inside the building, a pesticide-free aeroponic mist, packed with nutrients and oxygen, enables plants to grow more quickly—a full crop cycle is just 16 days. The facility can produce 2.2 million pounds of crops annually, 75 times as much as a traditional farm of similar size. And the factory recycles materials, uses less energy thanks to a photosynthetic lighting system, requires no soil and uses only 5% as much water as traditional farms.

Repairing Our Planet

How can we meet our energy needs and provide ourselves enough water without destroying the planet—and ourselves along with it? Improper disposal of hazardous materials and waste, industrial accidents and leaks and natural disasters all cause environmental disaster throughout the United States and the world, destroying forests, making water unsafe and killing wildlife—and sometimes ourselves.

Exponential technologies offer solutions to these problems, giving us the opportunity to enjoy longer, healthier lives supported by greater economic freedom.

Incidentally

Here are some examples of innovations in environmental remediation that are under development:

- Purdue University researchers have created a way to clean up oil spills using inexpensive materials found in everyday household cleaning products.

- Modern Mining Solutions has developed a water purification system that can be used for large lakes and underground aquifers that have been contaminated with pollutants.

- Researchers at Ohio State University have produced a stainless steel mesh, the result of 10 years of research, that can collect oil on a mass scale.

- Inventor Cesar Harada has invented a drone sailboat that cleans an oil spill by pulling an absorbent sleeve through it.

- MIT researchers have formed nanoparticles that attach themselves to oil when mixed into contaminated water, making it easier to collect and remove.

- A Canadian company has crafted a cleanup technology based on milkweed fibers, which naturally repel water and oil. The company says its kits remove oil twice as fast as the most proven methods.

- Yanko Design has developed a drone that releases bacteria that breaks down oil and prevents it from spreading. The device also transmits sound waves that keep wildlife from approaching infected areas—to protect fish, birds and other animals while making it easier to clean up spills.

- The National Center for Atmospheric Research can predict how fire will spread, using technology that analyzes weather data and topography. Researchers have discovered that fire patterns closely resemble those of severe storms, and they have partnered with NASA to create a smartphone app to help firefighters direct their resources.

Chapter Eight: Innovations in Education

Education in the future will be as different as today's college campuses are from the one-room prairie schoolhouse of yesteryear.

Good thing, too, because today's efforts to provide youth with college degrees aren't working. What you're about to read is a sharp condemnation of today's higher education system. I'm going to present you with a strong case that college is broken—and then I'll show you how innovations from exponential technologies will help us fix it.

Let's start with the cost of a college degree. The average cost of in-state tuition at public universities in the 1980–81 school year was $2,320, according to the College Board. The average cost for the 2015–16 school year was $9,140. That's an average annual increase of 4.08%, compared to an overall annual inflation rate of 3.01% for the Consumer Price Index, according to the Bureau of Labor Statistics. In other words, tuition has been rising 33% faster than the average rate of inflation.

This forces students to borrow heavily, unlike their parents and grandparents who went to college. Although most students graduated with no debt in 1990, more than 70% of the class of 2016 left school with debt, at a record average of $37,000 per graduate, according to the *International Business Times*. In total, 42 million people owe $1.3 trillion in student debt, representing 6% of the national debt, according to the Center for Investigative Reporting. As a nation, that's more than we collectively owe to credit cards.

And two-thirds of students don't know how interest rates work, according to a 2016 survey by LendEDU. Two-thirds don't realize that interest accrues while they're in school, and 8 in 10 don't know the repayment terms of their loans. That lack of knowledge costs them when they leave school: More than 8 in 10 adults—81%—say they have made financial or personal sacrifices due to their student loan debt, according to a survey by the American Institute of CPAs. Of the respondents:

- 50% delayed contributions to retirement accounts.

- 46% are moonlighting.

- 40% are living with roommates instead of living alone.

- 40% delayed the purchase of a house.

- 37% moved in with family members.

- 20% postponed marriage.

- 19% delayed having children.

And those with student loans need 10 years on average to accumulate enough money to make a down payment on a home—twice as long as it takes students who graduate without college debt, according to research by Apartment List.

All this might be tolerable if college were a good investment. But too often it's not. Of those surveyed, 71% would go to a different school if given a second chance—half to a community college for two years and half to a public university instead of a private one.

Their wistful wishes are understandable. It takes so long to pay off college loans that of parents aged 46 to 55 who are trying to save for college for their own teenage children, one in four is still paying off his or her own student loan, according to the College Savings Foundation.

All this might be tolerable if the spending got the results everyone is looking for. After all, lots of people buy cars they later realize they can't afford—but at least they get to drive them. But more than 35 million college students never graduate. Indeed, 21.5% of the U.S. adult population are college dropouts, according to the Census Bureau.

Only 39% of students graduate college in four years, according to the National Center for Education Statistics. Instead, 60% graduate in six years. From a financial perspective, that's almost as bad as never graduating. According to ACT, 31.5% of college freshmen—nearly one in three—drop out of school, and only about half graduate in four years; a great many take six years to graduate. An analysis by researchers at the University of Texas at Austin of students who took out loans found that those who graduate in four years owe an average of 40% less than those who graduate in six years. And by taking an extra two years to graduate, students cost themselves nearly $300,000 in additional tuition expenses, extra interest on loans, lost income and reduced retirement savings, according to a study by NerdWallet.

Incidentally

The federal government is the primary lender to student borrowers, providing 90% of all the money students receive in loans. The rest is provided by commercial lenders—and 90% of them require a creditworthy adult to cosign the loan on behalf of the undergraduate. Getting a cosigner can help the student obtain lower interest rates and fees because the loan's terms are based on the co-signer's credit score, which is almost certainly higher than the student's.

But three in four students don't know that cosigners are legally obligated to repay the loan if the student fails to make payments, according to a survey by LendEDU. Since cosigners, typically the student's parents or grandparents, are in their fifties, sixties or seventies, they are placed at significant financial risk. And for many, this risk becomes real, because 17% of all students—7 million Americans—are in default on their loans, according to the Department of Education. According to the College Savings Foundation, 15% of all the debt owed by retirees is for student loans—up from virtually zero 25 years ago. And a study by the Government Accountability Office found that more than 155,000 Social Security recipients had their Social Security checks garnished in 2013 because of this issue.

Incidentally

Yes, two extra years of college mean two more years of tuition expenses and two fewer years in the workforce. That means two fewer years that you can earn a salary and get matching contributions for your retirement plan, and two fewer years of compound growth for your savings. It also means two fewer years of retirement before you die. College costs are a problem, and the longer you take to get your degree, the bigger the problem becomes.

Students take more than four years to get their degrees because 80% of them change their majors at least once, according to the National Center for Education Statistics. And 37% transfer to a different school at least once, according to the National Student Clearinghouse Research Center, and when they do, their credits aren't always accepted by the new school—forcing them to retake classes. Changing majors and schools is why the average student obtains more credits than necessary, according to the book *College (Un)bound*.

Refusing to take credits earned at other colleges is one of the biggest scandals in higher education. If the education a student got from a class at another school isn't acceptable, why is the school willing to hire as a *professor* someone who graduated from there?

College has also become exclusionary, and a big reason is cost. According to *The Journal of Higher Education*, large numbers of in-state applicants are rejected by public universities because out-of-state students pay more. The result: Fewer low-income and minority students get to go to college.

Incidentally

And the problem is getting worse: Enrollment of out-of-state freshmen jumped by 20% from 2003 to 2013, says PRC. By 2016, one in four students at public universities were from another state. It's even worse at some schools; the University of

Incidentally

Some of the most lavish accommodations aren't even available to all students. Instead, they're reserved for the athletes. Football players at Clemson University have their own miniature golf course, volleyball courts, laser tag arena, movie theater, bowling lanes, barbershop and other amenities. The University of Tennessee's 145,000-square-foot training center has a two-story weight room, hydrotherapy room and amphitheater-style meeting room. Florida State and the University of Florida have indoor football practice facilities (something the NFL's Jacksonville Jaguars don't have—meaning the university's athletes are treated better than the pros).

These schools, like most others, charge every student—not just athletes—annual "activity fees" to pay for all this. And the bills are massive: Georgia Tech collects more than $5 million per year from students to help pay for its athletic department—whether or not those students go to any games or use any of its facilities. It's the same at many other schools.

Alabama student body, for example, is more than 50% nonresident.

So assuming you get accepted to attend, what are you getting in exchange for today's huge tuition bills? As we've seen, most graduates don't feel they got a great education. But they do get frills. At Boston University, they get to live in a 26-story glass-and-steel tower featuring walk-in closets and floor-length mirrors. The Indiana University of Pennsylvania spent $270 million on residence halls complete with private bedrooms and bathrooms, wireless Internet, microwave ovens, refrigerators and carpeting. Gettysburg College's $27 million, 55,000-square-foot recreation center has a rock-climbing wall.[40] Drexel University's $45 million, 84,000-square-foot rec center has a walking and jog-

Incidentally

College students aren't the only ones enjoying big perks on campus. So are college presidents. According to the *Chronicle of Higher Education's* **annual survey of compensation, the average salary of presidents of private colleges in 2013 (the most recent data available) was $436,429. Public school presidents earned an average of $428,250. And 34 college presidents (32 private, 2 public) earned more than $1 million per year. This doesn't include perks that college presidents often receive, such as free housing, a car and driver, tickets to sporting events, paid sabbaticals and even guaranteed employment for spouses.**

---

[40]In reviewing an early draft of this book, one of my researchers pointed out that a rock-climbing wall is not considered opulent. I thanked him for making my point.

ging track. The University of Memphis has a $50 million, 169,000-square-foot campus center with its own movie theater and food court. The University of Alabama, Boston University and Texas Tech each provides students with a lazy river. And High Point University offers students a first-run movie theater, a steakhouse, outdoor hot tubs, free food, a roaming ice cream truck and a concierge desk. It even employs a Director of Wow. No wonder *College (Un)bound* says college students spend 3.3 times as many hours on social and recreational activities as they do in classes, in labs and studying. With all that fun being offered, which would *you* rather do?

Incidentally

More than 35 million Americans are college dropouts, according to Ali Houshmand, the president of Rowan University. An internal study found that 2,600 students attended Rowan from 2006 to 2012 but left without obtaining a degree—even though they had completed 60 credits or more. And 550 of them—or 21%—had earned 120 credits or more.

Rowan decided to invite 175 of its former students back—and 10 percent of them accepted the offer. To support them, Rowan pays for up to 10 credits, provides additional tuition discounts and offers a general studies degree for students who didn't meet the course requirements of their major. Rowan is sharing its experience with other colleges and universities so they can help their dropouts as well.

Here's another problem with today's education system: Classes are priced without regard to the degree being sought. The typical student graduating with a degree in petroleum engineering earns $120,000; the typical student with a degree in counseling psychology earns an average of only $29,000. But when those two students attend the same college or university, their cost of tuition is identical.

The money being spent doesn't seem to be doing much. The study *Academically Adrift* found that 45% of students make no statistically significant gains in critical thinking, complex reasoning and writing skills in their first two years of college; 36% made no gains over four years. Small wonder, then, that one in four college graduates earning less than $50,000 a year says a degree was a bad deal.

And here's the most damning statistic: A 2013 study by the Federal Reserve Bank of New York found that only 27% of the nation's college graduates are working in a field closely related to their major.[41] (Those with graduate degrees were excluded from the study.) And only 62% had a job that required a degree at all. This strongly suggests that an overwhelming number of college students

---

[41]Are you? How about your kids?

are studying the wrong subjects—and that many are spending years, and hundreds of thousands of dollars, getting a degree they'll never use. How often do people buy cars they'll never drive or homes they'll never occupy?

Clearly, our higher education system is broken. It's hard to draw any other conclusion. And education is broken around the world, too.

According to the United Nations, 58 million children didn't go to primary school in 2015. Ninety-three countries have an acute shortage of teachers. In a third of countries, 25% of primary school teachers do not meet national standards. The world needs 2.7 million primary education teachers—1.3 million to fill new posts and 1.4 million to replace retirees. By 2020, says UNESCO, 10.9 million additional teachers will be needed.

Fortunately, solutions are being developed by exponential technologies. Venture capitalists invested $1.9 billion in education technology in 2015 alone, double the amount invested in 2014. The results: innovations including free textbooks, remote learning, self-paced learning, education without teachers and free education. Let's look at each one.

Incidentally

Half of recent college graduates are working at jobs that don't require a bachelor's degree, according to a 2014 study by the Federal Reserve Bank of New York, suggesting that half of all graduates may have wasted hundreds of thousands of dollars and four to six years of their lives—and negatively affecting countless more years of their lives.

Free Textbooks

The average cost of a new textbook is $82, according to the National Association of College Stores, and many titles cost more than $200.

It's easy to eliminate the cost of printing books: Put their content online. It's already happening: Achieving the Dream, a project serving community colleges, has 76,000 students in business administration, general education, computer science and social science use a digital library; 100,000 students attending community colleges in Virginia are using "open resources," saving students more than $3 million a year.

The University of Maryland's University College has eliminated printed textbooks in favor of online materials for its 64,000 undergraduates. And OpenStax College, a nonprofit supported by the Gates Foundation, Rice University and others, produces peer-reviewed digital textbooks for free. Nearly 700,000 students at 1,855 schools have saved more than $68 million using its materials since 2012.

©Glasbergen
glasbergen.com

"This book is defective. I tap the page and nothing happens!"

Research shows that free open-access materials not only lower costs (to $128 per course, on average, according to the Student Public Interest Research Groups), they lead to better grades, higher course completion rates and faster degrees (saving even more in tuition costs and accelerating the student's ability to get a job and start earning money).

Remote Learning

Stanford University rejects 9 in 10 applicants. This gave Sebastian Thrun an idea. A research professor in Stanford's computer science department, Thrun decided to create an online course on artificial intelligence for anyone who wanted to participate. Launched in 2011, the course attracted 160,000 people from 190 countries, aged 10 to 70. More than 23,000 students completed the class, and 250 earned perfect grades—none of whom was from Stanford.

Thrun used this experience to cofound Udacity, an online site that offers low-cost classes. In the process, Thrun and his colleagues created the first MOOC, or massively open online course. Udacity focuses on providing vocational courses for professionals—the kind of education needed to increase job skills and improve careers. In 2014, Udacity taught 1.6 million students from 203 countries. It also partners with the Georgia Institute of Technology to offer a master's degree in computer science.

Today, hundreds of colleges and universities around the world offer MOOCs. Many do so through Coursera, whose slogan is "An education in anything for anyone anywhere." Its CEO is Rick Levin, former president of Yale University. The site boasts 35 million students worldwide and offers more than 4,200 courses provided by 122 institutions, including some of the biggest names in higher ed both in the United States and abroad (such as Penn State, Johns Hopkins, Northwestern, Yale, Caltech and the University of Tokyo). Most MOOCs cost less than $100; a master's degree from Georgia Tech costs just $7,000 (compared with as much as $60,000 when obtaining it the traditional way).

> Move over, MOOCs. You're being bypassed by MOORs. Instead of merely taking online classes, students are now being invited to participate in online research. Through a MOOR, or massively open online research, students can work on research projects under the leadership of prominent scientists from around the world—learning by doing, not just by listening, reading and watching.

Technology isn't the only driver of lower costs; competition and social policies help. Pace Law School in New York offers tuition equal to the lowest-cost public law school in the student's home state. It's a bargain for many students.[42] And the state of Tennessee offers a free two-year associate's degree from any of its community or technical colleges.

Self-Paced Learning

If there's a problem with MOOCs, it's that, as they are college courses, there are schedules to maintain. Such rigidity doesn't work for many people. Your schedule might not let you attend on a regular basis, and if you need to review material, you could fall behind.

---

[42]And supports my criticism that tuition pricing is arbitrary.

The solution is self-paced learning. One of the first such sites was Khan Academy, a nonprofit organization created in 2006 by Salman Khan. While working as a hedge fund analyst, Khan produced a short online tutorial for his younger cousin who was struggling with math. She shared it with friends, who asked for more tutorials, so Khan started posting tutorials on YouTube. The videos' popularity led Khan to quit his job and create the academy, with the stated goal of providing a "free, world-class education for anyone, anywhere." He has since received funding from the Gates Foundation, Google, AT&T and others.

Although early Khan videos covered only mathematics, the academy now offers courses in history, health care, medicine, finance, physics, chemistry, biology, astronomy, cosmology, civics, art history, economics, music, computer programming and computer science—more than 5,000 in all and they've been translated into 26 languages (30% of users live outside the United States). Learners can move at their own pace and rewind or skip through lessons. And, recognizing the role gamification can play in education, Khan Academy offers six levels of badges to reward students for their progress. As of 2016, Khan Academy students had completed 3.8 billion exercises from 580 million lessons.

Another self-paced learning company is The Great Courses Plus, which offers more than 7,000 lectures. You can construct your own syllabus and view it anytime on demand. Cost: $16 to $500 per lecture, or $179.99 for an annual subscription to its streaming service.

©Glasbergen
glasbergen.com

"You have to attend classes. You can't just follow me on Twitter."

Still another is MasterClass, whose slogan is "access to genius." It has only one person teaching a given course. After all, how many psychology professors do we really need? Shouldn't we find the one psychology professor who is better at teaching psychology than every other psychology professor—and give that one psychology professor the world's biggest podium so he or she can reach not just 20 students but millions around the world?

That's the concept behind MasterClass. Kevin Spacey teaches acting. Annie Leibovitz teaches photography. Christina Aguilera teaches singing. Usher teaches performance. James Patterson teaches writing. And Serena Williams teaches tennis. The cost is $90 per course.

Education Without Teachers

Instead of eliminating all teachers per field but one, as MasterClass does, why not go a step further and eliminate *all* teachers—period. That's what 42, a university in Paris, did. Its goal is to teach 10,000 students how to create computer code by 2020. The university is completely free and has no teachers. No standardized testing, either. Just peer reviews and coding projects. Aspiring students aged 18 to 30 compete in groups of 1,000 in a four-week coding and logic competition; the best are admitted. When the school opened in 2013, it received 20,000 applications and admitted 2,500 students. It now has a campus in Silicon Valley as well.

Another program, launched in 1999, is the Hole-in-the-Wall Education Project (HiWEP), conceived by Sugata Mitra, chief scientist at NIIT, a global management training company based in India. Curious about whether computers could facilitate unsupervised learning, in 1999 Mitra's team cut a hole in the wall between NIIT's offices in Kalkaji, New Delhi, and the slum on the other side. The team inserted a computer into the hole—and waited.

Soon children living in the slum began using the computer on their own, and they quickly developed proficiency. Additional experiments confirmed the ability of children to develop computer skills without any instruction, supervision or coaching. At this writing, there are more than 100 Hole-in-the-Wall Learning Stations throughout India.

Free Education

When you combine capitalism and social policy, amazing things happen. Policy makers want more people to go to college, and employers want to attract good workers. Starbucks found a way to combine these goals: it gives all of its 135,000 employees who work at least 20 hours per week the opportunity to get a free online college education from Arizona State University.

Fiat Chrysler goes even further: not only can every employee working at a Fiat, Chrysler or Jeep dealership obtain a bachelor's degree for free, he or she can also obtain a master's degree for free—and so can every member of his or her family! The degrees are offered online through Strayer University.

At Arizona State University's W. P. Carey School of Business, all its MBA students attend for free, thanks to a $50 million donation from the real estate developer William Polk Carey. Instead of using the money to pay faculty salaries, which the school had been doing since 2003, administrators in 2015 started spending the money on their students instead—eliminating tuition, which had ranged from $54,000 to $90,000 for the two-year program.

> If Arizona State could do this with a $50 million donation, it makes you wonder what Harvard could do with its $38 billion endowment. Or Yale ($26 billion). Or Stanford, Princeton, MIT, Texas A&M, University of Michigan, University of Pennsylvania, Columbia and Notre Dame, which collectively are sitting on $162 billion.

Other opportunities for a free education are emerging, too. Tennessee lets every high school graduate attend one of its community or technical colleges for free. The University of the People is an accredited online institution built for underserved students worldwide—and is tuition free. Its initial class of 700 students, enrolled in 2014, hails from 180 countries; 30% are from Africa, only 25% are from the United States. The university's enrollment jumped to 4,000 students in 2016. Classes are 10 weeks long, include weekly homework and quizzes, and are taught by an almost entirely volunteer faculty. (The university needed 100 professors; 3,000 volunteered.) The university is funded by New York University, the Gates Foundation and others.

As a result of all these innovative ways to gain knowledge, you—and your children and grandchildren—need to rethink your approach to college. It's never been more important to obtain knowledge and skills and keep them current. Yet the traditional college experience is so expensive that the costs can be more harmful than the degree is helpful.

Therefore, you need to shift your focus from "college degree" to a new concept. And we'll explore that in chapter 15.

PERSONAL FINANCE IMPLICATIONS

1. Your children and grandchildren can ruin their lives by accumulating massive college debt or wasting years pursuing a degree they may never get or use.

2. It's therefore more important than ever that you develop for them an effective college savings strategy—not merely where and how to invest but how much to spend on the degree itself.

3. Although college tuition might be free in the future, room and board will never be. They will require more money than ever.

4. Unless you're already retired, plan on returning to college yourself to gain knowledge and skills you'll need to remain competitive in the workforce. This not only means you'll incur education expenses; it also means you might need to interrupt your career so you can return to school. That could mean losing income for months or years at a time. You'll need a financial plan to anticipate this, so you can maintain your lifestyle without destroying your long-term retirement plan while your career is on hiatus. This further increases the need to build your savings.

5. If you have cosigned student loans, talk with your financial planner about the risks and implications.

Chapter Nine: The Future of Leisure and Recreation

Of all the exciting innovations that exponential technologies will bring, one is particularly worth looking forward to: fun!

Leisure and recreation will make up a big part of your life in the future. You might find this hard to believe if, these days, all you do is work. And many people do: According to a study from the Center for Economic and Policy Research, 41% of employed Americans don't use all their vacation time. And according to Age Wave, 83% of working Americans regularly work while on vacation.

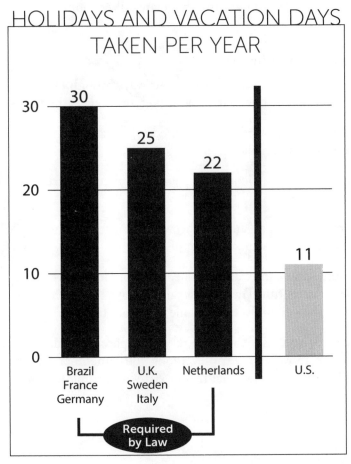

That's assuming you take a vacation at all. Americans take an average of just 11 vacation days per year, compared to 30 in Brazil, France and Germany; 25 in the United Kingdom, Sweden and Italy, and 22 in the Netherlands, according to Expedia. And the United States is the only country in the OECD (Organisation for Economic Co-operation and Development) whose government does not require paid vacation and paid holidays for workers, as shown in Figure 9.1.

If you're not used to being on vacation, plan on getting into the habit. Because, after all, retirement is really nothing but one looooong vacation.

FIGURE 9.1

Chances are, you need to focus on this. According to Age Wave, 53% of Americans have "hardly planned at all" for how they will spend their time in retirement. So let's look at a few leisure and retirement activities—so you can see how much fun they'll be.

Travel and Entertainment

With plenty of money, great health and lots of time, you'll want to see all that this wonderful planet has to offer. Retirees spent more on leisure travel than any other age group in 2016—$180 billion, according to Age Wave. It projects that figure to surpass $4.6 trillion by 2035. It's another huge area of economic growth.

Travel options you'll want to consider include:

- **Adventure travel.** Hike, bike, swim and paddle your way through exotic lands instead of sitting on a tour bus that stops at (yet another) cathedral.

- **Voluntourism.** Build houses, dig wells, provide medical assistance or teach children to read in impoverished villages.

- **Learning.** Travel with experts in paleontology, botany, archeology, art history, political science and more.

- **Cruising.** If you haven't been on an around-the-world cruise, you just might: 45% of retirees call cruise ships "very appealing."

- **Solo travel.** Don't assume you can't travel just because you don't have a travel partner. Overseas Adventure Travel, for example, says that 40% of its customers who are over the age of 50 travel alone. You can, too.

- **Multigenerational travel.** You might want to take your parents, children or grandchildren—or all the above—on a trip everyone will remember. About a third of retirees took a multigenerational trip in 2015, according to Age Wave.

Sports

Sports are probably a part of your life. Maybe not as a participant (only 15 million U.S. adults play sports, or 6% of the adult population, according to Playpass) but probably as a fan. Indeed, 6 in 10 U.S. adults are sports fans, according to Gallup's surveys on the subject, including two-thirds of men and half of women. And the more affluent you are, the more likely you enjoy watching sports: 68% of affluent adults are sports fans.

And if you're not a sports fan, exponential technologies may well turn you into one. Here's why, with a look at what's coming, from *The Future of Sports*, a report commissioned by Charlie Jacobs, the chief executive officer of Delaware North's Boston Holdings, the owner of the Boston Bruins professional hockey team.

Stadiums of the Future

First, going to games will be more fun than today's experience. Between now and 2040, stadiums will convert into megavenues accommodating 250,000 people. Complexes will feature everything from picnic tables, bars and restaurants to amusement park rides.

AI will improve your experience, too, via dynamic ticketing. Want to sit next to people of similar age who went to the same college as you did? Fine. Want to sit with others who share your interests in fashion, culture, politics or religion? Okay. Near neighbors? Away from your ex? No problem.

Wealthy fans will still enjoy luxury boxes, while families will watch the game from pavilions that feature high-definition jumbotrons. Tailgating will move inside the gates, because restaurants and stores will be inside, as they are at airports. And self-driving vehicles will eliminate parking hassles.

Some of the fun is already here. The Boston Celtics offer those at games video and audio they can't get at home. The Boston Bruins' mobile app tells season ticket holders which of their professional contacts are at the game. At home games of the New England Patriots, attendees see camera angles not available on TV; soon fans will be able to listen to radio communications between the coach and quarterback (you can already listen to drivers talking to their pit crews at NASCAR and Formula 1 automobile races).

> **Stadiums of the future will also be safer than ever. Using crowdoptics, security personnel will be able to see where fans are pointing their smartphones, so they can respond to incidents faster. And ticketing systems will use facial recognition technology so officials know who is attending.**

Inexpensive, family-friendly venues will feature augmented reality, holographic replays and 3D displays. And you won't simply watch a game—you'll participate, the way owners, coaches and journalists do now. If you don't like the play that just ran, you'll be able to activate a video game that instantly resets the game's conditions—and shows you what would have happened if the players had passed, pitched, swung, shot, run, thrown or kicked as you say they should have.

Playing Sports

And if you like to play sports, exponential technologies will help you become an athlete, or a better one. In chapter 3, we saw how bionics will help the least coordinated perform like pros. Technology is also creating perfectly weather-proof environments. I don't just mean lights that let you play golf at midnight. I'm talking about year-round skiing at Lake Tahoe (where a resort produces snow in the summer) and Dubai (which has indoor skiing facilities), as well as surfing (perfect waves are offered at an artificial lake in central California courtesy of the Kelly Slater Wave Company).

And then there are fantasy and electronic sports. You might decide to play both.

Fantasy Sports

When playing fantasy sports, you build a virtual pro team based on real players and "play" against other teams—games are won based on the statistical performance of the real players. IBISWorld says that fantasy sports is a $2 billion industry, and Eilers Research projected in 2015 that fantasy sports will grow by 41% annually, reaching $14 billion in 2020. Already, 20% of the U.S. population play, according to the Fantasy Sports Trade Association. Most players are college educated with incomes above $50,000 annually. So you might well get involved, if you're not already.

E-Sports

People love to play video games; they account for 26% of all growth in app use, according to Nielsen, and a large portion of app games are devoted to sports (more than 100 million copies of Madden NFL have been sold—and that's just one game).

Worldwide, 700 million people, including 159 million Americans (or more than half the U.S. population), play video games for an hour a day or more. The average young person racks up more than 10,000 hours of gaming by the age of 21—about the same amount of time spent in classrooms from middle school through high school. Clearly, playing games isn't just something young people do; it's a large part of who they are.

Don't assume that you're limited to playing football with your Xbox. Thousands of games are available, and many are more popular than Madden NFL. Millions of fans watched live, for example, as the world's best players of the video game Defense of the Ancients competed for $17 million in prize money at International DOTA 2 Championships. Fifteen thousand fans packed Seattle's KeyArena in 2016 to see the event in person. Similar competitions are held each year, including events at the Dallas Cowboys' AT&T Stadium (which sells out for an entire week at an average ticket

"THIS HAS BEEN FUN, DAD, BUT I NEED TO SPEND MORE QUALITY TIME WITH MY SMARTPHONE."

Cartoon by Harley Schwadron

price of $100) and the Seoul World Cup Stadium—Asia's largest soccer stadium, with 40,000 seats.

Don't assume that video games are just for kids. According to the Entertainment Software Rating Board, half of all gamers are age 35 or older.

And don't think e-sports aren't really sports. Robert Morris University offers 45 athletic scholarships to League of Legends video game players.

Player Connections

Technology will let you participate in real games, too. Social media will give you direct connection to players, and you'll even be able to invest in them. Fantex already sells securities linked to a pro's future earnings. (Pro football tight end Vernon Davis raised $4 million this way.)

Also, coaches will crowdsource plays, asking fans what play they think should be called. Social media will allow you to join with other fans to influence players, coaches and even entire leagues—everything from a team's player acquisition decisions to league rules. Hate the Redskins name? The fans—and only the fans—will decide whether it stays or goes.[43]

This is already happening. Scottish fans of the Rangers soccer team hired their own auditor to review the club's financials. Fans and players threatened to boycott the Los Angeles Clippers until the league banned team owner Donald Sterling for his racist statements. A boycott by soccer fans in Italy caused only 2,000 of 82,000 tickets to be sold at[44] a key match.

However much time you devote to sports, you'll likely maintain or increase it in the future—partly because you'll have the time, and partly because sports and games are going to be even more fun than they are now.

---

[43]Team owner Dan Snyder has little say in the matter, despite his babbling. If his season ticket holders were to boycott the team in protest over the name, he'd acquiesce—in a hurry.
[44]for? to? in? Sometimes, writing is hard. Get me Quill! (chapter 2)

PERSONAL FINANCE IMPLICATIONS

1. Expect to spend lots of money on travel and recreation—and this will need to be factored into your financial plan.

2. If you enjoy playing real sports (over virtual ones), you can expect injuries. This requires disability insurance as well as health insurance. But disability insurance is currently available only to those with an earned income—and under age 65—so you can't count on it to protect you for your entire life. This increases the importance of accumulating ample assets by saving and investing.

3. Increased travel options require you to consider ideas that may be new to you. More on this in chapter 9.

Chapter Ten: Financial Services Innovation

Nowhere is there more excitement about exponential technologies than on Wall Street. Just think of the profits from selling brand-new toilets to 7 billion people—yeah, investors want in on that.

Small wonder, then, that venture capitalists raised $187 billion to invest in tech start-ups in 2015 alone, according to CB Insights—a 187% increase over the prior year. And 10% of that amount, or $19 billion, was aimed at improving financial technology—fintech for short. This figure is ten times as high as the amount raised in 2010, as shown in Figure 10.1—a truly exponential rate of increase.

Indeed, hundreds of fintech companies have been formed, focusing on nontraditional funding sources, platforms, currencies and the storage and transfer of value.

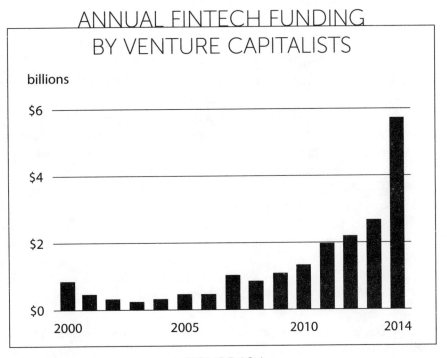

ANNUAL FINTECH FUNDING
BY VENTURE CAPITALISTS

FIGURE 10.1

It's not just new companies that are trying to make money in the financial services industry. Big, established ones are, too. Walmart, for example, now offers personal banking, ATMs and tax preparation services, and life insurance executives wonder if Amazon or Google might enter their business—disrupting a centuries-old industry.

We're already beginning to see the benefits of technological innovation in the financial services industry. Money transfers, which used to take days, now take minutes. Sending money is as easy as sending a text, and the cost is as little as zero. According to the World Bank, this is a $600 billion business. One of the largest players is M-PESA, a mobile payment system used in 70 countries to transfer billions of dollars every month. In Kenya, 25% of its GDP is transacted via M-PESA.

Lending is another major area for the financial services industry. A big target is small business owners; they need funds to support their ventures, but as they have few assets and even less of a track record, banks often reject their loan applications. This has created opportunities for Internet-based lenders.

Fundbox, for example, lends money to small businesses based on their invoices; small-business owners can borrow as little as $100 at low rates of interest, with no collateral—and receive funding within minutes. ZipCap loans money based on customer loyalty: if you're a small-business owner, you ask your customers to pledge to be frequent buyers. You send those pledges to ZipCap, and it will loan you money based on them. And Eastern Bank provides loans of up to $100,000 to small businesses in less than five minutes.

Small-business owners aren't the only ones who struggle to borrow. Consumers do, too—and the Internet offers solutions for them as well, along with an opportunity for investors. The concept is called *crowdfunding*. A borrower posts a request for a loan on a website, describing how much money he wants to borrow and what he'll use the money for. People willing to loan the money state the interest rate they want to receive and when they want their money returned. If the two parties agree, they complete a transaction.

Lendingclub.com, perhaps the largest such site, has arranged funding for more than $20 billion in loans since 2007. Each borrower can obtain from $2,000 to $40,000. Investors can loan the full amount or as little as $25 of it. So instead of making a single loan of $2,000 to one person, you can make $25 loans to 80 people, dramatically reducing your risk of loss should one borrower default. (Thus as many as 80 people might collectively provide $2,000; 1,600 strangers might collectively fund a maximum-sized loan request.)

Half of all borrowers on Lending Club say they use the money to refinance their mortgages, while 20% pay off more expensive credit card debt. The rest cite other uses. Interest rates range from about 5% to nearly 36%, depending on the borrower's creditworthiness. In other words, investors can earn far higher rates than offered by bank savings accounts, while borrowers can get loans they otherwise could not obtain or at lower interest rates than they otherwise would have to pay.

There are now hundreds of online lenders—and understandably so: Consumer lending is projected to be a $3 trillion market by 2025, according to Credit Suisse. And crowdfunding is revolutionizing it. Former Treasury secretary Larry Summers, a member of Lending Club's board, says that crowdfunding "has the potential to profoundly transform traditional banking over the next decade."

While 70% of Lending Club's borrowers use their loans to pay off other debts, crowdfunding also helps entrepreneurs start and grow their businesses. Kickstarter is perhaps the largest of these companies. From 2009 through 2016, its site was used to raise more than $2.5 billion from more than 11 million backers, providing funding to more than 111,000 projects. Nearly 200 projects raised more than $1 million; more than 3,000 raised more than $100,000 apiece. A study from the University of Pennsylvania says that money raised on Kickstarter has allowed entrepreneurs to start nearly 9,000 companies and create more than 300,000 jobs.

Crowdfunding is also used to raise money for charitable, social, civic and even personal purposes. The largest such site is gofundme.com, which lets people donate to well-known charities, including the American Heart Association, Red Cross, Boys & Girls Clubs of America, Make-A-Wish Foundation and National Wildlife Federation.

But gofundme.com also lets you create or fund a campaign to pay someone's medical bills, send their son to college, cover costs for their daughter's soccer league or pay for their father's funeral.

The site's "success stories" include 16-year-old Chauncy, whose mother is disabled. A friend started a campaign to buy Chauncy a lawn mower; it raised $334,700. After Blue Angels pilot Jeff Kuss was killed in a plane crash, leaving behind a wife and two small children, a campaign raised $371,246 for them. A family received $51,329 after their dog stopped a rattlesnake from biting their 7-year-old girl; a high school senior asking for money to pay for college got $26,131; a cancer patient in England seeking money for treatment got £452,563; and a Virginia elementary school student who tried to raise $500 so he could buy hand sanitizer for his school ended up raising $15,210. All told, gofundme.com says people have donated more than $2 billion since the site was launched in 2010.

Crowdfunding's popularity is growing at an exponential rate; such sites helped people raise more than $5 billion in 2015, twice as much as they did in 2012, and are projected to raise $100 billion by 2025—twice as big as the entire venture capital industry.

Rather than fearing crowdfunding, the federal government has embraced it. President Barack Obama signed into law the Jumpstart Our Business Startups (JOBS) Act of 2012, which lets companies raise up to $50 million online. Prior to the JOBS Act, only accredited investors[45] were allowed to invest in such offerings. Today, anybody can, via thousands of websites.

All this is becoming known as the Sharing Economy. And it's not just money that people are sharing, it's knowledge. This is the emergence of *crowdsourcing*—the notion of soliciting services, ideas or content from a large group of people.

We've already seen how UPS uses algorithms to increase efficiency. Now consider Allstate. Its data scientists have developed an algorithm to help the company set prices for its insurance policies. Allstate tries to hire the best scientists it can, but no company can claim it does. So in 2011, it offered, on the website Kaggle, $10,000 to anyone who could improve its algorithm. Within three days, applicants submitted 107 entries; the best improved Allstate's version by 271%, saving the company tens of millions of dollars annually.

---

[45]People who have a net worth of at least $1 million, not counting their primary residences, or income of at least $200,000 each year for the last two years ($300,000 if married).

If you're wondering how that happened, consider that more than half a million data scientists worldwide participate in Kaggle contests—and some of them are better than Allstate's.

Companies and studies using Kaggle include:

- State Farm: Can someone build an algorithm so computer sensors can spot distracted drivers? (1,115 teams have submitted entries)

- Grupo Bimbo, the world's largest baker: How can it maximize sales and minimize returns of its goods? (897 teams)

- Avito, the biggest site for online classified ads in Russia: How to detect duplicate ads? (509 teams)

- Shelter animal outcomes: How can it improve outcomes for shelter animals? (1,180 teams)

- Annual nominal fish catches: What is the impact of overfishing in the Northeast Atlantic region? (612 teams)

There are hundreds more.

The Sharing Economy has thus led to the rise of the On-Demand Worker. Researchers at Princeton and Harvard estimate that 16% of the U.S. workforce are now "contingent"—defined by the Department of Labor as independent contractors (self-employed individuals), on-call workers, temp workers and workers employed by contract firms. You already hire many of these people: your wedding photographer, housepainter, babysitter—all these workers come when summoned, perform a task, then depart when finished—and for a small fee compared to the cost of hiring a full-time worker.

Incidentally

Crowdsourcing sites are also being used to track the activities of drug dealers. Residents in inner cities are using websites to tell police about criminal activity in their neighborhoods.

Indeed, no grass cutter would be able to make a living if yours were the only lawn he mowed. That's why the grass cutter mows lots of lawns.

When I was a little kid, maybe six years old, I told my dad that trash collectors had the greatest job in the world. When he asked why, I replied that they only worked one day a week—the day they came to pick up our trash. Dad had to explain that on the other days they were busy collecting trash from other people's homes. It was my first awareness that the world extended beyond my front yard.[46]

In other words, people who mow lawns don't have a boss—they have dozens of bosses, each one a home owner. And home owners have dozens of workers—each hired to do a specific task, at a specific time and for a specific duration. When the task is finished, the relationship is over—until the next time.

Thus, our nation is moving from the New York model of employment to the Hollywood model. The New York model is the classic workplace scenario: employees work in huge skyscrapers for a single employer, doing the same work over and over for decades. In the Hollywood model, people gather for a specific project that is typically completed in a few months. Directors, actors, screenwriters, musicians, set and costume designers, film editors, publicists, caterers and chauffeurs work in a variety of locations to complete a specific assignment—and when that assignment is completed, they move on to another project.

Instead of drawing a single paycheck from one employer, those operating under the Hollywood model typically receive paychecks from a variety of sources. No single source might pay much money, but in the aggregate their total income can be even more than that received by those working under the New York model.

The Hollywood model suggests that workers must move from a focus of "having a job that makes me money" to "having skills that make me money." In other words, we're moving from ownership of jobs to access to jobs.

You can see these concepts deployed throughout today's economy. Instead of owning a car that sits idle 95% of the time, you can access a car on demand, through such companies as Zipcar and car2go. If you don't want to drive the vehicle yourself, you can order a car that comes with a driver, through such services as Uber and Lyft. In each case, you use the vehicles only as needed, for

---

[46]Dad also had to tell my older brothers to shut up and quit teasing me for being so dumb. So I started teasing them for getting into trouble for teasing me, which caused Dad to tell me to shut up, which caused my brothers . . . it was a long afternoon for Dad.

mere minutes or a few hours, freeing you from the responsibility of ownership and all the attendant costs, such as insurance, taxes, maintenance and parking—not to mention the cost of the automobile itself.

Thousands of websites now allow you to participate in the Sharing Economy. You no longer need to buy a dress for your sister's wedding; you can rent one instead via the website Rent the Runway. If the idea of wearing a $10,000 watch appeals to you but not its price, you can rent high-end watches for less than $250 a month via the website Eleven James. Other sites, such as Vinted.com, let you swap your clothing with others—so you don't have to spend lots of money to get a new wardrobe. You can even rent sheep (to cut your grass; Rocky Mountain Wooly Weeders), chickens (to get morning eggs; Rent-A-Chicken), falcons (to keep birds away from your crops; Falcon Force), bees (for honey; The Pollination Connection) and goats (to eat weeds and keep your lawn tidy; Rent-A-Ruminant).

You can even build an entire company via the Sharing and On-Demand Economy. The Internet offers more than 10,000 sites that help you create and operate your own business. If you'd like to help people who are moving pack up their belongings, the website Bellhops can help you market your business. If you're an interior designer, you can make your services available via the site Laurel & Wolf. Handy.com matches home owners who need work done around the house with independent contractors able to perform those tasks. Instacart pairs customers with personal shoppers, while other sites connect customers with people willing to clean their houses. If you have power tools gathering dust,

Open Shed lets you rent them to people in your neighborhood; and JustPark allows you to rent your driveway to people needing a place to park their car.

Postmates lets you deliver goods locally, while Shyp lets you make money by taking other people's packages to the post office so they don't have to. Borrow My Doggy is a site that lets you earn a living as a dog walker or sitter, and at TaskRabbit you can read listings that people have posted naming the task they need done and the price they're willing to pay for it—and you decide if you want the job.

If you have a nice wine collection and know you'll never drink it all, CorkSharing helps you invite people to your home to taste your wine collection—for which you'll charge a fee, of course. If you're a chef, people looking for a night out can hire you to cook and serve them a meal in your home via the site EatWith.

If you own a car but don't want to become an Uber driver, you can make money by taking other people's possessions with you when you're going somewhere. PiggyBee helps you do that. You can also rent your car for short periods of time when you're not using it, via the website Turo. There are even websites that help you start your own sharing websites.

Fiverr lets you offer your artistic and professional services for a fee. Through Vayable, you can be a guide to visiting tourists. Skillshare lets you teach what you know online to students wanting to learn; you can teach any course you want, and if your class has 25 students or more, you'll be paid to do it. (The average teacher earns $3,500 a year, according to Skillshare.) HourlyNerd helps you become a part-time business consultant; Quirky can help you get your invention to the marketplace within a month, and if you want to build a proto-type of an invention but lack the tools, there's no need to buy any gear. Instead, simply go to TechShop.

With a dozen locations around the country, TechShop lets you build or create just about anything. Available tools include computer-controlled vinyl and glass cutters, soldering irons, floor jacks, engine hoists, pneumatic tools, oscilloscopes, saws, presses, computer-controlled sewing and embroidery machines, hand and power tools, digital SLR cameras, large metal lathes and milling machines, calipers and micrometers, injection molders, routers, 3D scanners and printers, laser cutters, welding gear, sanders and polishers, painters and more. And if you don't know how to use the equipment, TechShop offers classes to teach you and staff to help you—and the facilities are open 24/7, letting you tinker whenever you want.

And when you're ready to start your company, you can turn to Gust Launch. With one click of a mouse, the site incorporates your startup and handles all back-office legal, financial, accounting and equity operations. And since Gust is one of the world's most prominent angel investing platforms, it plans to eventually let ordinary investors provide funding to these startups.

One-third of U.S. adults are making money in the sharing economy, according to a 2016 survey by *Success* magazine, including, according to the Pew Research Center, nearly 20% of those over age 65. After all, the Shared Economy makes easy. Airbnb, for example, which lets you rent a room in your house to travelers, says 13% of its listings are offered by hosts age 60 and older; the average senior earns about $6,000 by hosting travelers only 60 days per year. And *Success* says that more than 30% of the self-employed population is 55 or older.

Participants in the sharing economy earn money by selling items online, working as an independent contractor or consultant, renting assets they own (a room, car, clothes or tools) or working as a ride-sharing driver. Only 30% told *Success* they earn their primary income this way; the rest do it to make extra money—and they boost their income by as much as 20%.

Incidentally

Consumers who purchase products online are notorious for returning them. Often, customers will discover that the product doesn't fit or is the wrong color. When companies receive goods back, they can't resell them as new—so they offload them in bulk at sharply reduced prices. Some entrepreneurs have discovered that if they're willing to buy truckloads of returned products, they can resell them, one at a time, on sites such as eBay and Craigslist. *The Washington Post* cited one such individual in 2016, an out-of-work banker, who now earns $8,000 a month selling returned products online.

The sharing economy doesn't just make it easy to make money; it makes it easy to actually start a business. A variety of websites will conduct background checks of people you plan to hire and manage onboarding and personnel issues. You can even avoid hiring staff completely; virtual assistants from My Virtual

Incidentally

Every major automobile manufacturer realizes the importance of the sharing economy: BMW, for example, offers its own car-sharing program called DriveNow, which lets owners of Mini Coopers earn money with their automobile. And GM invested $500 million into Lyft.

Partner and Fancy Hands will develop your website, conduct market research and handle such administrative services as accounting and travel logistics. You can even find sites that provide specialized services. For example, if you need a temporary call center, LiveAnswer can serve you, while Routific and Zendrive will help you with vehicle route optimization and logistics.

If you decide you don't want to operate your business out of your home, the Internet can help you find companies that are willing to rent their extra space on flexible terms. PivotDesk, Desks Near Me and Share Your Office all do this. Other companies will share their underused business equipment, so you don't have to buy your own gear. FLOOW2 is one such outfit. And WeWork will give you access to common office space.

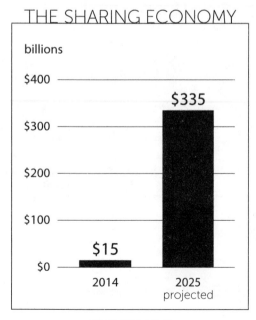

THE SHARING ECONOMY

FIGURE 10.2

For $350 per month, WeWork provides Internet access, printers, group health insurance and a social network (with free beer to enjoy while you're interacting with other entrepreneurs). There are so many people taking advantage of WeWork's service that it has become the world's fourth largest commercial landlord, with more than 5 million square feet of office space. As of 2016, WeWork had 50,000 users, with plans to grow to 2 million worldwide. A competitor is Regus, which controls more than 40 million square feet of office space globally.

The sharing economy is a $15 billion industry. By 2025, it's projected to exceed $335 billion.

Games and Gamification

Mary Poppins[47] was right. She said, "In every job that must be done, there is an element of fun. You find that fun, and *snap!*—the job's a game!"

This is the concept behind gamification: the use of games to motivate people to do something they otherwise wouldn't do.

We saw in chapter 9 how much time people spend playing video games. Wouldn't it be great if we could put those hours to doing something really useful, such as, oh, say, curing malaria?

9-12
© 2016 Bil Keane, Inc.
Dist. by King Features Synd.
www.familycircus.com

"When will I be old enough to have a phone I can stare at all day?"

© 2016 Bil Keane, Inc. Distributed by King Features Syndicate, Inc.

Now we can, and Mary Poppins has shown the way: Scientists have turned the fight against malaria into a game called MalariaSpot.

Here's how it works. Technicians upload images of a patient's blood sample to the site; players tag as many parasites as they can in just one minute. Traditionally, diagnosing malaria in a single child takes 30 minutes. But in one month, competing players from 95 countries played 12,000 MalariaSpot games, making 700,000 parasite diagnoses with 99% accuracy—exponentially accelerating the ability of doctors to treat their patients.

Foldit is another crowdsourcing computer game that helps scientists. It pertains to "protein folding." Proteins are essentially long chains of amino acids, and scientists need to understand how to get them to fold in predictable ways, to help them combat HIV/AIDS, cancer, Alzheimer's disease and other major illnesses. In this online game, players compete to design the best way to fold proteins;

---

[47]Oh, come *on*. Don't tell me you don't know who *she* is!

scores are publicly displayed. A quarter of a million people have played since 2008; players once solved a problem in three weeks that had stumped researchers for 15 years.

Sea Hero Quest is a game designed to spot early signs of dementia. Within a week of its launch in 2016, more than 150,000 people downloaded the game. In just two minutes, researchers accumulated the equivalent of 70 years of lab data on human spatial memory and navigation, according to Alzheimer's Research UK. It's easy to get people to do something when it's fun. But how can you motivate people to do something that's difficult or dangerous? The answer: offer a reward. Perhaps the earliest example of that comes from the story of David and Goliath. The book of Samuel, chapter 17, verse 25, states, "The king will give great wealth to the man who kills [Goliath]. He will also give him his daughter in marriage and will exempt his family from taxes in Israel." There's nothing like a reward to get things done.

Three thousand years later, Charles Lindbergh became the first man to fly an airplane nonstop across the Atlantic Ocean. It wasn't just fame he pursued; he was vying to win the Orteig Prize, a $25,000 reward for being the first person to achieve the feat.

The Orteig Prize inspired Peter Diamandis, who later cofounded Singularity University with Ray Kurzweil, to create the Ansari XPRIZE in 1996. It offered $10 million to the first team that could build and fly an aircraft into space, return it safely and repeat the achievement within two weeks. Twenty-six teams from seven nations spent $100 million trying to win that $10 million prize. Mike Melvill succeeded on October 4, 2004. Today, *SpaceShipOne* resides in the Smithsonian's Air and Space Museum alongside Lindbergh's *Spirit of St. Louis*.

What Peter realized is that people will collectively spend far more trying to win a prize than sponsors would ever pay for the effort. Instead of spending $100 million trying to build a spaceship, he used the concept of exponentiality to massively leverage the money. As a result, dozens of teams, not just one, collectively spent 10 times as much money as the prize was worth, producing far more research, knowledge and experience—and achieving success far more quickly—than could have occurred if one team had been granted $10 million to make the attempt.

Peter is now sponsoring a variety of other XPRIZEs, including $1.4 million to whoever develops a method to clean up oil spills at the rate of 1,100 gallons per minute, and $10 million to create a tricorder comparable to the one envisioned by *Star Trek*. Additional XPRIZEs are aimed at improving education around the world, curing Alzheimer's disease, even increasing happiness.

Congress, too, has recognized the benefits of gamification. Realizing that the U.S. savings rate is very low—47% of U.S. households would be unable to pay an unexpected bill of $400, according to the Federal Reserve—Congress passed, and President Obama signed into law, the American Savings Promotion Act of 2014. The law is based on a program conducted by 62 credit unions in four states that convinced 40,000 people—three-quarters of whom are financially vulnerable—to open a bank account.

How were the credit unions able to convince tens of thousands of people to save money when they had previously been unwilling to do so? Most of those people bought lottery tickets every day, so the credit unions turned bank deposits into raffles: for every $25 deposited, they were given the chance to win $3,750. So instead of throwing money away on lottery tickets, 40,000

Incidentally

The success of these programs has inspired the U.S. government to create similar prizes:

- To help the government thwart bioterrorism, the Defense Department is offering $1 million to anyone who can create an algorithm that analyzes genetic sequences and identifies its organisms.

- In conjunction with the National Football League, General Electric and Under Armor, the National Institute of Standards and Technology is offering $2 million to anyone who can develop ways to prevent and detect concussions.

- The Consumer Product Safety Commission is offering $6,500 to middle school students to create posters that warn about the dangers of carbon monoxide.

- The National Institutes of Health is offering $100,000 for the creation of new ways to fight drug use and addiction.

- The Environmental Protection Agency is offering $15,000 to anyone who can use existing government data to increase the awareness of nutrient pollution.

- The Interior Department is offering $20,000 to develop cheaper ways to track fish and aid in recovery efforts.

- The Agriculture Department will pay $63,000 to anyone who can creatively provide USDA data to farmers, researchers and consumers.

- NASA is offering $1,500 to anyone who can identify the elements needed to establish a continuous human presence on Mars.

people switched to putting that money into a bank account. Since 2009, they've accumulated $100 million in savings.

Thanks to the American Savings Promotion Act, banks and credit unions around the country are now able to offer similar programs.

The Key to Worldwide Economic Growth: Eliminating the Unbanked

If we're to increase worldwide economic growth sharply, we have to sell more of everything every year—more houses, cars, refrigerators, clothes, magazine subscriptions, chicken dinners and . . . well, everything.

But the amount of any given product we can sell is limited by the total number of potential customers. You're not going to buy many more refrigerators, for example, because you already own one. So does everyone else in the middle and upper classes. So if we want to sell a lot more of every product, we have to seek more customers.

There are billions of people in South America, Africa and Asia (and rural Kentucky, for that matter). But most of them are poor—and poor people don't buy houses, cars or refrigerators. So how can we turn them into consumers so they can buy the products we want to sell to them?

Simple: We have to elevate poor people to the middle class. If we can do that for the 3 billion people around the world who are impoverished, the world's economy will skyrocket.

Technologies such as M-PESA and the Gates Foundation toilet, along with strategies such as the American Savings Promotion Act, can help poor people improve their financial situation, but there's a more basic prerequisite: giving poor people access to a bank account.

A bank account?

Yes, indeed. You probably don't stop to consider how important it is—any more than you think about how many times your heart beats each day. But without a bank account, how would you manage your money?

Imagine having a job, and it's payday. Most employers want to send your paycheck directly to your bank account via direct deposit. This, of course, requires you to *have* a bank account. But let's say you don't have one. What should your employer do with your paycheck?

There's only one option: Hand it to you. What will you do with it?

You must cash the check. There are only two ways you can do this. You can either go to your employer's bank—assuming a local branch is available, convenient for you to reach and willing to cash a check for someone who is not a depositor—or you can go to a check-cashing store, such as a liquor store or pawnshop. Businesses willing to cash paychecks charge as much as 20% of the value of the check, a significant portion of your income. (Losing 20% of your income could prevent you from escaping poverty.)

But one way or another, you've cashed the check, and the money is in hand—hundreds, perhaps thousands, of dollars. What will you do with it?

That's the first problem faced by the unbanked: keeping their money safe. People without bank accounts have only three places to store their cash: in their home, in their car (if they have one) or on their person. All three are fraught with risks—and not merely the risk of theft but also the risk of bodily harm if they happen to be present when thieves, knowing they are unbanked, try to take the money.

And being forced to maintain physical possession of the cash means they can't earn interest on it. You would never consider burying your life's savings under a mattress, but that is precisely what the unbanked are forced to do. The inability to invest their money so it could earn interest, dividends and capital gains is one reason poor people stay poor.

A second reason the unbanked struggle to advance in society is that they have no access to credit. Credit is provided by banks and other lenders, and they want to know you have money, which shows your ability to repay the loan. You demonstrate this by having a bank account. Without one, it is virtually impossible to obtain a loan or even a credit card. Being unable to borrow money to buy a car, purchase a telephone plan, finance college education—or the clothes or tools you need to get and hold a job—is a third reason poor people stay poor.

Almost 30% of the world's population is unbanked—2 billion of the planet's 7 billion people, including 12% of the U.S. adult population. Two-thirds of the world's unbanked people live in Asia, as Figure 10.3 shows.

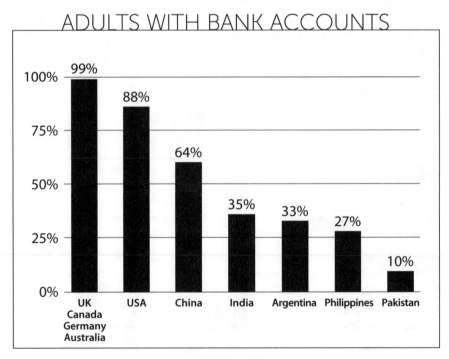

ADULTS WITH BANK ACCOUNTS

FIGURE 10.3

Access to bank accounts is so important for the world's economic growth that the World Bank has set a goal of making bank accounts available to everyone by 2020. Its plan is working: from 2011 to 2014, 700 million people obtained bank accounts—that's more than twice the U.S. population. India, for example, had only 5 million high-income middle-class households in 1995; today there are

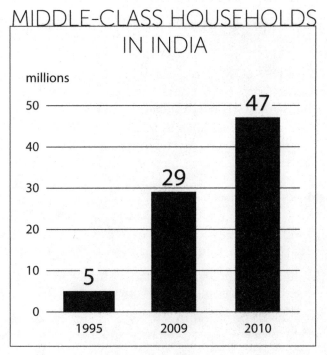

FIGURE 10.4

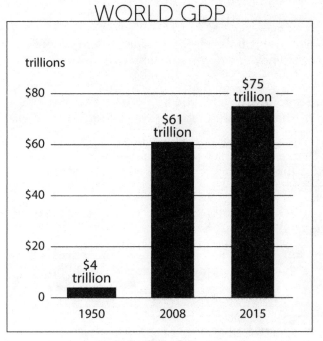

FIGURE 10.5

23.6 million. This helps explain why the size of the global economy[48] jumped from $61 trillion in 2008 to $75 trillion in 2015 and why it is projected to reach $86 trillion by 2020.

And as the world's largest economy, the United States will be the largest beneficiary of global growth. McKinsey Global Institute's December 2015 report said that digitization could add as much as $2.2 trillion to our GDP by 2025—an increase of more than 12% over our GDP in 2016.

McKinsey says our growth will include:

- **$850 billion through operations and supply chain optimization (real-time monitoring and control of production lines and better logistics routing through optimization and prioritization)**

- **$500 billion through increased labor supply and productivity, benefiting 41 million people (19% of the working-age population)**

- **$400 billion through improved asset efficiency (less downtime caused by preventive maintenance and increased asset utilization)**

- **$350 billion through improved research and development and better use of data (leading to new inventions and faster product development cycles thanks to better testing and quality control systems)**

- **$50 billion through resource management (improved energy and fuel efficiency and decreased waste of raw materials)**

McKinsey also says these estimates are low, because the scope of its report was limited. Therefore, it says, "the potential for technology-fueled growth is much wider" than its $2.2 trillion estimate suggests. For example, the report says that:

- **Big Data analytics in health care and government could generate $300 billion in cost savings and even bigger returns in the form of improved health and more effective public services.**

- **Selling through digital channels could generate productivity gains of up to 15%.**

- **Opportunities for new employment and increased income offered by the sharing economy could add $500 billion to U.S. GDP.**

---

[48]Measured by Gross Domestic Product, the value of all finished goods and services produced each year.

- **The U.S. government could benefit by $550 billion a year—$95 billion from productivity gains and up to $460 billion in savings by minimizing erroneous payments, improving procurement and making tax collection more effective.**

The result, McKinsey says, is that the United States has reached only 18% of its digital potential. Clearly, the opportunity for our economy is huge.

And we're not even one of the leaders in moving toward a digital economy. McKinsey's Country Digitization Index (which aggregates indicators measuring technology supply, innovation and use by businesses, consumers and government) ranks the United States 11th among the 34 member nations of the Organisation for Economic Co-operation and Development. U.S. households, McKinsey says, are less wired than those in northern Europe, Japan, South Korea, New Zealand and Israel. Nearly 80% of UK residents have purchased goods and services online, for example, compared to only 60% for households in the United States, and more than 95% of seniors (those over 65 years of age) in Scandinavia use the Internet, compared to fewer than 80% of U.S. seniors.

How will we achieve these gains?

Through exponential technologies, of course. Read on . . .

Mobile Banking, Brought to You by Free Wireless Internet

The World Bank isn't going to get Citigroup or Bank of America to open branches in remote African villages. So how can billions of unbanked people establish bank accounts?

They'll use apps on their smartphones, just as you can.

Mobile banking is already happening. In Kenya, mobile-based financial transactions comprise 40% of the country's GDP. And 10% of Bangladesh's 160 million people are using bKash, an online payments service; it processes 70 million transactions daily, according to *The Wall Street Journal*.

Only 21 percent of Kenyans have bank accounts, according to Financial Inclusion Insights, and of those who do, 77% manage their accounts via their mobile phones. The use of mobile devices is so common in Kenya that the government issued a bond in 2015 exclusively through mobile phones. The minimum investment was $28, compared to $477 for bonds issued the old way, greatly increasing the number of Kenyans who could afford to participate. And because the offering was executed digitally, all trades were completed instantaneously; conventional methods require an average of two days.

Clearly, mobile banking creates the platform for raising the standard of living for billions of people. But for a mobile phone to work, the world's unbanked must have access to the Internet. And, as we've already seen, 4 billion people around the world currently don't.

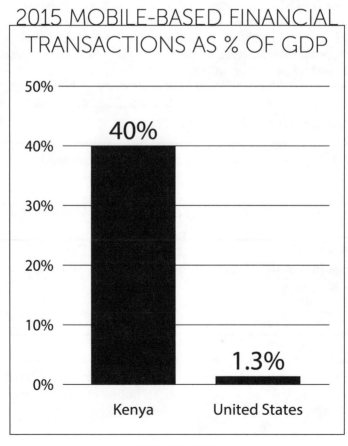

FIGURE 10.6

But if all goes according to plan, they all will by 2020. A variety of companies are working to make this happen:

- SpaceX is spending $10 billion to launch and maintain 400 satellites in low Earth orbit to provide Internet access worldwide.

- OneWeb is spending $3 billion to launch 900 microsatellites by 2019.

- Facebook is building unmanned solar-powered autonomous aircraft with wingspans wider than a Boeing 747 but weighing less than a car. The planes will fly at altitudes of 60,000 feet for months at a time, beaming Internet access from the sky.

- Google's Project Loon is launching thousands of balloons that will float 65,000 feet up to provide high-speed Internet access around the globe. Its first balloon was launched over Sri Lanka in 2016.

- Scientists in Estonia are developing Li-Fi, a wireless technology 100 times as fast as Wi-Fi. Because it transmits data via visible light, LED lightbulbs could become wireless routers.

With a smartphone and free high-speed Internet access, everyone around the world will be able to open and maintain a bank account. Billions of people will suddenly have educational and economic opportunities they never had before. Not only will they be able to earn more money than ever, they will spend more money than ever. As Peter Diamandis asks in his book *Abundance,* what might 3 billion people invent, discover and consume?

Thanks to these and other exponential technologies, we are at the earliest stages of what is clearly becoming the greatest period of innovation in human history. Not only will the lives of billions of people be dramatically—exponentially— improved, we'll see global GDP grow by tens of trillions of dollars.

Digital Currency

There's really only one reason currencies exist: to help governments facilitate commercial transactions both within their borders and with other nations. The alternative is for apple growers to trade their bushels for blankets—not a very efficient mode of commerce. But thanks to currency, farmers can trade those bushels of apples for cash and later trade some of that currency for a blanket.

The weaver can then exchange some currency for nails. Currency makes commerce easier, facilitating a growing economy.

All that's needed is for everyone to agree on the value of that currency.

And that's the problem: The governments that issue currencies also control them. Money, after all, is nothing more than paper—so if a government needs to pay its debts, it can simply print more paper.[49]

But the more paper the government prints, the less each bill is worth. If the government doubles the number of bills in circulation, the value of each is cut in half. That means you need twice as many bills to buy something as you needed before. This is called inflation, and when it gets really out of hand, you have absurdities such as Zimbabwe in the 2000s, where, according to the Cato Institute, hyperinflation at its peak in November 2008 hit the incomprehensible rate of 98% *per day*—meaning that whatever you didn't buy today would cost you twice as much tomorrow.[50] It caused the Zimbabwean government to print bills with a face value of—get this—$100 trillion. (Understandable, since a loaf of bread alone might cost several million bucks.)

© Hikupic / Alamy

To solve the problem of inflation, Satoshi Nakamoto created the world's first global digital currency in 2009. It's called *Bitcoin*. It exists only online; no one prints paper or mints coins. The software operating Bitcoin is open source, meaning it's available to anyone with an Internet connection. Thus, no

---

[49] Wouldn't you love to be able to print money whenever you needed to pay some bills?
[50] What, that's not incomprehensible? Well, try this: a daily inflation rate of 98% translates to an annual inflation rate of 89,700,000,000,000,000,000,000%. As I said, incomprehensible.

government, corporation, group or person controls the issuance, management or valuation of bitcoins, and transactions are as anonymous as when you use cash printed by the U.S. Treasury. Most important, the computer technology developed to create Bitcoin capped the number of bitcoins that could ever be produced, guaranteeing that bitcoins can't be eroded by inflation.

If no government issues the bitcoin, then who does? The answer: anybody who wants to. You can create your own bitcoins or purchase them from someone else. Most people choose the latter, because creating bitcoins (called "mining" by enthusiasts) is time-consuming and expensive. (Several dozen websites, such as Coinbase, CeX, Kraken, BTC-e, CoinDesk and GDAX, let you buy and sell bitcoins quickly and easily.)

Think of it this way: You could go into the forest and pick apples from a tree. The apples would be free except for the time and money you spend on the effort. Or you could go to the local market. Faster, easier—but you'll have to pay the merchant. You have the same options when obtaining bitcoins: dig into computer systems to create them or buy them from an online vendor.

Here's another way to think about it: When you vacation in Europe, you trade your U.S. dollars for euros. Both are currencies; you use one to make purchases in the United States and you use the other to make purchases in France. Likewise, you can trade your dollars for bitcoins so you can make purchases online.

Incidentally

Bitcoin ETFs are here. Applications for SolidX Bitcoin Trust and Winklevoss Bitcoin Trust have been filed with the SEC, and BitcoinETI is already trading in Europe. There are also bitcoin ATMs in Maryland, Virginia, Pennsylvania and Ohio, where you can trade dollars for bitcoins.

Why bother with using bitcoins to make online purchases when you can just use a debit card? Because bitcoins are free. By contrast, merchants pay up to 3% whenever you use a debit or credit card—and that cost is passed on to you in the form of higher prices for the products you buy. Widespread adoption of bitcoins would not only lower consumer prices, it would completely disrupt the card industry's business model.

No wonder Jason Oxman, the CEO of the Electronic Transactions Association, said in 2014 that the industry is undergoing "the single most important period of innovation since the invention of the magnetic strip [50 years ago]. It is truly a revolutionary time for payments."

Incidentally

There's a new version of Monopoly that doesn't use cash. Instead, players use credit cards. So even one of the most traditional board games has converted to digital currency. Guess what playing this version of the game is teaching your kids?

He's not alone. As far back as September 2014, the Bank of England said that bitcoin is "a significant innovation" that "opens up the possibility . . . to transform the financial system."

This is not to say that bitcoin will become the default currency worldwide. But some form of digital currency certainly will—and perhaps many forms, just as there are many currencies around the world.

Indeed, a 2016 research paper from economists at the Bank of England said that every central bank around the world should create its own digital currency. The paper says the global economy would rise by 3%, in addition to giving policy makers more effective tools to avert economic recessions and manias. Ecuador has already launched a digital currency, and China announced in 2016 that it is planning to do so as well.

Governments gain two big benefits from digital currencies. First, the elimination of cash would help the fight against drug dealers and terrorists. After all, criminals don't use credit cards to conduct business. Digital currencies can leave electronic footprints that law enforcement and military intelligence can use to find our enemies.

And there's another, more pedestrian form of criminal activity that digital currencies can eliminate: tax evasion. I'm not just talking about megazillionaires hiding money in offshore accounts, either. I'm referring to people who live in your neighborhood.

Ever had someone say to you, "The price is $20,000, but if you pay in cash I'll do it for $17,000"? Do you think the babysitter is paying taxes on the money she earned Saturday night?

Due to "under-the-table" deals, the federal government failed to collect $3 trillion in taxes over the past decade, according to the Treasury Department; collecting those unpaid taxes would wipe out the entire federal deficit—without having to raise tax rates on anyone!

So it's no surprise that U.S. agencies, including the Justice Department, Federal Reserve, Securities and Exchange Commission, Secret Service, and FinCEN (the Treasury Department's Financial Crimes Enforcement Network) have acknowledged that the IRS has declared that bitcoins are property and are to be taxed the same as stocks, bonds and mutual funds; the Commodity Futures Trading Commission has concurred, saying that from a trading perspective, bitcoins are no different than gold, oil, cattle or soybeans.

Cartoon by Harley Schwadron

So if you aren't using bitcoins yet, you probably will. More than 100,000 U.S. businesses accept bitcoins, including the NBA's Sacramento Kings, the online retailer Overstock.com, the Las Vegas hotel-casinos D and the Golden Gate, cheapair.com, an online travel agency, the photo-sharing website Reddit, the dating website OKCupid, a bar in midtown Manhattan and a Subway sandwich shop in Allentown, Pennsylvania. The American Red Cross, Save the Children and other charities accept donations in bitcoins (they use BitPay, a site that converts bitcoin donations back into dollars). The Federal Election Commission allows political donations to be made in bitcoins. And Great Britain lets consumers pay each other in bitcoins using a mobile app.

Banks, too, recognize the benefits of digital currency. UBS is working on one; its research found that the financial industry could save $20 billion a year by 2022 in cross-border payments, securities trading and regulatory compliance. Barclays Bank is testing bitcoin as a payment system as well, as are JP Morgan Chase and Credit Suisse. And Citibank, one of the largest movers of money in the world, is experimenting with its own digital currency, which it calls Citicoin.

Incidentally

Dozens of colleges and universities, including Stanford, Princeton, Duke and NYU, offer courses on cybercurrencies and bitcoin.

Despite this activity, we are in the earliest stages of adoption. Only about 100,000 retailers around the world are known to accept bitcoins. As few Americans have ever heard of them—let alone used them.

Still, the use of bitcoins is rising. There were 1.3 million users in 2014, and that figure is expected to reach 4.7 million by 2019, according to Juniper Research. Wall Street certainly supports the movement: Venture capital firms have invested $550 million in bitcoin companies so far, while total fintech funding has skyrocketed from $4 billion in 2013 to $23.5 billion in 2015, according to estimates from Santander, Oliver Wyman and Anthemis Group.

Incidentally

The Sacramento Kings NBA team in 2014 became the first professional sports team to let fans make ticket and concession purchases with bitcoins.

If you want to get a sense of where all this is going, consider Sweden. In that country, bills and coins are used in just 2% of its financial transactions overall, and in about 20% of consumer payments (compared with an average of 75% for the rest of the world), according to Euromonitor International. More than half of its banks don't accept cash deposits, and no cash is kept at many branches; those wanting withdrawals in cash must make arrangements in advance and are charged a fee. It won't be long before Sweden gets to 100%—and the rest of the world catches up.

If all this still finds you unconvinced, if you still insist on believing that you will never use digital currencies, please understand that you already are. Every time you buy something with a credit or debit card, you are making a digital transaction. Airline miles and hotel points are forms of digital currency, as are Disney Dollars (currency issued by the Walt Disney Company for exclusive use at its theme parks and stores). Even casino chips are a form of privately created and operated currency.

You can accept this statement or not, but the fact is that soon the only place you'll see currency is in a museum.

The Blockchain

When Satoshi Nakamoto created Bitcoin, everyone initially focused on the digital currency itself. But over the past decades, attention shifted to the underlying technology that allows bitcoin to operate.

Some are calling this technology the most significant advance since the creation of the Internet.

Strike that. Some are calling the blockchain the most important invention since *the wheel*.

Wow.

Why is the blockchain being treated with such reverence and admiration? Because it can eliminate the trust industry.

You probably don't know what that industry is or even that there is such an industry, demonstrating how ingrained it is in every aspect of commerce.

So let's explore the trust industry—what it is, why it exists, its inherent problems and how life can be vastly improved by replacing it with something better.

The trust industry exists because we have no choice but to trust others whenever we engage in a financial transaction. It is because of trust that you are willing to hand someone your money today in exchange for their promise to deliver you a product later (whether a pizza in a half hour, a mattress next week or a house in three months). It is because of trust that the business accepting your money today has confidence that the currency will retain its value and be transferable.

Without this trust, we would be forced to return to the days when people traded apples for blankets—an unwieldy, cumbersome system abandoned long ago.

To make trust work, an entire trust industry has been established, and 10 million people work in this field. You know them by their other name: *middlemen*. Commercial bankers, securities brokers, insurance providers, real estate agents and lawyers are all really nothing more than middlemen.

Think about buying a home. You're trusting that the seller in fact owns the house he's selling to you. That's the first point of trust. And because your trust might be misguided, you buy title insurance.

You see the problem: You're forced to trust others, and that's risky. So you incur an expense solely because you can't *trust* the seller. If you could *authenticate* his ownership of the property, you wouldn't need to buy title insurance. This example illustrates both the problem (trust) and its solution (authentication).

The above example also explains why we need so many middlemen: a real estate agent represents the seller; the title settlement company represents the title insurance company; the mortgage broker acts on behalf of the lender. All these middlemen explain why you incur so many fees when buying a house.

Cartoon by Harley Schwadron

The trust industry isn't limited to real estate. Indeed, middlemen are everywhere. After all, Bruce Springsteen doesn't personally sell you tickets to his concerts. Instead, you buy them from a ticket agent. That's a middleman. So is a travel agent who gets you a hotel room. The list is a long one of occupations that are little more than middlemen.

The blockchain that Satoshi Nakamoto invented to create bitcoin can digitize and automate all the services of all those middlemen and greatly reduce the transaction costs. Buying a house will take minutes, not months, and the transaction costs will fall from tens of thousands of dollars to near zero.

Understanding the Blockchain

Think of the blockchain as, well, a chain. Each link represents data. Once added to the chain, links (data) cannot be altered, copied or deleted. Instead, they are immutable—but they are also always visible by everyone.

To illustrate, imagine placing the deed to your house onto the blockchain. You are the first link in the chain. When you attach your deed to yourself, it becomes the second link in the chain. Let's call you Link A and the deed Link B. The two are linked together forever.

When you sell the house, the deed connects to the buyer. Thus, Link B attaches to Link C (the buyer). We now have *you-deed-buyer*. That's a block of links in the chain. Hence, *blockchain*.

The links of *you-deed-buyer*, or Links A-B-C, are forever connected, and all the world knows it. Anyone can see this chain anytime, just as you can view a photo of Beyoncé whenever you want. But that's all anyone can do: view it. The chain can be lengthened by adding links, but existing links cannot be altered, and as a result, the deed can never be lost, manipulated, copied or stolen.

Thus, when the owner (Link C) wants to sell the house, Buyer D is certain that the transaction is legitimate. That's because only one link can connect to Link C; if the buyer can become Link D, it means no one else has done so. If the buyer can't, it means someone else already did. Either way, confidence is 100%. Thus the transaction isn't simply trustworthy, it's *authenticated*.

David Mondrus and Joyce Bayo, who married in Orlando in October 2015, became the first couple in history to place their wedding vows onto the blockchain. Because anyone can access the blockchain—but never change, alter or erase its information—it is arguably the only man-made product that will truly last forever. David and Joyce thus considered the blockchain the ultimate testament of their enduring love for each other.

This authentication feature is what has everyone so excited about the blockchain. Although it was created to facilitate bitcoin transactions—I give 50 bitcoins to you, and you give 20 bitcoins to the next person (creating the chain)—everyone now realizes that the blockchain can be used to track *any* transaction. After all, the blockchain is just a data warehouse. Thus you can upload any data into it—deeds, patents, contracts, insurance policies, votes, concert tickets, even marriage certificates. And once uploaded, you can transfer ownership of that data or append new data to it at any time.

If you're not sure how profound this is, consider what the Bank of England thinks of it. The blockchain, it says, "enables verification of payments to be decentralised, removing the need for a trusted third party. It may reshape the mechanisms for making secured payments: instead of settlement occurring across the books of a single central authority (such as a central bank, clearing house or custodian), strong cryptographic and verification algorithms allow everyone in a DLT network to have a copy of the ledger, and give distributed authority for managing and updating that ledger to a much wider group of agents."

If that's incomprehensible, try this statement from *Billboard* magazine. It said blockchain technology "offers solutions to multiple, previously intractable, problems of the industry, such as song rights monitoring and complex, but transparent and reliable, royalty distribution." It cites one platform that let consumers "exchange digital assets for everything from financial industry (shares, bonds, stocks), records (certificates, copyrights, documentation) to ownership (event tickets, vouchers, gift cards)."

Gift cards might seem like small potatoes.[51] So how about the entire U.S. stock market? NASDAQ is developing blockchain software to let private companies issue and trade shares faster and more cheaply than other means currently allow. NASDAQ CEO Robert Greifeld said in 2015, "Blockchain technology holds great promise in allowing capital markets to operate more efficiently with greater transparency and security."

---

[51]They aren't; the gift card industry was a $130 billion market in 2015, according to CEB TowerGroup. Sales are expected to hit $160 billion by 2018.

Congress is showing support, too. In 2016, a bipartisan resolution in the House of Representatives called for the federal government to promote blockchain technology. States are exploring the opportunities as well; Vermont passed a law allowing the blockchain to be used as a legal method of record keeping.

Business is helping the effort. IBM has a blockchain innovation center in Singapore that fosters collaboration among government, academic and industry to create applications for use in finance and trade, and Deloitte has a partnership with five blockchain technology companies to provide digital identity programs, manage digital banking, handle cross-border payments, offer loyalty and rewards and more.

A 2016 study by Goldman Sachs says that blockchain technology could add as much as $37 billion to the U.S. economy by 2020. Its breakdown:

- $11 billion to $12 billion in savings for the securities clearing and settlement business

- $3 billion to $9 billion for the Sharing Economy

- $2.5 billion to $7 billion for the electricity industry

- $3 billion to $5 billion in cost savings associated with federal anti-money laundering and "know your customer" compliance regulations

- $2 billion to $4 billion in cost savings for the title insurance industry

You can expect radical changes in how you engage in every type of transaction thanks to the blockchain—including the use of money itself.

The financial services industry is the world's largest. The world's bank, insurance, securities and credit card companies are among the biggest employers in the world. And consumers interact with those companies on a daily basis. With so much money involved and so many people affected, it's not surprising that technologists see this industry as a huge opportunity for transformative innovation.

Incidentally

The blockchain will radically transform many industries and services, not just real estate. Here are 20 more examples:

- **Academic records.** Schools could use the blockchain to show that students have passed certain courses or obtained degrees. It would be impossible for anyone to lie about his or her academic record.

- **Banking.** The blockchain essentially does what banks do—safely store and transfer instruments of value. That's why many banks are investing in blockchain start-ups.

- **Car leasing and sales.** A customer could choose a car, sign a lease or sales agreement and obtain an insurance policy in minutes.

- **Cloud storage.** Centralized servers are vulnerable to attacks by hackers. But the blockchain is decentralized, reducing the risk of data loss due to cyberterrorists.

- **Cybersecurity.** By removing human intermediaries, and because of its cryptographic properties, the blockchain could dramatically reduce the theft of digital data.

- **Energy management.** The only way for most households and businesses to get electrical power is to buy it from a power company. But solar power lets customers generate their own energy, and the blockchain lets them sell it to their neighbors.

- **Fighting counterfeiting.** Fake goods account for 8% of world trade—about $1.7 trillion in 2015, according to NetNames. It's not just handbags sold on New York City streets; approximately 10% of airplane parts are counterfeit—raising questions of public safety. The blockchain can label and track everything, virtually eliminating the ability for counterfeit goods to be sold. If 3D printing makes it easy to produce counterfeit products, the blockchain renders them worthless.

- **Gift cards and loyalty programs.** These are cheaper to produce and more secure to use with blockchain technology.

- **Government and public benefits.** The blockchain can make it easier, cheaper and safer to distribute everything from Social Security checks to payments to government contracts.

- **Health care.** Blockchains can help hospitals share data without compromising security, which could lead to more accurate diagnoses and more effective treatments at lower cost.

- **Insurance.** Stratumn, Deloitte and Lemon Way are creating a blockchain solution to let people insure high-value items that individuals exchange with each other (for example, vacation home swapping via the sharing economy).

- **Networking.** IBM and Samsung are working on a way to use the blockchain so huge numbers of devices can communicate without the need for a central hub.

- **Online music.** The blockchain could make it possible for users to listen to music and pay artists directly, with no intermediary.

- **Payments and money transfers.** The blockchain could be used to instantaneously connect payers and payees worldwide without middlemen and at extremely low cost.

- **Ride sharing.** Uber and Lyft use centralized hubs to dispatch cars, but an Israeli start-up uses the blockchain to find people traveling the same routes.

- **Smart contracts.** The blockchain could write and administer legal contracts, such as real estate contracts, mortgage loans, employment agreements and wedding licenses without human intervention.

- **Sports management.** Want to own an athlete? The Jetcoin Institute lets fans fund players' salaries in exchange for a portion of the players' income, using the blockchain to decentralize the process. (More on this in chapter 9.)

- **Stock trading.** Overstock.com, the online retailer, has already used the blockchain to issue bonds. In 2016, the company announced plans to trade its stock and others online, using blockchain technology.

- **Supply chain management.** Supply chains are links in the manufacturing process that involve moving, say, auto parts from a supplier to a car manufacturer's assembly facility. The blockchain can document the process faster and more cheaply, without human error.

- **Voting.** With the blockchain, future voters might cast ballots via their mobile devices. Because data are entered into a public ledger without intermediaries, the votes would be unalterable and secure.

PERSONAL FINANCE IMPLICATIONS

1. Crowdfunding and crowdsourcing offer you unprecedented opportunities to earn money and find solutions to problems in your everyday life.

2. Crowdfunding and crowdsourcing are still largely unregulated industries, creating fertile environments for scam artists and crooks. Though it's probably okay to borrow money from an online crowdfunding site, you shouldn't lend, invest or give money to people trying to raise money from these sites with any expectation of getting your money back.

3. If you are employed in the traditional New York model, look for opportunities to become involved in the Hollywood model. Chances are that your employer will impose that on you in coming years, anyway, so it's better to act on your timetable instead of your employer's.

4. Mobile banking is changing the very nature of the financial services industry. If you still visit your local bank branch, ask the staff to show you how to make your next visit the last. Learn how to make all deposits and withdrawals online using your mobile device.

5. Blockchain technology will revolutionize every aspect of money as you currently understand it. It will also destroy millions of jobs—and not just clerical and entry-level positions but highly skilled, high-paying jobs. Consider if your occupation is threatened by this technology so you can decide if you need training in a new field. More on this in chapter 14.

Chapter Eleven: Safety and Security

There is no question that we face unprecedented threats, some a result of technological innovation itself. Fortunately, technology is also providing solutions to many of today's challenges.

Your smartphone, for example, will feature sensors alerting you to chemical, biological and radiological threats—and automatically call police, who will know, thanks to the GPS chip inside your phone, exactly where the threat is.

Wearables will protect you, too—from wristbands that provide alerts to clothing that protects you against viruses and harmful radiation, just as many clothes help you avoid getting a sunburn. Social media will analyze their networks to identify and warn likely victims of threats, too—so you'll know if someone's stalking you.

It will get harder for crooks to steal your identity, too. Proteus Digital Health, for example, has created a pill powered by stomach acid that creates an 18-bit signal—it essentially turns your body into an authentication token. No more passwords or ID cards needed! And the United Kingdom's National Physical Laboratory has developed a gait recognition system that can identify people based on the way they walk; you'll be able to pass through checkpoints without having to show ID.

Checkpoints are designed to prevent people with guns from entering certain areas. But you can't rope off an entire city or college campus. So there's little that police can do but wait until a firearm is used. The key, then, is to ascertain where the shots are being fired as quickly as possible. One solution is ShotSpotter, software used by dozens of police departments across the country. It identifies the specific location where gunshots were fired, enabling officers to reach the scene faster.

Still, police would love to know who's firing a gun—or who the gun is being fired at—*before* the trigger is pulled. That's why the Chicago Police Department uses an algorithm that helps predict who will commit, or be the victim of, gun violence. Created by a professor at the Illinois Institute of Technology, the algorithm scores people based on their criminal records, gang affiliations, employment status, drug histories and connections to friends and family who are in prison in gangs or have been killed.

The algorithm identified 1,400 people; in 2016, according to the CPD, 117 of the 140 people arrested during a citywide gang raid were on the list. So were more than 70% of the people shot in the city and 80% of the shooters. So in addition to using the list to arrest people, the police distributed it to social workers and community leaders so they could intervene before violence occurred.

This isn't the only instance of law enforcement turning to the community for help. After 140 people, including nine police officers, were injured during the Vancouver Stanley Cup riot of 2011 (which began after the Boston Bruins defeated the Vancouver Canucks), a police investigative team collected more than 1 million photographs and 1,600 hours of video from citizens—including some from rioters themselves who had posted their exploits on Facebook and YouTube. The police used facial recognition software to compare people in the images against DMV records and, in an act of crowdsourcing, posted photos on social media sites, asking the public for help in identifying the hoodlums. As a result, more than 200 people were identified and arrested; some hoodlums became the targets of online shaming campaigns that resulted in their being fired from their jobs or removed from athletic teams.

Cartoon by Harley Schwadron

In a digitally connected world, you can run, but it's increasingly difficult to hide.

These and other innovations are helping to protect you and your private information. This explains why safety and security are a huge growth industry; according to Gartner, annual worldwide spending on security software is expected to hit $94 billion in 2017, up from $20 billion just five years earlier.

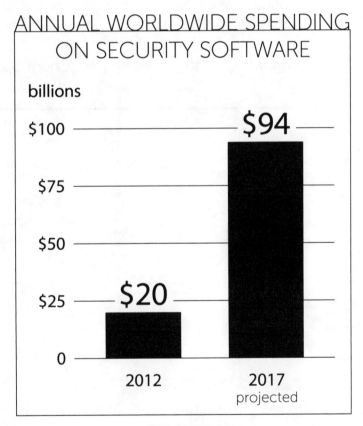

ANNUAL WORLDWIDE SPENDING ON SECURITY SOFTWARE

FIGURE 11.1

PERSONAL FINANCE IMPLICATIONS

1. You'll spend more for security than you used to; these costs need to be factored into your housing budget.

2. Because of digitization, security now applies to your money as well as your person. We'll talk about ways you can protect your-self in chapter 16.

3. Security is a growth industry, offering investment opportunities.

Chapter Twelve: The Dark Side

The future I've shared with you so far is exciting and hopeful. But let's not kid ourselves: Exponential technologies create issues that cannot be ignored. So let's look at the dangers and pitfalls of exponential technologies—subject by subject, as we've explored them thus far.

The Dark Side of the Internet

You use websites to hire a cab; crooks use websites to hire getaway cars. You use sites to find a date; criminals use sites to find hit men.

There are sites to help people stalk women, have extramarital affairs and share sexually explicit photos and videos of ex-lovers (a practice so common it now has a name: *revenge porn*).

There are sites that let you illegally download music and movies. One such site had 50 million users a day, representing 4% of global Internet traffic, before it was shut down by authorities.

Crime is as old as civilization, and the Internet has created new ways to commit them. Thieves have perused newspaper obituary columns for centuries, for example, knowing that families leave their homes empty and unprotected when attending funerals. In Marc Goodman's outstanding book *Future Crimes,* the former futurist-in-residence for the FBI reveals that 78% of convicted burglars in the United Kingdom say they used Facebook and other social websites to find out when people were going on vacation.

Swindlers are also trolling for victims on dating sites. They post fake profiles to meet people looking for romance—and eventually ask for money, often using a sob story about Mom needing an operation or a cash crunch in his business. The FBI says victims lost $120 million in the first half of 2016, a 23% increase from the prior year.

In South America, kidnappers use Google to ensnare victims. They go to airports and read the names on signs waved by chauffeurs looking for their fares. The kidnappers google the names, and when they identify a big-shot executive, they pay the chauffeur to leave so they can impersonate him. The arriving executive happily gets into the car—not realizing he's facilitating his own kidnapping. According to Cognizant, $1.5 billion was paid in ransom in 2015, explaining why K&R insurance[52] is a $10 billion market and growing by 12.3% per year.

You can't necessarily avoid kidnappers merely by staying away from Brazilian airports. Your computer programs can be hijacked just as easily. When hackers succeed in planting a virus on your computer called ransomware, you'll see a pop-up screen demanding payment of a few hundred dollars. If you fail to pay within 48 hours, all your data will be destroyed. The FBI says 250,000 victims paid $30 million in ransom through 2015.[53]

And people today are not just being attacked by people; they're being attacked by their computers and mobile devices. For example, 30% of all devices are infected with viruses called *botnets* that send spam to your entire address book.

Criminals also use viruses to take over other computers, instructing them all to access a specific website at the same time. This overloads the sites, causing them to crash. These *denial-of-service attacks*, which have hit BBC, British Airways, IMDB and others, disrupt commerce and create fear among consumers.

The scariest disruption caused by technology to date was the infamous "flash crash" that hit the stock market on May 6, 2010. That Thursday morning, the Dow Jones Industrial Average opened at 10,862. In all respects, it was a normal trading day—until 2:45 p.m. Suddenly, and without warning, the Dow plunged 600 points. But as Figure 12.1 shows, the Dow fully regained its loss within five minutes. A colleague who monitors market activity all day long had coincidentally left his desk to get a cup of coffee and missed the entire event—that's how fast it happened.

What wasn't fast was how long it took the Securities and Exchange Commission, the Commodities Futures Trading Commission, the Federal Bureau of Investigation and the Justice Department to figure out the cause of the incident. Their conclusion after five years of investigation: a guy in London did it.[54]

---

[52]Kidnap and ransom. Yeah, there is such a thing.
[53]Even the payments have gone high tech. Ten years ago, ransom had to be paid with prepaid debit cards sold by Walmart and CVS. Now, the extortionists demand payment in bitcoins.
[54]I agree, that *is* ridiculous.

Navinder Sarao, an investor who liked to trade futures contracts, built an algorithm to enter fake sell orders that would artificially drive down the market so he could buy while prices were low. During the flash crash, Sarao traded 62,077 contracts with a notional value of $3.5 billion—and made a profit of $879,018, according to regulators. But in doing so, he temporarily wiped out more than $1 trillion of equity value in the U.S. stock market. Investors who sold securities during that five-minute interval were never reimbursed for their losses. And regulators haven't said that they know how to prevent another such incident.

Everything I've described so far involves ordinary computers and commonplace technology. In a bit, you'll see what might happen when artificial intelligence is developed.

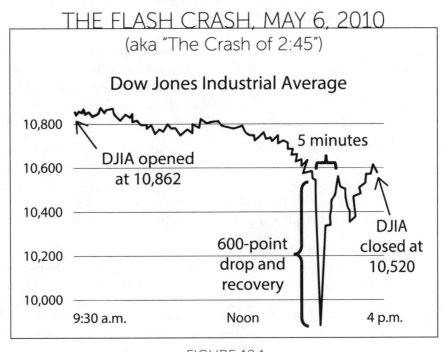

FIGURE 12.1

The Dark Side of Mobile Tech

It's not just desktop computers that are vulnerable. Today, 21% of fraud cases occur on mobile devices, and annual losses exceed $6 billion. In 2012, Kaspersky Lab found 67 fake banking apps; a year later, it found 1,300—a 1,900% increase that can only be called exponential. Likewise, in 2013, Juniper Networks found 4 million mobile phone malware apps—a 614% increase over a year earlier. Antivirus software stops only 5% of these programs.

The camera on your mobile phone or laptop can be hacked. Viruses and Trojans[55] can give attackers access to your device's microphone, recording what you say even when you're not using the phone. Likewise, your phone's video camera can be turned on without your knowledge to record what you're doing. Anything you do and any data on your mobile phone can be forwarded without your being aware of it. And because your phone has a GPS inside it, your location can be tracked by others in real time.

The more you use your mobile phone, the more likely you're going to fall for a scam conducted through it. You're not just getting robocalls by aggressive marketers, either—you're getting phone calls from outright crooks. In 2015, 11% of U.S. consumers lost money to telephone scams, according to a Harris poll. Total cost: $7.4 billion. The top scams, according to the Federal Trade Commission:

- **Business listing scam:** A small-business owner is told his listing on Google (or Yahoo! or Bing) is not up to date, or that his firm's location on online maps is about to be deleted (or conversely, that there's an opportunity to have it added). These problems can be quickly rectified by paying a small fee. "If you'll just give me your credit card number . . ."

- **Free vacations:** A caller says you've won a free trip, and all you need to pay are the taxes—in advance, of course. So "if you'll just give me your credit card number . . ."

- **Loan scams:** Got a loan that's past due? Want to get rid of a high interest rate? The callers offer to let you apply for loans over the phone. Sometimes they threaten to have you arrested if you don't cooperate. All you need to do is "give me your credit card number . . ."

---

[55]Malignant software that piggybacks on benign programs you download.

- **Surveys:** You get a call inviting you to participate in a survey. It will take only a few minutes, you're told, and you'll be entered into a drawing where you might win a free cruise or even a new car. So you answer some questions about politics, the economy or some social issue. A couple of days later, you get a phone call announcing you've won the prize! But taxes are due up front, so "if you'll just give me your credit card number . . ."

Your mobile phone gives you access to the world. It also gives the world access to you.

The Dark Side of AI and Machine Learning

Some of the most brilliant people on the planet, including such luminaries as Stephen Hawking, Elon Musk and Bill Gates, fear artificial intelligence. In 2015, along with hundreds of other technologists, the three signed a letter warning that artificial intelligence might be more dangerous than nuclear weapons.

"Success in creating AI would be the biggest event in human history," Hawking wrote in 2014. "Unfortunately, it might also be the last, unless we learn how to avoid the risks." Musk calls AI "our greatest existential threat," while Gates, in a 2015 interview, said he's "in the camp that is concerned about super intelligence."

They and others have called for limiting advances in AI until greater understanding and protections can be devised.

Wondering what has these folks so spooked? You can get an idea by watching sci-fi movies. Spend some time with HAL 9000 from *2001: A Space Odyssey*; Skynet from *The Terminator*; or WOPR from *WarGames*. I bet you can name your favorite[56] flicks of this genre, too.

---

[56]That might be a poor word choice.

The Dark Side of AR and VR

If donning a pair of glasses can make you feel as though you're anywhere in the world, why would you ever get out of bed? The movie *Surrogates*, starring Bruce Willis, or *Avatar*, starring a bunch of blue Na'vis from the planet Pandora, offer opportunities for you to contemplate the answer to this question.

The Dark Side of Wearables

If you wear clothing that measures your heart rate and other physiological data, who owns the information? The manufacturers, apparently.

At least that's the case with the University of Michigan. As part of its $170 million deal with Nike, the sportswear manufacturer provides gear to all of UM's athletes. But the contract also lets Nike collect personal data from wearable technology, including heart-rate monitors, GPS trackers and other sensors. There's no saying what Nike might do with the data or whether players would be compensated—or even informed. In the future, you might buy a shirt, but the manufacturer or retailer might own the data it collects about you.

And let's keep in mind that wearables aren't always clothes. If a grain-of-rice-sized Watson can be implanted into your brain, is there a risk that your mind could be hacked? You can decide if you'd like to live in *The Matrix* or not.

The Dark Side of Big Data

Then there's the issue of personal privacy. Our examination of Big Data in chapter 2 demonstrated that your personal information has not only already been collected, it's been widely distributed. But there's one element of your personal information that hasn't yet been collected by anyone: your innermost thoughts.

Those days may be ending. Functional magnetic resonance imaging (fMRI) machines can identify when an area of the brain is in use, because blood flow to that region increases. At least two companies claim they can thus determine whether an individual is telling the truth.

How long will it be before fMRIs are placed alongside witness stands—or in your kitchen, where your spouse might sit you down in a straight-backed wooden chair with no arms and, with a bright light shining in your eyes, ask, "Are you lying?" or the more horrifying question "Have you *ever* lied to me?"

I'm not sure we're ready to live in a society where everyone's true thoughts are always known by everyone else.

And if you think such technologies might be disruptive to your relationships, consider the disruptive impact exponential technologies are already having on businesses—strike that, entire industries—around the country.

Newspapers, including the *Baltimore Examiner, Cincinnati Post* and *Tampa Tribune,* have gone out of business, unable to compete against the instantaneous reporting capabilities of the Internet. Tower Records was killed by iTunes, Blockbuster by Netflix.

The demise of those companies has led to the creation of the sharing economy and the rise of the on-demand worker, but many economists note that contingent workers lack protections and benefits traditional employees have historically enjoyed. These include unemployment insurance, workers comp, pensions and liability safeguards. So although many workers are enjoying newfound freedom and the ability to generate multiple revenue streams, they are obtaining them in exchange for greater economic risk.

The Dark Side of Robotics

What happens when robots start making robots? This is not hypothetical, because at Cambridge University, they already are. A "mother bot" creates another to perform a specific task. Mom evaluates its creation's performance, then modifies its manufacturing process so the next bot it builds performs even better. The result of 2015 tests: the tenth generation bot performed twice as well as the first gen did.

You know what you call a robot that can make copies of itself, with each one more advanced than its predecessor?

The Terminator.

The Dark Side of SDVs

Self-driving vehicles will cause the loss of millions of jobs—and not just those of cabbies and truck drivers. After all, if you don't have truck drivers, you don't need truck stops. SDVs also eliminate the need for parking valets, garage attendants, toll booth operators, driving schools, car rental companies and public transit systems.

Not only that, the entire "crash economy" goes away. With no automobile accidents, there might be no need for automobile insurance, so that industry could disappear. That's a big deal: auto insurance represents about a third of all the premiums collected each year by the property-casualty insurance industry. Cincinnati Financial Corporation, in its 2015 filing with the Securities and Exchange Commission, noted that it receives 25% of its revenue from the sale of automobile insurance policies—and that that revenue is at risk. "Disruption of the insurance market caused by technology innovations such as driverless cars could decrease consumer demand for insurance products," the company wrote.

Allstate issued similar warnings in its 2016 annual report to shareholders: "Potential technological changes, such as driverless cars or technologies that facilitate ride or home sharing, could disrupt the demand for our products from current customers, create coverage issues or impact the frequency or severity of losses, and we may not be able to respond effectively." The chief executive officer of Allstate, Tom Wilson, told *The Wall Street Journal*, "Change is coming and we need to get ahead of it." That's why Allstate created Arity, a company that's hired more than 200 data scientists and other tech experts. Its goal: to figure out how to keep Allstate in business.

Wilson's sentiment was echoed in a regulatory filing by the Mercury Insurance Group, which told the SEC, "The advent of driverless cars and usage-based insurance could materially alter the way automobile insurance is marketed, priced and underwritten."

The Travelers Indemnity Company agrees; its 8-K filing stated, "Driverless cars, assisted-driving technologies or technologies that facilitate ride or home sharing, could disrupt the demand for our products from current customers, create coverage issues . . . and we may not be able to respond effectively."

These views are widely shared: A 2015 survey of insurance company executives found that 84% agreed that self-driving vehicles will greatly impact their businesses by 2025—and 90% admitted that they do not have a strategic plan to deal with it.

The same dilemma faces the automotive aftermarket parts business, as well as claims adjusters, collision repair companies and auto paint shops. LKQ, an aftermarket parts manufacturer, told the SEC, "If the number of vehicles involved in accidents declines or the number of cars being repaired declines, our business could suffer."

The elimination of automobile accidents could even force many chiropractors out of business. After all, more than 35% of spinal injuries are caused by automobile accidents, says the Mayo Clinic.

Indeed, it's hard to tell where the dominoes will stop falling. Consider the fact that state and local governments generate $6.5 billion a year in revenue from moving violations, parking tickets and towing fees. Many small towns across America are notoriously dependent on speed traps to generate the revenue they need to provide basic community services. But self-driving vehicles don't speed, run red lights, go the wrong way on one-way streets or ignore stop signs. They don't double-park or stand where prohibited. If these municipalities suddenly lose the $6.5 billion they're currently receiving each year from hapless human drivers, how will local governments pay their bills?

And since one of the bills they pay is the interest they owe on the municipal bonds they've issued, might we experience the largest series of muni bond defaults in U.S. history? And if that happens, what will be the impact on all the retirees who bought $3.6 trillion worth of bonds and who are dependent on the income they produce?

There are other issues to consider as well. One is liability: If a self-driving vehicle is involved in an accident, is the vehicle's owner financially responsible, or does liability belong to the occupants of the vehicle, the vehicle's manufacturer or the sensory system's designer?

There are also ethical considerations: If a child suddenly runs into the road, should the car be programmed to swerve into a tree, killing its occupant, or continue forward and kill the child?

Then there's the question about hackers: Should the computer systems be designed to allow police to commandeer your car and take you directly to jail?

This isn't as far-fetched as it might seem. After all, in 2015, Cathy Bernstein was arrested for being a hit-and-run driver. The informant was her car.

When she left the accident scene, her Ford automatically called 911. It's a safety feature designed to help police find accident victims who might be unable to call for help. When police phoned her, she denied being in an accident, according to news reports, but the car's GPS placed her at the scene, and a police inspection found damage to her vehicle consistent with the incident. It was the first time a car tattled on its owner. It won't be the last.

Want to hear more concerns? Okay, how about this one: Will car enthusiasts no longer be permitted to tinker with their cars?

And what of the automobile manufacturers themselves? Uber predicts that most current automakers will be bankrupt by 2030, replaced by new companies such as Tesla and Local Motors. What will happen to the defunct companies' shareholders, workers—and their dealers and all the people they employ?

As I said, it's hard to tell where the dominoes will stop falling.

Incidentally

One of the biggest challenges with SDVs is getting them to operate safely on roads filled with cars driven by humans.

The accident rate for Google's self-driving cars is 0.66 per 100,000 miles, or almost double the 0.38 rate for cars driven by humans, according to the National Highway Traffic Safety Administration. That sounds as though SDVs are worse than human drivers—but keep in mind that only one of the Google car's accidents was the car's fault (it was traveling at less than 5 mph and bumped into a bus). Instead, cars driven by humans keep crashing into them.

One reason: SDVs obey all traffic laws all the time, without exception. That means they occasionally get hit from behind by inattentive or aggressive human drivers who aren't expecting the car in front of them to actually stop when approaching a yellow traffic light.

The Dark Side of Drones

It's illegal for anyone to walk across your lawn without your permission, but it's perfectly legal for someone to hover a drone over it and take pictures of your children playing in the yard while you cook burgers on the grill. Or hover outside your bedroom window with its camera focused on . . .

And North Dakota has taken the ethical debate to, ahem, new heights: The state legislature has legalized the use of armed police drones. For now, authority is restricted to tasers, tear gas, pepper spray and rubber bullets, but are real bullets next?

And who decides when to shoot—a police officer or the drone itself?

Indeed, many wonder whether the military will one day give the "kill decision" to robots. The Pentagon has made it clear that humans are required to authorize the firing of a weapon, but some wonder how long that policy can survive. Consider a U.S. Army robot carrying an M-16, facing an enemy robot armed with an AK-47. If the Army's robot can't fire until given permission by a human, it will lose the fight if the enemy's robot has no such restriction. Eventually, some say, the Pentagon will have no choice but to permit robots to fire their weapons autonomously.

Such a future may be getting closer. Following the horrific murder of five police officers in Dallas in 2016, local police used a robot to kill the terrorist. It was the first such use of bots in U.S. law enforcement history, and though few have expressed disapproval, many are wondering whether this introduces a new era in police response to shootings.

The Dark Side of Bionics

If you could enjoy eyesight that gave you both telescopic and microscopic vision, why wouldn't you obtain it?

Maybe you wouldn't do this for yourself. But would you do it for your child?

Lots of parents do everything they can to give their children advantages: enrolling them in private schools, having them wear braces to straighten their teeth and improve their smiles, and hiring coaches, trainers, tutors and teachers to improve and develop their athletic, intellectual or artistic talents. Parents often fear that failing to do "whatever it takes" could place their children at a competitive disadvantage.

Are you willing to be passed over for a promotion or have your child's college application denied because you refused to take full advantage of every opportunity to enhance your or your child's qualifications and abilities?

I remember watching Oscar Pistorius compete in track events at the 2012 Olympics—despite the fact he has no legs. Frankly, when I saw that, I wondered, "Why not just strap rocket boosters to his knees and catapult him to the finish line?"

© Paul Gilham/Getty Images Sport/Getty Images

Yeah, I know, his artificial legs are supposed to be equal substitutes for real ones. But how can we know they don't provide him with an advantage?

Athletes are prohibited from ingesting performance-enhancing drugs, so why can Pistorius wear prosthetics that clearly enhance his running ability?

Obviously, my view isn't widely shared; Pistorious competed in the 2012 Games—and reportedly plans to do so again, in the 2020 Games.[57]

You have to wonder if "natural" sprinters might one day voluntarily choose to replace their legs with artificial ones so they can run faster or longer. And if ath-

---

[57]Yeah, despite the fact that he's a convicted murderer. But let's try to stay with the point I'm making here, okay?

letes make that the norm, it won't take long for fans and the rest of society to follow suit. Eventually, everyone will have performance-enhancing bionic implants. Could bionics spell the end of humanity as we know it?

There's a name for people who are a mix of humanity and technology: *the Borg*.

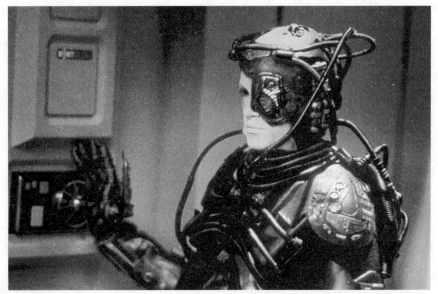

© AF archive / Alamy

The Borg are bad guys in the *Star Trek* sci-fi series. They "assimilate" humans into their culture by surgically adding tech to them.

Think you might never agree to such procedures? As a Borg once said, "Resistance is futile."

So the real question raised by bionic technology is this: At what point do humans cease to be . . . human?

The Dark Side of Nanotech and Materials Science

The lack of history is making it difficult to understand the risks of nanotechnology. A report by Ernst & Young said, "The emerging applications of nanotechnology in the manufacture or use of medicine, cosmetics, drug delivery, robotics, materials science and other products and systems create potential liability exposures. Examples include bodily injury (analogous to asbestos exposure) and environmental damage from nanoparticles escaping uncontrolled into the air or water supply."

"Thalidomide babies"—children with severe birth defects—were born in the 1950s when their mothers took the new "wonder drug" thalidomide for anxiety while pregnant. Might nanotech products cause similar problems—and do we want to find out before or after we begin marketing such products?

I'd say more on this topic, but . . . the lack of history is making it difficult to estimate the risks.

The Dark Side of 3D Printing

3D printing is expected to cause $100 billion in intellectual property losses by 2018, according to a report from Gartner. That's because this technology makes it easy to make an exact copy of someone else's design.

People are also using 3D printers to print things most of us would prefer they didn't print, such as weapons that can get through security checkpoints without being detected, handcuff keys and ATM skimmers.

In 2013, Cody Wilson, a 25-year-old Texas law school student, 3D-printed a gun to prove it could be done. He successfully fired six shots before the gun broke.

By the way, Wilson uploaded his design files onto the Internet, and more than 100,000 people downloaded them before the State Department required him to take the files down. More recently, Wilson has displayed an AR-15 assault rifle built with 3D-printed parts that is capable of firing hundreds of rounds. Wilson has even started his own company, Defense

Incidentally

Digital pirates aren't just using 3D printers to steal intellectual property. In 2014, they generated $220 million in ad revenue by getting people to watch stolen video content such as television shows, movies and sporting events. This problem will likely get worse, since younger Americans see nothing wrong with the practice. According to the report, more than half of Americans aged 18 to 34 watch pirated content. They are unlikely to change their, uh, view. The primary reason they watch pirated content: it's free.

Distributed, which sells a device for just $1,500 that can make gun parts to complement 3D-printed gun parts.

Meanwhile, the Bureau of Alcohol, Tobacco, Firearms and Explosives says it's not yet possible to produce a "consistently reliable" firearm via a 3D printer.

Counterfeit handbags for sale at a street-front tourist shop in St. Thomas, U.S. Virgin Islands.

The more that federal and state governments increase their efforts to prevent criminals and suspected terrorists from legally purchasing firearms, the more those people will turn to manufacturing them themselves. With 3D printers already costing less than $500 and the materials needed to print a gun costing as little as $25, it's easy to see why nefarious individuals won't bother trying to buy guns the way law-abiding citizens do.

Of course, this isn't solely a domestic issue. In 2016, police in Australia found a 3D-printed pistol of unknown design when they busted a meth lab.

Are you envisioning unkempt terrorists lurking in dimly lit rooms to jigger 3D designs? You might want to look instead at the goofy teenager next door. Mattel has rereleased ThingMaker, the 1960s toy that let kids create Creepy Crawlers by pouring melted plastic into molds. The device is now a 3D printer—and it retails for under $300. In collaboration with Autodesk, kids can download thousands of designs for free from thingiverse.com to make pretty much anything they want, whether you're watching or not.

What might a hormone-driven, bullied teenager create?

The Dark Side of Medicine and Neuroscience

We've seen how more people than ever are living with good health during old age. But not every elder in good health engages in socially acceptable activities.

In 2015, Brian Reader, age 76, was arrested by police after masterminding one of the most brazen jewel heists in British history. The youngest of his four main accomplices was 60 years old.

Reader's case isn't isolated. In South Korea, crimes committed by people 65 years of age and older rose by 12% from 2001 to 2013, including a 40% increase in violent crime. Crime in Japan by people over the age of 65 doubled from 2003 to 2013, where more elderly are now caught shoplifting than teenagers. The Netherlands has also experienced a sharp rise in arrests and incarceration of elderly people, while in London, the number of elderly prison inmates is increasing three times faster than the overall prison population.

Medical innovations aren't just helping criminals extend their careers; they could lead to murders on a truly horrific scale.

CRISPR and other genetic modification technologies might one day be used to weaponize the H5N1 flu bug so it kills people on a mass scale. The technology might also be used to genetically create a virus designed to kill a single individual—your ex-spouse, say, or a head of state. In 2012, *The Atlantic* published an article claiming that the Secret Service destroys or wipes down everything the president ever touches, to prevent enemies from collecting his DNA. The article also claimed that U.S. embassies have been collecting the DNA of foreign nationals, including heads of state, for unstated purposes. The Secret Service, Pentagon and intelligence agencies refused to comment on that story.

It's not just a lone scientist/inventor working in a basement we need to worry about. Rogue nations (such as North Korea), secret government agencies and loosely regulated commercial laboratories all might do something the rest of us consider, well, stupid.

And one of those stupid acts might be to genetically modify DNA in a way that passes on the altered genes to offspring. Currently, CRISPR doesn't do that. But some scientists want to, in an effort to fight inherited diseases.

And they may be getting their way. The Human Fertilisation and Embryology Authority, Great Britain's fertility regulator, has given a scientist permission to edit human embryos, and Chinese researchers are doing likewise. (U.S. agencies won't fund such research on human embryos, but private funding is allowed.)

This is so worrisome that in 2015, scientists who are members of the National Academy of Sciences, the Royal Society of London and China's Academy of Sciences—including Jennifer Doudna, the scientist credited with discovering the CRISPR/Cas9 technology—called for a moratorium on making inheritable changes to the human genome.

If it's possible to design a virus at the molecular level that can travel the bloodstream to hunt for and kill cancer, might it not also be possible for a virus to be designed that will kill you instead?

And it might not even be an act of bioterrorism—state-sponsored or not—we need to fear. The British cosmologist Martin Rees predicted in 2002 that an act of *bioerrorism* would kill 1 million people by 2020. Rees's point is that well-intentioned scientists—or some high school kid playing with tech tools in his parents' basement—might inadvertently or mistakenly unleash a virus that produces casualties on a ghastly scale before it is stopped.

Even deliberate, well-intentioned acts are worrying some people. A 10-year project launched in 2016 aims to chemically manufacture DNA without sperm or eggs—yes, the goal is to synthetically create an entire human genome. The project, run by the Center of Excellence for Engineering Biology, will cost billions of dollars. Proponents say the ability to fabricate DNA would enable huge scientific and medical advances. Ethicists worry it would mean the end of humanity.

The Dark Side of Energy and Environmental Systems

We've seen how new energy systems can disrupt established companies, threatening workers and shareholders alike. But what if an innovation starts killing people?

The safety of genetically modified foods is hotly debated. Although there is little evidence of any problems, GMO supporters were set back in 2015 when

Christopher Portier, a former director of Risk Assessment Research at the National Institute of Environmental Health Sciences, part of the National Institutes of Health, said he is certain that glyphosate, a weed killer used on genetically engineered crops, is "definitely genotoxic." Spraying it on crops can damage human DNA in ways that could lead to cancer. "There is no doubt in my mind," he said. And the World Health Organization's International Agency for Research on Cancer agrees, saying glyphosate is "probably carcinogenic to humans." While the debate rages, consumers are left wondering if their food is safe to eat.

The Dark Side of Crowdfunding and Crowdsourcing

Ever seen the TV show *Who Wants to Be a Millionaire*? Contestants are asked a series of increasingly difficult questions—the more they answer, the more money they make, but answering any question incorrectly ends the game. When faced with a multiple-choice question, contestants are allowed to poll the audience. Hundreds of people vote, and whenever 70% or 80% of the audience agree that one of the choices is the correct answer, the contestant always goes with the audience's recommendation—and invariably the audience is correct.

That, of course, was an early version of crowdsourcing. Today this form of crowdsourcing is routinely provided by hundreds of websites. Millions of people offer their opinions, giving you the opportunity to learn from their experiences. Deciding which movie to see, which restaurant to dine at and which plumber to hire are all made much easier thanks to the prevalence of online reviews posted by your fellow consumers. Indeed according to Neilsen, 90% of consumers are influenced by online reviews, and 70% of those surveyed say they trust online reviews as much as reviews provided by their friends.

"I WASN'T COPYING OFF OTHERS. I WAS CROWDSOURCING THE ANSWERS."

Cartoon by Harley Schwadron

Unfortunately, many of the reviews are worthless. And I don't mean that people lack good taste in movies, I mean that people really aren't involved in the first place. According to Yelp, 25% of the reviews appearing on its website are "suspicious" or even "not recommended"—meaning the site considers the reviews to be fake, placed there by the companies being reviewed. In 2014, a federal appeals court ruled in part that it was legal for Yelp to manipulate reviews. Users are not necessarily aware of these alterations, nor of the basis for Yelp's ratings.

Facebook's 2015 filings with the SEC admit that 2% of its accounts are fake, too. That's 20 million monthly active users, equal to the entire population of the state of New York. If you want to make your company look like a big deal, you can buy 100,000 fans for $1,500. Likewise, you can buy 4,000 Twitter followers for five dollars.

Crowdsourcing and crowdfunding can be a hub of criminal activity as well. A Chinese online lender stole more than $7.6 billion from more than 1 million investors from 2014 to 2016 in what Chinese officials called a massive Ponzi scheme. And the credibility of the biggest U.S. peer-to-peer lender, Lending Club, was damaged in 2015 when an investigation found that $22.3 million worth of loans had been sold to single investors without all of them meeting the buyer's criteria. (Reportedly, the loan applications had been altered to appear as though they did.) As a result, the CEO was fired and the company was being investigated by the Justice Department and the Securities and Exchange Commission.

Even legitimate crowdfunding sites raise concerns: when a 13-year-old was killed by a drunk driver in 2015, a neighbor launched a fund-raiser on youcaring.com. Relatives, friends, neighbors and even strangers contributed $2,700 to help the family pay for funeral expenses. But the family soon learned that the neighbor had kept more than $1,000 of the money. There've been other reports of funding requests created by people with no connection to victims; the creators' campaigns can easily keep all the money for themselves. With little accountability and few laws governing these sites, it's easy for deceptive behavior to occur.

Even when everything is above board, fund-raisers never receive all the funds collected. GoFundMe, for example, the largest fund-raising site, keeps 5% of the money it raises. It also charges a processing fee of 2.9% plus 30 cents per donation. This total cost of about 8% is considered by many to be exorbitantly high.

Critics also say that cash-strapped state and local governments are taking undue advantage of crowdfunding sites. Agencies aren't raising money themselves on the sites; instead, their employees and citizens are—due to budget cuts. Schoolteachers frequently establish fund-raising campaigns on such websites as donorschoose.org to raise money for books, field trips and classroom supplies. At Citizinvestor, community activists can raise money to pay for such municipal services as recycling facilities and park maintenance.

Crowdsourcing has been used for an even more nefarious purpose: a "flash rob." Someone anonymously posts the name and address of a liquor or convenience store. At a designated time, a mob swarms the store, overwhelming the shopkeeper and stealing as much as they can carry within a minute or two. The crime is over almost as quickly as it begins, and the perpetrators scatter as rapidly as they had assembled. Because they don't know one another, they are unable to implicate others if caught. Flash robs have occurred in large cities, such as Chicago, Houston and Jacksonville, as well as small towns, such as Germantown, Maryland.

Don't assume you'll make money by investing via crowdfunding sites. Many projects fail, some borrowers default—and some sites are crooked.

The Dark Side of Games and Gamification

Gamification manipulates behavior. It reduces us to demanding rewards and refusing to perform when none is offered. It removes the ability for people to act out of kindness and generosity—to act solely in support of others.

Poorly designed games can also waste money and time and damage relation-ships. Employees, customers, ballplayers, students and children—whoever your target is—could have the opposite reaction if they believe your motives aren't pure.

The desire to achieve results can indeed cause both game creators and partici-pants to suffer ethical lapses. Wanting higher profits, Wells Fargo created a bonus program to reward employees who opened a certain number of accounts. The result: Over a five-year period, 5,300 employees created millions of fake bank and credit card accounts in an effort to collect bonuses or meet quotas; the head of the unit received $125 million in compensation upon retiring in 2016 even though the bank itself paid a $185 million fine that year and faced criminal prosecution.

Or consider Volkswagen. Its executives were so determined to say that their cars produced low emissions that its engineers installed software so cars being tested would appear to emit fewer emissions than they actually did. At this writing, the company has paid $14.7 billion in fines and still faces thousands of lawsuits and criminal charges in several countries.

Finally, gamifying everything can embarrass or even humiliate those who don't perform well, especially if failures are well publicized.

So although motivation is a laudable goal, technology makes it so easy to turn everything into a reward system that we must be careful not to destroy the human experience.

The Dark Side of Unbanked/Mobile Banking

As we've seen, it's hard to keep secrets on the Internet. But keeping secret is exactly what you want to do when it comes to your bank account and balance.

Unfortunately, many wireless networks are easily monitored by hackers, especially if reception is poor. And losing your phone is a much bigger deal than it used to be. Anyone finding (or stealing) your phone could pick it up, log in to your banking app, and access your money. Sure, passwords can help—unless you autosave them.

Spammers send you emails that appear to be from your bank with ominous warnings that your account has been breached—hoping you'll click on a link in the email. Do that, and you'll be providing the crooks with the exact information they need to access your real account. Some crooks don't even bother with high-tech gadgetry; they just engage in "shoulder surfing"—looking over your shoulder as you log on to your mobile device.

Crooks also use the fact that you make virtual deposits to cash your checks twice. It's called "double presentment" and can happen thanks to "remote deposit capture," which has become a staple of mobile banking.

Instead of going to the bank and physically handing the teller a check that you want to deposit into your account, you can now simply take a photo of it and email or text the photo to the bank via the mobile app. It's convenient, but because you keep the check, it creates the opportunity for you to forget that you've made the deposit, causing you to deposit it again. The result: the bank will eventually get it corrected, but in the meantime you might think your balance is higher than it really is, causing you to bounce checks. Hello, overdraft fees.

The example I've just described is accidental. But criminals do it deliberately. If they manage to get you to send them a check—or if they merely get your account number so they can create fake checks of your own account themselves—they'll deposit the same check repeatedly. By the time you realize what's happening, your money could be gone.

And these problems refer only to crooks attacking you. When they decide to attack a bank itself, every account at the financial institution can be compromised. The result can be inconvenience if you're denied access to your account for a few hours—or economic chaos if the bank's entire system was destroyed. That's never happened. Does that mean it can't?

The Dark Side of Digital Currency

Everyone in the world knows what an American dollar is, and everyone is willing to accept it in exchange for goods and services. That certainly can't be said of Bitcoin (or any digital currency). With so few merchants currently willing to accept them, you have to wonder if there's any point to owning bitcoins.

And there are some pretty basic risks to owning or using digital currencies. Since you're not likely to attempt mining your own, you'll buy them from an exchange. That means you need to be confident that the exchange is a legitimate business. (Exchanges have to register with the Treasury Department's Financial Crimes Enforcement Network, so make sure the one you're planning to work with has done that. Go to www.fincen.gov/financial_institutions/msb/msbstateselector.html.)[58]

---

[58]Registration does not ensure that an exchange is trustworthy or consumer-friendly; some exchanges charge transaction fees of as high as 7% plus exchange fees.

Also, digital currency prices are known to fluctuate wildly. Bitcoin prices rose from pennies in 2009 to $1,216.73 in November 2013 before falling to about $400 in 2014. In September 2016, the price was $600. Clearly, there's not yet sufficient stability to have confidence that the dollars you convert into bitcoins can be converted back into dollars of the same amount.

This point was highlighted by the experience of Laszlo Hanyecz, who on May 22, 2010, used bitcoins to buy two Papa John's pizzas. Bitcoins, which had existed for only a year, were still worth pennies—which is why it took Hanyecz 10,000 BTC to pay for $25 worth of pizza. But six years later, those 10,000 BTC were worth $6 million, making those pies the most expensive pizzas of all time. Because price fluctuations persist, you could find yourself wildly overpaying when using bitcoins too.[59]

In addition to losing bitcoins by overpaying for goods, you also have to be careful not to lose them by, well, losing them. When you buy bitcoins from an exchange, you create an encryption code—a private key to your account (called an electronic wallet). If you lose that key, you'll never be able to access your account again, meaning your money will be gone forever (as though you had lost your wallet). Forgetting the password isn't the only way to lose the key; a crash of your hard drive will do it, too, if you haven't backed up your files.

Using bitcoins requires careful attention as well. To send bitcoins to another person, you must enter his or her key; if you mistype it, you could end up sending your BTC to the wrong person. Depending on the exchanges involved, you might not be able to stop the transaction or claw it back.

And then there's the tax implication. When you spend $10 to buy a pizza, you simply hand the delivery guy a ten-dollar bill. End of transaction. But using bitcoins is far more complicated. Remember when I told you that the IRS treats bitcoins as property? That means you have to track the price you paid for each bitcoin—as you do for individual shares of stock and compare that cost to the price you got when "selling" the bitcoin (using it in a transaction). If you used, say, $10 to buy 10 BTC but later used only eight BTC to buy $10 worth of pizza, you have made a profit—and you must report that profit and pay taxes on

---

[59]Because Laszlo's purchase was the first real-world transaction involving bitcoins, enthusiasts revere May 22 as "Bitcoin Pizza Day." It's the currency's version of the Fourth of July. Kinda chokes me up.

it on your federal tax return. Imagine asking your pizza guy to hand you Form 1099 along with the bread sticks![60]

So far, we've addressed risks associated with your personal use of digital currencies. Let's shift now to some bigger issues. After all, it's one thing for you to lose your private key. It's quite another for your exchange to go belly up—which is what happened to the Mt. Gox exchange in February 2014. When it collapsed, almost $400 million of customer funds, representing nearly 6% of all Bitcoin then in circulation, were lost. If you had been storing your bitcoins at Mt. Gox, your only recourse would have been to file a claim in its bankruptcy proceeding. At this writing, no one has recovered any bitcoins or received any refunds.

It might not even take a hacker or the collapse of an exchange to destroy the world's bitcoins: Since it operates as electronic code, a bug in the program could wipe out everyone's holdings—immediately and worldwide. Imagine if all of the nation's hundred-dollar bills all over the world suddenly vanished!

Here's another risk. Bitcoin brags that it is immune to inflation, thanks to its fixed supply. But it doesn't say anything about *deflation*. You know what we called the last deflationary period that occurred in the United States? The Great Depression.

Digital currencies are inevitable. No one is certain what the risks will be.

The Dark Side of the Blockchain

The Treasury Department's Financial Stability Oversight Council warned in 2016 that blockchain technology and marketplace lending could present risks to the nation's financial stability.

The FSOC warned that blockchain technology is so new that the risks aren't clear. Thus, premature adoption by the financial industry could pose a "significant risk" to financial stability. The FSOC also says some blockchain systems could be vulnerable to fraud if a large portion of participants were to collude to defraud the rest. And because firms using blockchain systems operate worldwide, over multiple regulatory jurisdictions and national boundaries, regulators would have to coordinate their efforts to identify and monitor risks.

---

[60]I wonder how many of today's bitcoin users are actually doing this—or even know about it.

The whole point of the blockchain—authentication via an open-source ledger that everyone can see—means that no transaction activity would be private. Hello, accountability, good-bye, personal privacy. Although transactions would be secure, your neighbors would be able to see that you had bought adult diapers.

You might not know who created the blockchain system you're using. Was it your friendly neighborhood bank or some outfit funded by the Russian government? And what might the implications of that be? No one yet knows.

So far, blockchain technology can't match the speed of systems used by today's credit card companies. Your Visa transaction is completed in milliseconds, but bitcoin transactions currently take far longer. According to Thomson Reuters, 13% of transactions take longer than 20 minutes; some take more than an hour. The more time it takes to complete a transaction, the more time hackers have to interfere with it. Also, this increases the risk of double presentment.

And then there's the risk of a "51% attack," the only known way to wreck a blockchain. It requires a majority of users to collude, but if they managed it, they would gain control of the blockchain. If the world's financial institutions were depending on that hijacked blockchain, it would be, uh, a problem.

The Dark Side of Investments

The word that best describes the impact exponential technologies will have on investments is *disruption*.

Do not take that word lightly. Seismic disruption can cause a painting to hang off kilter—or a skyscraper to collapse.

Technological innovation can bring an exciting new product or service to the marketplace—and destroy an entire industry, throwing millions of people out of work and causing investments to become worthless. And it can occur with shocking speed.

Consider photography. In 1995, 710 million rolls of film were developed. Almost all of them had been manufactured by Kodak, a company founded in 1888. The company was one of the country's largest, with 140,000 people on its payroll and $28 billion in annual revenues.

Then came digital photography. By 2012, Kodak had just 17,000 employees, and it filed for bankruptcy. But in that same year, a two-year-old digital photography company with 13 employees called Instagram was sold for $1 billion.

That, my friends, is *disruption*. And it's not just Kodak and its employees and shareholders that are being threatened. As the Silicon Valley investor David Rose has said, "Any company designed for success in the 20th century is doomed to failure in the 21st."

Tower Records was disrupted by iTunes. Borders was disrupted by Amazon. com. Blockbuster was disrupted by Netflix. Classified ads in newspapers were disrupted by eBay, Craigslist, monster.com and CareerBuilder. *Encyclopaedia Britannica* was disrupted by Wikipedia and Google.

Even disruptors can become disrupted. Consider MySpace, launched as a social networking site in 2003. News Corporation bought it in 2005 for $580 million, and in 2006 it surpassed Google as the most visited website in the country. But you may never have heard of MySpace, because you use Facebook.

There's nothing new about disruption destroying companies, of course. After all, the horse-and-buggy business was disrupted by the Ford Model T.

Workers of disrupted companies often suffer displacement. They lose income while searching for new work, and they might have to relocate. But it usually works out; the people who built those buggies probably found employment in Henry's factories.

But the *owners* of those buggy manufacturers were financially decimated. Their product became obsolete, so the value of their businesses fell to zero. Any inventory they had was suddenly worthless. And if they had planned to pass on their business to their sons, that plan was destroyed.

This problem persists today for all investors. When you purchase stock in a company, you become one of its owners—and if the company goes bankrupt, as Kodak did, your investment becomes worthless.

Many big companies today are threatened with extinction due to exponential technologies.

Consider the hotel industry. Hyatt, for example, founded in 1957, has 45,000 employees and 155,000 hotel rooms in 54 countries. As of November 30, 2016, investors valued the company at $7.8 billion. By comparison, Airbnb, with 1 million rooms in 34,000 cities around the world, was valued at $24 billion—even though it doesn't manage a single hotel property.

Or consider Quicken Loans. Without any branch offices, it's become the second largest mortgage lender in the United States. Bill Emerson, the company's CEO, says, "We are a technology and marketing company that happens to do mortgages."

Emerson isn't the only CEO who draws a distinction between his company's product and the business his company is in. Elon Musk, the CEO of Tesla Motors, refers to his company's Model S as "a very sophisticated computer on wheels."

With thinking like this, it's easy to understand how a social networking upstart that lets users share photographs could blindside a company that had been manufacturing film for 124 years.

And Kodak isn't an aberration; it's the canary in the coal mine. Many more huge companies will go bankrupt just as it did. In 1920, the average company in the S&P 500 Index remained on the list for 65 years before it was acquired, merged or went out of business, according to a study by professors at Yale University. But as of 2015, the average life span is just 15 years. And a study by the Olin Graduate School of Business says that 40% of the Fortune 500—the 500 largest publicly traded U.S. companies—won't exist by 2025.

And all the CEOs of the Fortune 500 know it. In 2015, when *Fortune* magazine asked those executives, "What is your company's greatest challenge?," 72% replied, "The rapid pace of technological innovation."

Should you hope you're investing in the other 28%? Or are their CEOs oblivious to what's coming? Either way, disruption is a significant threat that investors must consider. For example, in a 2015 survey by LIMRA, 57% of insurance executives said an outside source such as Google or Amazon will be a disruptive force in the life insurance market by 2020. Those executives have reason to be concerned: according to LIMRA, 21% of consumers say they're willing to buy life insurance online from a nontraditional source—and that number can only be expected to grow.

What other industries are susceptible, and what might this mean for investors and the future value of their investments?

The Dark Side of Safety and Security

Arresting people identified by an algorithm as likely to commit a crime—which is what police in Chicago do—is the ultimate form of profiling. This raises important questions about civil liberties, no?

And if police can do this, so can criminals. After all, the data used by that law enforcement algorithm are available to anyone—meaning that crooks can put the data to nefarious use.

Thieves, child molesters, estranged spouses, disgruntled employees and others already use technology to do nasty things. Thieves can easily hack the electronic lock on your hotel room door or monitor your thermostat. (Knowing your home's temperature helps a crook know if you're away.) Thieves also use laptop computers to steal cars; the National Insurance Crime Bureau says crooks are hacking electronic systems to open car doors and start engines. In 2015, Fiat Chrysler recalled 1.4 million vehicles to fix software after hackers remotely took control of the Jeep Cherokee, activating the vehicle's engine, air-conditioning, radio and windshield wipers.

Meanwhile, child molesters can hack into Bluetooth-enabled baby monitors so they can eavesdrop; an estranged spouse or other person could remotely alter your blood glucose meter to send you into hypoglycemic shock or manipulate your pacemaker.

And then there are disgruntled employees. A notorious case occurred in 2010, when the Texas Auto Center was hacked by a former employee. The dealership sells used cars to people with poor credit if they allow the installation of a device that lets the dealership disable the vehicle if loan payments aren't made on time. An unhappy former employee broke into the company's computer system and activated the device on more than 100 cars, essentially turning them into bricks. Although the devices were designed so a vehicle whose ignition is on can't be "bricked"—to avoid the risk of an accident—many car owners missed work, had to pay for tow trucks and suffered other inconveniences. Both the auto dealership and the manufacturer of the devices were embarrassed.

Even those we can't label as "crooks" are hacking you. If your coffee machine is connected to the Internet, for example, your brewing habits are the property of the machine's manufacturer; the data can be used by the manufacturer or sold to others for them to use as they wish.

You know this is true, because you read it in the terms of service agreement you received when you bought the item.[61]

The Darkest Side of All

Crime, loss of privacy, existential threats—the negative side of exponential technologies can be summed up in a single word.

Disruption.

People fear the unknown, and they resist change. And if there's one statement we can make about exponential technologies that is absolutely undeniable, it's this: They will change almost everything.

So it's no surprise that dissent is rising. But it's not the first time we've experienced resistance to technological innovation. In the early 1800s, textile workers in England reacted angrily when power looms threatened their jobs. Weavers burned mills and factory machinery in 1811, 1816 and 1817, and threshing machines were destroyed during riots in 1830. Those acts were not spontaneous; workers practiced drills, and they executed coordinated attacks. Such opponents of technology became known as Luddites, in honor of Ned Ludd, who had reportedly smashed two looms in 1779.

---

[61]Yeah, as if you read ToS documents. Proving that you almost certainly don't, look what happened to thousands of people who downloaded purchases on April 1, 2010, from Gamestation, a British computer game retailer. The company revealed that its ToS agreement contained a clause giving the company legal rights to their souls. "By placing an order via this Web site on the first day of the fourth month of the year 2010 Anno Domini, you agree to grant Us a non transferable option to claim, for now and for ever more, your immortal soul. Should We wish to exercise this option, you agree to surrender your immortal soul, and any claim you may have on it, within 5 (five) working days of receiving written notification from gamesation.co.uk or one of its duly authorised minions." It was an April Fool's Day joke, but it proved that few people read ToS agreements. (Customers had the opportunity to nullify the clause—and get a £5 voucher for doing so—but only 12% did, suggesting that the other 88% didn't read the ToS. And even if you do read every ToS, what are you going to do if you disagree? It's not as though Apple will be willing to modify your ToS when you buy an iPhone.

You can find Luddite behavior throughout modern history. In the 1800s, locomotives were steam powered; workers called firemen kept the boilers burning. Although diesel engines rendered their jobs obsolete in the 1930s, it wasn't until 1963 that railroads were able to eliminate those positions, thanks to legislative protections secured by unions.

If you want to see a modern-day boiler keeper, just look at a guy driving a taxi. Cab drivers in cities around the world have been demonstrating against Uber, staging sick-outs, blocking major highways and access to airports and even destroying Uber cars and attacking Uber drivers, all in an effort to stop the proliferation of a competitor they regard as destructive to their careers.

© GERARD JULIEN/AFP/Getty Images

© Gonzalo Fuentes / Reuters Pictures

They're not the ones trying to protect themselves. If you own a mutual fund, you know your investment generates a lot of mail: monthly or quarterly statements, trade confirmations, semiannual and annual reports and that prospectus you never bother reading.[62] Every fund company is capable of emailing this

---

[62]The ultimate ToS!

material to you or texting a link so you can view the documents on a secure website. Imagine the money fund companies could save every year in printing, postage and handling costs—or rather, imagine the money *you* would save, since those costs are merely passed along to you. So why hasn't Congress changed the law, or the U.S. Securities and Exchange Commission its regulations, so the industry can stop producing paper and instead provide the information digitally?

Because the industry is fighting the change.

Not the mutual fund industry. The paper industry.

Consumers for Paper Options is a lobbying organization that opposes the elimination of paper. Its members are the American Forest & Paper Association and the Envelope Manufacturers Association, in partnership with the National Association of Letter Carriers and the National Rural Letter Carriers' Association. CPO opposes the SEC's proposal to let mutual funds transmit information to investors electronically. (According to the group's website, allowing digital distribution of documents "will potentially harm millions of investors.") The group also wants the IRS to continue distributing all its forms via paper, wants the Treasury Department to resume issuing paper versions of EE savings bonds and wants the Social Security Administration to restart mailing annual Social Security statements to workers aged 25 to 60 and to mail Social Security checks to retirees instead of having those checks direct-deposited into bank accounts electronically.

It's blatant job protectionism, and that's all that many Luddites are. Others are simply pandering. The editors of *Car and Driver*, for example, flatly stated in July 2016, "The fully automated car will never happen." Do the editors truly believe this, or are they simply saying what their subscribers want to hear?

SMITH & HOBSON

"PEOPLE REPLACING PEOPLE WITH APPS AND ROBOTS SINCE 2009"

Cartoon by Harley Schwadron

Regardless of the answer, there is no doubt that many of the people who support efforts to abandon or restrict technological advances are those who feel threatened. Highlighting disruption and "the unknown," Luddites often gain public support, and although they sometimes score political victories, they always lose in the end.

Consider President George W. Bush's curtailment of stem cell research in 2001. The research didn't stop; it simply moved—to South Korea and Israel, which became the world's hub for this technology. In 2009, President Obama removed the restrictions, and by 2016, the United States was once again the world leader in this field, with twice as many clinical trials under way as all other nations combined, according to the National Institutes of Health. So much for efforts to halt the technology.

Although the Luddites failed to stop progress in stem cell research, they succeeded in losing American jobs and delaying the introduction of medical cures for millions of people who need them.

Indeed, Luddites often exacerbate the very disruption they claim to oppose. Any taxi driver could switch to Uber; if he doesn't own a car, websites can help him obtain a vehicle he can use. Instead, many cabdrivers seem to prefer lining up on interstate highways, shutting down major arteries that keep a city's economy moving. They seem to have no regard for the thousands of people they've disrupted: first responders unable to reach those in need, for example, or small-business owners who lose money because they can't deliver products on time—all because a taxi driver doesn't like the fact that a competitor is providing a comparable service that is faster, cheaper, more reliable, more comfortable, more enjoyable and safer.

This is why many people use only one word to describe Luddites: selfish.

Some Luddites, though, aren't trying to protect their own jobs. They regard themselves as altruistic. Consider Greenpeace International. Its website calls genetically modified food "genetic pollution." But few in the scientific community agree with this assessment. In fact, more than 5,000 scientists, including more than 100 Nobel laureates, signed a letter in 2016 urging Greenpeace to end its opposition against genetically modified food.

"We urge Greenpeace and its supporters to re-examine the experience of farmers and consumers worldwide with crops and foods improved through biotechnology, recognize the findings of authoritative scientific bodies and regulatory agencies, and abandon their campaign against "GMOs" in general and Golden Rice in particular," the letter stated, noting that the World Health Organization estimates that 250 million people suffer from vitamin A deficiency (VAD), including 40 percent of the children under age 5 in the developing world. UNICEF says VAD kills 1 million to 2 million children annually and is the leading cause of childhood blindness globally (as many as 500,000 children each year; half die within 12 months of losing their eyesight).

A scientifically proven solution is golden rice. It's genetically engineered to produce beta-carotene (which white rice doesn't have), which the body converts into vitamin A. Beta-carotene, which gives the grain a golden color, is a natural component of many edible plants, including all green vegetables and carrots, and can be ingested in large quantities without causing more than orange discoloration of the skin (if ingested in excess). The body converts only as much beta-carotene into vitamin A as it needs; the rest is stored in body fat or excreted.

Golden rice was invented in 1999 by scientists at the Institute for Plant Sciences of the Swiss Federal Institute of Technology in Zurich and the Centre for Applied Biosciences at Germany's University of Freiburg. It received the blessing of Pope Francis in 2013 and won the Patents for Humanity award from the White House Office of Science and Technology Policy and the U.S. Patent and Trademark Office in 2015.

Greenpeace, apparently, is unimpressed.

"Greenpeace [has] . . . repeatedly denied these facts and opposed biotechnological innovations in agriculture," the Nobel laureates' letter says. "They have misrepresented their risks, benefits, and impacts, and supported the criminal destruction of approved field trials and research projects."

The letter also notes that "Scientific and regulatory agencies around the world have repeatedly and consistently found crops and foods improved through biotechnology to be as safe as, if not safer than those derived from any other method of production. There has never been a single confirmed case of a negative health outcome for humans or animals from their consumption. Their environmental impacts have been shown repeatedly to be less damaging to the environment, and a boon to global biodiversity."

Yet, for inexplicable reasons, Greenpeace advocates opposition. It is a prime example of Luddites in action.

By rejecting innovation, Luddites interfere with others' lives. They delay access to improvements that can vastly enhance individual experience, society at large and the planet as a whole.

PART TWO

What Exponential Technologies Mean for Personal Finance

Now that you have a basic background in exponential technologies, we can explore what all this means for your personal finances.

Your financial plan must anticipate the future you're likely to experience, not the one your parents did. Although the elements of your financial plan will look familiar—with an emphasis on housing, retirement, long-term care, estate planning and investments—your lifestyle will be profoundly different from your parents'. That means your strategy for all the above must be different from your parents'—and even different from what you have done up to this point.

So let's begin.

Chapter Thirteen: The Financial Plan You Need Now for the Future You're Going to Have

Your current financial plan is probably fatally flawed.

And don't give me any nonsense that you don't even have a financial plan. Yes, you do, and you know you do, so stop kidding around. Even if you've never hired my firm or some other financial advisor to prepare a personal financial plan for you, you have a financial plan.

You have a plan because you have goals, such as saving for college for your children, buying a home, retiring by a certain date or caring for aging parents. And if you work with a firm like ours, you have a specific plan in place to achieve those goals and your planner is helping you save the money you'll need to achieve those goals, helping make sure you're saving that money in investments that are right for you and, best of all, helping you do all this with a minimum of drudgery, hassle and fuss.

But even if you don't have a formal financial plan, you have a financial plan nevertheless. It goes something like this: "I'm going to work until I die." Or "I'm a federal employee [or schoolteacher, police officer, firefighter, in the military or union member], so I'm going to work until I qualify for pension benefits. At that point, I'm going to retire. Maybe I'll go work somewhere else for a while, but by the time I'm 55 [or 60, 62, 65, 70 or whatever] I'm going to retire for good—and I'll go to Florida [or Arizona or Texas or wherever]."

As vague as such a plan is—after all, it requires no more time to develop than it takes to drink a beer[63]—it's probably fairly accurate.

Whether formal or informal, though, your plan is probably fatally flawed, because it's using assumptions based on historical data that won't prove accurate or relevant for your life.

When I started creating financial plans in the 1980s, I routinely set my clients' life expectancies at age 85. It wasn't long before I increased that to age 90, and today we routinely tell our clients that they should assume they'll live to age 95.

---

[63]And, in fact, it probably was completed in the course of drinking a beer.

This is a key number, because the longer you live, the more money you're going to need. We tend to be conservative financial planners, so we project a long life expectancy for our clients. Indeed, by increasing the amount of money they need to accumulate, we reduce the risk that they might run out. And assuming a long life means you must save more or earn a higher return (net of inflation and taxes) than a shorter life expectancy would require.[64]

It's not uncommon for clients to pause when we tell them they should assume a life expectancy of age 95. They dispute the notion that they'll live so long— usually because their parents and grandparents didn't—and they cringe at the thought of doing so (because their heads are filled with images of nursing home residents staring out a window while drooling in a wheelchair). This helps explain why many financial planners still provide their clients with financial plans that assume 90-year life expectancy: It's easier to give clients what they want (even if it's wrong) than give them what they need.

But our society's work-life paradigm never contemplated living in an exponential world. Indeed, when the Social Security system was created in the 1930s, the concept was simple: Pay into the system for 40 years, then collect benefits. The government knew that most workers wouldn't survive to age 62, and actuarial data at the time suggested that those who did would live for only 12 years longer. Franklin D. Roosevelt never envisioned that my grandmother would collect benefits for 39 years (she passed away at age 101).

If you live into your nineties, you're in trouble if your financial plan assumes you will retire in your sixties. And you're in *big* trouble if you live to age 100, 110, 120—or even longer.

Yet that is precisely the future you are likely to experience. If the Society of Actuaries says today's life expectancy is 86.6 for men and 88.8 for women, guess what the SoA will be saying when you reach age 86.6 or 88.8 in twenty, thirty or forty years?

---

[64]This is one of the tricks some financial salespeople play on their unsuspecting clients. By using a shorter life expectancy (age 85, say), the amount of money you need to save and/or lower the rate of return you need to earn on your savings is significantly reduced. As a result, a 3% return on an annuity or life insurance contract suddenly looks good. What the hapless people who buy those products based on that sales pitch don't realize (until decades later) is that they didn't die as soon as was projected—and they now find themselves out of money.

Obviously, the Social Security system was never designed to provide retirement benefits for 60 years. Neither was your pension plan. Or the annuity that someone is trying to sell you. Nor are you likely to accumulate enough money by age 65 to allow you to live off it for four to six decades or more.

But don't be dejected if you think I'm suggesting that your future is certain to be a financial failure. I'm not saying that at all. All I'm saying is that it's unreasonable to expect that Social Security, pensions and savings will be sufficient to allow you to retire at 65 and never again earn an income.

In fact, it's not only unreasonable, it's undesirable. This is another paradigm shift, because we've gotten used to the notion of retirement (even though it was a 20th-century invention; it didn't exist prior to that). People liked the idea of retiring in their sixties because they knew they'd be dead by 70—and they wanted a chance to relax and enjoy themselves before their health deteriorated and they died.

But as I predicted in 1997 in my book *The Truth About Money*, retirement won't exist in the 21st century; it is outliving its relevancy.

Incidentally

Some researchers now believe everyone could live to 120, thanks to the drug metformin. It's the world's most widely used diabetes drug and costs only 10 cents a day. In 2015, a UK study found that diabetes patients treated with metformin not only lived longer than other diabetic patients, they lived longer than the healthy control sample. When Belgian researchers tested metformin on a species of roundworms, the worms aged more slowly and stayed healthy far longer. Studies with rodents produced similar findings.

The Food and Drug Administration has approved a clinical trial, sponsored by the American Federation for Aging Research, to see if the drug can slow or stop degenerative diseases and heart conditions. If the drug works, people could soon have biological ages decades lower than their actual ages.

The demise of retirement is something not to lament but to celebrate. The fact that you're going to work during your seventies, eighties and nineties is extraordinarily exciting—because it means not only that you are going to live an extraordinarily long time but that you're going to be healthy enough to do so.

In fact, you're not only going to need to work, you'll want to. Instead of doing jobs that are physically difficult, dangerous, demeaning or just plain boring, a world enhanced by exponential technologies will create occupational opportunities that will enable you to earn money while working as many or as few hours as you wish, spending the rest of your time in activities that interest you. You'll wake up each morning excited about how you're about to spend your day. And best of all, you'll earn the money you need to sustain your lifestyle—no matter how long you live.

So you need to work with a financial planner who can help you develop *three* kinds of financial plans, not just one like most financial planners provide their clients today—and now you understand this book's title.

Your Plan **for Now**

You need a financial plan *for now*: to help you deal with the issues you are currently facing: protecting your identity, paying off your credit card debts, building cash reserves and dealing with the risk that you might suffer illness, injury, death or lawsuits (with financial implications not just for yourself but for your spouse/ partner and children as well). Thus your financial plan *for now* must solve your need for long-term care insurance (which we'll cover in chapter 20), estate planning (chapter 21) and investing (chapter 17).

Your Plan **for Later**

This plan is the conventional planning process you're more familiar with and might even have completed. While the plan you created *for now* is focused on where you are today, the plan you need *for later* is focused on where you're going—or, rather, at least on where you think you're going.

Your financial plan *for later* thus needs to address future education expenses for yourself as well as your children (see chapter 15): your future retirement income needs, the likelihood and costs of your own long-term care and the cost of providing financial support to aging parents or other relatives. It is at this point that conventional financial planning stops.

Your Plan **for Much Later**

But you must not stop there. You need a plan to help you anticipate and plan for the life that a world filled with exponential technologies suggests you are going to live. And although this plan is *for much later*, you need to obtain this plan right now, and you need to obtain it from a financial planner who is well versed in exponential technologies and all that that phrase means.

The plan *for much later* will take into consideration the fact that you are going to live not just another 20 or 40 years but perhaps 50 or 100 more. And because it's impossible to say with any degree of specificity what your life will be like, one thing is certain: The more money you have in the future, the better prepared you will be to handle any financial situation.

And here's some good news for you: In many ways, you'll find it easier to pay your way in the future than you might think. There are two reasons for this: Much of what you buy will become cheaper, and your savings will grow larger, making it easier to pay for everything. Let's look at both of these factors.

Prices Will Fall

Don't assume that all the products and services you currently buy will cost as much in the future. Many will become obsolete—you don't buy eight-track cassettes anymore—and others will become less expensive (or even free). It's all thanks to exponential technologies, and it's called *demonetization*.

To get an idea of how you'll likely spend money in your seventies, eighties and nineties, let's look at how people of those ages spend their money today. Housing is their number one expense (including utilities and cellular service), according to the 2015 Consumer Expenditure Survey, published by the Bureau of Labor Statistics, followed by transportation, health care, food, entertainment, insurance, clothing and personal care products/services. Figure 13.1 shows the breakdown.

From a retirement-planning perspective, your primary concern is figuring out how to pay these bills. If you live as long as I've suggested, you're worried that inflation, which we covered in chapter 10, will make it difficult to pay those bills.

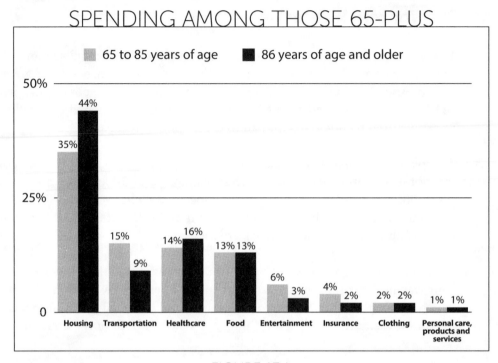

SPENDING AMONG THOSE 65-PLUS

FIGURE 13.1

But inflation might not be a big problem for many areas of spending. You've already seen why: Moore's Law tells us that technology costs fall by 50% every two years.

We've seen lots of examples throughout this book. You probably spent $500 on your current smartphone, but Amazon is offering one to members of its "Prime" service for just $50—or one-tenth the cost. Even that's expensive when compared to the phone offered by Ringing Bells, an India-based company. Its Android smartphone costs just four dollars. It has a four-inch screen, 1 GB of RAM, 8 GB of storage and both front and rear cameras. A Canadian company sells tablets in India for under twenty bucks. Soon tablets will be free; businesses will give them away as they do with coffee mugs, pens and pads of paper.

Or consider your smartphone. It has a Global Positioning System to track where you are and an accelerometer to measure your speed and acceleration. When introduced in 1981, GPS systems weighed 52 pounds and cost $120,000; in the 1960s, accelerometers weighed 50 pounds and cost millions of dollars. Today, both fit on computer chips that cost less than two bucks.

The famed physicist Richard Feynman said it best: "There's plenty of room at the bottom." As things get smaller (thanks to nanotechnology) they also get cheaper. In *Bold*, Peter Diamandis showed how the components of your smartphone would've cost you $900,000 if you had purchased those products between 1969 and 1989. His list included a camera, videocamera, CD player, video games, cell phone, watch, calendar, alarm clock, timer, encyclopedia and more. You use all these features today for free, and you probably haven't even noticed that you long ago (okay, 10 years ago) stopped paying for them.

We've shown how housing is going to become far less expensive by communities being built on cheap land that was once used for agriculture and ranching. Ride-handling and ride-sharing services such as Uber and car2go are demonetizing the automotive industry. Why own a car and incur all its attendant costs, such as insurance, repairs, parking and fuel, when you can summon a car on demand and pay only for the time you are actually using it? This can cut your transportation costs as much as 90%. And as we've seen, energy and education will both be virtually free.

The cost of health care will come down sharply, too, as we become able to prevent and cure diseases with unprecedented ability. Diagnostics done with the aid of your smartphone will be fast, accurate and free. Robots will perform surgery with microscopic precision, using data from millions of previous surgeries to obtain the best results. Prescription drugs will be will be uniquely matched to your physiology, and they'll be cheap thanks to low research, development and manufacturing costs.

We can expect similar reductions in the cost of food. For every dollar we spend growing food, we spend another 34 cents transporting it, according to the Department of Agriculture. Vertical farming eliminates much of this extra cost, and genetic improvements that increase crop yields will do much to further reduce the cost of the food we eat.

Entertainment is already largely free—you can play games online and on your phone, watch tens of millions of videos on YouTube and more. Smart fabrics that never get dirty will extend the life of clothing while eliminating the drudgery of doing laundry, saving you money both ways.

This is not to suggest that life will actually become free, of course; you don't pay to make phone calls anymore, but you do pay lots of money in monthly subscription services related to your smartphone. You don't buy personal computers anymore, but you do buy phones, tablets and laptops. And you haven't bought any robots yet. (You'll probably own lots of them, each with a price tag.) And I haven't even mentioned all the money you'll spend on leisure and recreation.[65] Just as there are lots of things we never had in the 1970s or 1980s that we consider indispensable today, you'll have many necessities you've yet to purchase— because they haven't been invented yet.

So, yes, you will need money in the future. Lots of it. We just can't say for sure how you'll spend it. Therefore, the need to save for your future is as important as ever, and you may well need more than ever.

Your Savings Will Grow

Many people who contemplate what it means financially to live to age 110 worry that they will run out of money. This fear is misplaced. You see, living for 70 more years means you can invest for 70 more years, too. This can make it easier than ever to accumulate wealth.

Here's why. Historically, most people who save do so for only 20 or 30 years, because they don't get started until they're in their forties or fifties and they spend their money in their sixties, seventies and eighties. Saving for two or three decades isn't enough time for compound growth—exponentiality—to work its magic, even if you earn the highest returns that you can reasonably expect.

Here's why. Say you sock away $500 per month in an investment that charges no fees whatsoever.[66] Let's assume the investment somehow manages to earn 10% per year. And let's further pretend that you never have to pay taxes on the profits. Yep, this is quite an investment![67]

If you start the above at age 45 and continue to 65, you'll accumulate $382,848, as shown in Figure 13.2. This is why people in their fifties often say to us at our seminars, "I wish I'd started 20 years ago!"[68]

---

[65]Oops! Just did.
[66]There's no such investment, of course. Work with me here, people.
[67]It's also completely fictitious. There is no such investment that earns 10% per year with no fees and no taxes. Don't let anyone make you think otherwise. This illustration is purely hypothetical.
[68]You've probably said that, too.

But you *will* have those extra 20 years, due to living longer and healthier and working longer, thanks to exponential technologies. That means you can save money until 85, not just 65. By doubling the amount of time you invest, from 20 years (45–64) to 40 years (45–84), guess how much more you'd accumulate?

You wouldn't merely double the results to $750,000. Instead, doubling the time *octuples* the results—you'd end up with $3,188,390! Figure 13.2 shows you the exponential growth curve.

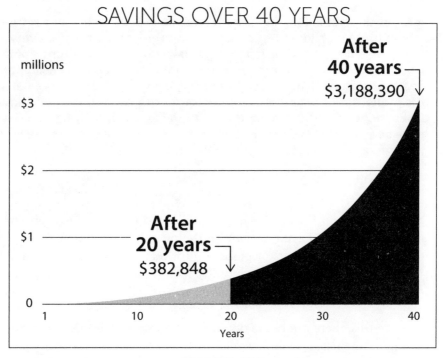

SAVINGS OVER 40 YEARS

FIGURE 13.2

My wonderful Aunt Bea, who passed away in 2015, is a perfect example of so many themes we've covered in this book. She was 94 when she died and lived alone until she moved into an assisted living facility a few months prior to her passing. My brothers and cousins had been worried how she'd pay for the facility—after all, Aunt Bea hadn't worked in decades.

But as her executor, I was aware of her financial situation. I also knew something the others didn't: Aunt Bea had been letting her savings grow for 50 years. She was living in the house her parents (my grandparents) had left to her; thus her housing expenses were minimal. She was still driving (!) the same car she'd bought in the 1980s, and because she didn't eat much, her grocery bill was small. Her medical bills were paid mostly by Medicare. So when she passed, the family was shocked to learn how much money she left. I wasn't surprised, because I understand the power compound growth can have over many decades.

It is this understanding, in fact, that led me in 1999 to invent a retirement saving tool for children. It's called the Retirement Income for Everyone Trust®, and it's been awarded two U.S. patents. Under the terms of the trust, the child can't access the money until retirement age (except for death or disability). If you establish the trust when the child is a newborn, the money in the account can grow for more than 60 years! The minimum investment is $5,000, and, at this writing, more than 4,000 RIC-E Trusts have been established for children and grandchildren across the country. (For important information on the RIC-E Trust®, refer to the last page of this book.)

So although your financial plan *for later* would have you focus on saving enough money to make a down payment on the purchase of a home, saving for your children's education costs or preparing for retirement, your financial plan *for much later* will, admittedly, be more vague. The reason: We know you'll incur expenses in the future, but we can't be certain what those expenses will be.

Despite this, there can be no doubt that you need to accumulate more savings and investments, so you'll have the money you need to support yourself. You'll also need massive revisions to your estate planning—and we'll cover all those subjects in the chapters that follow.

Chapter Fourteen: Career Planning

Ready to sell your house? If so, you're probably going to hire a real estate agent, to whom you'll pay a 6% commission. That's $60,000 to sell a million-dollar home.

Instead, imagine a website that lets you post photos of your house. Potential buyers are drawn to the site by machine-learning algorithms that know exactly what kind of house they want, and they can tour your house via virtual reality whenever they want, without disturbing you. Their VR goggles let them see what each room would look like with their furniture in them, and they can even "virtually" change the color of your walls—so you don't have to "really" paint everything beige before putting your house on the market. If they have questions about the house and neighborhood, the website's virtual sales agent will answer them, even providing remodeling costs instantaneously. When they're ready to make an offer, you'll get a text—and when you agree to sell, AI will write the contract and secure their mortgage loan within minutes. Closing will be in days, not months as it does today.

Sound futuristic? A lot of this already exists, either free or for very low cost (in the hundreds of dollars), and what isn't yet available is expected to arrive by 2025. Will you still choose to pay a human real estate agent $60,000 to sell your million-dollar house?

This is why real estate brokers are becoming obsolete. If you doubt this, ask yourself this question: When's the last time you spoke to a travel agent?

Indeed, the jobs of real estate agents and travel agents are being threatened by technology. And they're not the only ones. Lawyers are at risk, too. In 2016, the global law firm Baker Hostetler became the first in the legal profession to "hire" an AI attorney. Named ROSS, it reads thousands of legal documents to find the ones that support the firm's cases.

Traditionally, recent law school graduates are hired to perform such work. But ROSS, which is based on IBM's Watson, is faster and more accurate. It can find almost instantly any obscure but relevant court ruling no matter how old it might be and offer opinions in plain English. As intuitive as human lawyers, ROSS can understand questions and respond with a hypothesis backed by references and citations. It provides only the most relevant answers out of thousands of results it collects, and it keeps its human colleagues updated on the latest court decisions that affect their cases.

Although ROSS's technology was initially focused on bankruptcy law, the firm that created it says ROSS will eventually be used in virtually every area of legal practice. Ryan Calo, a University of Washington law professor, was quoted as saying failure to use systems such as ROSS "will come to be viewed as irresponsible, like writing a brief on a typewriter."

Incidentally

You might be worried that robots are replacing jobs, but many employers are thankful they can. An aging population has created a serious labor shortage for Komatsu of Japan, one of the world's largest construction companies. The company is solving the problem by using robots in some of its operations. For example, drone-guided robotic vehicles survey and map construction sites, a job humans need two weeks to complete but that the machines can do in 30 minutes.

Teaching assistants at universities are also at risk. During the 2016 spring semester at the Georgia Institute of Technology, Jill Watson, another IBM-designed robot, responded to students' questions over email with a casual, colloquial tone. The students didn't know they were having conversations with a computer—and when told after the semester ended, they felt that Jill's help had been as good as the assistance they got from the school's human TAs. How long will those humans be needed?

Lawyers and teaching assistants are just the start. In fact, hundreds of occupations are going to be eliminated, and millions of jobs along with them. How severe will this be? Well, according to a study by Oxford University, 47% of all occupations in the United States are at high risk of being taken over by exponential technologies over the next 20 years. Figures 14.1 and 14.2 show the most and least likely jobs to be lost, according to the study.

"Bad news—some kid just created an app that creates apps."

Alex Gregory/The New Yorker Collection/The Cartoon Bank

THE 175 JOBS **LEAST** LIKELY TO BE LOST TO AUTOMATION

Probability is 10% or less, least likely listed first

Recreational Therapists
First-Line Supervisors of Mechanics,
    Installers and Repairers
Emergency Management Directors
Social Workers
Audiologists
Occupational Therapists
Orthotists and Prosthetists
Health Care Social Workers
Oral and Maxillofacial Surgeons
Supervisors of Firefighters
Dietitians and Nutritionists
Lodging Managers
Choreographers
Sales Engineers
Physicians and Surgeons
Instructional Coordinators
Psychologists
Supervisors of Police
Dentists
Elementary School Teachers
Medical Scientists
Administrators, Elementary and
    Secondary School
Podiatrists
Clinical and School Psychologists
Mental Health Counselors
Fabric and Apparel Pattern Makers
Set and Exhibit Designers
Human Resources Managers
Recreation Workers
Training and Development Managers
Speech-Language Pathologists
Computer Systems Analysts
Community Service Managers
Curators
Athletic Trainers
Medical and Health Services Managers
Preschool Teachers, Except Special Ed
Home Management Advisors
Anthropologists and Archeologists
Special Education Teachers
Clergy
Foresters
Guidance Counselors
Career/Technical Education Teachers
Registered Nurses
Rehabilitation Counselors
Teachers and Instructors, All Other
Forensic Science Technicians
Makeup Artists
Marine Engineers and Naval Architects
Education Administrators
Mechanical Engineers
Pharmacists
Logisticians
Microbiologists
Industrial Psychologists
Coaches and Scouts
Sales Managers
Hydrologists
Marketing Managers
Marriage and Family Therapists
Engineers, All Other
Training and Development Specialists

First-Line Supervisors of Office and
    Administrative Support Workers
Biological Scientists, All Other
Public Relations Managers
Multimedia Artists and Animators
Computer and Information Scientists
Chief Executives
Education Administrators, Preschool
Music Directors and Composers
Supervisors of Production Workers
Securities, Commodities and Financial
    Services Sales Agents
Conservation Scientists
Special Education Teachers
Chemical Engineers
Architectural and Engineering Mgrs
Aerospace Engineers
Natural Sciences Managers
Environmental Engineers
Architects
Physical Therapist Assistants
Civil Engineers
Health Diagnosing
Soil and Plant Scientists
Materials Scientists
Materials Engineers
Fashion Designers
Physical Therapists
Photographers
Producers and Directors
Interior Designers
Orthodontists
Art Directors
Supervisors of Correctional Officers
Directors, Religious Activities
Electronics Engineers
Biochemists and Biophysicists
Chiropractors
Occupational Therapy Assistants
Child School Social Workers
Health and Safety Engineers, Except
    Mining Safety Engineers
Industrial Engineers
First-Line Supervisors of
    Transportation and Material-
    Moving Machines and Vehicles
Veterinary Technologists
Industrial Production Managers
Industrial Engineering Technicians
Computer Systems Administrators
Database Administrators
Purchasing Managers
Postsecondary Teachers
Environmental Scientists and
    Specialists, Including Health
Substance Abuse Counselors
Lawyers
Craft Artists
Operations Research Analysts
Information Systems Managers
Commercial and Industrial Designers
Biomedical Engineers
Meeting, Convention and Event
    Planners
Veterinarians

Writers and Authors
Advertising and Promotions Managers
Political Scientists
Credit Counselors
Social Scientists and Related Workers,
    All Other
Astronomers
Ship Engineers
Software Developers, Applications
Fine Artists, Including Painters,
    Sculptors and Illustrators
Psychiatric Technicians
Landscape Architects
Health Educators
Mathematicians
Floral Designers
Farmers, Ranchers and Other
    Agricultural Managers
Forest Fire Inspectors and Prevention
    Specialists
Emergency Medical Technicians and
    Paramedics
Editors
Prosthodontists
Health Care Practitioners and
    Technical Workers, All Other
Travel Guides
Licensed Practical and Licensed
    Vocational Nurses
Sociologists
Arbitrators, Mediators and Conciliators
Animal Scientists
Residential Advisors
Aircraft Cargo Handling Supervisors
Respiratory Therapists
Broadcast News Analysts
Financial Managers
Nuclear Engineers
Construction Managers
Musicians and Singers
First-Line Supervisors of Nonretail
    Sales Workers
First-Line Supervisors of Personal
    Service Workers
Food Scientists and Technologists
Compliance Officers
Fish and Game Wardens
Graphic Designers
Food Service Managers
Child Care Workers
Fitness Trainers and Aerobics
    Instructors
Gaming Managers
Electrical Power Line Installers and
    Repairers
Police and Sheriff's Patrol Officers
Travel Agents
Chefs and Head Cooks
Animal Trainers
Radio and Television Announcers
Electrical Engineers
Chemists
Respiratory Therapy Technicians
Physicists

FIGURE 14.1

THE 171 JOBS **MOST** LIKELY TO BE LOST TO AUTOMATION

Probability is 90% or more, most likely listed first

Human Resources Assistants, Except Payroll and Timekeeping

Medical and Clinical Laboratory Technologists

Reinforcing Iron and Rebar Workers

Roofers

Crane and Tower Operators

Traffic Technicians

Transportation Inspectors

Patternmakers, Metal and Plastic

Molders, Shapers, and Casters, Except Metal and Plastic

Appraisers and Assessors of Real Estate

Pump Operators, Except Wellhead Pumpers

Signal and Track Switch Repairers

Gaming and Sports Book Writers and Runners

Musical Instrument Repairers and Tuners

Tour Guides and Escorts

Mechanical Door Repairers

Food and Tobacco Roasting, Baking and Drying Machine Operators and Tenders

Gas Compressor and Gas Pumping Station Operators

Medical Records and Health Information Technicians

Coating, Painting and Spraying Machine Setters, Operators and Tenders

Multiple Machine Tool Setters, Operators and Tenders, Metal and Plastic

Rail Yard Engineers, Dinkey Operators and Hostlers

Electrical and Electronics Installers and Repairers, Transportation Equipment

Dining Room and Cafeteria Attendants and Bartender Helpers

Heat Treating Equipment Setters, Operators and Tenders, Metal and Plastic

Geological and Petroleum Technicians

Automotive Repairers

Patternmakers, Wood

Extruding and Drawing Machine Setters, Operators and Tenders, Metal and Plastic

Office Machine Operators, Except Computer

Pharmacy Technicians

Loan Interviewers and Clerks

Dredge Operators

Insurance Sales Agents

Cabinetmakers and Bench Carpenters

Painting, Coating, and Decorating Workers

Fence Erectors

Plating and Coating Machine Setters, Operators, and Tenders Metal and Plastic

Retail Salespersons

Combined Food Preparation and Serving Workers, Including Fast Food

Production Workers, All Other

Helpers–Carpenters

Cooling and Freezing Equipment Operators and Tenders

Fiberglass Laminators and Fabricators

Service Unit Operators, Oil, Gas and Mining

Conveyor Operators and Tenders

Outdoor Power Equipment and Other Small Engine Mechanics

Locomotive Firers

Machine Feeders and Offbearers

Model Makers, Metal and Plastic

Radio, Cellular, and Tower Equipment Installers and Repairs

Butchers and Meat Cutters

Extruding, Forming, Pressing, and Compacting Machine Setters, Operators and Tenders

Refuse and Recyclable Material Collectors

Tax Examiners and Collectors and Revenue Agents

Forging Machine Setters, Operators and Tenders, Metal and Plastic

Industrial Truck and Tractor Operators

Accountants and Auditors

Drilling and Boring Machine Tool Setters, Operators and Tenders, Metal and Plastic

Mail Clerks and Mail Machine Operators, Except Postal Service

Waiters and Waitresses

Meat, Poultry, and Fish Cutters and Trimmers

Budget Analysts

Cement Masons and Concrete Finishers

Bicycle Repairers

Coin, Vending and Amusement Machine Servicers and Repairers

Welders, Cutters, Solderers and Brazers

Couriers and Messengers

Interviewers, Except Eligibility and Loan

Cooks, Short Order

Excavating and Loading Machine and Dragline Operators

Helpers–Painters, Paperhangers, Plasterers and Stucco Masons

Hotel, Motel and Resort Desk Clerks

Tire Builders

Door-to-Door Sales Workers, News and Street Vendors and Related Workers

First-Line Supervisors of Housekeeping and Janitorial Workers

Agricultural Inspectors

Paralegals and Legal Assistants

Manicurists and Pedicurists

Weighers, Measurers, Checkers, and Samplers, Record Keeping

Textile Cutting Machine Setters, Operators, and Tenders

Bill and Account Collectors

Nuclear Power Reactor Operators

Gaming Surveillance Officers and Gaming Investigators

Library Assistants, Clerical

Operating Engineers and Other Construction Equipment Operators

Print Binding and Finishing Workers

Animal Breeders

Molding, Core Making and Casting Machine Setters, Operators and Tenders, Metal and Plastic

Electrical and Electronic Equipment Assemblers

Adhesive Bonding Machine Operators and Tenders

Landscaping and Groundskeeping Workers

Grinding, Lapping, Polishing and Buffing Machine Tool Setters, Operators and Tenders, Metal and Plastic

Postal Service Clerks

Jewelers and Precious Stone and Metal Workers

Dispatchers, Except Police, Fire and Ambulance

Receptionists and Information Clerks

Office Clerks, General

Compensation and Benefits Managers

Switchboard Operators, Including Answering Service

Counter Attendants, Cafeteria, Food Concession and Coffee Shop

Rock Splitters, Quarry

Secretaries and Administrative Assistants, Except Legal, Medical and Executive

Surveying and Mapping Technicians

Model Makers, Wood

Textile Winding, Twisting and Drawing-Out Machine Setters, Operators and Tenders

Locomotive Engineers

Gaming Dealers

Fabric Menders, Except Garment

Cooks, Restaurant

Ushers, Lobby Attendants and Ticket Takers

Billing and Posting Clerks

Bridge and Lock Tenders

Woodworking Machine Setters, Operators and Tenders, Except Sawing

Team Assemblers

Shoe Machine Operators and Tenders

Electromechanical Equipment Assemblers

Farm Labor Contractors

Continued

Continued from previous page

Textile Bleaching and Dyeing Machine Operators and Tenders
Dental Laboratory Technicians
Crushing, Grinding and Polishing Machine Setters, Operators and Tenders
Grinding and Polishing Workers, Hand
Pesticide Handlers, Sprayers and Applicators, Vegetation
Log Graders and Scalers
Ophthalmic Laboratory Technicians
Cashiers
Camera and Photographic Equipment Repairers
Motion Picture Projectionists
Prepress Technicians and Workers
Counter and Rental Clerks
File Clerks
Real Estate Brokers
Telephone Operators
Agricultural and Food Science Technicians
Payroll and Timekeeping Clerks
Credit Authorizers, Checkers and Clerks

Hosts and Hostesses, Restaurant, Lounge and Coffee Shop
Models
Inspectors, Testers, Sorters, Samplers and Weighers
Bookkeeping, Accounting and Auditing Clerks
Legal Secretaries
Radio Operators
Driver/Sales Workers
Claims Adjusters, Examiners and Investigators
Parts Salespersons
Credit Analysts
Milling and Planing Machine Setters, Operators and Tenders, Metal and Plastic
Shipping, Receiving and Traffic Clerks
Procurement Clerks
Packaging and Filling Machine Operators and Tenders
Etchers and Engravers
Tellers
Umpires, Referees and Other Sports Officials

Insurance Appraisers, Auto Damage
Loan Officers
Order Clerks
Brokerage Clerks
Insurance Claims and Policy Processing Clerks
Timing Device Assemblers and Adjusters
Data Entry Keyers
Library Technicians
New Accounts Clerks
Photographic Process Workers and Processing Machine Operators
Tax Preparers
Cargo and Freight Agents
Watch Repairers
Insurance Underwriters
Mathematical Technicians
Sewers, Hand
Title Examiners, Abstractors and Searchers
Telemarketers

FIGURE 14.2

THE FLYING MCCOYS ©2016 Glenn and Gary McCoy. Dist. By UNIVERSAL UCLICK. Reprinted with permission. All rights reserved.

In case you're wondering, personal financial advisors have only a 42% probability of being replaced by automation.[69]

It's important to note that these lists refer only to occupations we'll be losing. They don't refer to the occupations we'll be *inventing*. Indeed, we've been through this before. In 1870, 50% of American employees worked on farms, according to the Bureau of Labor Statistics and the Census Bureau. By 1950, that number had dropped below 10%. Today, only 1% of Americans work on a farm.

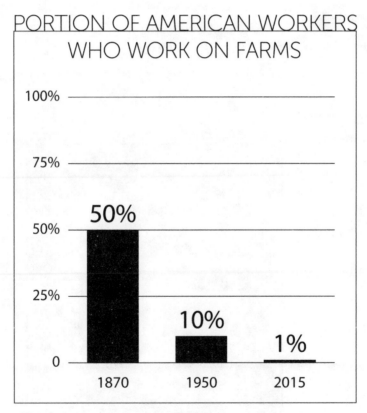

PORTION OF AMERICAN WORKERS WHO WORK ON FARMS

FIGURE 14.3

---

[69]You weren't wondering. But I was.

But no one is suggesting that 99% of Americans are out of work; they merely migrated to new occupations. Machines eliminated agricultural jobs, but they also created brand-new ones—in factories, thanks to the Industrial Revolution. Indeed, by 1976, nearly 20% of the workforce worked in them.

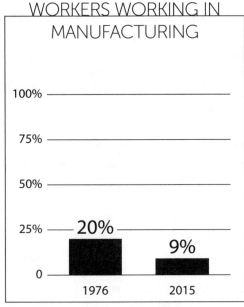

FIGURE 14.4

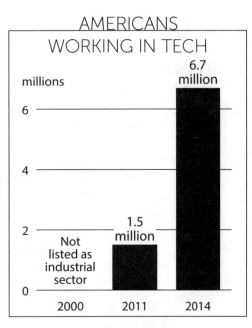

FIGURE 14.5

But manufacturing jobs now comprise only 9% of the U.S. workforce. Again, no one is suggesting that 91% of the workforce is unemployed. We simply underwent another transformation—this time, to the Information Age. By 2014, 6.7 million people worked in technology jobs, up from 1.5 million in 2011. (In 2000, the Bureau of Labor Statistics didn't even list "technology" as an employment category.)

Consider travel agents and app developers. From 2000 to 2014, online hotel booking revenue increased more than tenfold, from $14 billion to more than $150 billion, but the number of U.S. travel agents fell by 48% during that time, from 124,000 to 65,000, according to McKinsey. And although there weren't any smartphone app developers in 2000 (because the smartphone hadn't been invented yet), there were 300,000 people working in that occupation by 2016—twice the number of travel agents in 2000. And app developers earn a lot more than travel agents as well ($100,000 median salary versus $36,000, according to the Bureau of Labor Statistics). And though job opportunities for travel agents are expected to decrease, job opportunities for app developers are expected to grow by 17% in 2024 compared to 2014. Pretty good trade-off.

A study of Germany's automotive industry shows similar results. Although the industry's use of robots rose by 17% between 2010 and 2014, according to the International Federation of Robotics, employment in the sector rose by 3% in 2014, according to the German Automotive Industry Association. So although automation might have prevented more jobs from being created, it didn't stop job growth from occurring, let alone eliminate all current jobs.

A separate study from Boston University's School of Law using government data further endorses this notion. Studying the impact of computer automation affecting 317 occupations from 1980 through 2013, researchers found that "employment grows significantly faster in occupations that use computers more." Although automation removes some jobs—notably lower-level, dangerous, labor-intensive, repetitive and otherwise undesirable jobs—it creates more jobs than it removes.

Bank tellers are proof of this. Automated teller machines were supposed to render bank tellers obsolete—and ATMs have indeed cut the average number of tellers per bank branch, from 20 in 1988 to 13 in 2004, according to an economist at Boston University. But the reduction in payroll costs meant that bank branches became cheaper to operate, enabling banks to open more branches than ever. As a result, the number of bank branches rose 43% during that period, maintaining the overall employment of bank tellers. So rather than destroying jobs, ATMs created them. ATMs have also improved their roles, shifting mundane tasks to machines so humans can do more interesting work, such as sales and customer service.

Thus the advent of exponential technologies does not mean that jobs will be lost; it means that they will change. Consider ROSS. Andrew Arruda, the CEO and cofounder of ROSS Intelligence, the company that developed ROSS, says his company's bot will allow law firms to charge lower fees, enabling them to serve the nearly 80% of Americans who currently can't afford an attorney when they need one. By creating more affordable options for clients, the legal profession could enter its biggest growth phase in decades.

The 900-plus attorneys at Baker Hostetler seem to agree with that assessment. Bob Craig, a spokesman for the firm, says, "ROSS is not a way to replace our attorneys—it is merely a supplemental tool to help them." He says that the chief value of ROSS is that it allows the firm's human attorneys to focus on advocating for their clients and being creative, instead of spending hours poring through hundreds of cases looking for relevant passages of law.

So although McKinsey says 60% of occupations could have 30% of their activities automated (with 15% of jobs completely eliminated) by 2025, all those people won't be out of work forever. In fact, McKinsey projects a global shortage of 40 million workers with college or postgraduate degrees by 2020. And the recruiting firm Manpower says that more than a third of global employers can't find the talent they need.

But transitions aren't seamless. Many occupations will be lost before new ones are created. Likewise, many people will lose their jobs before they find another. A study by the Hackett Group says world-class (read: technologically proficient) finance organizations require 48% fewer full-time employees per billion dollars of revenue. This trend can only be expected to accelerate and broaden throughout business and commerce worldwide.

In all of these companies, automation is taking over. Foxconn, a company that assembles iPads, Wiis, Kindles, laptops and mobile phones, employs 1.2 million people—and says that automation of its workforce will cause it to eliminate 500,000 jobs by 2018.

So you need to prepare yourself for this coming transition. If you want to know if your current job is safe or what type of job will be available to you in the future, realize that four skills will be valued the most:

- **Thinking**
- **Communicating**
- **Creating**
- **Managing**

Let's illustrate by looking at the creative arts. The following occupations will be huge beneficiaries of technology:

- actors
- animators
- architects
- art directors
- choreographers
- commercial and industrial designers
- composers
- dancers

- directors
- editors
- fabric and apparel patternmakers
- fashion designers
- film and video editors
- graphic designers
- interior designers
- landscape architects

- musicians
- photographers
- producers
- radio and TV hosts[70]
- set and exhibit designers
- singers
- writers

According to the Department of Labor, the number of artists working in the United States increased by 20% from 1999 to 2014—from 1.5 million to 1.8 million; both the number of jobs and the average incomes of those workers rose more than the overall U.S. job market.

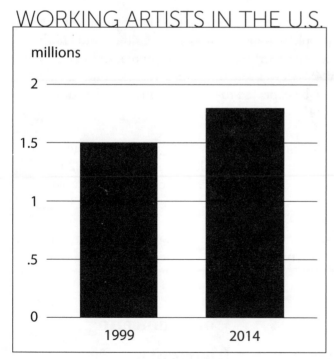

WORKING ARTISTS IN THE U.S.

FIGURE 14.6

The Future of Music Coalition says that technology is creating new types of jobs, too; of the 46 distinct sources of revenue it tracks for musicians, 13 didn't exist in 2000. Video game designers, for example, hire actors, composers and writers, and they pay song license fees and royalties. Musicians now earn income by giving lessons on YouTube, earning both ad revenue and subscription fees, and they make money from royalties on ringtones they create.

Musicians are also using software, such as that produced by Native Instruments, to mimic the sound a Steinway grand

[70]Yay!

piano makes in a Vienna concert hall, to replicate the sounds of hundreds of guitar amplifiers or to simulate the Mellotron used by the Beatles on *Strawberry Fields Forever*. In 2000, such equipment cost millions of dollars; today it costs thousands.

There's more. Writers can now self-publish and earn royalties from Amazon's Kindle platform. Filmmakers can use crowdfunding to raise money for their projects; through 2016, they've raised more than $290 million on Kickstarter alone. And they shoot HD-quality films on an iPhone, using GoPro and drones that cost less than $1,000 to get aerial shots that couldn't be produced in the past. They're also using Apple's editing software ($299) to make Oscar-winning films.

Those in the creative arts aren't the only ones benefiting from the technological revolution. Technology will create demand in many other jobs as well. These include:

Agents	Database Managers	Mental Health Counselors
Animal Trainers	Dietitians and Nutritionists	Microbiologists
Anthropologists	Engineers and Construction Workers	Nurses
Applications Developers	of All Kinds, Including Carpenters,	Operations Research Analysts
Arbitrators, Mediators and Conciliators	Plumbers and Electricians	Physical and Occupational Therapists
Archaeologists	Ethicists	Physicians, Surgeons And Dentists
Astronomers	Firefighters	Political Scientists
Athletes and Sports Competitors	Fitness Trainers	Private Detectives
Athletic Trainers, Coaches and Scouts	Flight Attendants	Project Managers
Biochemists and Biophysicists	Floral Designers	Psychologists
Business and Systems Analysts	Food Scientists	Public Relations Specialists
Business Intelligence Analysts	Fund-Raising Managers	Recreational Workers
Business Managers	Gamification Designers	Rehabilitation Counselors
Chief Executives	Geographers	Religious Educators
Child Care Workers	Hairdressers	Robotics Specialists
Clergy	HR and Labor Specialists	Sales Reps
Community Service Managers	Hydrologists	Social Scientists
Compliance Officers	Lawyers	Social Workers
Computer and Information Systems	Lodging Managers	Sociologists
Analysts	Logisticians	Speech-Language Pathologists
Computer Scientists	Market Research Analysts	Substance Abuse Counselors
Concierges	Marketing Managers	Teachers
Construction Managers	Marriage and Family Therapists	Veterinarians
Credit Counselors	Mathematicians	Web Developers
Curators	Meeting and Event Planners	Zoologists

FIGURE 14.7

The key for you to be able to continue earning an income, therefore, is to make sure you have the knowledge, training and skills that will allow you to perform in an occupation that a society shaped by exponential technologies will need and value.

It's quite possible that your current training and experience have not prepared you for the jobs of the future. Therefore, you might need to go back to school. And for that, we move on to the next chapter. As you'll see, how and where you'll get the education you need and what you'll pay for it are not what you might think. The implications are enormous—and not just for you but also for your children and grandchildren who are headed to college for the first time.

Chapter Fifteen: College Planning

It's time to shift our thinking about education, because obtaining a college degree is no longer the proper goal. Even if you manage to obtain a degree in the field in which you ultimately gain employment—and we saw in chapter 8 that many people can't get admitted, while many of those who do aren't able to pay, fail to graduate or wind up with degrees unrelated to their eventual careers—the skills and knowledge you obtain from that degree quickly become stale in a world in which information grows exponentially.

So it's no longer enough to say you got a college degree from umpty-dump university one or two (or three or four) decades ago. Instead, you have to make sure your knowledge and skills are current. And that means we must replace the notion of college degrees with a new concept: *lifelong learning.*

So your children will not go to college for a single stretch that lasts four to six years. Instead, they will go to college, get a job—and then go back to college. And instead of trying to learn more about the field they're already in, they'll seek an entirely new set of skills so they can embark on a completely new career in a totally different field from the one they were in before.

After engaging in this new career for a period of time, they will return to college again—and they will repeat this cycle perhaps half a dozen times during their lives. Along the way, they will interrupt this *education-job-education* cycle with extended periods of unemployment—an *education-job-education-job-sabbatical-job-education-sabbatical-job-job-education-job* type of experience. And those sabbaticals won't be for four weeks each but for two or three *years* apiece—truly extended periods during which they will raise children, travel globally, serve their communities, support charities, undertake entrepreneurial activities and focus on wellness, personal growth and self-fulfillment.

Indeed, the college experience of the 2020s, 2030s and beyond will look nothing like it ever did.

That said, one thing that will remain constant is your need to save, so you can afford to engage in lifelong learning. Not only will you incur educational expenses, you'll likely interrupt your career, meaning you'll experience long periods where you're not earning an income. Between spending more money than before (on education) and earning less (because you're unemployed during that time), the need for savings is vital, so you can get through those periods without plummeting yourself into the depths of debt.

This also explains why you need to continue saving in a 529 College Savings Plan—but with a new twist.

> Because I explained these state-run programs in great detail in my book *The Truth About Money*, I won't do so here, although I summarize their advantages and disadvantages for you in Figures 15.1 and 15.2. And I will add that my colleagues and I have long regarded 529 College Savings Plans as the best way to save for college; I have been a vocal supporter of them since their inception. Virtually all our clients who have school-age children have 529 accounts (or at least have been advised by us to start one), and on my radio show I have long blasted any suggestion that people should be saving for college in any vehicle other than a 529 plan.[71]

Actually, there are two twists. First, stop saving for college for your kids and grandkids as though a bachelor's degree is all they'll ever need. Recognize instead that their bachelor's degree will be the *start* of a lifelong learning experience, not the end of one.

This means you need to consider the future costs of education. And I'm not talking about graduate degrees (which may or may not be needed or pursued) but classes and programs designed to enhance and extend knowledge and skills. We can't begin to guess the form or format of that learning—or the cost. But it is safe to expect that a cost will be incurred—if not a direct tuition expense, then an opportunity cost in the form of lost wages while that knowledge is pursued and obtained. So as you save for education expenses, don't assume all those savings will be spent when the student is 18 to 24 years of age. You'll want to keep a lot of that money in reserve for spending when the student is in his or her thirties, forties, fifties and sixties.

---

[71]My commentaries have objected most ferociously to pitches by insurance agents that consumers should sell all their assets and use that money to buy life insurance. For the purported purpose of saving for college!!

Second, don't think solely about the kids. Lifelong learning might apply to you, too. Depending on your age, health and occupation, *you* are going to need to return to school. You must also consider the possibility that you will need (or merely want) to engage in lifelong learning as well.

This trend is well under way. Two examples: More than 150,000 adults 50-plus attend the Osher Lifelong Learning Institutes, which offer adult education programs at colleges and universities across the country. And at George Washington University, nearly 1,000 of the students are age 50 or older. Like those folks, you, too, may engage in lifelong learning.

This means you, too, might leave your current field and enter a new one. If so, you are likely to go (or return) to college to learn new skills so you can maintain or enhance your ability to earn an income. And that means you, like your kids, might experience significant economic disruption as you undergo this transition. Therefore, you need a completely new kind of financial plan, one that can accommodate and help you prepare for this shift.

This is new territory for you. It's also new for most financial planners, so make sure the one you choose to work with understands exponential technologies and their implications for financial planning—so you can get the plan you need for the future you're going to have.

ADVANTAGES OF A 529 PLAN
UNDER CURRENT LAW

- Money placed into the account grows tax-deferred for years (and potentially decades). No annual tax reporting is required. In many states, you also get an income tax credit or deduction for your contributions.

- Withdrawals are free of federal income tax when used for qualified education expenses (including tuition, room and board and books) at accredited institutions worldwide. Withdrawals are often free of state income tax as well (depending on the state in which you live and, in some states, whether you participate in your home state's plan or a different state's plan).

- Segregating your education funds in a separate account such as a 529 plan helps you set a target of how much you need to save and monitor your progress. It also helps prevent you from using the money for other purposes.

- As account owner, you decide who the account is for (called the beneficiary) but you maintain control of the asset—and you can change the beneficiary at any time and for any reason. (Changes are restricted to the initial beneficiary's siblings, cousins, children or parents.)

- Having money in a 529 plan instead of an ordinary taxable account can increase the student's ability to obtain financial aid. That's because the qualification criteria does not count assets in 529 plans the same way as taxable accounts.

- The creation or existence of a 529 account might encourage relatives to contribute, since the account is designated for college.

FIGURE 15.1

DISADVANTAGES OF A 529 PLAN
UNDER CURRENT LAW

- Withdrawals not used for qualifying college expenses are subject to federal and state income taxes at your top marginal tax bracket, plus a 10% IRS penalty.

- Multiple accounts are required if multiple children in your household attend college at the same time.

- Unlike taxable accounts, 529 plans do not qualify for a step-up in basis. Thus, if the account owner dies, taxes could be due on the entire account's profits.

- You can reallocate the money in the account to other investments only twice per year.

- Investment costs can be high, depending on the state plan selected.

- Investment options in every state plan are limited, and many states impose asset allocation models you might not prefer, such as placing significant amounts of your money into foreign securities, emerging markets and high-yield bonds.

- Some states (California, Delaware, Hawaii, Kentucky, Massachusetts, Minnesota, New Hampshire, New Jersey and Tennessee) do not provide a tax deduction for contributions.

- The amount you can contribute each year is limited.

- Congress or the states might change the features of the program, including the tax benefits.

- Limited advice on the program is available from financial planners.

- The ability to qualify for financial aid is impacted if the account is owned by the student.

- Accounts owned by grandparents can reduce the student's eligibility for financial aid.

- The account offers minimal returns unless the money is held for many years (ideally, 10 or more).

FIGURE 15.2

© MARK ANDERSON, WWW.ANDERTOONS.COM

"I appreciate the text, Kate, but next time you
can just raise your hand."

For example, at our firm, the financial planners of Edelman Financial routinely recommend that clients place a portion of education-earmarked savings into a special Lifelong Learning account that we've created specifically for this purpose. Although the money remains fully available to our clients at any time (subject to current market values, of course) the account is designed to hold assets that the client expects not to use for 10 years or more. By having such a long-term holding period, we can invest the money more aggressively than we otherwise might, and by having an account specifically designated for lifelong learning, we reduce the risk that the client might spend the money on something else. If your financial advisor is not considering ideas like these to help you prepare for the future, it may be time to find a new advisor.

Chapter Sixteen: Protecting Your Privacy

It's far better to prevent identity theft than have to recover from it, so here's how you can help keep your information safe:

To Protect Your Identity

1. Shred papers that contain personal information, including credit card offers you get in the mail. And I don't mean tearing paper in half. Buy a shredder and use it. Review your credit report at least once a year. If you find errors, don't call the creditor that filed the information. Instead, contact the credit-reporting agency:

    TransUnion 800-888-4213; fraud division: 800-680-7289
    Equifax 800-685-1111; fraud division: 888-766-0008
    Experian 888-397-3742; fraud division: 888-397-3742

2. Put a lock on your mailbox or rent a post office box. Better yet, have bills delivered to a secure website and checks deposited directly to your bank account instead of having them mailed to your home.

3. Never put information about yourself on a postcard or envelope other than your return address.

4. If your mail doesn't arrive, contact the local post office immediately.

5. Contact the Direct Marketing Association's Mail Preference Service at www.dmachoice.org to place your address on the "do not mail" list.

6. Never give personal information to someone you don't know, whether in person or over the phone.

7. Don't enter contests that demand your name, address or other information.

8. Get a new "nonpublished" telephone number from the phone company.

9. Secure your computer by installing a firewall and software to prevent and detect viruses and spyware.

10. Never include personal information in an email.

Cartoon by Harley Schwadron

11. Never click on a link or open an attachment you receive in an email—even if it's from a friend.

12. Don't cut and paste links from an email into your web browser. Instead, find the website on your own to help ensure that you don't visit a fake site.

13. When you use a credit card to make a purchase online, make sure the website's address begins with the letters https://. (The "s" means "secure.")

14. Don't disclose your birth date or other facts about yourself on social networks.

15. Don't leave passwords where others can see them.

16. Photocopy all the documents you carry with you, and on the copies, write the phone number and email address of each source. Also carry with you the credit-reporting agency phone numbers listed above.

17. Never use your Social Security number, address or birth date as a PIN or ID number. *Never carry your SS card with you.*

18. Limit the information on your checks. Use an initial instead of your first name, and exclude your middle name. Don't include your driver's license number, Social Security number, or telephone number.

19. Use checks only when paying bills through the mail; in stores, use credit or debit cards and take your receipt with you so you can match it to your statement when it arrives.

20. Never disclose your mother's maiden name.

21. Don't fill out warranty cards. They are just data collection tools; you're covered without sending in the card.

22. Keep important papers in a bank safe-deposit box or fire- and burglar-resistant home safe.

23. If a family member has died, send a copy of the death certificate to the IRS and cancel the deceased's driver's license and credit cards.

24. Check the credit records of your minor children. Thieves assume you won't.

25. Use financial sites that require two-factor authentication, so crooks need both your account password and your phone number to access your accounts.

26. Remember that identity thieves can include coworkers, friends, relatives, children and roommates. They think you won't suspect or punish them. Be willing to do both.

If Your Identity Has Been Stolen

If someone has forged a check, your bank owns the loss, provided you notify it in a timely manner.

If someone uses your credit card, your liability is limited to $50 if you report your card's theft within 50 days.

Your liability on debit cards is also $50, but only for two days. Your liability is $500 for the next 58 days, and after 60 days, your liability is unlimited.

"Yesterday my ID was stolen. This afternoon, after they checked my credit score, it was returned."

From The Wall Street Journal, permission
Cartoon Features Syndicate

So notify your bank or card company as soon as you discover a problem. Follow these steps:

1. Phone the institution's fraud division. Keep notes about the call, including the date and time of the call and the name and title of the person you talked to. Keep your records for seven years after you resolve the problem.

2. Send a copy of your notes to the person you spoke with, via certified mail, return receipt requested. If you send an email, require confirmation of receipt.

3. Replace all affected accounts with new ones. Ask each institution to note that accounts were "closed at customer's request."

4. Issue "stop payment" orders on all missing or outstanding checks.

5. Notify the check verification companies TeleCheck (800-710-9898) and Certegy (800-237-3826) that your checks were stolen.

6. If you're not satisfied with your bank's response, complain to the Federal Financial Institutions Examination Council at ffiec.gov.

7. Tell the three credit-reporting agencies to place a fraud alert on your credit record.

8. File a police report where the problem occurred.

9. If the thief got your Social Security number, contact a local Social Security office.

10. If the thief got your driver's license, contact your state's department of motor vehicles.

11. Never pay a credit card bill for goods bought by thieves who used your card. The liability belongs to the card company, not you.

Chapter Seventeen: The Investment Strategy You Need for the Future

As much as our world is changing, one constant will remain: the need for you to adopt and maintain the right investment strategy so you can generate the income you need from your investments. This will be key to helping you maintain your standard of living no matter how long you live.

Indeed, your investment strategy must be designed to prepare you for the future, for if you continue to hold investments designed to do well in the last century, your portfolio may very well fail to perform as well as you need it to in our new one. And helping you make sure your portfolio is designed for exponential times is what this chapter is all about.

Traditionally, people needing income from their investments tended to favor income-producing products, such as government, corporate and municipal bonds; bank CDs; and annuities. That approach worked fine in the 1970s, when interest rates were double digit—but those investments are woefully insufficient in the low-interest-rate economy of the 21st century.

The problem facing income-oriented investors is obvious: The income you get from those vehicles is low, is eroded by taxes and doesn't keep up with inflation.

Indeed, you face a three-part challenge: You have to produce the income you need, sustain it for as long as you live and make sure it keeps pace with inflation.

"O.K. The forward rate for marks rose in March and April, combined with a sharp increase in German reserves and heavy borrowing in the Eurodollar market, while United States liquid reserves had dropped to fourteen billion dollars, causing speculation that the mark might rise and encouraging conversion on a large scale. Now do you understand?"

James Stevenson/The New Yorker Collection/The Cartoon Bank

Incidentally

Has someone suggested that you buy a fixed or equity-indexed (or equity-linked) annuity?

They might tell you that if you buy one, you'll get income for life, with no risk from the stock market.

That might sound appealing, but they might not tell you that if you withdraw money from such an annuity you might incur surrender charges of 10% or more, and if you make any withdrawals prior to age 59½ you'll incur taxes plus a 10% IRS penalty on any interest earned.[72]

And they might not tell you that by "annuitizing" your annuity (meaning receiving monthly checks on a systematic basis):

- The monthly income you'll receive is often quite low

- You give up all rights to your principal forever (you can't ever ask to receive a lump sum of any amount)

- The income doesn't rise with inflation, meaning its value will be eroded over time

- The income stops upon your death[73]

- The income is only as safe as the insurance company's ability to pay it[74]

- The amount of income you'll receive is determined by the insurance company, using actuarial data that generally assume that you—and every other contract owner—will live to only age 85, 90 or 95. But if everyone lives to 110, will the insurance company be able to keep paying everyone "for life" as it promised?

Because of the way they are often pitched by insurance salespeople, those annuity products routinely appear on the "top fraud" lists of federal and state regulators. So if someone has told you to buy one of those annuities, get a second opinion from a fee-based, independent financial planner.

---

[72]That's right: annuities produce interest—not profits, not capital gains, not dividends. And unlike the others, interest is subject to taxes at your top marginal tax rate.

[73]You can request to have the monthly checks continue for your surviving spouse, but that means the checks you each receive will be less than they otherwise would—and potentially a lot less, depending on how much younger your spouse is.

[74]If the insurance company collapses, your checks could stop. Each state has a fund to protect owners of insurance contracts, but you should expect to receive less (perhaps a reduction of 50% or more) from those guaranty funds than you were receiving from the insurance company itself.

Figure 17.1 shows the challenge faced by investors today. If you had placed $100,000 into a one-year bank CD in 1982, you would've earned 15% in annual interest. By 2016, due to inflation (based on the Consumer Price Index as reported by the Bureau of Labor Statistics), you'd have needed to earn $43,845 in interest to purchase the same goods and services you bought in 1982. But in 2016, the average U.S. bank was paying only 0.3%, according to bankrate.com— meaning that if you were that CD depositor, you would have found it virtually impossible to maintain the same standard of living without spending your principal, perhaps even to the point of spending it all, leaving you penniless.

And that's just the impact of inflation. If we add taxes to the equation, the situation becomes dire. Say you manage to find a bank willing to pay you 1.5% in annual interest. Let's further say you pay 33% in combined federal and state income taxes. That means you would lose one-third of your earnings, leaving

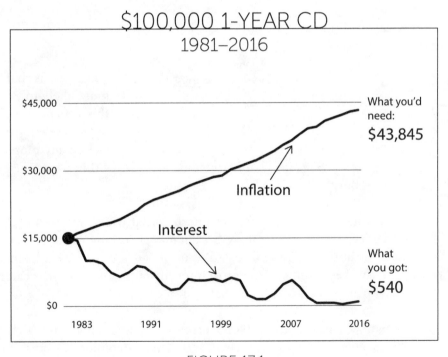

FIGURE 17.1

HOW TAXES AND INFLATION CAN HURT OVER 20 YEARS

Hypothetical interest rate	1.5%	$100,000
33% fed/state tax rate	− 0.5%	
	1.0%	
Hypothetical inflation	− 3.0%	
Real annual return	− 2.0%	
	× 20 yrs	
	− 40%	$60,000

OVER 40 YEARS

Hypothetical interest rate	1.5%	$100,000
33% fed/state tax rate	− 0.5%	
	1.0%	
Hypothetical inflation	− 3.0%	
Real annual return	− 2.0%	
	× 40 yrs	
	− 80%	$20,000

FIGURE 17.2

you with 1% after taxes, as shown in Figure 17.2. And if inflation is 3% annually,[75] your actual return in real economic terms would be -2% per year. If you were to do that for 20 years, you would lose 40% of your money's buying power.

In other words, if you start with $100,000 and leave it in that account for 20 years, you'll watch it "grow" to $60,000. If you do so for 40 years, you'll lose 80% of your money—meaning your hundred grand would fall, in real terms, to only $20,000.

The irony is that the people most likely to experience this situation are risk-averse investors. They don't want to lose any money, so they put their life's savings into bank accounts, which they think are safe. Sadly, they go broke—but they do it *safely*!

Clearly, that approach isn't what you need. What you really need is an effective investment management strategy. So I'm going to show you the strategy we use to manage the $16 billion entrusted to us by our firm's 30,000 clients coast to coast. We've been using this approach for my entire 30-plus-year career as a financial planner and investment advisor.

Our strategy is based on the Nobel prize–winning academic research of Modern Portfolio Theory, behavioral finance and neuroeconomics. If that sounds complicated or intimidating, in practice it's remarkably simple, affordable and easy to

---

[75]It's actually been 3.15% annually since 1913, according to inflationdata.com, but that's being picky.

implement. You can do this on your own, or, if you lack the time, knowledge or desire to deal with this chore, you can hire a financial planner to do it for you.

Let's not gloss over those three words.

Successfully managing your personal finances takes a significant amount of *time*. Researching investments, staying current with the latest tax laws, executing transactions and handling tax record-keeping and reporting requirements can be daunting tasks.

You also need to know what you're doing. That's where *knowledge* comes in. You might feel knowledgeable about investing, but do you know which registration type is best (individual, joint tenancy, tenants by the entirety, joint tenants with rights of survivorship, trust, and so on)? Do you know which of the three types of IRA accounts that are available (Deductible, Non-deductible and Roth) is best for your situation? Making the wrong decisions on issues like these can prove costly.

Even if you have the time and the know-how, do you really want to do all this work? Without the *desire* to do so, your personal finances won't get the attention they need.

If you lack one or more of these key attributes, you should hire a financial planner. But if you have all three, you can proceed on your own. Indeed, everyone needs a financial plan, but not everyone needs a financial planner. Only those who lack time, knowledge or desire need a planner.

There are three simple steps involved in this approach, and I'll explain what they are and why we follow them.

Step 1: Diversify Your Investments

We've already seen that putting your life savings into bank CDs isn't going to provide you the income you need to maintain your lifestyle on a long-term basis. That means we must put your money somewhere else.

But if "somewhere else" means the stock market, you might cringe. Lots of people think the stock market is risky, volatile and unpredictable—and it's the last place they'd want to put all the hard-earned money they've worked a lifetime to accumulate.

If you are among this group, you're not alone. A 2015 survey by bankrate.com found that more than half of Americans have *zero percent* of their money in stocks precisely because they're afraid of the stock market.

There's a reason so many people believe stocks are risky, volatile and unpredictable—and it's reflected by Figure 17.3. It shows the monthly performance of the S&P 500 Index from 1926 through 2015. The chart confirms the highly unpredictable nature of the stock market. Extreme volatility appears to be the norm—and since you have no idea what the market is going to do in the months to come, your conclusion might be that you're taking a big risk to invest in stocks.

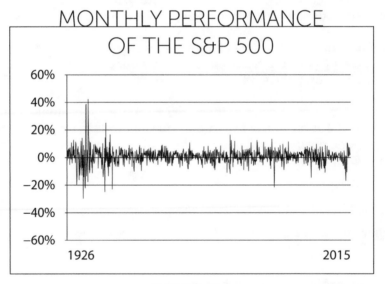

FIGURE 17.3

Frankly, the graph in Figure 17.3 looks like an EKG readout—and we all know that the stock market has caused heart attacks.

But let me ask you a question: Why are we looking at a chart showing stock market performance in 30-day intervals? After all, is it your intention to invest your life's savings for just a month?

I doubt it—and that means Figure 17.3 is a distraction. What we should look at instead is a timeline that is truly relevant to you and your goals. So answer this question: How long will your money remain invested?

If you're planning to withdraw all your money in one year, look at Figure 17.4, which shows the annual performance of the S&P 500 since 1926. If you intend to leave the money invested for five years, look at Figure 17.5, which shows every five-year rolling interval since 1926. If you think you will still own investments 10 years from now, look at Figure 17.6, which shows all the 10-year rolling intervals since 1926, and if you expect to have money invested 20 years from now, look at Figure 17.7, which shows all the 20-year rolling intervals for the past 90 years.

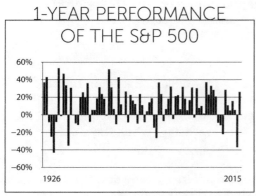

FIGURE 17.4

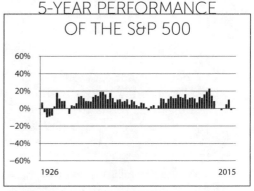

FIGURE 17.5

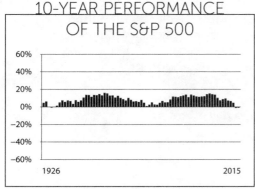

FIGURE 17.6

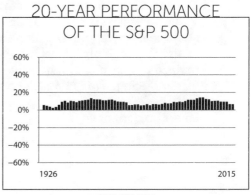

FIGURE 17.7

As you can see, the longer you remain invested, the less risky, volatile and unpredictable the stock market becomes. It's the same stock market in all these charts; the only difference is the time frame.

That's how we can turn something as risky, volatile and unpredictable as the stock market into something remarkably stable: the wild monthly swings in value disappear over longer periods.

So if you are a long-term investor—and you are if you are saving money to use over your life expectancy—you can dismiss the stock market's short-term volatility as completely irrelevant.

This is why evening newscasts that recap the market's daily results make me crazy. During the broadcast, the anchor tells you how the stock market performed today. The only number you get—today's performance—is certain to be different from the number you got yesterday. This reinforces fears that the market is risky, volatile and unpredictable.

But that's not news. That's noise.

Once, just once, I would like to hear a news anchor say, "Based on the results of today's stock market activity, the average annual return of the S&P 500 since 1926 is 10%." Every TV news anchor would be able to make that statement on every broadcast; even on those rare days when the stock market crashes, its average annual return since 1926 remains 10%.

So if we're all supposed to act like long-term investors, why do the media insist on talking to us as if we were a bunch of day-trading market timers?

The answer is obvious: If the statistic that "the stock market has produced a 10% annual return since 1926" never changes, it isn't news. So there'd be no reason for you to watch the show if they merely repeated the same statistic in each broadcast. So to get you to tune in each evening, they replace that important, helpful, consistent statistic with a meaningless, fear-inducing, ever-changing one.

Smart, experienced investors know not to pay attention.

This conversation might be causing you to conclude that I am arguing for you to own a portfolio fully invested in stocks. I am not suggesting that; I'm simply trying to get you comfortable with the idea of placing some (indeed, perhaps just a little) of your money into stocks.

For sure, you don't have to put a significant portion of your money into stocks to enjoy a significant improvement in your overall results. Let me illustrate what I mean.

Consider two investors. Both have $100,000 to invest for 25 years. The first investor places the entire $100,000 into a bank CD earning 2016's average annual rate, which according to bankrate.com is 0.6%. After 25 years, this investor's $100,000 will be worth $116,131.[76]

The second investor takes a different approach and instead chooses to diversify her $100,000 by making five separate investments of $20,000 each. The first block of $20,000 is used to purchase lottery tickets. Just as you would expect, the tickets all prove to be worthless—resulting in a loss of $20,000.

"Help! I haven't saved enough for retirement!"
Christopher Weyant/The New Yorker Collection/The Cartoon Bank

She hides the second block of $20,000 under her mattress. By not earning any interest at all, this money remains $20,000 after 25 years.

She places the third block of $20,000 in the same place as the other investor did: into a bank CD. And she earns the very same 0.6% per year for the entire 25-year period. This block of $20,000 therefore grows to $23,226.

---

[76]We're ignoring taxes in this hypothetical illustration.

With her fourth block of $20,000, she invests in U.S. Treasuries, widely regarded as the safest investment in the world. And she manages to earn 2.1%, which is the average return of U.S. Treasuries in 2016. As a result, after 25 years, this fourth block has grown to $33,626.

She now has one block of $20,000 left to invest. And she decides to gamble by placing it into a fund replicating the returns of the S&P 500 Stock Index. (Frankly, I'm not sure we can consider the S&P 500 a "gamble," but that's what she calls it.) And although the S&P 500 has earned an average of 10% per year since 1926, she's not going to be so fortunate. Her return will be just 8%. Even so, this block of $20,000 grows to $136,970 after 25 years.[77]

The total value of all five blocks of money: $213,822. That's nearly twice as much as the investor who placed his entire life's savings into bank CDs.

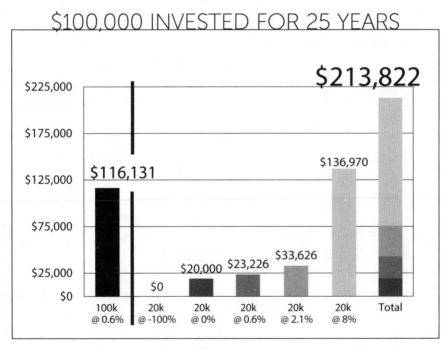

FIGURE 17.8

---

[77]This is a hypothetical illustration meant to demonstrate the principle of compounding and is not representative of past or future returns of any specific investment vehicle. My Compliance Department made me say so.

She was able to accomplish this despite making lots of unprofitable investment decisions: She threw away one-fifth of her money on lottery tickets, buried a second fifth under her mattress, earned a low bank-CD rate on the third block, and got a meager rate from U.S. Treasuries from the fourth block. Even though she earned market-based returns on only one-fifth of her money, she still ended up with nearly twice as much as a "completely safe" strategy would have produced.

And that's my point. You don't need to take high risks to enjoy the potential for higher returns. Just be willing to accept occasional short-term volatility with some of your money. Truly, that's sufficient to make a material difference in your wealth.

Okay, you get it: You need to invest your money in a diversified fashion. You're not foolish enough to put 20% of your money into lottery tickets, of course, or bury 20% of your money under your mattress, so how *should* you invest your money?

Welcome to the world of professional money management. You are now facing what is perhaps the most important investment management challenge there is: the asset allocation decision. How will you *allocate* your *assets* among the many asset classes and market sectors offered by the global financial marketplace?

"Your mother called to remind you to diversify."
Mike Twohy/The New Yorker Collection/The Cartoon Bank

And *many* is indeed the apt descriptor, as Figure 17.9 shows.

Stocks
    By company size (large, mid-size, small)
    By industrial sector (consumer, energy, financials, health care, IT, manufacturing, materials, telecom, utilities)
    By style (growth, value)
    By geography (U.S., foreign —with the latter further defined by developed vs. emerging markets)

Bonds
    By maturity date or duration (short-term, intermediate-term, long-term)
    By issuer (corporate or government—with the latter defined by federal or state/local)
    By quality (investment grade bonds graded AAA–BBB) vs. speculative grade, otherwise known as junk bonds, or those graded BB and below)
    By geography (U.S., foreign —with the latter again defined by developed vs. emerging markets)

Real Estate
    By type (commercial, residential, retail, industrial, agriculture)
    By quality (price point)
    By leverage (the amount of money being borrowed to purchase the property)
    By geography (U.S., foreign —with the latter still defined by developed vs. emerging markets)

Natural Resources
    Oil
    Natural gas
    Water
    Timber
    Precious metals
    Gold
    Silver
    Copper
    Platinum
    Others
    Commodities (livestock, wheat, soybean, corn, sugar, coffee, cotton, cocoa, cattle, hogs)

Cash
    FDIC-insured accounts
    U.S. Treasuries (bills, notes, bonds)

FIGURE 17.9

Stymied by which of these to choose? Figure 17.10 solves this riddle for you. It ranks 16 major asset classes and market sectors in each of the 10 years from 2006 to 2015. Start by looking at the box in the upper-left corner—this is the best performer of 2006. If you were trying to decide what investment to purchase for 2007, you might have decided to pick this one. After all, it was best for the year!

ASSET CLASS PERFORMANCE
2006–2015

Rank	2006	2007	2008	2009	2010	2011	2012	2013	2014	2015
1 BEST	Real Estate 34.6	Emerging Markets 39.4	Intermediate Govt Bonds 15.4	Emerging Markets 78.5	Mid Cap Growth 30.6	Intermediate Govt Bonds 13.0	Real Estate 19.3	Small Cap Growth 42.7	Real Estate 28.6	Large Cap Growth 5.7
2	Emerging Markets 32.1	Natural Resources 34.4	International Bonds 10.5	Mid Cap Growth 41.1	Real Estate 28.0	Intermediate Corp Bonds 8.2	Mid Cap Value 18.5	Small Cap Value 40.0	Large Cap Value 13.5	International Growth 4.1
3	International Value 30.4	International Growth 16.5	Short-term Govt Bonds 6.7	Natural Resources 37.5	Small Cap Growth 28.0	Real Estate 7.4	Emerging Markets 18.2	Mid Cap Value 34.3	Large Cap Growth 13.1	Small Cap Growth 2.8
4	International Growth 22.3	Mid Cap Growth 13.5	Short-term Corp Bonds 0.3	Large Cap Growth 37.2	Small Cap Value 24.7	International Bonds 4.3	Small Cap Value 18.2	Large Cap Growth 33.5	Mid Cap Value 12.1	Mid Cap Growth 2.0
5	Large Cap Value 22.2	Large Cap Growth 11.8	Intermediate Corp Bonds −4.7	International Value 34.2	Natural Resources 23.9	Small Cap Growth 3.6	International Value 17.7	Mid Cap Growth 32.8	Mid Cap Growth 7.6	Intermediate Govt Bonds 1.9
6	Small Cap Value 19.6	International Bonds 11.3	Small Cap Value −29.5	Mid Cap Value 33.7	Mid Cap Value 22.8	Large Cap Growth 2.6	Large Cap Value 17.5	Large Cap Value 32.5	Small Cap Value 7.54	Real Estate 1.7
7	Natural Resources 16.8	Intermediate Govt Bonds 9.8	Small Cap Growth −32.9	International Growth 29.4	Emerging Markets 18.9	Short-term Corp Bonds 1.8	Mid Cap Growth 17.3	International Value 23.0	Intermediate Corp Bonds 7.4	Short-term Corp Bonds 0.9
8	Mid Cap Value 14.6	Short-term Govt Bonds 7.3	Mid Cap Value −34.9	Real Estate 28.8	Large Cap Growth 16.7	Short-term Govt Bonds 1.6	International Growth 16.9	International Growth 22.5	Intermediate Govt Bonds 6.4	Intermediate Corp Bonds 0.7
9	Small Cap Growth 10.5	Short-term Corp Bonds 6.0	Large Cap Value −36.8	Small Cap Growth 28.4	Large Cap Value 15.5	Large Cap Value 0.4	Large Cap Growth 15.3	Natural Resources 16.5	Small Cap Growth 3.9	Short-term Govt Bonds 0.6
10	Large Cap Growth 9.1	International Value 6.0	Mid Cap Growth −37.6	Small Cap Value 22.8	International Growth 12.2	Mid Cap Growth −0.9	Small Cap Growth 14.6	Real Estate 4.3	Short-term Corp Bonds 1.1	International Bonds −3.3
11	International Bonds 6.1	Small Cap Growth 5.6	Real Estate −37.6	Large Cap Value 19.7	Intermediate Corp Bonds 10.5	Small Cap Value −1.4	Intermediate Corp Bonds 11.3	Short-term Corp Bonds 1.5	Short-term Govt Bonds 0.6	Large Cap Value −3.8
12	Mid Cap Growth 5.8	Intermediate Corp Bonds 5.0	Large Cap Growth −38.4	Intermediate Corp Bonds 19.0	Intermediate Govt Bonds 8.6	Mid Cap Value −2.4	Intermediate Govt Bonds 3.7	Short-term Govt Bonds 0.4	Emerging Markets −2.2	International Value −5.7
13	Short-term Corp Bonds 4.7	Mid Cap Value 2.6	Natural Resources −42.6	Short-term Corp Bonds 11.6	International Bonds 5.7	Natural Resources −7.4	Short-term Corp Bonds 3.7	Intermediate Corp Bonds −2.0	International Growth −4.4	Mid Cap Value −6.7
14	Intermediate Corp Bonds 4.3	Large Cap Value −0.2	International Growth −42.7	International Bonds 3.9	Short-term Corp Bonds 4.2	International Growth −12.1	Natural Resources 2.2	Emerging Markets −2.6	International Bonds −5.1	Small Cap Value −6.7
15	Short-term Govt Bonds 3.9	Small Cap Value −5.5	International Value −44.1	Short-term Govt Bonds 0.8	International Value 3.2	International Value −12.2	International Bonds 0.5	International Bonds −3.8	International Value −5.4	Emerging Markets −14.9
16 WORST	Intermediate Govt Bonds 3.3	Real Estate −16.9	Emerging Markets −53.3	Intermediate Govt Bonds −3.6	Short-term Govt Bonds 2.4	Emerging Markets −18.4	Short-term Govt Bonds 0.4	Intermediate Govt Bonds 0.4	Natural Resources −9.8	Natural Resources −24.3

FIGURE 17.10

But take a look at how it performed in the following year: It ranked dead last. That's the folly of trying to pick investments based on their past performance. As every prospectus says, "Past performance does not guarantee future results. Any assertion to the contrary is a federal offense."

Trying to pick next year's winners is a fool's game. As Figure 17.10 shows, returns are random. So instead of trying to predict which of these 16 asset classes and market sectors is going to perform best, just pick them all!

Here's an illustration of what can happen if you fail to own everything all the time. As Figure 17.11 shows, owning all of Figure 17.10's sixteen asset classes and market sectors equally for the entire 10-year period ending December 31, 2015, would have produced an average annual return of 7% per year. But if you had missed the top three performers in each year, your average annual return would have been only 2.2%. In other words, the combined average returns of each year's top three outperformed the combined average returns of the other 13! Unless you think you're capable of picking the top three out of 16 each year, you'll be much better off owning all 16 instead.

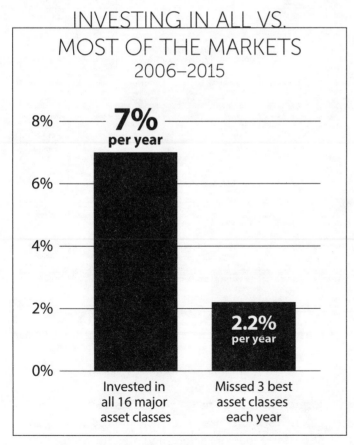

FIGURE 17.11

That's why we provide our clients with highly diversified portfolios. Of course, diversification does not guarantee better performance and cannot eliminate the risk of investment losses, and no one can legitimately guarantee that a diversified portfolio will outperform a nondiversified portfolio.

Congratulations! You've just solved the most important investment management challenge there is. You now realize that you need to allocate your money among the many asset classes and market sectors offered by the global financial marketplace.

But this raises a second challenge: In what combination should you own these various investments? After all, the data in Figures 17.10 and 17.11 suggest that you should own each in equal amounts. Clearly, that can't be the correct answer (because if it were, every investor on the planet would use the same asset allocation model). Obviously, because everyone's situation is different, some investors need to have more of their portfolio in stocks while others need to have less.

So how much of *your* portfolio should be placed into each of these asset classes and market sectors?

The answer is . . . it depends.

I wish I could provide you a more specific answer right here, right now, but this is just a book on personal finance—it's not a private, in-depth meeting with a financial planning professional. That's why this book is no substitute for that meeting. Either on your own or with a financial planner, you need to consider your personal circumstances, including your goals and objectives, risk tolerance, need for income, investment time horizon, income and expenses, assets and debts, family issues and more.

By going through that process, you'll be able to determine what your asset allocation model should be (and it's quite possible that you might end up with several asset allocation models—one for your own IRA, another for your spouse's, a third for your joint account and so on). Figure 17.12 shows examples of asset allocation models, reflecting the needs of different clients based on their individual circumstances.

There's one way I can help you right here, right now: Go to RicEdelman.com and click on the Guide to Portfolio Selection. You'll answer a few questions and instantly receive an asset allocation model based on your answers. It's fast, fun and free!

One warning: Like other such tools you'll find on the Internet, our GPS is a risk-based asset allocation algorithm, *not* a financial planning–based program. That means the allocation model you'll get is based predominantly on how you feel about risk, which, as every financial planner knows, is an approach vastly inferior to one based on your goals and other important personal circumstances. So although the GPS can give you a quick and easy picture of an asset allocation model, you shouldn't consider it a substitute for going through the financial planning process.

A MORE EFFECTIVE APPROACH
TO ASSET ALLOCATION

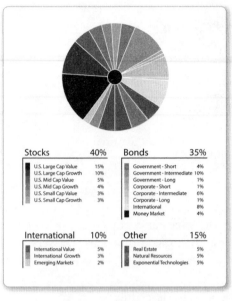

Stocks	40%	Bonds	35%
U.S. Large Cap Value	15%	Government - Short	4%
U.S. Large Cap Growth	10%	Government - Intermediate	10%
U.S. Mid Cap Value	5%	Government - Long	1%
U.S. Mid Cap Growth	4%	Corporate - Short	1%
U.S. Small Cap Value	3%	Corporate - Intermediate	6%
U.S. Small Cap Growth	3%	Corporate - Long	1%
		International	8%
		Money Market	4%

International	10%	Other	15%
International Value	5%	Real Estate	5%
International Growth	3%	Natural Resources	5%
Emerging Markets	2%	Exponential Technologies	5%

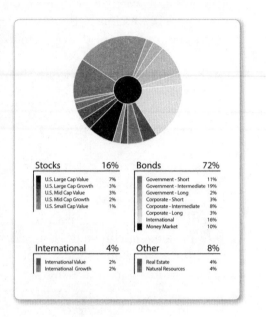

Stocks	16%	Bonds	72%
U.S. Large Cap Value	7%	Government - Short	11%
U.S. Large Cap Growth	3%	Government - Intermediate	19%
U.S. Mid Cap Value	3%	Government - Long	2%
U.S. Mid Cap Growth	2%	Corporate - Short	3%
U.S. Small Cap Value	1%	Corporate - Intermediate	8%
		Corporate - Long	3%
		International	16%
		Money Market	10%

International	4%	Other	8%
International Value	2%	Real Estate	4%
International Growth	2%	Natural Resources	4%

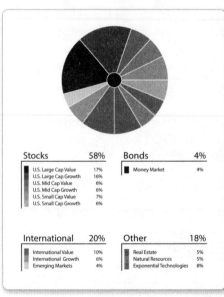

Stocks	58%	Bonds	4%
U.S. Large Cap Value	17%	Money Market	4%
U.S. Large Cap Growth	16%		
U.S. Mid Cap Value	6%		
U.S. Mid Cap Growth	6%		
U.S. Small Cap Value	7%		
U.S. Small Cap Growth	6%		

International	20%	Other	18%
International Value	10%	Real Estate	5%
International Growth	6%	Natural Resources	5%
Emerging Markets	4%	Exponential Technologies	8%

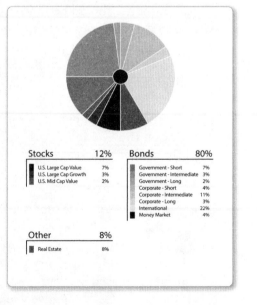

Stocks	12%	Bonds	80%
U.S. Large Cap Value	7%	Government - Short	7%
U.S. Large Cap Growth	3%	Government - Intermediate	3%
U.S. Mid Cap Value	2%	Government - Long	2%
		Corporate - Short	4%
		Corporate - Intermediate	11%
		Corporate - Long	3%
		International	22%
		Money Market	4%

Other	8%		
Real Estate	8%		

FIGURE 17.12

Step 2: Maintain a Long-Term Focus

Once you construct your asset allocation model, it's vital that you maintain it for a long time. And when I say long, I don't mean weeks or months. I mean decades.

Within this context, let me ask you this question: Are you:

1. a long-term investor?

2. a market-timer?

If you're like most of the people whom I meet at our seminars and who visit our offices, you probably consider yourself a long-term investor. You're not trying to double your money in the next few hours or days; you'd be very happy to double it over the next 10 years.[78]

So let's find out if you really are a long-term investor. Think about the investments you own in your retirement plan at work, IRA or joint account, and answer one question.

How long have you owned them?

I'm not referring to the accounts themselves—I want to know how long you've owned the actual investments that are inside those accounts. How long have you owned them?

In 1950, according to the New York Stock Exchange, people held their investments for an average of seven years. Today, the average investor's holding period is about eight months. What can an investor expect to achieve in just eight months?

There's no denying it: Holding investments merely for months makes you a market timer. Sorry to be blunt, and sorry if this upsets you, but if your behavior is contrary to both your best interests and your own self-description, it's best to acknowledge it so you can fix it.

---

[78]That would be a 7.2% average annual return.

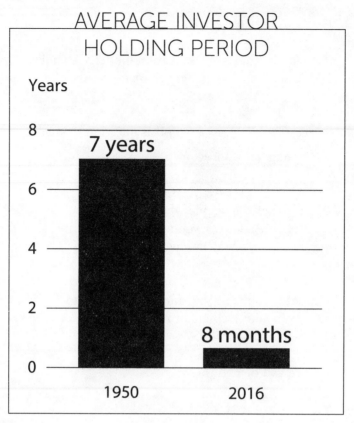

FIGURE 17.13

The importance of maintaining a long-term focus is best illustrated by Figure 17.14. If you had been invested in the stock market from 2011 through 2015— that's 1,258 trading days—you would have earned 10% per year. But if you had missed that period's best 15 days, your average annual return would have been . . . zero. Yep, the entire profit of five years came in just 15 days.

Could you have picked the best 15 days out of 1,258?

Do you think some magazine columnist or television pundit could have?

I know you think it's hard to do. But in fact it's *twice* as hard as you think. That's because not only must you know when to get out of the market, you must also know precisely when to jump back in.

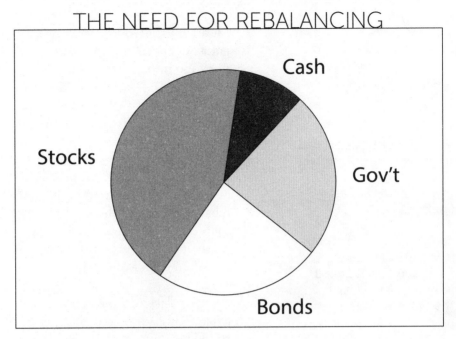

FIGURE 17.16

In Figure 17.16's example, that means we'd reduce the stocks and add more cash to bring everything back into balance.

By periodically rebalancing the portfolio in this fashion, we reduce the risk of having too much of one asset class or market sector and too little of another.

When should you rebalance? You have two choices: by time or percentage. When you rebalance by time, you simply execute your trades on a calendar basis—monthly, quarterly or annually. The interval doesn't matter, provided you are consistent.

Calendar rebalancing is easy, but it's not as effective as you might like. If you rebalance quarterly, for example, you'll execute a rebalance on June 30 whether the portfolio needs it or not. And you might miss opportunities that occur during the quarter.

This is why my firm doesn't rebalance our clients' accounts based on time. Instead, we do it by percentage. You can do it this way, too—but I'll warn you: You have to monitor your portfolio *every day*.

Incidentally

If you're retired, you may be wondering if these three steps are applicable to you.

They are.

The alternative is to put your life's savings into bank CDs, bonds, U.S. Treasuries or annuities—and as we've seen, that approach fails over long periods.

But how can you generate monthly income from a globally diversified portfolio? The solution is called a Systematic Withdrawal Plan. It can give you the opportunity to generate current income today while laying the foundation for increasing that income over time, to keep pace with inflation.

It's easy to do: Simply reinvest all interest and dividends back into the portfolio. Then withdraw a monthly amount from your account. That's all there is to it.

I explain SWPs in greater detail in my book *The Truth About Retirement Plans and IRAs*, so if you're near or in retirement and trying to figure out how to generate long-term income from your portfolio, adjusted for inflation, give that a read.[80]

Here's how it works: Begin by setting your target asset allocation. Say you place 10% of your portfolio into a given asset class. You then set a certain range—say, 8% to 12%. You let the investment drift within that range, and you rebalance whenever it drifts beyond either threshold.

This is highly effective, but it's also a pain because you never know when you'll need to rebalance. (Hence the need to watch the portfolio every day.) You also have to know how to set drift parameters—otherwise you'll rebalance too often or not often enough.[79]

Properly designed portfolios usually need rebalancing only a few times each year. But during turbulent times, such as those we experienced in 2008, you might need to rebalance a dozen times or more.

So the choice is yours: rebalance by time or by percentage. But do it.

Building Your Portfolio

Once you've settled on your asset allocation model, you need to buy investments to construct it. But don't buy individual securities. Instead, put your money into funds that invest in them. The reason: Studies show that buying individual stocks and bonds is riskier than buying funds of stocks and bonds. Here are the data:

---

[79]This probably helps explain why investors choose to hire financial planners like us: We do all this work for them, relieving themselves of the drudgery while assuring them that their investments are being rebalanced skillfully. Remember that time-knowledge-desire thing?

[80]Just $19.95 at booksellers everywhere. Shameless plug.

For the five years ending December 31, 2015, as shown in Figure 17.17, only 49% of all stocks listed on the New York Stock Exchange made money. But during that same period, 99% of stock mutual funds did. And as Figure 17.18 shows, the average return of stock mutual funds was 9.8% during that period, while the average stock price *fell* 6.5%!

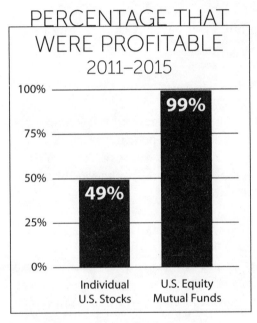

FIGURE 17.17

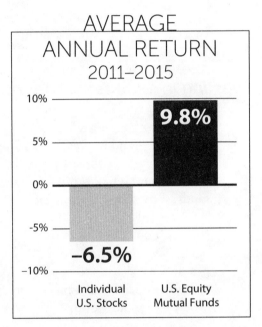

FIGURE 17.18

How are mutual funds and exchange-traded funds able to offer these results? Simple: They are diversified. Even the least diversified funds own dozens of securities, while the most diversified own thousands.

But—and here's an important distinction—we don't use retail mutual funds in the Edelman Managed Asset Program®. One reason: They're expensive. The average cost is 2.63% per year. (The breakdown is as follows: 1.19% per year for the annual expense ratio, according to Morningstar, plus 1.44% per year in trading expenses, according to a 2013 study published in the *Financial Analysts Journal*.)

So we instead provide our clients with exchange-traded funds and institutional mutual funds. These investments are significantly less expensive than the average retail mutual fund.[81] And these funds tend to trade very little, incurring far lower costs than 1.44% per year. That's important, because trading can trigger capital gains, which in turn can generate a tax liability. All told, lower cost and funds that do less trading can save you money, which in turn let you keep more of your investment's annual returns![82]

Indeed, investing isn't just about making money; it's equally about saving money.

Investing in Exponential Technologies

Everything you've read thus far about investment management reflects how my wife and I—and all the financial planners at our firm—personally handle our own money. Jean and I have been managing our money this way for more than 30 years, and it's how my firm manages billions of dollars for the tens of thousands of middle-class and high-net-worth families who are our clients.[83]

But this book has introduced new concepts from the field of exponential technologies. Networks and computer systems, Big Data, robotics, nanotechnology, 3D printing, medicine and neuroscience, energy and environmental systems, education technology, leisure and recreation and financial services innovation—all of these are changing our world, and they offer new investment opportunities (and risks).

In chapter 12, we saw how quickly big companies can be disrupted, and that surely sounded scary.[84] But there's more to the story: When a billion-dollar company disappears, it's replaced by a *new* billion-dollar company. And it's getting easier than ever to create one. As Figure 17.19 shows, it took Kodak 100 years to reach a billion-dollar valuation, but Instagram did it in two years.

---

[81]There are also some low-cost funds available from some retail mutual fund companies, and we're not averse to recommending them to our clients when appropriate.

[82]You can buy investments like these on your own or through a financial advisor. If you hire a financial planner, the planner's fee will offset some or all of the savings. Some would say it's worth it—that the savings essentially pay for all of the planner's advice and services. Others would say they're better off doing it themselves. Time-knowledge-desire, folks.

[83]As I mentioned earlier, we invest the same way as our clients. Not just Jean and I, but every financial planner in our firm as well. You might want to ask if your financial advisor owns the same investments he or she is recommending for you. Many don't. We do.

[84]It was supposed to; the chapter is called "The Dark Side."

TIME TO CREATE A $1B COMPANY

Kodak	**100 years**
Whirlpool	**86 years**
Mattel	**25 years**
Nike	**24 years**
Starbucks	**24 years**
Google	**8 years**
Facebook	**5 years**
YouTube	**18 months**
Groupon	**18 months**
Instagram	**2 years**

FIGURE 17.19

There are so many billion-dollar start-ups that they now even have a name: *unicorns*. The typical unicorn is less than 10 years old, as shown by Figure 17.20 (compared to 85 years for the average Fortune 500 company).

So how can you invest in companies that are exploiting exponential technologies instead of being disrupted by them?

You know we like to use mutual funds and exchange-traded funds,[85] so you won't be surprised that we turned to the fund industry to see what it offers. We closely examined and extensively researched every fund available that focuses on technology (there are 425 of them), to find the one fund we could place into our own accounts and also recommend to our clients for theirs.

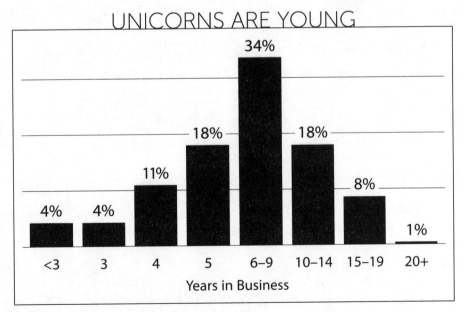

UNICORNS ARE YOUNG

FIGURE 17.20

---

[85]Recall Figures 17.17 and 17.18 on page 225.

Our analysis left us dismayed and disappointed. We discovered that every tech stock fund is essentially the same: They all invest exclusively in tech stocks.

But that's not what we were looking for. I'm not interested in just buying a bunch of tech stocks—heck, anyone can do that. Intel, Microsoft, IBM, Oracle, Apple—it doesn't take a genius to create a list of the country's biggest technology stocks. And that's all those tech funds do. As you can see from Figure 17.21, the average tech stock fund has nearly 80% of its holdings in technology stocks. Well, duh.

SECTOR DIVERSIFICATION

Market Sector	Avg Tech Fund	XT
Technology	77.4%	28.1%
Consumer	6.6	5.4
Industrials	4.9	13.2
Financial	3.4	6.3
Healthcare	2.6	30.3
Communication	2.0	11.9
Real Estate	0.6	0.0
Energy & Materials	0.2	4.0
Utilites	0.2	0.0
Cash	2.1	0.8

FIGURE 17.21

I was not looking for a fund that merely buys a stereotypical list of companies that are creating technology. I also want a list that includes companies that are *using* technology to grow in new, exciting and, yes, exponential ways. But our research discovered that no such fund existed.

So I asked BlackRock to build it. BlackRock is the world's largest money manager with more than $5 trillion in assets under management. It owns iShares, the largest ETF provider in the industry. I explained what I was looking for. BlackRock liked my idea and agreed to create an ETF based on it.

But BlackRock does not provide securities analysis, so it needed someone who could say which securities ought to be included in this new ETF. So it approached Morningstar, the world's preeminent resource of mutual fund and ETF research, and asked if its research team could create an index of securities based on my idea. Morningstar also liked the idea and agreed to participate. It took its analysts about a year, and in early 2015, it launched the Morningstar Exponential Technologies Index. BlackRock promptly licensed the index and in March 2015 launched the iShares Exponential Technologies ETF (ticker symbol: XT) based on it.

My firm's portfolio management team and I worked closely with Morningstar and BlackRock as they developed the index and the ETF. We're proud of their accomplishment, which according to BlackRock made me the first financial planner in history to inspire the creation of an ETF.

XT is unlike any other technology fund. Instead of investing solely in the companies that *create* technology, this fund is equally focused on companies that *use* technology. Morningstar's process was brilliant: After identifying major themes (big data and analytics, nanotechnology, networks and computer systems, energy and environmental systems, medicine and neuroscience, robotics, 3D printing, bioinformatics and financial services innovation) it examined publicly traded companies around the world to determine the degree to which is each engaged in the development or usage of these technologies. The result is an ETF unlike any other tech fund.

"EDDIE, TAKE IT FROM ME... INVEST IN ROBOTICS."

Cartoon by Harley Schwadron

XT is more diversified than the average tech fund.

- It has 200 stocks in its portfolio, compared to just 85 for the average tech fund. (All the data you're seeing here is as of December 31, 2016. Some data changes daily, so this information might not be current by the time you read it.)

- Other tech funds invest 100% into tech stocks, but XT's portfolio is only about 30% tech. The rest of the portfolio consists of companies from other market sectors.

- XT has only about two-thirds of assets in large-cap stocks. The rest are in mid-cap and small-cap stocks, as shown in Figure 17.22.

- And though the average tech fund has 85% of its assets in U.S. stocks, XT has less than two-thirds of its assets invested domestically. The rest is invested around the globe, as shown in Figure 17.23.

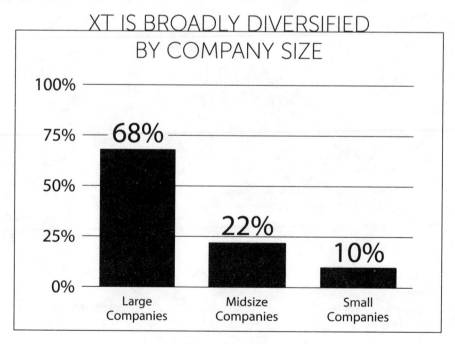

FIGURE 17.22

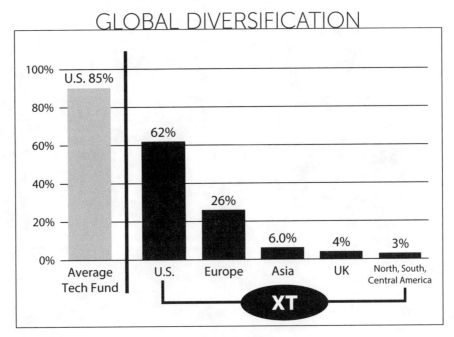

GLOBAL DIVERSIFICATION

FIGURE 17.23

XT owns shares in both *developers* and *users* of technology. This is crucially important—and the basis of my desire to have XT created.

"How come Jasper's mutual fund is up twelve per cent and mine's only up eight?"
Robert Weber The New Yorker Collection/The Cartoon Bank

XT is also equally weighted. This means it places an equal amount of money into each of those 200 stocks. That's not how other tech funds do it. Instead, they are cap-weighted, meaning that the amount they invest in each stock depends on how big each company is. (The bigger the company, the more it gets of the fund's money.) As a result, although the average tech fund owns 85 stocks, nearly half (46%) of its money is held in just 10 stocks—and those 10 stocks can render the other 75 irrelevant. XT instead places just one-half of one percent of its assets into each stock, as Figure 17.25 shows. Thus there's no big risk caused by allocating lots of money to just a few stocks.

THE INVESTMENT STRATEGY YOU NEED FOR THE FUTURE **CHAPTER SEVENTEEN**

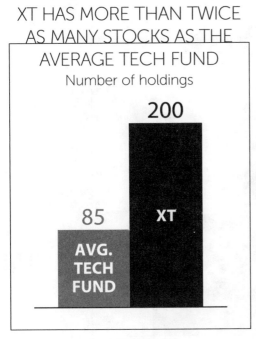

FIGURE 17.24

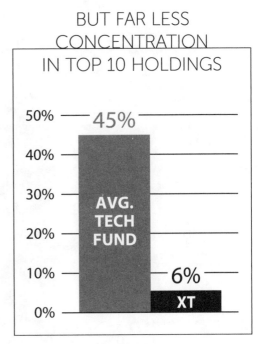

FIGURE 17.25

XT's expense ratio is half that of the average technology fund. According to Morningstar, the annual expense ratio of the average tech fund is 0.94%. XT's cost is just 0.47%.

XT is tax-efficient. Morningstar revises its index on an annual basis; the low turnover reduces trading expenses and minimizes the need to distribute capital gains. It also helps to reduce the annual tax liability.

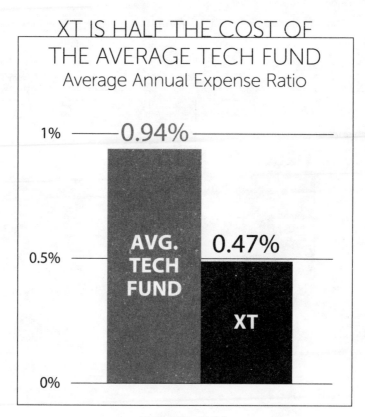

FIGURE 17.26

The unique attributes of XT have generated positive reaction from the investment world. Zacks Investment Research called XT "a good opportunity for investors to play the niche area of the booming technology sector. . . . This ETF stands out from the rest and in our view holds a lot of potential. . . . This ETF could be a solid choice for long-term investing." StreetAuthority wrote that XT "deserves clear consideration for your portfolio." And etfdb.com, in a June 2016 report called "The 5 Technology ETFs You Should Consider" wrote, "XT makes for a great long-term play on technology's biggest potential themes."

At this writing, clients of Edelman Financial Services collectively own more than 90% of XT's shares. I mention this because my bragging about the fund could be interpreted as self-serving and a conflict of interest.

So . . . should you invest in XT? And if so, how much of your portfolio should you place into it?

The answer, of course, depends on your individual circumstances. As we showed earlier, your portfolio's asset allocation model needs to reflect your goals and objectives, risk tolerance, time horizon, need for liquidity, and a great many other aspects pertaining to your personal financial situation. We must also take into consideration other aspects of your financial life—not just your investments but also your need for education and retirement planning, estate planning, insurance, tax advice, the role of home ownership and mortgages, employee benefits, and more.

In short, you need to engage in personal financial planning. That's the only way you can be confident that you are creating an asset allocation model correctly designed to help you achieve your goals in a manner that doesn't subject you to any more risk than necessary.

So there you have it. To construct a portfolio for the future, you should:

1. Invest in a globally diversified portfolio.

2. Maintain that portfolio for a very long time.

3. Strategically rebalance the portfolio as needed.

4. Include companies that are using or developing exponential technologies to help them become, and remain, unicorns of the 21st century.

Incidentally

Disclosure: Neither I nor any of the financial planners of Edelman Financial Services, nor the firm itself, has ever received any compensation of any kind from BlackRock, Morningstar or any other third party for the creation, launch, distribution or management of the iShares Exponential Technologies ETF.

My goal in having XT brought to the marketplace was so that everyone could have access to the fund, not just our clients. We are proud of our work in XT's development and pleased that it is available to all investors through the open marketplace.[86]

---

[86]Investors interested in XT should carefully consider the investment objectives, risks, charges and expenses of the investment. This and other important information is contained in the fund's prospectus, which can be obtained from your investment advisor or by calling BlackRock at 800-474-2737 and should be read carefully before investing. My Compliance Department made me say this, too.

Chapter Eighteen: Where You'll Live in the Future

If you're going to be alive 30 or 40 years from now, will you want to live where you're living now?

I suspect not—and it's not just because you'll want to move to a warmer climate or get a smaller place that doesn't have a lawn that needs mowing. Sure, they might be factors in your decision to move. But equally so will be the emergence of homes and communities that offer features, advantages and opportunities you'll embrace. Let's explore them.

Naturally Occuring Retirement Communities

My parents found themselves living in a retirement community even though they hadn't moved from their home of 40 years. Mom and Dad bought their home in 1957 in one of those sprawling new bedroom communities of the post-war era. With a mortgage provided by the G.I. Bill, they were able to attain the American dream: a home of their own, a 2,000-square-foot, split-level house on a postage-stamp-sized lot in a brand-new neighborhood. They were in their early thirties, with two kids and a dog (I wouldn't arrive for another two years), just like every other family in the neighborhood. There was a brand-new elementary school down the street. A new swim club, too.

Fast-forward 40 years. My parents are still living in that house. Almost all their neighbors are still living in their houses, too. But instead of having trucks delivering reusable cloth diapers to the moms and soft-serve ice cream to the kids, Meals on Wheels is delivering food to elderly home owners who lack the mobility to shop for food or cook. The local swim club has adults-only hours, and the elementary school is now a senior center.

Without intending it, and without even knowing it, my parents found themselves living in a NORC (naturally occurring retirement community). You might, too. Or you might decide to move to a neighborhood that offers services needed and desired by people in their second or third half-century.

In my parents' case, they didn't live in their NORC for long. Dad had shifted his company's business activities to Las Vegas, so instead of commuting a couple thousand miles every couple of weeks (as he had found himself doing for a few years), my parents decided to relocate.

And they chose a new home in a—you guessed it—over-55 community. This is another kind of NORC, and they are much more common. Rather than evolving to serve seniors, these communities are designed for seniors from their inception.

Over-55 communities and NORCs house 36% of U.S. seniors, according to AARP. They offer a variety of services, including yard work, household chores, transportation services, social programs—even health care management. Monthly dues range from $100 to $1,000, in addition to the cost of the home itself. Some communities are apartment buildings; others feature mansions.

But saying you built a community on purpose isn't the same as saying you've built an intentional community. That is something entirely different.

Intentional Communities

Intentional communities are for people who identify with one another. The affinity could be based on any commonality—geography, history, vision, purpose, philosophy or common social, economic or political interests. They are designed for sustainable living, personal and cultural transformation and social evolution—and they've been around a long time: the Fellowship for Intentional Community, which provides support services to intentional communities, has roots dating to 1937. As of 2016, ic.org lists 2,234 intentional communities in 78 countries, including 1,546 in the United States.

Cohousing

Cohousing has a misleading name, because it refers to an entire community, not just one house.

When you buy a house in a cohousing development, the home itself is yours. It will probably be in a cluster and small (700–1,200 square feet), with cars parked on the perimeter of the community. The largest structure is the common house, which typically features a communal kitchen and dining area, as well as living rooms and parlors, game room, library, gym, media room, workshop and hobby/craft room. Some even have guest rooms. Keeping the homes small and the common house large encourages residents to socialize.

When these units are new, buyers participate in designing the community's grounds and features. Unlike in typical apartment and condominium buildings, there is no resident manager; instead, the residents work together to maintain the community.

At this writing, there are 160 cohousing communities (of which 28 are restricted to seniors) in 25 states. To learn more, go to cohousing.org, the website of the Cohousing Association of the United States.

Shared Housing

This is defined as elders (usually unrelated) living together for companionship. They typically share expenses.

If you're having trouble envisioning this, simply recall *The Golden Girls*.[87] In the TV sitcom,[88] Dorothy (played by Bea Arthur) lives in a house with her spunky mother Sophia (Estelle Getty); the sex-crazed southern belle Blanche (Rue McClanahan); and ditzy Rose (Betty White), a Norwegian American from St. Olaf, Minnesota. The girls support each other financially and emotionally, and enjoy friendships and relationships that only roommates can develop.

Shared housing is very common, accounting for about 4 million U.S. households, according to AARP and the National Shared Housing Resource Center.

---

[87] You gotta be kidding me.
[88] Yes, it was a TV sitcom. It aired from 1985 to 1992 on NBC. You do know what NBC is, don't you? I mean, it's not Crackle. But still.

Before You Cohabit

If you're going to cohabit with anyone other than a spouse, you should obtain the services of an attorney, who can draft a contract stipulating the legal and financial rights, responsibilities and penalties associated with the arrangement. Details will vary based on who owns the property; who pays for maintenance, repairs, capital improvements, taxes and insurance; and even who has the right to use shared facilities and under what circumstances. The agreement should also stipulate what happens if a member of the household fails to live up to his or her obligations.

Incidentally

Crafted properly, your housemates' agreement should enhance and protect your relationships, not harm or interfere with them. If you want an idea of how contracts can go a little too far, though, consider the Roommate Agreement signed by Sheldon Cooper, the theoretical physicist from TV's *The Big Bang Theory* who may or may not have Asperger's syndrome, and his friend and roommate, Leonard Hofstadter, an experimental physicist at CalTech.

Among other things, their roommate agreement stipulates that:

- One must help if an artificial intelligence the other has created takes over Earth.

- The shower can have at most one occupant, except in the event of an attack by water-soluble aliens.

- If either party suspends their friendship, their surviving responsibilities to each other would be only rent, utilities and a perfunctory chin-jut of recognition as they pass in the hall.

- Sheldon will be Leonard's sidekick should he ever get superpowers.

- If one of the roommates ever masters time travel, he must appear in the apartment exactly five seconds after the clause is signed.

It is not necessarily the recommendation of this book that the agreement between you and your housemates contain these or similar clauses. But I gotta admit, they are worth considering.

Ecovillages

Ecovillages are for people concerned about the environment. Named by the United Nations as one of the world's 100 Best Practices for Sustainable Living in 1998, ecovillage residents grow as much of their own food as possible, create homes using local materials, operate renewable energy systems, protect nature and safeguard wilderness areas. Many communities even create their own currencies, which helps them support each other's small businesses. The Global Ecovillage Network lists hundreds of ecovillages worldwide.

Housing Cooperatives

Just about everyone in New York City knows what a co-op is. More than 1.5 million New Yorkers live in one, and the concept is spreading to the rest of the country.

In almost every other real estate concept, including all those we've discussed so far, you buy and own your property, whether it's a single-family home or an apartment in a larger building. But that's not the case with co-ops. Instead, a corporation owns both the building and your apartment. You therefore buy membership in the corporation; doing so gives you the right to live in a specific apartment.

And because it's a membership-based corporation, the members of that corporation get to decide who's allowed to join (and thus move into the building). When you bought and moved into your current home, your neighbors had no say. But in a co-op, they have *lots* of say. In fact, they'll require you to submit to a background check and a series of interviews with other residents. If they don't like you—they don't have to say why—you won't be allowed to purchase your home (uh, er, your membership in the corporation). Madonna and Richard Nixon had their applications rejected by co-op boards.

Many co-ops were constructed by trade unions, to ensure that their members— and only their members—had places to live. Student housing co-ops are also common at colleges throughout the country. And that's a key appealing aspect of co-ops: once you're in, you can help make sure that only folks you'd enjoy living with come in, too![89]

You can learn more at coophousing.org, the website of the National Association of Housing Cooperatives.

---

[89]Unless you have the view of Groucho Marx, who said he would never join a club that would have him as a member.

Niche Communities

Niche communities are designed for people who share a common identity. This could be union membership, artistic inclination, religious faith, sexual orientation—or even being alumni of the same university. Entrance fees range from $1,000 to $500,000 or more, and monthly fees can be thousands of dollars. Two examples are the Fountaingrove Lodge, an LGBTQ community in Santa Rosa, California, and the Village at Penn State, a residence for the school's alumni.

The Village Model

The concept is simple: Instead of leaving your home to move into senior housing or assisted living, you and others in your neighborhood form a nonprofit organization that provides services so you can all keep living at home.

A 2012 study published by *The Gerontologist* found 42 villages across the United States; by 2016, according to the Village to Village Network, that number had tripled. There are now 205 such villages in 38 states, and more are being established each year.

Some villages comprise just a few city blocks; those in rural areas might cover a 20-mile radius. Typical services include modifications to make your home accessible, transportation, meal delivery, dog walking, health and wellness programs, social activities, nurses and care managers.

Most villages have 150 to 200 members. Entrance fees can range from $1,000 to $500,000 or more, depending on whether the price includes the cost of the property. Monthly fees range from $50 to $1,500. The average resident is a middle-class, 74-year-old woman.

To learn more, visit vtvnetwork.org.

Don't Just Choose the Type–Choose the Location, Too

All the housing environments described on these pages can be found in the Midwest as well as on the coasts. So be sure to consider location when considering which type of community appeals to you. An ideal location might be one you have never considered.

For example, 39% of the U.S. population lives in a county that borders an ocean, according to the National Oceanic and Atmospheric Administration, suggesting that lots of folks want to be near the water. Even if that describes you, you can't ignore the Midwest. After all, being far from an ocean doesn't mean you're far from water. Millions of Americans live on or near a lake or river, with benefits they say strongly outweigh being next to an ocean: Lakes and rivers contain freshwater, not seawater and don't suffer from sharks, jellyfish or seaweed. Many lakes even offer waves (Lake Michigan gets two- to four-foot waves in the summer and four- to eight-footers in the winter; Lake Superior's waves can hit 20 feet). And water sports and boating on both are common.

The Midwest offers another advantage, too: When we no longer need tens of millions of acres for farming and ranching, thanks to the innovations described earlier, all that land will become available for redevelopment. This suggests it will be both cheap and plentiful.[90]

And if you regard living in the Midwest as being in the middle of nowhere and a million miles from anywhere, fear not—thanks to self-driving vehicles. You won't mind spending two or three hours in a car to get to a major urban center, according to research by the Global Cities program at the Nature Conservancy. Its study says that the easier it is to get from one place to another, the more willing people are to travel.

In other words, if you can enjoy a luxurious commute that allows you to read, watch a video, listen to music, play a game, interact with others—or even sleep—you won't mind being in a car for long periods. And I haven't even mentioned the productivity opportunities a long commute will provide you: you can study, participate in meetings virtually, and do as much work as you wish, undisturbed by others.

So as you contemplate the kind of community you'd like to live in, give some thought to where you'd like to live as well. Your ideal location might surprise you.

---

[90]Maybe it will be cheap *because* it will be plentiful.

Chapter Nineteen: A Second Home

For many, the American dream is not owning a home. It's owning a *second home*—a vacation home.

If you're thinking about buying a second home, proceed cautiously. This is not a conversation about investing in real estate; according to the National Association of Realtors, only 7% of vacation homes produce rental income. I'm also not suggesting that rental property is a terrible investment; it's simply not what most second-home buyers have in mind. So we're going to talk about buying a second home that you can enjoy with[91] family and friends.

Before you even start looking for a second home, be aware of all the reasons *not* to buy one. These include:

- **Cost.** Think of everything you have in your house. Got a picture? Good— because you'll have to buy all that stuff all over again for your second home. Furniture, consumer electronics, dishes, pots and pans, cutlery, bedsheets and bath towels—even toothbrushes and tinfoil. You'll need two of pretty much everything. You'll also incur maintenance and repair costs, taxes, condo or association fees and more. Mortgage interest rates are higher for second homes than for primary residences, too. And most of the costs you incur won't translate into higher market value when you sell the property.

- **Worries.** Owning a house that's hundreds or thousands of miles away can keep you up at night. Has someone broken in? Did the pipes freeze? Will the air-conditioning operate when I arrive? You have none of these thoughts when you're planning to visit a hotel.

- **Work.** When you go to your vacation home, you're supposed to be . . . on vacation. But when you show up at a property you last saw many months ago, you might discover that the gutters need cleaning, the windows need washing, the lawn needs mowing, the filters need replacing, the fridge needs stocking and more—in other words, everything you do to maintain your primary home must be done for your vacation home. At home-home, you can do these chores here and there throughout the year. But since you're at your vacation home infrequently, all chores must be done in the

---

[91]Or away from.

compacted period of your visit. Many owners of second homes discover that they spend much of their vacation working around the house instead of playing golf or going to the beach.

- **Boredom.** Sitting on the porch of a second home, gazing at the peaceful lake as the sun sets, sounds wonderful. But after the sixteenth time you do it, you might find it boring. Will you want to travel to the same place for years, do the same things, and eat at the same restaurants?

- **Value.** If you were *certain* that the house was going to fall in value, you wouldn't buy it. So you are assuming it will maintain its value or grow. But neither is guaranteed. Vacation homes tend to suffer greater swings in price than suburban and urban houses, because people tend to buy them during boom times (when they're flush with cash) and sell them during recessions (when they're out of work and struggling to pay their bills). Banks know you're more likely to default on the mortgage on your second home than the one on your primary residence (because suffering a foreclosure on your main home could render you homeless, while losing your second home would be merely a financial setback). That's why lenders demand higher down payments and charge higher interest rates for mortgages on second homes (see "Cost" above).

- **Future utility.** That second home might be the perfect size and location for you, with perfect amenities and community service. But will that still be true when your children get older? Teens and college undergrads are more likely to want to spend time at the vacation home with their friends, not with you—or not go there at all. And when your kids get married and have kids of their own, you might discover that your second home can't accommodate the needs and interests of your growing family.

All these issues help explain why so many people who can afford to buy second homes refuse to do so—and why many who own second homes happily become *former* owners of second homes. But refusing to buy a second home means you're stuck going to hotels and resorts. You have to research properties and check availability, take your clothes with you, wonder who's been sleeping in the bed before you arrived—and what germs they might have left behind—and hope the property will be as enjoyable as you and your family hope. And one thing is for sure: the place won't be *Cheers*. No one will know your name, and no one will know who you are.[92]

Fortunately, there are now alternatives to owning a second home: you can own part of one, and you can join clubs that grant you access to many of them—giving you the benefits of a second home without the headaches and at a lower cost. Let's look at both options.

Fractional Ownership

You could vacation at a Four Seasons or Ritz-Carlton resort, staying in a hotel room and dining in the hotel restaurants. Or you could buy a one-sixteenth interest in a two- or three-bedroom condo at one of their properties, complete with living room, dining room and kitchen, with balconies overlooking the beach or ski slopes. Property management does everything—from building the condo to furnishing it (from sofas to linens and everything you need in the kitchen) to handling all maintenance and repairs. All you do is show up (and pay your share).

For each one-sixteenth share you purchase, you get the right to occupy the condo for two or three weeks per year. Since you own the condo, you're free to let friends and family use it (even if you're not present). You can even rent out the property (or rather, rent out the days you're entitled to use it) to generate income.

Although fractionals avoid the problems of cost, worry and work associated with ownership of second homes, they suffer from four problems:

- **The value can fall.** This can happen because of overall economic conditions, poor maintenance of your resort by the property's manager or a decline in interest in its location.[93] If you purchase a fractional unit from a new resort, you have to wonder if the property will be as desirable in 10 or 15 years as it is now.

---

[92]Aw, gee. Again? Go ask your parents. Again.
[93]In 2016, the Zika virus curbed many people's interest in traveling to the Caribbean, for example.

- **Fractional shares always sell to the lowest bidder**. Since every condo at the property is identical, buyers always choose the one with the lowest price. This dampens resale value.

- **You're still returning to the same place every vacation**. Thus you haven't solved the boredom factor. (You can reduce this problem by purchasing a fractional unit from a property manager that lets you swap your time for use at their other properties.)

- **You have to pay annual dues**. You must pay the dues even if you don't visit the condo.

Destination Clubs

A more flexible (and possibly more expensive) vacation alternative is the club model. Instead of owning legal title to a (portion of) a property, as you do with a fractional unit, a vacation club is literally that: membership in a club. Just as you don't own the barbells you use at a health club, you generally don't own the real estate when you join a destination club. Instead, you merely purchase the right to use the property—just as you get to use the weights in the health club.

When you join a club, you gain access to all the properties it owns for a certain number of days or weeks each year. Properties can be freestanding homes, villas or condos, and they might or might not be located within a resort. Many clubs own hundreds or even thousands of properties, both in the United States and around the world; others own just a few. In almost every case, each home is worth millions of dollars, giving you the ability to enjoy homes far more luxurious than you probably could purchase on your own.[94]

Destination clubs are ideal if you want variety and amenities. The service level is typically high, with concierge services and housekeeping—even private chefs. The clubs handle all maintenance and repairs, decorating and furnishing, and they stock the kitchen for you prior to arrival. Some clubs even provide a car for your use during your visit.

---

[94]And even if you did, you'd have only one. But through a club, you have access to a complete inventory of high-end properties.

Prices vary widely. Some clubs charge $25,000 to join, while others demand more than a million dollars. The less you pay up front, the more you'll pay to use any of the properties. And all charge annual dues, which can reach five figures. Still, compared to the initial and ongoing costs of owning a second home, destination clubs can be a bargain.

There are downsides to destination clubs, however. They include:

- **No ownership rights**. You're joining a club, not buying real estate. If the properties grow in value, the profits belong to the club, not you. If you quit, you generally can't get your money back—just as when you fail to go to the gym.

- **No transfer rights.** Many clubs refuse to let your friends and family use the properties unless you're present. (They want them to buy their own memberships.)

- **Limited property availability.** Many clubs have a poor member/property ratio. Others have tiered membership, meaning that those who pay higher dues get first rights to book locations. These ratios and rules can make it difficult for you to book a property—either at all or in high season (you might never get to go to that ski resort, for example, or you might be able to book a house there only in the summer).

- **Advance reservations required.** Some clubs require you to book properties as much as two years in advance. This is a problem for people who don't know their schedules that far out, as well as for travelers who like to be spontaneous.

- **Use or lose.** As with fractional ownership, you must pay the annual dues whether you use the program or not.

Incidentally

There are clubs that let you share luxuries other than homes. Some clubs allow you to drive exotic cars, wear expensive jewelry, wear designer clothing and fly on private jets—all at a fraction of what it would cost to own these products outright.

Indeed, it's all part of the sharing economy. Life is becoming more about experiences, not ownership.[95]

---

[95]If that sounds confusing, consider that you used to buy videocassettes of movies for $89.99. Now you pay just a few dollars or you pay a monthly subscription fee, and you get to watch your favorite flicks whenever you want without having to own them. Why not do that with a Maserati? Drive it whenever you want for a few hundred dollars a day, without having to plunk down $150,000 for it.

DESTINATION CLUBS INCLUDE

Club	Locations	Website
Banyan Tree Private Collection	Worldwide	btprivatecollection.com
Equity Residences	North America	equityresidences.com
Exclusive Resorts	Worldwide	exclusiveresorts.com
G2G Collection	North America	g2gcollection.com
The Hideaways Club	Worldwide	thehideawaysclub.com
Inspirato	North America	inspirato.com
Luxus Vacation Properties	North America	luxusgroup.com
Destination M	Worldwide	destination-m.com
The Quintess Collection	North America	quintess.com
Rocksure Property	Worldwide	rocksure.com

FIGURE 19.1

I haven't mentioned time-shares. That's because there's not a lot of reason to recommend them.

Time-shares emerged in the 1960s as a way for resort operators to maximize profits by selling blocks of time—typically in increments of a week—to guests willing to return every year. If the boredom factor exists with full or fractional ownership of a property, it's even worse with a time-share—because you not only have to return to the same property each year, you have to go the very same week every year as well.

Many people buy time-shares on impulse, after attending a sales presentation by a resort's marketing staff. Sometimes you're invited to attend the session while you're vacationing at the resort. In other cases, you are invited to a free trip provided you agree to attend the sales presentation. Time-share salespeople have reputations for aggressive and manipulative sales practices, and many buyers are convinced to finance the purchase, saddling them with payments they can't afford. Time-shares are also notoriously difficult to sell—partly because there are so many remorseful owners trying to unload their purchases and partly because many properties are of poor quality. Consider that there are far more websites about time-share rip-offs than opportunities.

The bottom line: never buy a time-share.

If you are interested in these ideas, talk with your financial planner for help deciding if any of them is right for you.

Incidentally

The IRS considers time-shares to be personal property, like your car. They are not classified as real estate investments, so never let any sales agent persuade you otherwise.

Chapter Twenty: Long-Term Care in the Future

We've looked at several types of communities you may occupy in the future, and even second-home concepts. I'm not sure which of these you might choose to live in in the future, but there's one place you *won't* live 20 years from now: in a nursing home.

Medical science is going to render nursing homes obsolete. As we saw in chapter 6, older Americans are living healthier lives than ever, and it's only going to get better. Continuing advances in nanotechnology, biotechnology, bioinformatics, neuroscience and robotics means doctors will be able to repair or replace just about anything that goes wrong with you. After all, we're already replacing an astonishingly long list of body parts: not just teeth, knees and hips but kidneys, livers, hearts and lungs—and of course, genes themselves. For all these reasons, living in a nursing home is probably not in your future.

The trend is already under way: according to AARP, the number of people over age 65 who are living in nursing homes is down by 20% since 2010, while the number of U.S. households headed by someone over age 65 is up by 24% since 2003—now totaling 27 million households. And the number of households headed by someone 75 or older is up by 13% since 2003. In fact, there are now more women over 75 living alone than with relatives.

This has huge implications for what has until now been one of the biggest challenges in the financial planning field: how to pay the costs of long-term care. It's safe to say that virtually every professional financial planner routinely recommends LTC insurance. And appropriately so, considering that the costs of long-term care are responsible for more bankruptcies among senior citizens than any other cause.

The average cost of long-term care in a private nursing home in 2016 was $7,698, according to Genworth, the largest seller of LTC insurance. The cost of care is not covered by health insurance or, after 100 days, by Medicare. Yet, according to the Department of Health and Human Services, 7 in 10 Americans over age 65 can expect to need long-term care services. Small wonder, then, that financial planning practices—including mine—advise middle-class clients to purchase long-term care insurance.[96]

That recommendation was never popular, partly because no one wants to contemplate such a future and partly because no one wants to spend money buying expensive insurance policies. That said, responsible people (the kind who are likely to hire financial planners in the first place) recognize the importance of owning LTC insurance—especially when you consider that the cost of just one month in a nursing home is more than the annual cost of an LTC insurance policy.

Or at least it used to be.

Unfortunately, the long-term care insurance industry has done a terrible job of pricing its policies. With little actuarial data to rely on, it failed to accurately predict how many policyholders would file claims and how much money those claims would cost. As a result, it has been stung: Far more claims than it expected have been filed, and the cost per claim has been higher as well.

Consequently, many insurance companies have quit the business. Those that remain—and there aren't many left—have dramatically increased the premiums they charge. And when I say dramatically, I mean it: Policies today are routinely 75% to 200% more expensive than they were 10 years ago. And these price increases don't apply solely to new customers; they apply equally to people who purchased their policies many years ago.

This is perhaps the most shocking aspect of being a LTC policyholder. Unlike life insurance contracts, where the annual cost is guaranteed never to rise, the cost of an LTC policy can go up. Insurance companies write their contracts this way precisely because they know their actuarial data are suspect. So they give themselves a hedge: the ability to increase prices as needed.

This has created a crisis for many retirees who have dutifully paid their LTC insurance premiums for many years. If it was difficult to get a couple to agree to

---

[96]People who are poor generally don't have to worry about LTC costs; being poor, they qualify for Medicaid, which pays for most LTC expenses. Rich people don't have to worry about these costs, either, because, well, they're rich. And people who are single can often skip LTC insurance because, with no spouse or partner to worry about, they can divert all their financial resources to providing for their care. This is why the ones struggling with this issue are, for the most part, married and middle class.

pay $4,000 a year for policies protecting both the husband and wife, imagine their reaction when they receive a letter informing them that the price has doubled. For someone living on $40,000 or $50,000 a year in retirement, this news is worse than shocking; it is *unaffordable*.

In doing research for this book, we checked our files and found an LTC policy that provided adequate, appropriate protection for a client back in 1994. The policy cost about $1,500 per year—annoying but tolerable. Today, that client is paying $6,500 for the same policy.

Thus, many retirees who own long-term care insurance are in a quandary: pay for a policy they can't afford (putting themselves under financial pressure) or go without it and face the risk of incurring long-term care costs that are so massive they will push them into personal bankruptcy in your seventies or eighties?

For the past decade, financial planners have been wrestling with this conundrum on behalf of (and along with) their clients. We have dealt with this issue far too many times in our own firm's financial planning practice. Sometimes we are able to help a client find the resources to keep the policies in force. (That's a euphemism for saying that the client cuts other expenses.) In other cases, we help the client restructure the policy: by reducing the benefits (by reducing either the daily benefit or the number of years that benefits will be paid), we can reduce the price, albeit at the risk that their remaining coverage might be insufficient.

There is no ideal solution to this situation. But thanks to exponential technologies, this entire dilemma is going to solve itself. By 2035, experts predict, medical science will eliminate the maladies that force people to move into nursing homes—eliminating not just the nursing homes and the costs associated with them but virtually any need for long-term care services and, by extension, the need for long-term care insurance itself.

Therefore, my firm's financial planners and I have established a new protocol regarding long-term care advice. We continue to recommend the purchase of long-term care insurance for those of our clients for whom this expense would impose financial hardship, but we are now advising our clients to expect to need this coverage only until the mid-2030s.

In other words, if in 2017 you have a spouse or partner, are in the middle class and are age:

- **65 or older:** You likely need to obtain coverage and maintain it for the next two decades or so.

- **40 or younger:** You can probably assume that you will never need to own LTC insurance.

- **Ages 41-64:** You might need to buy a policy, but you can expect to cancel it at some point instead of owning the policy for the rest of your life. Because you won't need the policy forever, you can pay more for benefits you might need now (or soon), knowing you will be able to eliminate the policy when medical advances eliminate the conditions requiring long-term care. And being able to plan for the elimination of long-term care insurance costs makes it easier to create an overall financial plan—for now, later and much later—that you can actually achieve.

What Type of LTC Policy Should You Buy?

If you are in the age range that suggests you need to consider buying an LTC insurance policy, you must balance your need for coverage against the rising costs of that coverage. If you talk with me or my colleagues, we'll give you advice tailored to your specific circumstances and personal situation. That said, generally speaking, our advice will often reflect the following viewpoints—and if you've read my prior books or been a longtime listener of my radio show, you'll see that the advice that follows is different from what I've said in the past. That's because the changes in pricing discussed above have forced us to modify our recommendations.

By permission John L. Hart FLP and Creators Syndicate, Inc.

> ***If you are under age 50 with good personal and family health histories and do not own LTC insurance***

We now generally do not recommend that you purchase LTC insurance. Instead, you should consider self-insuring, meaning saving as much as possible (including what you would have paid in LTC insurance premiums) so you have the funds to pay for long-term care services, should you or your spouse or partner need it.

> ***If you are under age 50 and do not have a good family health history***
>
> **OR**
>
> ***If you are age 50 or older but don't currently own LTC insurance***

We continue to recommend that you consider the purchase of LTC insurance. However, in addition to comparing traditional LTC insurance policies against LTC state partnership plans, we also now recommend that you consider hybrid LTC policies. We never recommended these types of policies in the past, reflecting another change in our advice.

Let me elaborate. When you buy a traditional LTC policy, you pay monthly, quarterly or annual premiums. When you need assistance with two or more activities of daily living (generally defined as eating, bathing, toileting, dressing and transferring from bed or chair), you qualify for benefits from your policy. Your policy will dictate how much money you will receive and how long you'll receive it—along with other features, such as whether your benefits will rise with inflation. The more benefits you want, the more the policy will cost. If you exhaust your policy's benefits but still need care, you'll have to use your savings and investments. If you run out of those, you'll become eligible for Medicaid.

It's that running-out-of-money part that caused states to create partnership LTC plans. After discovering that many people were going broke paying for care—forcing state-funded Medicaid programs to take over the costs—states created an incentive for you to buy LTC insurance, thus reducing your reliance on Medicaid. The incentive: Instead of having to spend all but about $2,000 of your own money on care in order to qualify for Medicaid, states now let you keep as much money as you received in LTC insurance benefits. So if your policy pays you $300,000 in benefits over several years before reaching its limit, you get to keep $300,000 in assets and still qualify for Medicaid.

Partnership policies can be complicated,[97] and in some states, they are ridiculously more expensive than traditional policies. This is why a careful analysis of each type of policy is required to determine which is best for you. And both types of policies suffer a mutual drawback: They are both pure insurance. If you never file a claim, you never get any money back, regardless of how much you'd spent in premiums.

That fact has always been annoying. Add the concerns that premiums have soared in cost and are likely to rise further, and toss in our expectation that LTC services will become extinct in the coming decades—and it's easy to see that hybrid policies are more attractive than they used to be.

Strike that. They're not more attractive than before. It's just that, comparatively speaking, we like traditional and partnership policies less. In other words, hybrids haven't gotten better; the others have gotten worse—making hybrids more worthy of consideration than they used to be.

What makes a hybrid different from traditional and partnership policies? Life insurance. Instead of offering benefits that are payable only if you incur LTC costs, hybrid policies offer the opportunity to get back some of the money you've paid in premiums. Money is returned if you cancel the policy without having received LTC benefits; either you get the check or your heirs do (if you die without having received LTC benefits).

Hybrid policies often cost more in the first year than traditional or partnership policies. But over time, thanks to the ability to get some or all of the money back, hybrids prove to be cheaper. Hybrids also let you lock in the cost; once purchased, the annual premium is guaranteed never to rise—eliminating the worry that costs might escalate beyond affordability. And because of the cash-value/death-benefit features embedded in these policies, medical underwriting for them is sometimes more lenient than for traditional and partnership policies. All these factors contribute to making hybrids worth considering today.

[97] Just like the above paragraph.

If you currently own an LTC policy

Talk with a financial planner to determine if you still need the policy. If you do but you feel your current policy is unaffordable, your planner can help you determine if you can save money by reducing your policy's benefits.

Indeed, many insurance companies are letting policyholders alter their contracts to make them more affordable. Changing the waiting period, daily benefit, years of coverage or other features could reduce the annual cost while making sure you still have some protection.

It might also be worth comparing your policy to others, including hybrids, to see if switching to a new policy might be in your best interests. Ask your insurance agent or financial planner to give you proposals. But be careful that an agent doesn't try to persuade you to buy a new policy simply so he can earn a fresh commission. For many policyholders, keeping your policy might be your cheapest and best option. Keep in mind that you're older than you were when you bought your policy and the prices for LTC policies are based on age. The longer you've owned your policy, the more expensive it will be to purchase a replacement. This is why those who don't already own an LTC policy are better candidates for hybrid policies than those who are currently insured. You should probably consider a hybrid policy only if you can no longer afford your current policy, and a financial planner can help you with this analysis.

If you don't currently own an LTC policy

Talk to an independent financial planner, not an agent who works for a particular insurance company, for help in reviewing your financial situation to determine whether a policy is in your best interests and, if so, to recommend a policy that is affordable and meets your needs.

Quite frankly, if it weren't for exponential technologies, I don't know how society would solve the problem of the enormous costs associated with a vastly growing old-age population.

Chapter Twenty-one:
Estate Planning for the Family of the Future

You're likely to be around for a very long time. And not just you but everyone else in your family. So instead of three generations gathering at Thanksgiving, you may well have five, six or seven.

Your family tree won't just be bigger; it'll be more complex. Some adults won't be married, while others will marry often. Children will have parents who've never married (or never married each other), are no longer married to each other, are married to people of the same gender or of different races or cultures (or all three), who have been married more than once—or aren't their biological parents (thanks to adoption and sperm and egg donors). This is all becoming so normal that it's not even worth writing about—any more than it's noteworthy today to meet a couple who met online (according to a study by professors at Stanford University, 35% of all marriages between 2005 and 2012 were among people who met on dating websites).

But since I am writing about it, you might as well see the data. In the United States:

- 40% of all births in 2014 were to unmarried women, according to the CDC's National Center for Health Statistics.

- The number of women giving birth for the first time in their thirties rose by 28% from 2000 to 2014, according to the CDC.

- There are 12 million single-parent households with at least one child under age 18, according to the Census Bureau.

- 95 million adults—42% of the adult population—have a steprelationship, according to smartstepfamilies.com.

- 10% of grandparents live with a grandchild, according to the Census Bureau.

- Approximately 150,000 children are adopted each year, according to the Department of Health and Human Services, suggesting that there are millions of adopted children in the United States. More than 40% of all adoptions in 2013, the most recent year for which data are available, were transracial.

- 42 million adults over age 25, or 20% of the adult population, have never married, according to the Pew Research Center.

- 24% of never-married adults ages 25 to 34 are living with a partner, according to the Pew Research Center.

- 70% of all women ages 30 to 34 have lived with a boyfriend, according to professors at UNC–Greensboro. Only 40% married them.

- 17% of adults have married more than once, and 4% have married three or more times, according to the Census Bureau.

- 21% of recent marriages involve both spouses marrying for the second time or more, according to the Census Bureau.

- More than 8% of all marriages in 2015 were interracial, according to the Brookings Institute.

- 22% of adults are divorced, according to Public Discourse.

- 28% of the people who divorced in 2011 were age 50 or older, according to the Census Bureau.

"I MET SOMEONE WONDERFUL IN A CHAT ROOM...
AND THEN I FOUND OUT SHE'S A CAT!"

These statistics demonstrate that family trees are becoming unconventional compared to those of prior generations. But all the stats involving children have one common element: The babies have all been made the way babies have always been made.

Thanks to technology, that's changing. In 2014, more than 65,000 babies—nearly 2% of all births in the United States—were conceived by in vitro fertilization. The number of IVF procedures jumped from 113,000 in 2003 to more than 165,000 in 2016—an increase of 46%, according to Peter Diamandis's October 2, 2016 article "Are We Moving Closer To Having Designer Babies?" Costs have dropped by 50% during this period, to just $10,000 per procedure, while success rates have risen from 20% to more than 50%. Thus not only are couples spending less, they're more likely to get a baby from the effort.

Although this science is letting men and women conceive who otherwise couldn't, at least the process still involves a man and a woman.[98] But this might not always be the case in the future. In 2016, the first baby was born from a procedure that combined the DNA of three people. And scientists at the University of Bath are trying to make babies without using eggs (they've already done it with mice), which could let two men (or even a sole male) produce a child (all that's needed is one ordinary cell and sperm).

Indeed, the family tree of the future will have branches unlike any we've ever seen. So it's an understatement to say that estate planning is getting complicated. It's one thing to say you'll give money to your grandchildrens' education funds equally, quite another when you have a daughter who is in her third marriage and has had a child with each husband but has no custody of her eldest child and shared custody of the middle child; another daughter

©Glasbergen
glasbergen.com

GLASBERGEN

"I asked my dad where babies come from. He says you download them from the Internet."

[98] Although not necessarily a man and woman who are married to each other. Many IVF babies result from eggs or sperm donated by third parties, and some babies are carried to term by a surrogate mother. These variations further complicate the family tree.

in a gay relationship who's raising a child born by a surrogate mother who used sperm from an anonymous donor and an egg from your daughter's partner; and a son, who's dad to his unmarried partner's child, whom she adopted from Croatia.

I'm not making any judgment calls here. But you will. And that's why you need effective estate documents. Without them, your money might go to people you don't consider to be "family members"—people who may or may not have any biological link to you. Conversely, without these documents, your money might not go to people you love and adore—and perhaps helped raise—merely because there is no legal connection between you and them.

Legal is the operative word here. Attitudes change, circumstances evolve, and promises are forgotten or inaccurately recollected. So the only thing that matters is what's written down and signed—and attested to by witnesses in the states where that's required.

It's those state laws that matter. Many provide automatic rights to those who are legally married and deny them to those who aren't. Was your significant other rushed to the hospital? Doctors won't talk to you. They might not even let you see the patient. And they certainly won't allow you to make decisions regarding your loved one's care. Those rights are limited to spouses and blood relatives.

Buying a home with someone you're not married to? If the co-owner dies, his or her relatives might be your new roommate, because automatic transferal to you of the decedent's share is available only if you were married.

Own a business jointly with someone else? If the person dies or becomes incapacitated, your new partner could be your old partner's spouse.

With people living longer and creating all sorts of family dynamics that Norman Rockwell never imagined, it all underscores the importance of dealing with estate planning as part of your financial plan *for much later.*

Digital Assets

As if all this weren't enough reason to update your estate documents, here's another: digital assets.

Prior generations stored photographs in photo albums. Jean and I have dozens stacked away in closets and bookcases in our home, and I bet you do, too. But would you care to guess how many photographs you've stored on your computer or in the cloud? My guess is that you have far more digital photographs than physical ones.

If you die, your surviving spouse or children can grab your wedding album from the closet or bookcase where it resides. But what about the photos you've placed on Facebook, Pinterest or the multitude of other social media sites you might be using?

Due to federal privacy laws, most Internet companies won't grant your family access to your online accounts after you die—and some simply delete your files upon news of your death. Few states have passed laws to solve this problem, although Delaware, Florida and Virginia let parents and guardians manage their deceased children's accounts. Elsewhere, families must obtain a court order to obtain the rights to view a deceased's account. The process can take years, during which time online services might delete the accounts due to inactivity.

"Think long-term. Like, if you ever have kids and they decide to have kids, this could really pay off for their kids' kids."

© Cornered by Mike Baldwin

Losing your loved one's photos can be as tragic as death itself. After a 29-year-old woman died, her mother tried to access her daughter's online account in order to preserve all the photos, emails and other content her daughter had accumulated. Instead, the provider deleted everything, citing privacy laws. "It was like experiencing my daughter's death a second time," she told me.

Some sites offer ways for you to avoid such problems. Facebook, for example, lets you name a "legacy contact"—a person who can post your obituary on your Timeline. This person can't log in as you or read your private messages, but can respond to new friend requests and update and archive your posts and photos. Google lets you select "trusted contacts"; they can receive data from your Gmail or Google+ accounts.

Other sites have similar features. But they all require that you take action: You must activate these features, inform your designee that you've assigned them this responsibility *and* give them your passwords (or tell them where those passwords can be found following your death or incapacity, such as in your estate attorney's files or your bank safe-deposit box).

You must also tell this person how you want him or her to handle your account after you die or become incapacitated. Do you want others to continue receiving your birthday reminders, or do you want this feature turned off? Should your account be deleted or, as some sites permit, left as a memorial? How should information that might violate your privacy be handled? (Perhaps you have visited sites or friended people you'd rather not have your family members know about.)

All this pertains only to social media. What about your bank and brokerage account and your personal IT gear—home computer, laptop, tablet and smartphone? Without passwords, the data on all those devices and in all those accounts could be lost forever.

Make sure you work with a financial planner and an estate attorney who are knowledgeable about dealing with digital assets, so your estate-planning documents can include them.

If you haven't reviewed your estate plan in the past few years, do so now. And plan on revisiting it every few years from now on, to make sure it stays current and continues to reflect your wishes.

Epilogue:
Welcome to the Greatest
Time of Your Life

Thanks to exponential technologies, you are likely to experience a longer and healthier life span and you'll be able to earn money easily on a part-time basis. Imagine a future where you're free to pursue any activities you wish! Indeed, the future will be the greatest time of your life.

That future is already here. According to Age Wave, people over 65 are the happiest, most relaxed, most content and least anxious of any age group—and having the most fun, as shown in Figures E.1–E.5.

These data are supported by a 2014 survey of more than 85,000 adults by Gallup. As Figures E.6–E.9 show, compared to every other age group, adults 65+ report having more supportive relationships and love in their lives, have far less financial stress and far greater economic security, have the most pride in their community, and have better health and more energy to enjoy their day.

In Age Wave's survey, recent retirees reported "an enormous sense of liberation and relief," and nearly every retiree surveyed (92%) said they now have the freedom to do whatever they want. In fact, retirees are 10 times as likely to say that life is more fun, enjoyable and pleasurable than it was before they retired. They report experiencing less stress and having more freedom to do what they want, when they want and on their own terms. In other words, they're having a great time.

Most (72%) spend that time involved in lifelong learning, travel, volunteering and new activities. And as we've seen from our look at the sharing economy, you probably won't stop working altogether. Indeed, according to Age Wave's research, 68% of retirees work part-time.

I'M HAVING FUN

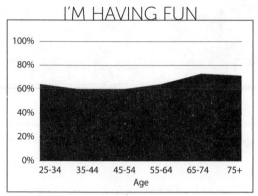

FIGURE E.1

I'M HAPPY

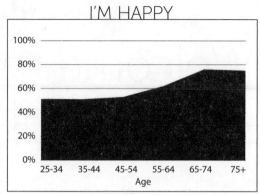

FIGURE E.2

I OFTEN FEEL RELAXED

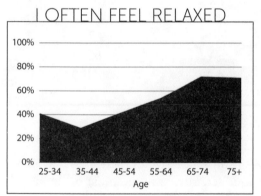

FIGURE E.3

I'M CONTENT

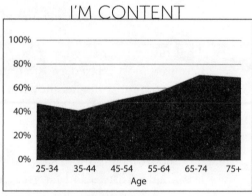

FIGURE E.4

I'M ANXIOUS

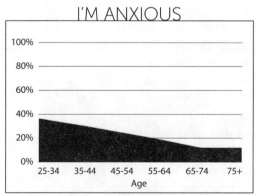

FIGURE E.5

And the longer you're retired, the better it gets, according to Age Wave. As retirement decades ensue, enjoyment improves and deepens. Spontaneity peaks, and feelings of happiness, contentment and confidence reach their zenith.

"Being" will replace "doing" as well, as you find yourself playing, exercising, shopping, reading, volunteering and socializing.

The outlook is clear: The future will likely be the greatest time of your life.

And throughout all these stages, you'll have unprecedented amounts of time and ample opportunity to engage in discovery and learning. You'll learn about history, art, science, religion and much more. But the one subject you may well take time to learn the most about will be . . . yourself.

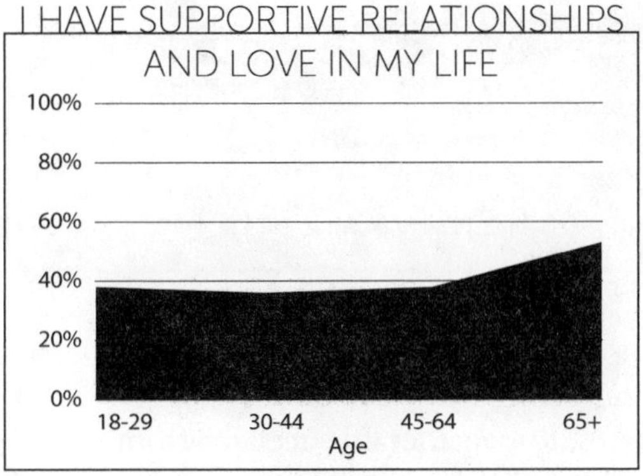

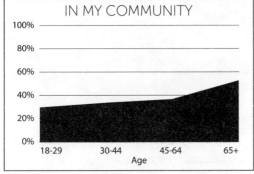

FIGURE E.6

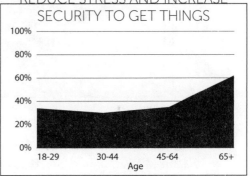

FIGURE E.7

I LIKE WHERE I LIVE, I FEEL SAFE AND I HAVE PRIDE IN MY COMMUNITY

FIGURE E.8

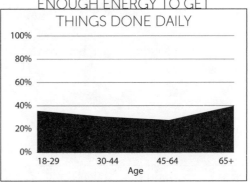

FIGURE E.9

What I'm talking about is *The Other Side of Money*.

Each month, my wife, Jean, who cofounded our financial planning and investment management firm with me more than 30 years ago, writes a column for our 16-page client newsletter. Her column is called "The Other Side of Money," and in it she focuses on being self-aware and explains how to achieve contentment and happiness. With a degree in nutrition and consumer economics, she's far more the expert in this subject than I—and with a lot of pride (and a tinge of jealousy) I note that our clients frequently tell me that her column is their favorite part of the entire newsletter.[99]

Jean also self-published her book *The Other Side of Money: Living a More Balanced Life Through 52 Weekly Inspirations*, to considerable acclaim from a great many of our clients. As she says, "Personal finance is more personal than finance." So I asked her to share with you her perspective on how, at its most fundamental and personal level, exponential technologies will provide you the opportunity to engage in the most untechnical yet important of all activities: your own personal development and growth.

The following are her words.

---

[99]Not quite sure why I bother with the other 15 pages!

The Other Side of Money *by Jean Edelman*

What do we want to be when we grow up?

With technology doing the work for us, we will find ourselves with open time, more than we've ever had before.

What will we do? Who will we be? Our jobs will no longer define us, so it will be our philanthropy and contributions to our families and friends, our community and ourselves that will fulfill us. In order to be productive and helpful to others, as well as happy inside, we need to get to know ourselves.

We will want to go back to school and take time for a deeper study of our interests. We will want to engage in many hobbies. And our long, healthy lives will let us change our interests every decade if we wish.

We'll have no fears, and we'll live in a world where we are not judged, instead free to be whoever we want to be. What will we choose to do? Who will we choose to be? We'll devote decades to answering these questions, and we'll discover that we enjoy changing the answer as decades pass by.

These are big questions, to be sure, and only we have the answers.

People use a lot of words to describe this journey. Mindfulness, self-awareness, being conscious, being in the moment. What do these all mean, and how can they help us make ourselves a better person?

The first step is to realize that to have a more fulfilling life we need to wake up to our inner journey—our own very personal life and all the hard lessons that come with it. How can we become more conscious, self-aware and mindful in our day-to-day life? How do we connect with our emotions so that we control them and they don't control us?

First, we must realize we have control of our breath, our thoughts and actions. This control will help us relax and enjoy the ride more.

It may sound simple, but breath really is the answer. And although it sounds simple, it can be hard to master. It's worth doing, because staying connected to our breath connects us to our body, to our mind, to our emotions.

The practice is to simply breathe in one long inhalation, breathe out one long exhalation. We are being very aware that we are breathing in and breathing out. We want to be conscious of our breath while we walk, while we cook, while we brush our teeth. When life gets all whipped up, we want to connect to our breath so we don't get pulled into the drama around us.

Connecting to our breath lets us step back, so we can make a smart decision—or, better yet, decide we don't need to get involved in the issue of the moment and just walk away. When we stay connected to our breath as we move through our day, we are in the moment and we are able to fully take in that moment.

What we want is a day full of rich moments. A day where we notice everyone and everything. We can have more peace and gratitude when we understand this and use our breath to enrich our moments.

Being connected to our inner self puts forth a lot of questions we don't always want to answer. What are our strengths and weaknesses? What do we like to do? Where do we want to live? What are our core beliefs? It takes time and patience to uncover the answers. The beauty is that they will change as we live our lives.

To find answers, we need to process our thoughts. In order to process our thoughts we need to find different outlets. Here are just a few:

Time outside with nature. Long walks to think about whatever is on our mind. The best way to process our emotions is to take long walks outside. Good deep breaths at a nice, easy pace can help us process any big decision. Nature is a great friend and will absorb our anger and our fears and help bring clarity to our life. No matter the time of year or time of day, nature is ready and waiting for us to share our deepest thoughts.

Quiet time. This will be new for some, but quiet time is essential. We cannot process life without quiet time. This can be sitting with a cup of tea, meditating, taking quiet walks. This is a time to plug into our heartbeat and breathe. The quiet helps us reset our nervous system. A pause between activities or before we start one will help us be more connected to whatever it is we are doing.

Journaling. Writing heals. Writing a long letter to ourselves is very helpful to process big questions. No one needs to see our journal. We just need to set aside a time every day to write our thoughts and feelings so we can process the changes that are occurring. This is a free-form style of writing. Whatever comes into our mind, we write down. We will surprise ourselves at how intuitive we really are. Freestyle writing will give us insights into ourselves we never knew. This writing helps us find gratitude and peace in our life that was deep within us and is waiting to come out.

Giving back. We will find ways to give to others. It can be to the elderly or children or animals. There will be many opportunities to give our time and our hearts.

Mentoring. This is a wonderful way to help others learn from our experiences, and we always get back more than we give.

Wherever technology takes us, our road will feel better if our moments are more fulfilling. We will have the time, so we must take the time.

We will have wonderful new experiences. To be fully connected to our life. To have patience, to show kindness, to have gratitude. All this comes to the surface when we know ourselves, when we connect to our breath and embrace the moment. Let the technology whiz by us; we will be enjoying the roses. How wonderful it will be.

Conclusion

This book has provided you with a window into the world in which you will soon find yourself. You'll be doing things you've never done before, going places you've never been, traveling in ways you've never experienced. There will be risks, and some of the dangers are unknown. And many of our traditions will be disrupted.

But the potential upside far exceeds any such worries. Billions of people's lives will be vastly improved, and that will most likely include those of you and your loved ones.

Because all this will be new to you, make sure you have a guide who can help you navigate. You can derive tremendous value from a financial planner who understands the future and who can develop projections and offer guidance for the future you're going to live in. I must warn you, though, having spoken on the subject of exponential technologies to thousands of financial planners at conferences across the country over the past six years, that the overwhelming majority of financial planners are not merely untrained about the impact of exponential technologies on financial planning—they are *oblivious* to it. So choose your advisor carefully.

With effective financial planning and an accurate, realistic perspective on the future, I believe the next several decades can be the most fulfilling, rewarding and satisfying time of your entire life, giving you the opportunity to engage in a variety of new pursuits.

And one of those pursuits, perhaps the most important one of all, is the one that our nation established above all else upon our founding in 1776. Profoundly and presciently articulated by Thomas Jefferson in the Declaration of Independence, it states what exponential technologies will ultimately allow us to do, and we'll do it on a grander scale and in greater ways and by more people than we ever could have imagined before. We will each be able to engage in:

the pursuit of happiness.

Further Reading

I recommend the following if you'd like to learn more about exponential technologies:

100 Plus: How the Coming Age of Longevity Will Change Everything, From Careers and Relationships to Family and Faith, by Sonia Arrison.

Abundance: The Future Is Better Than You Think, by Peter Diamandis and Steven Kotler.

The Age of Cryptocurrency: How Bitcoin and the Blockchain Are Challenging the Global Economic Order, by Paul Vigna and Michael Casey.

Bold: How to Go Big, Create Wealth and Impact the World, by Peter Diamandis and Steven Kotler.

College (Un)bound: The Future of Higher Education and What It Means for Students, by Jeffrey Selingo.

The End of College: Creating the Future of Learning and the University of Everywhere, by Kevin Carey.

Exponential Organizations: Why New Organizations Are Ten Times Better, Faster, and Cheaper Than Yours (and What to Do About It), by Salim Ismail.

Future Crimes: Everything Is Connected, Everyone Is Vulnerable and What We Can Do About It, by Marc Goodman.

The Future of Violence: Robots and Germs, Hackers and Drones—Confronting A New Age of Threat, by Benajmin Wittes and Gabriella Blum.

How to Create a Mind: The Secret of Human Thought Revealed, by Ray Kurzweil.

The Infinite Resource: The Power of Ideas on a Finite Planet, by Ramez Naam.

The New Digital Age: Reshaping the Future of People, Nations and Business, by Eric Schmidt and Jared Cohen.

Pardon the Disruption: The Future You Never Saw Coming, by Clayton Rawlings and James Randall Smith.

The Singularity Is Near: When Humans Transcend Biology, by Ray Kurzweil.

Superintelligence: Paths, Dangers, Strategies, by Nick Bostrom.

Figure Sources

P.1   Intel.

P.2   "Supercomputer Timeline," *George Mason University*, mason.gmu.edu.

P.3   *The Hamilton Project*.

P.4   This is a hypothetical illustration meant to demonstrate the principle of compound interest and is not representative of past or future returns of any specific investment vehicle.

P.5   Futuretimeline.net.

P.6   This is a hypothetical illustration meant to demonstrate the principle of compound interest and is not representative of past or future returns of any specific investment vehicle.

P.7   Peter H. Diamandis and Steven Kotler, "Abundance: The Future Is Better Than You Think," *Abundance the Book*, February 21, 2012, abundancethebook.com.

1.1   University of Michigan, Transportation Research Institute, umtri.umich.edu.

1.2   IHS Markit.

1.3   International Telecommunication Union, Google.

1.4   ICT Data and Statistics (IDS) Division, International Telecommunication Union.

1.5   Salim Ismail, "Exponential Organizations: Why new organizations are ten times better, faster, and cheaper than yours (and what to do about it)," *Exponential Organizations*, October 18, 2014, exponentialorgs.com.

3.1   CB Insights, McKinsey & Company, Uber, Business Insider, IHS Global Insight.

3.2   Uber.

4.1   National Science Foundation.

5.1   Google.

5.2   Gartner.

6.1   National Human Genome Research Institute, National Institutes of Health.

9.1   Expedia.

10.1   Bain Capital Ventures, CB Insights.

10.2   PricewaterhouseCoopers.

10.3   Paul Vigna and Michael J. Casey, "The Age of Cryptocurrency: How Bitcoin and the Blockchain Are Challenging the Global Economic Order," *Macmillan Publishers*, January 27, 2015, macmillan.com.

10.4   Peter H. Diamandis and Steven Kotler, "Abundance: The Future Is Better Than You Think," *Abundance the Book*, February 21, 2012, abundancethebook.com.

10.5   Statista.

10.6	*The Economist.*
11.1	Marc Goodman, "Future Crimes," *Future Crimes*, February 24, 2015, futurecrimesbook .com.
12.1	Wall Street Journal Market Data Group.
13.1	"2015 Consumer Expenditure Survey," U.S. Bureau of Labor Statistics.
13.2	This is a hypothetical illustration meant to demonstrate the principle of compound interest and is not representative of past or future returns of any specific investment vehicle.
14.1	University of Oxford.
14.2	University of Oxford.
14.3	Bureau of Labor Statistics, Census Bureau.
14.4	Bureau of Labor Statistics, Census Bureau.
14.5	Bureau of Labor Statistics, Census Bureau.
14.6	"Occupational Employment Statistics," Bureau of Labor Statistics.
14.7	University of Oxford.
17.1	"Certificates of Deposit," Federal Reserve of Economic Data - Economic Research Federal Reserve Bank of St. Louis, Bloomberg 12-Month Deposit Index.
17.2	This is a hypothetical illustration meant to demonstrate the principle of compound interest and is not representative of past or future returns of any specific investment vehicle.
17.3	Ibbotson Associates. Past performance does not guarantee future results.
17.4	Ibbotson Associates. Past performance does not guarantee future results.
17.5	Ibbotson Associates. Past performance does not guarantee future results.
17.6	Ibbotson Associates. Past performance does not guarantee future results.
17.7	Ibbotson Associates. Past performance does not guarantee future results.
17.8	This is a hypothetical illustration meant to demonstrate the principle of compound interest and is not representative of past or future returns of any specific investment vehicle.
17.10	Dimensional Fund Advisors. Past performance is not a guarantee of future results.
17.11	Morningstar. Past performance is not a guarantee of future results.
17.13	Ned Davis Research Group.
17.14	Morningstar. Derived from Morningstar Direct data.
17.15	This is a hypothetical illustration meant to demonstrate the principle of compound interest and is not representative of past or future returns of any specific investment vehicle.
17.16	This is a hypothetical illustration meant to demonstrate the principle of compound interest and is not representative of past or future returns of any specific investment vehicle.
17.17	Morningstar.

17.18   Morningstar.

17.19   Salim Ismail, "Exponential Organizations: Why new organizations are ten times better, faster, and cheaper than yours (and what to do about it)," *Exponential Organizations*, October 18, 2014, exponentialorgs.com. Laura Montini, "Then and Now: How Long It Takes to Get to a $1 Billion Valuation (Infographic)," *Inc.*, October 8, 2014, inc.com.

17.20   *Fortune, Wall Street Journal*

17.21   iShares, Morningstar. Data as of December 31, 2016

17.22   iShares, Morningstar. Data as of December 31, 2016

17.23   iShares, Morningstar. Data as of December 31, 2016

17.24   iShares, Morningstar. Data as of December 31, 2016

17.25   iShares, Morningstar. Data as of December 31, 2016

17.26   iShares, Morningstar. Data as of December 31, 2016

19.1   SherpaReport.

E.1   Age Wave.

E.2   Age Wave.

E.3   Age Wave.

E.4   Age Wave.

E.5   Age Wave.

E.6   Age Wave.

E.7   Age Wave.

E.8   Age Wave.

E.9   Age Wave.

Sources

Prologue: Yogi Berra Was Right

"The Future Is Not What It Used to Be," *Quote Investigator*, December 6, 2012, quoteinvestigator.com.

"Intel Timeline: A History of Innovation," *Intel*, 2016, intel.com.

"Moore's Law: What is Moore's Law," *Investopedia*, 2016, investopedia.com.

"50 Years of Moore's Law: Fueling Innovation We Love and Depend On," *Intel*, 2016, intel.com.

John Markoff, "Smaller, Faster, Cheaper, Over: The Future of Computer Chips," *The New York Times*, September 26, 2015, nytimes.com.

Max Chafkin and Ian King, "How Intel Makes a Chip," *Bloomberg Businessweek*, June 9, 2016, bloomberg.com.

Don Clark, "Nvidia Shows Off Its New Titan X Chip for Gamers," *The Wall Street Journal*, July 22, 2016, wsj.com.

Ed Ram, "How will the 5G network change the world?," *BBC News*, December 1, 2014, bbc.com.

Clayton R. Rawlings, James Randall Smith and Rob Bencini, "Pardon the Disruption: The Future You Never Saw Coming," *Wasteland Press*, November 11, 2013, wastelandpress.net.

Elsa Wenzel, "Scientists create glow-in-the-dark cats," *CNET*, December 12, 2007, cnet.com.

Matt McFarland, "The $75,000 problem for self-driving cars is going away," *The Washington Post*, December 4, 2015, washingtonpost.com.

Mary E. Shacklett, "LiDAR and the Driverless Car," *POB-Point of Beginning*, May 15, 2014, pobonline.com.

Peter H. Diamandis and Steven Kotler, "Abundance: The Future Is Better Than You Think," *Abundance the Book*, February 21, 2012, abundancethebook.com.

Vivek Wadhwa, "It's a beautiful time to be alive and educated," *The Washington Post*, August 25, 2014, washingtonpost.com.

"Digital Birth: Welcome to the Online World," *Business Wire*, October 6, 2010, businesswire.com.

Ray Kurzweil, "The Law of Accelerating Returns," *Kurzweil Accelerating Intelligence*, March 7, 2001, kurzweilai.net.

Ray Kurzweil, "The Singularity Is Near: When Humans Transcend Biology," *Singularity*, September 26, 2006, singularity.com.

Cliff Saran, "Apollo 11: The computers that put man on the moon," *ComputerWeekly.com*, July 17, 2009, computerweekly.com.

"Buy iPad mini 2," *Apple*, apple.com.

"Computing at the speed of light: Team takes big step toward much faster computers," *Phys.org*, May 18, 2015, phys.org.

William Herkewitz, "Meet The Memcomputer: The Brain-Like Alternative to Quantum Computing," *Popular Mechanics*, July 3, 2015, popularmechanics.com.

Fabio Lorenzo Traversa, Chiara Ramella, Fabrizio Bonani and Massimiliano Di Ventra, "Memcomputing NP-complete problems in polynomial time using polynomial resources and collective states," *Science Advances*, July 3, 2015, advances.sciencemag.org.

Massimiliano Di Ventra and Yuriy V. Pershin, "Memcomputers: Faster, More Energy-Efficient Devices That Work Like a Human Brain," *Scientific American*, February 1, 2015, scientificamerican .com.

Will Knight, "Robots Learn to Make Pancakes from WikiHow Articles," *MIT Technology Review*, August 24, 2015, technologyreview.com.

Part One: A Tour of Exponential Technologies

Chapter One: Connecting with Each Other

"Domino's Pizza, Ford Unveil Latest Ordering App Innovation Using SYNC AppLink System," *Ford*, January 7, 2014, media.ford.com.

"More Americans of all ages spurning driver's licenses," *University of Michigan, Transportation Research Institute*, January 20, 2016, umtri.umich.edu.

Amy Chozick, "As Young Lose Interest in Cars, G.M. Turns to MTV for Help," *The New York Times*, March 22, 2012, nytimes.com.

Jacqueline Detwiler, "The Generation That Doesn't Remember Life Before Smartphones," *Popular Mechanics*, November 19, 2015, popularmechanics.com.

Kyle Chayka, "To Absolutely No One's Surprise, Gamers Ordered $1 Million of Pizza on Xbox in Four Months," *Time*, January 9, 2014, time.com.

James B. Stewart, "Facebook Has 50 Minutes of Your Time Each Day. It Wants More," *The New York Times*, May 5, 2016, nytimes.com.

Felix Richter, "Americans Use Electronic Media 11+ Hours A Day," *Statista*, March 13, 2015, statista.com.

Kia Kokalitcheva, "WhatsApp now has 700M users, sending 30B messages per day," *VentureBeat*, January 6, 2015, venturebeat.com.

"YouTube Company Statistics," *Statistic Brain*, July 7, 2016, statisticbrain.com.

Jim Edwards, "Google Is Now Bigger Than Both the Magazine and Newspaper Industries," *Business Insider*, November 12, 2013, businessinsider.com.

"iTunes and Netflix already dwarf » Future of Digital 2014," *BI Intelligence*, December 5, 2014, slideshare.net.

"Future of Digital 2014," *BI Intelligence, LinkedIn Slideshare*/slideshare.net.

Monica Anderson, "Technology Device Ownership: 2015," *Pew Research Center*, October 29, 2015, pewinternet.org.

Dave Chaffey, "Mobile Marketing Statistics compilation," *Smart Insights*, October 26, 2016, smartinsights.com.

"Industry leaders discussed possibilities of more consumer centric mobile marketing campaigns," *MMA—Mobile Marketing Association*, April 19, 2010, mmaglobal.com.

Cheryl Conner, "Fifty Essential Mobile Marketing Facts," *Forbes*, November 12, 2013, forbes.com.

Robin Sidel, "Wallet War: Banks, Stores Slug It Out With Phone-Pay Apps," *The Wall Street Journal*, July 14, 2016, wsj.com.

Gloria Dawson, "At Sweetgreen, a Suitcase Full of Cash Won't Buy You Lunch," *The New York Times*, July 30, 2016, nytimes.com.

"Mobile Shopping Becomes A Larger Piece of the Pie," *PYMNTS.com*, July 26, 2016, pymnts.com.

Alice Hart-Davis, "Welcome to the new wave of wearable technology," *Newsweek*, June 21, 2015, europenewsweek.com.

Ray A. Smith, "Ralph Lauren to Sell Wearable-Tech Shirt Timed for US Open," *The Wall Street Journal*, August 19, 2015, wsj.com.

Dave Smith, "Google: Pill Passwords And Electronic Tattoos in the Works As Motorola Focuses on Innovating Authentication Methods [VIDEO]," *International Business Times*, May 30, 2013, ibtimes.com.

Shane Walker and Roeen Roashan, "Smart Clothing in Wearable Technologies Report—2015," *IHS Markit*, August 25, 2015, technology.ihs.com.

Clinton Nguyen, "Chaos Theory, Tech Tats: Vice Geeks Out Over Chaotic Moon's Coolest Biowearables," *Chaotic Moon*, November 23, 2015, chaoticmoon.com.

"U.S. and World Population Clock," *United States Census Bureau*, 2016, census.gov.

"Gartner Says 6.4 Billion Connected "Things" Will Be in Use in 2016, Up 30 Percent From 2015," *Gartner*, November 10, 2015, gartner.com.

"Internet Users," *Internet Live Stats*, 2016, internetlivestats.com.

"Cisco Visual Networking Index: Global Mobile Data Traffic Forecast Update, 2015–2020 White Paper," *Cisco*, February 1, 2016 cisco.com.

Evgeny Morozov, "Is Smart Making Us Dumb?," *The Wall Street Journal*, February 23, 2013, wsj.com.

Melanie Anzidei, "Running low on milk? Let your fridge tell you," *North Jersey*, January 7, 2016 northjersey.com.

Jane L. Levere, "Smart Luggage for the Connected Age," *The New York Times*, March 9, 2015, nytimes.com.

Maria Konovalenko, "Artificial Intelligence Is the Most Important Technology of the Future," *Institute for Ethics and Emerging Technologies*, July 30, 2013, ieet.org.

"Major Retailers Driving Growth In Mobile Augmented Reality Apps," *ScreenMedia Daily*, September 4, 2012, screenmediadaily.com.

Eli Rosenbergaug, "Concerns Over Rule Banning Sex Offenders From Playing Pokémon Go," *The New York Times*, August 21, 2016, nytimes.com.

SOURCES

Miho Inada, "'Pokémon Go'-Related Car Crash Kills Woman in Japan," *The Wall Street Journal*, August 25, 2016, wsj.com.

Tim Kelly, "Japanese truck driver playing Pokemon Go kills pedestrian," *Reuters*, August 25, 2016 reuters.com.

Nick Wingfield and Mike Isaac, "Pokémon Go Brings Augmented Reality to a Mass Audience," *The New York Times*, July 11, 2016, nytimes.com.

Sarah E. Needleman, "'Pokémon Go' May Leave Rivals Hunting for Gamers' Attention," *The Wall Street Journal*, July 26, 2016, wsj.com.

Paul Fontaine, "Icelandic Tour Bus Company Offers Pokémon Go Hunting Trips," *Reykjavík Grapevine*, July 28, 2016, grapevine.is.

Heather Kelly, "Pokemon Go breaks Apple download records," *CNN*, July 22, 2016, cnn.com.

Polly Mosendz and Luke Kawa, "Pokémon Go Brings Real Money to Random Bars and Pizzerias," *Bloomberg*, July 11, 2016, bloomberg.com.

Shona Ghosh, "How a French furniture brand activated Pokémon Go across 200 stores," *Campaign*, July 26, 2016, campaignlive.co.uk.

Kate Stalter, "Three Investing Secrets I Learned From Pokémon GO," *Forbes*, Jul 28, 2016, forbes .com.

Rebecca Hersher, "Holocaust Museum, Arlington National Cemetery Plead: No Pokémon," *NPR The Two-Way*, July 12, 2016, npr.org.

Elad Benari, "Pokemon craze hits Holocaust memorials," *Arutz Sheva*, July 25, 2016, israelnationalnews.com.

Luke Plunkett, "Sick Of Pokémon Go Disturbances, Local Government Asks Game To Remove Pokestops," *Kotaku*, July 24, 2016, kotaku.com.

Emily Zanotti, "Government Considers First Pokemon Go Regulations," *HeatStreet*, July 14, 2016, heatst.com.

Matthew Levinson, "Sberbank Helps Catch Pokémon and Provide Free Insurance for Pokémon Go Players," *Fintech Collective*, July 19, 2016, news.fintech.io.

Mike DiRocco, "Jaguars host 15,000 Pokemon Go fans at EverBank Field," *ESPN*, July 25, 2016, espn.com.

Nick Statt, "Hillary Clinton is holding a campaign event at a Pokémon Go gym," *The Verge*, July 14, 2016, theverge.com.

Brian Crecente, "Japanese government releases warnings, advice ahead of Pokemon Go arrival," *Polygon*, July 21, 2016, polygon.com.

Amelia Warshaw, "Real Dangers in the Fake Pokemon World," *The Daily Beast*, July 16, 2016, thedailybeast.com.

Rachel Vorona Cote, "Kids Illegally Cross Border Between Canada and U.S. in Pursuit of Pokémon," *Jezebel*, July 24, 2016, jezebel.com.

Ken Moritsugu, "Why the Pokemon-McDonald's deal in Japan could be big," *Japan Today*, July 23, 2016, japantoday.com.

Sadie Levy Gale, "Pokemon Go: Man 'impaled on metal fence' while playing game in Stockholm," *Independent*, July 25, 2016, independent.co.uk.

Samit Sarkar, "Pokémon Go player hits cop car while playing behind the wheel, all caught on camera," *Polygon*, July 19, 2016, polygon.com.

Terri Peters, "Baby Pikachu, is that you? Pokemon Go inspires baby names, BabyCenter reports," *Today*, July 26, 2016, today.com.

Brian Cantor, "The Band Perry Performs Via Hologram on "Jimmy Kimmel Live" (Watch Now)," *Headline Planet*, November 4, 2015, headlineplanet.com.

Daniel Kreps, "Andy Kaufman, Redd Foxx Holograms to Tour," *Rolling Stone*, October 23, 2015, rollingstone.com.

Matt Brian, "New smartphone chip will beam high-definition holograms as early as 2015," *Engadget*, June 3, 2014, engadget.com.

Steven Levingston, "Internet Entrepreneurs Are Upbeat Despite Market's Rough Ride," *The New York Times*, May 24, 2000, nytimes.com.

Chapter Two: Big Data

Bernard Marr, "Big Data: 20 Mind-Boggling Facts Everyone Must Read," *Forbes*, September 30, 2015, forbes.com.

"Email Statistics Report, 2015-2019," *The Radicati Group*, March 2015, radicati.com.

Artyom Dogtiev, "App Usage Statistics: 2015 Roundup," *BusinessofApps*, December 14, 2015, businessofapps.com.

"Twitter Usage Statistics," *Internet Live Stats*, internetlivestats.com.

"Percentage of all global web pages served to mobile phones from 2009 to 2016," *Statista*, 2016, statista.com.

"VNI Mobile Forecast Highlights, 2015-2020," *Cisco*, 2016, cisco.com.

"10th Annual Cisco Visual Networking Index (VNI) Mobile Forecast Projects 70 Percent of Global Population Will Be Mobile Users," *Cisco*, February 3, 2016, newsroom.cisco.com.

Joseph Bradley, Joel Barbier and Doug Handler, "Embracing the Internet of Everything to Capture Your Share of $14.4 Trillion," *Cisco*, 2013, cisco.com.

"Out of the box," *The Economist*, November 21, 2015, economist.com.

"What is big data?," *IBM*, 2016, ibm.com.

Salim Ismail, "Exponential Organizations: Why new organizations are ten times better, faster, and cheaper than yours (and what to do about it)," *Exponential Organizations*, October 18, 2014, exponentialorgs.com.

"The Rapid Growth of Global Data," *CSC*, 2012, csc.com.

"The Digital Universe of Opportunities: Rich Data and the Increasing Value of the Internet of Things," *EMC*, April 2014, emc.com.

"Gearing Up For Data Deluge from World's Biggest Radio Telescope," *ICRAR*, March 6, 2012, icrar.org.

"SKA Project," *Square Kilometre Array*, 2016, skatelescope.org.

"5 reasons why your data center is everywhere," *Cisco*, 2015, cisco.com.

"5 ways all-in-one minis deliver mighty IT solutions," *Cisco*, 2015, cisco.com.

"5 tips to ensure that big data has a big impact on your organization," *Cisco*, 2015, cisco.com.

"5 steps to aligning IT to the needs of your organization," *Cisco*, 2015, cisco.com.

"6 TB Hard Drive," *Amazon*, 2016, amazon.com.

"Samsung Mass Producing Industry's First 512-Gigabyte NVMe SSD in a Single BGA Package for More Flexibility in Computing Device Design," *Samsung Newsroom*, May 31, 2016, news.samsung.com.

Jennifer Langston, "UW team stores digital images in DNA—and retrieves them perfectly," *University of Washington—UW Today*, April 7, 2016, washington.edu.

James Bornholt, Randolph Lopez, Douglas M. Carmean, Luis Ceze, Georg Seelig and Karin Strauss, "A DNA-Based Archival Storage System," *University of Washington*, 2016, homes.cs.washington.edu.

Leo Hickman, "How algorithms rule the world," *The Guardian*, July 1, 2013, theguardian.com.

Yaniv Taigman, Ming Yang, Marc'Aurelio Ranzato, Lior Wolf, "DeepFace: Closing the Gap to Human-Level Performance in Face Verification," *Facebook*, June 24, 2014, research.facebook.com.

Penny Crosman, "Narrative Science Applies AI to Suspicious Activity Reports," *American Banker*, November 12, 2013, americanbanker.com.

"Welcome to the new era of data storytelling," *NarrativeScience*, 2016, narrativescience.com.

Rich McCormick, "AP's 'robot journalists' are writing about Minor League Baseball now," *The Verge*, July 4, 2016, theverge.com.

"Did a Robot Write This? Or a Wall Street Analyst?," *The Wall Street Journal*, July 7, 2015, wsj.com.

Shelley Podolny, "If an Algorithm Wrote This, How Would You Even Know?," *The New York Times*, March 7, 2015, nytimes.com.

"A Report From Singularity: Big Bright Minds," *Filene*, 2012, Filene.org.

John Markoff, "Synthetic DNA Is Seen as Way to Store Data for Centuries," *NewsDiffs*, December 3, 2015, newsdiffs.org.

Marc Goodman, "Future Crimes," *Future Crimes*, February 24, 2015, futurecrimesbook.com.

Matt Wrye, "Jumiya: There's a Direct Link Between Health and Finances," *CUNA—Credit Union National Association*, April 8, 2014, news.cuna.org.

Brian Caulfield, "Big Brains Introduced to Big Problems at Singularity U," *Forbes*, June 19, 2012, forbes.com.

Deena Coffman, "Senate Committee Looks To Regulate Private Data Collection Firms," *IDT911*, December 20, 2013, idt911.com.

Kate Murphy, "Web Photos That Reveal Secrets, Like Where You Live," *The New York Times*, August 11, 2010, nytimes.com.

Caitlin Bronson, "Allstate wants to spy on its auto insurance clients, patent reveals," *Insurance Business*, August 31, 2015, ibamag.com.

Tom Simonite, "Robot Journalist Finds New Work on Wall Street," *MIT Technology Review*, January 9, 2015, technologyreview.com.

"AP expands Minor League Baseball coverage," *AP*, June 30, 2016, ap.org.

Chris Matthews, "Why your car insurance company wants to track your heart rate," *Fortune*, June 19, 2015, fortune.com.

"FTC Recommends Congress Require the Data Broker Industry to Be More Transparent and Give Consumers Greater Control over Their Personal Information," *Federal Trade Commission*, May 27, 2014, ftc.gov.

"Data Brokers: A Call for Transparency and Accountability," *Federal Trade Commission*, May 2014, ftc.gov.

Laurie L. Sullivan, "Global Bioinformatics Efforts to Tame Big Data," *BCC Research*, February 8, 2016, bccresearch.com.

Tina Hesman Saey, "Body's bacteria don't outnumber human cells so much after all," *ScienceNews*, January 8, 2016, sciencenews.org.

"Wireless Medical Devices," *U.S. Food and Drug Administration*, April 7, 2016, fda.gov.

"Software speeds detection of diseases and cancer-treatment targets," *Los Alamos National Laboratory*, December 1, 2014, lanl.gov.

Leo Kelion and James Gallagher, "Google is developing cancer and heart attack detector," *BBC*, October 28, 2014, bbc.com.

Spela Kosir, "Wearables in Healthcare," *Wearable Technologies*, April 15, 2015, wearable-technologies .com.

Aaron Saenz," Smart Toilets: Doctors in Your Bathroom," *SingularityHub*, May 12, 2009, singularityhub.com.

"The best stories come from the heart," *AliveCor*, 2016, alivecor.com.

"Help from above," *The Economist*, July 2, 2016, economist.com.

Seth Berkley, "In Global Shift, Poorer Countries Are Increasingly the Early Tech Adopters," *MIT Technology Review*, May 11, 2016, technologyreview.com.

"MEGA Evolutionary Software Re-Engineered to Handle Today's Big Data Demands," *Oxford University Press*, May 2, 2016, mbe.oxfordJournals.org.

"Apple Introduces ResearchKit, Giving Medical Researchers the Tools to Revolutionize Medical Studies," *Apple*, March 9, 2015, apple.com.

Tracie White, "Stanford launches smartphone app to study heart health," *Stanford Medicine*, March 9, 2015, med.stanford.edu.

Jennie Dusheck, "Genetic research now integrated into MyHeart Counts app," *Stanford Medicine*, March 24, 2016, med.stanford.edu.

Lydia Polgreen, "Scanning 2.4 Billion Eyes, India Tries to Connect Poor to Growth," *The New York Times*, September 1, 2011, nytimes.com.

Basel Kayyali, David Knott, and Steve Van Kuiken, "The big-data revolution in US health care: Accelerating value and innovation," *McKinsey & Company*, April 2013, mckinsey.com.

Tami Deedrick, "It's Technical, Dear Watson," *IBM Systems Magazine*, February 2011, ibmsystemsmag.com.

Betsy Cooper, "Judges in Jeopardy!: Could IBM's Watson Beat Courts at Their Own Game?," *The Yale Law Journal*, August 23, 2011, yalelawjournal.org.

Seth Earley, "Is Watson Technology Practical for Business?," *Baseline*, December 6, 2011, baselinemag.com.

David Gondek, Ph.D., "IBMWatson: What is Watson?" *Predictive Analytics World*, 2011, predictiveanalyticsworld.com.

Toh Kar Inn, "HLB introduces IBM Watson to give fast answers to customers," *The Star Online*, January 12, 2016, thestar.com.

Karen Klinger, "'Jeopardy!' Man vs. Machine Match Draws Crowd at MIT," *CCTV—Cambridge Community Television*, February 15, 2011, cctvcambridge.org.

Lauren F. Friedman, "IBM's Watson Supercomputer May Soon Be the Best Doctor in the World," *Business Insider*, April 22, 2014, businessinsider.com.

Bill Murdock, "How to select a threshold for acting using confidence scores," *IBM Developer Works*, June 23, 2016, developer.ibm.com.

"Watson supercomputer comes to 14 hospitals," *Advisory Board*, May 7, 2015, advisory.com.

"IBM Watson Hard at Work: New Breakthroughs Transform Quality Care for Patients," *IBM*, February 8, 2013, ibm.com.

"WatsonPaths," *IBM*, 2016, research.ibm.com.

Amelia Heathman, "IBM Watson creates the first AI-made film trailer—and it's incredibly creepy," *Wired*, September 2, 2016, wired.co.uk.

Lucas Mearian, "IBM: Watson will eventually fit on a smartphone, diagnose illness," *Computerworld*, March 5, 2013, computerworld.com.

"Big Surge in Social Networking Evidence Says Survey of Nation's Top Divorce Lawyers," *American Academy of Matrimonial Lawyers*, February 10, 2010, aaml.org.

Lindsay Goldwert, "Facebook named in a third of divorce filings in 2011," *NY Daily News*, May 24, 2012, nydailynews.com.

Elizabeth Dwoskin, "Lending Startups Look at Borrowers' Phone Usage to Assess Creditworthiness," *The Wall Street Journal*, November 30, 2015, wsj.com.

Ron Sender, Shai Fuchs and Ron Milo, "Revised estimates for the number of human and bacteria cells in the body," *bioRxiv*, January 6, 2016, biorxiv.org.

"The Internet knows what you did last summer," *Popular Mechanics*, September 16, 2016, popularmechanics.co.za.

"IBM Watson," *IBM*, 2016, ibm.com.

Don Reisinger, "Why Facebook Profiles are Replacing Credit Scores," *Fortune*, December 1, 2015, fortune.com.

Steven Rosenbush and Laura Stevens, "At UPS, the Algorithm Is the Driver," *The Wall Street Journal*, February 16, 2015, wsj.com.

"ICT Facts and Figures 2016," *ITU*, 2016, itu.int.

Chapter Three: Robotics

Chris Boyette, "Robots, drones and heart-detectors: How disaster technology is saving lives," *CNN*, October 5, 2015, cnn.com.

"50 years Industrial Robots," *International Federation of Robotics—IFR*, 2012, ifr.org.

Dylan Love, "10,000 Robots Will Be Fulfilling Your Amazon Orders Before the End of This Year," *International Business Times*, November 20, 2014, ibtimes.com.

Alex Nixon, "Robinson-based TUG maker Aethon builds on health care trend," *TRIB LIVE*, February 3, 2014, triblive.com.

Terence Chea, "Telepresence Robots Help Physicians Make Diagnoses Remotely," *Gastroenterology Group of Naples*, 2016, ggn-gec.com.

Jonathan O'Callaghan, "Ebola-killing ROBOT destroys the virus in minutes: 'Little Moe' uses flashes 25,000 times brighter than sunlight to kill diseases," *Daily Mail*, October 7, 2014, dailymail .co.uk.

Angad Singh, "'Emotional' robot sells out in a minute," *CNN*, June 23, 2015, cnn.com.

"Hilton and IBM Pilot "Connie," The World's First Watson-Enabled Hotel Concierge," *IBM*, March 9, 2016, ibm.com.

"Lowe's Introduces LoweBot—The Next Generation Robot to Enhance the Home Improvement Shopping Experience in the Bay Area," *Lowes*, August 30, 2016, newsroom.lowes.com.

"RQ-4 Global Hawk," *U.S. Air Force*, October 27, 2014, af.mil.

"Detect and diffuse—The top 5 military robots for explosive ordnance disposal," *Army-Technology*, September 15, 2014, army-technology.com.

Aaron Saenz, "2000+ Robots in US Ground Forces in Afghanistan," *SingularityHub*, February 17, 2011, singularityhub.com.

Jonathan Silverstein, "The BEAR: Soldier, Nurse, Friend and Robot," *ABC News*, December 20, 2006, abcnews.go.com.

Sharon Gaudin, "U.S. military may have 10 robots per soldier by 2023," *Computerworld*, November 14, 2013, computerworld.com.

"Volvo: Refuse Truck Driver is Supported by Robot," *Business Wire*, September 16, 2015, businesswire.com.

"Shipboard Autonomous Firefighting Robot (SAFFiR)," *Office of Naval Research Science & Technology*, 2014, onr.navy.mil.

Laura Wagner, "WATCH: Golf Robot Named LDRIC Hits A Hole-In-One," *NPR*, February 5, 2016, npr.org.

Marty Biancuzzo, "The Only Two Robots Humans Should Be Afraid Of," *Wall St. Daily*, February 5, 2014, wallstreetdaily.com.

Georgina Prodhan, "Europe's robots to become 'electronic persons' under draft plan," *Reuters*, June 21, 2016, reuters.com.

Katherine Heires, "Rise of the Robots," *Risk Management*, September 1, 2016, rmmagazine.com.

Laura Hautala, "Hello Barbie: She's just insecure," *CNET*, December 4, 2015, cnet.com.

"Jupiter Forecasts Commercial Sales To Increase By 84% In 2016," *DroneBusiness.center*, January 19, 2016, dronebusiness.center.

Maria Kirby, "New FAA drone regulations mean new business opportunities," *BetaNews*, September 2016, betanews.com.

Pierluigi Paganini, "Why civilian drone use is a risky business," *FOX News*, March 31, 2015, foxnews .com.

"Johanna Zmud Named Head of Transportation, Space, and Technology Program at RAND Corporation," *RAND*, January 5, 2011, rand.org.

"Science, Technology, and Policy," *RAND*, 2016, rand.org.

James M. Anderson, "Autonomous Vehicle Technology: A Guide for Policymakers," *RAND*, 2014, rand.org.

James M. Anderson, Nidhi Kalra, Karlyn D. Stanley, Paul Sorensen, Constantine Samaras, Oluwatobi A. Oluwatola, "Autonomous Vehicle Technology: A Guide for Policymakers," *RAND*, 2014, rand.org.

"Motor Vehicle Crash Injuries," *Centers for Disease Control and Prevention*, October 2014, cdc.gov.

"Traffic Safety Facts: 2014 Crash Data Key Findings," *National Highway Traffic Safety Administration*, November 2015, crashstats.nhtsa.dot.gov.

"10 Leading Causes of Death by Age Group Highlighting Unintentional Injury Deaths, United States – 2014," *Centers for Disease Control and Prevention*, February 25, 2016, cdc.gov.

Sean Smith and Patrick Harris, "Truck Driver Job-Related Injuries in Overdrive," *U.S Department of Labor Blog*, August 17, 2016, blog.dol.gov.

Nidhi Kalra and Susan M. Paddock, "Driving to Safety," *RAND*, April 12, 2016, rand.org.

"National Economic Accounts: Current-Dollar and "Real" Gross Domestic Product," *Bureau of Economic Analysis*, September 29, 2016, bea.gov.

Alyssa Abkowitz, "Do Self-Driving Cars Spell Doom for Auto Insurers?," *Bloomberg*, September 10, 2014, bloomberg.com.

"Historical Tables: Table 4.1—Outlays by Agency: 1962–2021," *The White House*, 2016, whitehouse .gov.

Jen Wieczner, "Study: Self-driving cars crash five times as much as regular ones," *Fortune*, October 29, 2015, fortune.com.

Michele Bertoncello and Dominik Wee, "Ten ways autonomous driving could redefine the automotive world," *McKinsey & Company*, June 2015, mckinsey.com.

Lance Whitney, "Google's self-driving cars tear up 3 million miles a day," *CNET*, February 2, 2016, cnet.com.

David Shepardson and Paul Lienert, "Exclusive: In boost to self-driving cars, U.S. tells Google computers can qualify as drivers," *Reuters*, February 10, 2016, reuters.com.

Chris Ziegler, "Elon Musk says next year's Tesla cars will be able to self-drive 90 percent of the time," *The Verge*, October 2, 2014, theverge.com.

Jay Ramey, "Watch an autonomous Audi RS7 fly around the Hockenheim circuit," *Autoweek*, October 21, 2014, autoweek.com.

Cadie Thompson, "Volvo's first self-driving car has a big edge over the competition—and it's coming sooner than you think," *Business Insider*, May 31, 2016, businessinsider.com.

Michael Liedtke, "The Renault-Nissan Alliance is entering the race to build robotic cars with a plan to introduce 10 different models capable of temporarily relieving humans of their driving duties on highways and city streets," *U.S. News & World Report*, January 7, 2016, usnews.com.

"Investment Into Auto Tech on Pace to Break Annual Records," *CB Insights*, July 14, 2016, cbinsights.com.

David Curry, "Google and Ford may partner on self-driving cars at CES 2016," *Digital Trends*, December 22, 2015, digitaltrends.com.

Brooke Crothers, "Google Is Leader in 'Revolutionary' Self-Driving Cars, Says HIS," *Forbes*, November 12, 2015, forbes.com.

"Analyzing the Auto Tech investment Landscape," *CB Insights*, May 19, 2016, cbinsights.com.

"Startups to Watch," *CB Insights*, June 23, 2016, cbinsights.com.

"Who's Who in the Rise of Autonomous Driving Startups," *CB Insights*, June 9, 2016, cbinsights.com.

"Corporates in Autotech," *CB Insights*, April 18, 2016, cbinsights.com.

"Drones and Disrupting Auto," *CB Insights*, June 16, 2016, cbinsights.com.

"Disrupting the Auto Industry: The Startups That Are Unbundling the Car," *CB Insights*, May 26, 2016, cbinsights.com.

"Mcity Test Facility," *University of Michigan—Mobility Transformation Center*, 2016, mtc.umich.edu.

Drew Douglas, "Self-driving Tesla SUV saves Branson man's life," *KY3*, Aug 06, 2016, ky3.com.

Zack Kanter, "How Uber's Autonomous Cars Will Destroy 10 Million Jobs and Reshape the Economy by 2025," *Zack Kanter*, January 23, 2015, zackkanter.com.

David Z. Morris, "Today's Cars Are Parked 95% of the Time," *Fortune*, March 13, 2016, fortune.com.

"Self-Driving Vehicles Offer Potential Benefits, Policy Challenges for Lawmakers," *RAND*, January 6, 2014, rand.org.

Donald Shoup, "Cruising for Parking," *University of California, Los Angeles*, 2007, shoup.bol.ucla.edu.

Chris Roberts, "San Francisco transit agency says drivers seeking parking account for 30 percent of traffic, but data questioned," *The San Francisco Examiner*, September 17, 2013, sfexaminer.com.

David Gilbert, "World's First Driverless Car Insurance Policy Launched in the UK," *International Business Times*, June 8, 2016, ibtimes.com.

"Prevalence of Self-Reported Aggressive Driving Behavior: United States, 2014," *AAA Foundation for Traffic Safety*, 2014, aaafoundation.org.

SOURCES

Robert Wall, "Flying Cars Try to Take Wing," *The Wall Street Journal*, July 8, 2016, wsj.com.

Mike Stevens, "Terrafugia's flying car to launch in 2021," *CarAdvice*, July 27, 2015, caradvice.com.au.

Jon LeSage, "Flying cars grabbing attention and funding right up there with autonomous vehicles," *Green Auto Market*, June 13, 2016, greenautomarket.com.

"9 Companies Building Flying Cars," *Nanalyze*, June 14, 2016, nanalyze.com.

"Flying Car Makes Successful Maiden Flight," *PAL-V*, February 15, 2014, pal-v.com.

Kristin Tablang, "Park Your Private Jet in Your Own Backyard with This New Aircraft Concept," *Forbes*, June 1, 2016, forbes.com.

Ashlee Vance and Brad Stone, "Welcome to Larry Page's Secret Flying-Car Factories," *Bloomberg Businessweek*, June 9, 2016, bloomberg.com.

Jeanne Marie Laskas, "Helium Dreams," *The New Yorker*, February 29, 2016, newyorker.com.

Robert Wall and Costas Paris, "Pilotless Sailing Is on the Horizon," *The Wall Street Journal*, September 01, 2016, wsj.com.

Robert Wall and Costas Paris, "Ship Operators Explore Autonomous Sailing," *The Wall Street Journal*, August 31, 2016, wsj.com.

"History of Velcro Brand and George De Mestral," *Velcro*, 2016, velcro.com.

"Skycar 400," *Moller International*, 2016, moller.com.

Benjamin Snyder, "North Face Will Start Selling Parkas Made from Fake Spider Silk for $1,000," *Fortune*, May 11, 2016, fortune.com.

"Iowa State engineers develop micro-tentacles so tiny robots can handle delicate objects," *Iowa State University*, June 19, 2015, news.iastate.edu.

Peter Reuell, "A swimsuit like shark skin? Not so fast," *Harvard Gazette*, February 9, 2012, news.harvard.edu.

Abigail Doan, "BIOMIMETIC ARCHITECTURE: Green Building in Zimbabwe Modeled After Termite Mounds," *Inhabitat*, November 29, 2012, inhabitat.com.

Dave Smith, "This insane device promises to give you perfect vision for the rest of your life," *Business Insider*, May 22, 2015, businessinsider.com.

"EBR Systems Receives FDA Approval to Begin U.S. Pivotal Study of Wireless Cardiac Pacing System for Heart Failure," *Business Wire*, September 13, 2016, businesswire.com.

Tanya Lewis, "Prosthetic Hand Restores Touch, Heals Phantom Pain," *Live Science*, October 8, 2014, livescience.com.

Melissa Davey, "'Bionic spine' could enable paralysed patients to walk using subconscious thought," *The Guardian*, February 8, 2016, theguardian.com.

Agata Blaszczak-Boxe, "Lab-Grown Skin Sprouts Hair and Sweats," *Scientific American*, April 4, 2016, scientificamerican.com.

Kelly Hodgkins, "DARPA's ElectRx program seeks to cure ailments with electricity, not drugs," *Digital Trends*, October 7, 2015, digitaltrends.com.

Eliza Strickland, "Exoskeleton Could Quell the Tremors of Parkinson's Disease Patients at Crucial Moments," *IEEE Spectrum*, June 29, 2016, spectrum.ieee.org.

"Amy's Story," *Amy Purdy*, 2016, amypurdy.com.

Marianne Meadahl, "SFU researchers build better bionic hand," *Simon Fraser University*, May 3, 2016, sfu.ca.

Sara Reardon, "Welcome to the Cyborg Olympics," *Nature*, August 3, 2016, nature.com.

"The Future of Sports," *The Future of Sports*, September 2015, futureof.org.

"The Athlete," *The Future of Sports*, 2016, futureof.org.

Tanya Lewis, "World's First Robot-Staffed Hotel to Open in Japan," *Live Science*, February 5, 2015, livescience.com.

"Military Robots Tools And Weapon," *Armyofrobots.com*, 2016, armyofrobots.com.

Jonathan Silverstein, "The BEAR: Soldier, Nurse, Friend and Robot," *ABC News*, December 20, 2006, abcnews.go.com.

"SAFFiR Firefighting Robot," *Virginia Tech*, March 31, 2014, me.vt.edu.

Michael Liedtke, "The Renault-Nissan Alliance is entering the race to build robotic cars with a plan to introduce 10 different models capable of temporarily relieving humans of their driving duties on highways and city streets," *U.S. News*, January 7, 2016, usnews.com.

"Investment into Auto Tech on Pace to Break Annual Records," *CB Insights*, July 14, 2016, cbinsights.com.

"Carplane®—built for reality," *Carplane*, February 2, 2016, carplane.de.

Margaret Rhodes, "The North Face's 'Moon Parka' Is Spun from Faux Spider Silk," *Wired*, December 2, 2015, wired.com.

Cadie Thompson, "The world's largest air purifier is about to travel across China sucking in smog," *Business Insider*, June 30, 2016, businessinsider.com.

Chapter Four: Nanotechnology and Materials Science

"Size of the Nanoscale," *United States National Nanotechnology Initiative*, 2016, nano.gov.

"What is Nanotechnology?," *United States National Nanotechnology Initiative*, 2016, nano.gov.

Sebastian Anthony, "7nm, 5nm, 3nm: The new materials and transistors that will take us to the limits of Moore's law," *Extreme Tech*, July 26, 2013, extremetech.com.

"The new Nature Research solution for Nanotechnology," *A*STAR/Nanowerk*, May 29, 2014, nanowerk.com.

Alexa Liautaud, "Stanford engineers reach breakthrough in nanotechnology advancement," *The Stanford Daily*, October 2, 2013, stanforddaily.com

Nancy S. Giges, "Top 5 Trends in Nanotechnology," *The American Society of Mechanical Engineers*, March 2013, asme.org.

"Silicon dioxide," *BBC*, 2016, bbc.co.uk.

"Nanotechnology in sports equipment: The game changer," *Nanowerk*, May 27, 2013, nanowerk.com.

Wei-xian Zhang, "Nanoscale Iron Particles for Environmental Remediation: An Overview," *Journal of Nanoparticle Research*, August 2003, link.springer.com.

Bhupinder Singh Sekhon, "Nanotechnology in agri-food production: an overview," *US National Library of Medicine, National Institutes of Health*, May 20, 2014, ncbi.nlm.nih.gov.

Mallanagouda Patil, Dhoom Singh Mehta, and Sowjanya Guvva, "Future impact of nanotechnology on medicine and dentistry," *US National Library of Medicine National Institutes of Health*, May–August 2008, ncbi.nlm.nih.gov.

"The Story of Graphene," *Manchester 1824—The University of Manchester*, 2016, graphene.manchester.ac.uk.

Roni Peleg, "Strengthening Solar Cell Performance with Graphene," *Renewable Energy World*, June 15, 2015, renewableenergyworld.com.

David Burgess, "Graphene: the patent landscape in 2015," *Intellectual Property Office* blog, March 25, 2015, gov.uk.

Michael Andronico, "5 Reasons Graphene Will Change Gadgets Forever," *Laptop*, April 14, 2014, laptopmag.com.

Dexter Johnson, "Graphene and Perovskite Lead to Inexpensive and Highly Efficient Solar Cells," *IEEE Spectrum*, September 8, 2015, spectrum.ieee.org.

Jesus de La Fuente, "Graphene Applications & Uses," *Graphenea*, 2016, graphenea.com.

Mike Williams, "Another tiny miracle: Graphene oxide soaks up radioactive waste," *RICE University News & Media*, January 8, 2013, news.rice.edu.

Kristine Wong, "Filtering water with graphene," *Berkeley Engineering*, January 15, 2016, engineering.berkeley.edu.

"IU scientists create 'nano-reactor' for the production of hydrogen biofuel," *Indiana University Bloomington Newsroom*, January 4, 2016, news.indiana.edu.

"High-strength lightweight fabric for inflatable structures US 8663762 B2," *Google*, March 4, 2014, google.com.

Tibi Puiu, "Graphene proves to be fantastic radio waves absorber," *ZME Science*, February 26, 2014, zmescience.com.

Andrew Myers, "Straintronics: Engineers create piezoelectric graphene," *Stanford Engineering*, March 15, 2012, engineering.stanford.edu.

Qin Zhou, Jinglin Zheng, Seita Onishi, M.F. Crommie, and A. Zettl, "Graphene Electrostatic Microphone and Ultrasonic Radio," *University of Nebraska–Lincoln*, 2016, engineering.unl.edu.

Zhong Yan, Guanxiong Liu, Javed M. Khan and Alexander A. Balandin, "Graphene quilts for thermal management of high-power GaN transistors," *Nature Communications*, May 8, 2012, nature.com.

Kelly Lignos Ziv, "Is Graphene the New Steel?," *Fieldlens*, May 5, 2014, fieldlens.com.

Jared Sagoff, "Graphene proves a long-lasting lubricant," *Phys.org*, October 14, 2014, phys.org.

López-Dolado, González-Mayorga, and Gutiérrez, Serrano, "Immunomodulatory and angiogenic responses induced by graphene oxide scaffolds in chronic spinal hemisected rats," *US National Library of Medicine National Institutes of Health*, May 10, 2016, ncbi.nlm.nih.gov.

Michael Berger, "Graphene nanosensor tattoo on teeth monitors bacteria in your mouth," *Nanowerk*, March 29, 2012, nanowerk.com.

Jim Pomager, "Graphene Biosensors—The Next Frontier in Medical Diagnostics?," *Med Device Online*, September 18, 2014, meddeviceonline.com.

"Could elastic bands monitor patients' breathing?," *University of Surrey*, August 15, 2014, surrey.ac.uk.

"PEN Inc. Develops Graphene-Based Product for Use in Medical Imaging," *Yahoo! Finance*, October 28, 2015, finance.yahoo.com.

"Graphene shown to safely interact with neurons in the brain," *University of Cambridge*, 2016, cam.ac.uk.

Michael Tinnesand, "Graphene: The Next Wonder Material?," *ACS—American Chemical Society*, 2016, acs.org.

David Hochman, "An ethical diamond venture that has backing from Leonardo DiCaprio," *CNBC*, June 8, 2016, cnbc.com.

Blaine Friedlander, "Nanotech transforms cotton fibers into modern marvel," *Phys.org*, July 8, 2015, phys.org.

Brad Jones, "New optical chip can switch between states 90 billion times each second," *Digital Trends*, July 27, 2015, digitaltrends.com.

"New research uses nanotechnology to prevent preterm birth," *EurekAlert!*, February 1, 2016, eurekalert.org.

Nanostructure 'Cages' Could Capture Cancer-Fighting Drugs and Deliver Them to Diseased Cells," *HNGN—Headlines & Global News*, September 02, 2013, hngn.com.

Alessandro Pirolini, "Producing Unstainable T-Shirts with the Help of Nanotechnology," *AZoNano*, November 26, 2014, azonano.com.

"Risk of nanotechnology difficult for insurers to assess: Ernst & Young," *Canadian Underwriter*, December 17, 2013, canadianunderwriter.ca.

"Nanotechnology to outer space: ten top tech innovations of 2014," *The Conversation*, December 16, 2014, theconversation.com.

Dexter Johnson, "Graphene and Perovskite Lead to Inexpensive and Highly Efficient Solar Cells," *IEEE Spectrum*, September 8, 2015, spectrum.ieee.org.

Mike Williams, "Graphene composite may keep wings ice-free," *RICE University News & Media*, January 25, 2016, news.rice.edu.

Zhong Yan, Guanxiong Liu, Javed M. Khanx and Alexander A. Balandin, "Graphene-Graphite Quilts for Thermal Management of High-Power GaN Transistors," *Cornell University Library*, March 27, 2012, arxiv.org

"A new way to treat and prevent acne through nanotechnology," *George Washington University Medical Center*, July 15, 2015, nanowerk.com.

"MRI Probe Pairs Magnetic Nanostructure with Antibody for Early Detection of Alzheimer's Disease," *AZoNano*, December 23, 2014, azonano.com.

"Nanotechnology treatment reprograms immune cells to reverse autoimmune disease," *Medical Xpress*, February 17, 2016, medicalxpress.com.

"Nanotechnology Revolutionizes Eye Drops," *University of Reading*, October 6, 2014, cemag.us.

"New nanoparticle reveals cancer treatment effectiveness in real time," *Phys.org*, March 28, 2016, phys.org.

"Terminal Breast Cancer Treatment via Nanotechnology Produces 'Astounding' Results; Vanishes Disease Completely," *Latin Post*, March 15, 2016, latinpost.com.

"Nanoparticle therapy that uses LDL and fish oil kills liver cancer cells," *UT Southwestern Medical Center*, February 8, 2016, utsouthwestern.edu.

Megan Fellman, "First genetic-based tool to detect circulating cancer cells in blood: NanoFlares light up individual cells if breast cancer biomarker is present," *Northwestern Now*, November 17, 2014, news.northwestern.edu.

"Scientists use nanoparticles to fight ovarian cancer (w/video)," *Florida International University*, October 23, 2014, nanowerk.com.

"Son of Ex-Minister Malima in historic medical discovery," *Jamii Forums*, August 11, 2014, jamiiforums.com.

Sharon Gaudin, "MIT uses nanotech to hit cancer with one-two punch," *Computerworld*, May 9, 2014, computerworld.com.

Renu, "Nanotechnology may prevent Cancer from spreading," *Jagran Josh*, January 15, 2014, jagranjosh.com.

"UCLA Nanotechnology Researchers Prove Two-Step Method for Potential Pancreatic Cancer Treatment," *University of California, Los Angeles, Health Sciences*, November 12, 2013, newswise.com.

"Nanotherapy effective in mice with multiple myeloma," *Washington University School of Medicine*, May 21, 2015, nanotech-now.com.

"Nano-scaffolds made for converting stem cells into cells," *Mehr News Agency*, January 25, 2016, en .mehrnews.com.

"Nanotechnology delivery system offers new approach to skin disease therapies," *EurekAlert!*, February 29, 2016, eurekalert.org.

Andy Walker, "Bionic biospleen uses nanotechnology to eradicate bloodborne diseases," *Gearburn*, September 15, 2014, gearburn.com.

Richard Harth, "A nanotechnology fix for nicotine dependence," *The Biodesign Institute*, July 2, 2013, nanowerk.com.

Jasmine Sola, "New nanoscale imaging agent provides better picture of the gut," *University of Wisconsin-Madison*, July 24, 2014, nanowerk.com.

Michelle Starr, "Sony patents contact lens that records what you see," *CNET*, May 2, 2016, cnet.com.

"Nanocomposite sensors detect toxic gases," *Mehr News Agency*, February 14, 2016, en.mehrnews .com.

Darwin Malicdem, "New nanotechnology sends molecules to injury site to 'tell bone to repair itself,'" *International Business Times*, January 15 2016, ibtimes.com.

"Strong teeth: Nanostructures under stress make teeth crack resistant," *Helmholtz Association of German Research Centres*, June 10, 2015, nanotech-now.com.

Brian Mastroianni, "'Spermbots': Scientists design tiny motor to help sperm swim," *CBS News*, January 18, 2016, cbsnews.com.

Liz Ahlberg, "Tiny electronic implants monitor brain injury, then melt away," *University of Illinois at Urbana-Champaign*, January 19, 2016, nanotech-now.com.

"New ceramic firefighting foam becomes stronger when temperature increases," *ITMO University*, December 14, 2015, nanotech-now.com.

"Researchers use nanotech. to repair oil, gas pipelines," *Mehr News Agency*, December 6, 2015, en .mehrnews.com.

"Hygienic Nano Floor Coverings with Application in Production Lines, Therapeutic Centers Head to Market," *Fars News Agency*, November 3, 2015, nanotech-now.com.

Jennifer Chu, "Hydrogel superglue is 90 percent water: New 'water adhesive' is tougher than natural adhesives employed by mussels and barnacles," *MIT News*, November 9, 2015, news.mit.edu.

Sharon Gaudin, "Cornell team building heart-monitoring, bug-fighting smart clothes," *Computerworld*, October 17, 2013, computerworld.com.

Luke Dormehl, "High-tech shirts change their pattern and color in response to pollution or radiation," *Digital Trends*, July 29, 2016, digitaltrends.com.

"Silver Replaced with Copper Nanoparticles to Produce Antibacterial Fabrics," *Fars News Agency*, August 25, 2014, nanotech-now.com.

"Scientists Invent New Nanotech Smartphone Jeans," *PRWeb*, April 16, 2014, prweb.com.

Andrea Alfano, "Nanotechnology Makes It Possible to Print Extremely Bright Colors Without Using Ink," *Tech Times*, June 12, 2015, techtimes.com.

"Nano memory cell can mimic the brain's long-term memory," *RMIT University*, May 14, 2015, nanotech-now.com.

"Total recall: Missing memories have been restored in mice with Alzheimer's disease," *The Economist*, March 19, 2016, economist.com.

"Adept Armor Unveils Nanotechnology-Based Fabric Guard and Glass Guard," *AZoNano*, January 31, 2014, azonano.com.

"Smart keyboard cleans and powers itself—and can tell who you are," *American Chemical Society*, January 21, 2015, acs.org.

David Szondy, "Tiny gel tags indicate when packages food has spoiled," *New Atlas*, March 19, 2014, newatlas.com.

Grant Banks, "Magnetic nanosponges more effective at soaking up spills," *New Atlas*, January 20, 2014, newatlas.com.

"New Nanotechnology Tool Detects Avian Flu Virus on Farms," *The Poultry Site*, April 13, 2015, thepoultrysite.com.

"Smartphone battery fully charges in thirty seconds," *StoreDot Ltd*, April 17, 2014, energyharvestingjournal.com.

Iqbal Pittalwala, "Chemists use nanotechnology to fabricate novel rewritable paper," *University of California, Riverside*, Dec 2, 2014, nanowerk.com.

Billy Hallowell, "'Virtually Indestructible' Bible Built With 'Space Age Nanotechnology' Might Last You a Lifetime: It 'Literally Walks on Water,' *The Blaze*, August 4, 2014, theblaze.com.

"Nanotechnology researcher develop fire resistant paper coated with nanowires," *Chinese Academy of Sciences*, January 16, 2014, nanowerk.com.

"Patent awarded for genetics-based nanotechnology against mosquitoes, insect pests," *Kansas State University*, November 12. 2014, nanowerk.com.

"New solar power nanotechnology material converts 90 percent of captured light into heat," *University of California, San Diego*, October 29, 2014, nanowerk.com.

"Physicists build reversible laser tractor beam," *Australian National University*, October 20, 2014, nanowerk.com.

A'ndrea Elyse Messer "Tailored flexible illusion coatings hide objects from detection," *Penn State*, October 13, 2014, nanowerk.com.

Mary-Ann Russon, "Nanotech 'Nose' Sniffs Out Bombs From Five Metres Away," *International Business Times*, July 1, 2014, ibtimes.co.uk.

"Nanotechnology coating signals when equipment is too hot to handle," *New Jersey Institute of Technology*, July 4, 2014, nanowerk.com.

Karen M. Koenig, "Singing Paint and Other Attention-Grabbing Marketing," *Woodworking Network*, April 1, 2014, woodworkingnetwork.com.

"Using nanotechnology to protect grain exports," *University of Adelaide*, February 5, 2014, nanowerk .com.

Catherine Townsend, "CSI Canal Street: How scientists are using nanotechnology to crack down on fake designer bags, *Daily Mail*, December 24, 2013, dailymail.co.uk.

"Holtec Completes Nuclear Fuel Storage Basket That Use Nanotechnology," *Holtec*, November 29, 2013, nuclearstreet.com.

"Nanomechanical sensor detects levels of antibiotics in blood," *University College London*, March 2, 2014, nanowerk.com.

Michael B. Farrell, "Blood tests in minutes, not days or weeks," *Boston Globe*, September 30, 2013, bostonglobe.com.

Daniel Rapcencu, "Nanotechnology Comes to High Tech Building Environments [video]," *Device Magazine*, August 5, 2013, devicemag.com.

"Baldness Remedies Could Get Boost from New 3D Hair Follicle Model," *Genetic Engineering & Biotechnology News*, July 19, 2013, genengnews.com.

"Nanotechnology approach could lead to 'artificial skin' that senses touch, humidity and temperature," *American Technion Society*, July 8, 2013, nanowerk.com.

"Nanotechnology researchers use graphene to develop ultra-strong nanocomposite," *KAIST*, August 26, 2013, nanowerk.com.

Caroline Winter, "Material Progress: Five Substances of the Future," *Bloomberg*, June 9, 2016, bloomberg.com.

Chapter Five: 3D Printing

Bob Tita, "How 3-D Printing Works," *The Wall Street Journal*, June 11, 2013, wsj.com.

"How does 3D printing work?," *3DPrinting.com*, 2016, 3dprinting.com.

Scott J. Grunewald, "The Rolls-Royce Phantom Now Has More Than 10,000 3D Printed Parts, BMW Looks to Expand Use Across Entire Line of Cars," *3DPrint.com*, July 15, 2016, 3dprint.com.

George Putic, "Metal 3-D Printers May Revolutionize Industry," *VOA*, June 5, 2015, voanews.com.

Bulent Yusuf, "20 Best Cheap 3D Printers Under $500/$1000 in Fall 2016," *All3DP*, November 2, 2016, all3dp.com.

"Aviation," *3DPrinting.com*, 2016, 3dprinting.com.

Martin LaMonica, "Harvard Spin-off Voxel8 Takes 3D Printing Into Electronics," *Xconomy*, January 5, 2015, xconomy.com.

"First FDA-Approved Medicine Manufactured Using 3D Printing Technology Now Available," *Aprecia Pharmaceuticals*, March 22, 2016, aprecia.com.

TJ McCue, "3D Bioprinting BioBots Wants Piece of $50 Billion Pharmaceutical Industry Research Spend," *Forbes*, March 11, 2015, forbes.com.

Jay Cassano, "Matching People Who Have 3-D Printers with Children Who Need Prosthetic Hands," *Fast Company & Inc.*, February 2, 2015, fastcoexist.com.

Bob Yirka, "Tiny Robotic Swimmers Could Travel Through Bloodstream to Deliver Drugs," *Robotics Trends*, November 6, 2014, roboticstrends.com.

"Micro-camera can be injected with a syringe," *Phys.org*, June 27, 2016, phys.org.

"At Nike the Future is Faster, and it's 3D," *Nike News*, May 17, 2016, news.nike.com.

J. Rafael Tena, Moshe Mahler, Thabo Beeler, Max Grosse, Hengchin Yeh and Iain Matthews, "Fabricating 3D Figurines with Personalised Faces," *Disney Research*, November–December 2013, disneyresearch.com.

"Forecast: 3D Printers, Worldwide, 2015," *Gartner*, September 17, 2015, gartner.com.

Clare Scott, "3D Printing is So Last Week . . . Say Hello to '5D Printing' at Mitsubishi Electric Research Labs!," *3DPrint.com*, June 24, 2016, 3dprint.com.

"What is 3D printing?," *3DPrinting.com*, 2016, 3dprinting.com.

Scott J. Grunewald, "The Rolls-Royce Phantom Now Has More Than 10,000 3D Printed Parts, BMW Looks to Expand Use Across Entire Line of Cars," *3DPrint.com*, July 15, 2016, 3dprint.com.

"3D printing scales up," *The Economist*, September 7, 2013, economist.com.

Megan Gannon, "How 3D Printers Could Reinvent NASA Space Food," *Space.com*, May 24, 2013, space.com.

Priyanka Dayal McCluskey, "3-D printer helps doctors prep for complex surgeries," *Boston Globe*, January 18, 2015, bostonglobe.com.

Rob Stein, "Doctors Use 3-D Printing to Help a Baby Breathe," *NPR*, March 17, 2014, npr.org.

Mary-Ann Russon, "Beijing Doctors Implant World's First 3D-Printed Vertebra into 12-Year-Old Boy," *International Business Times*, August 19, 2014, ibtimes.co.uk.

"Cancer patient receives 3D printed ribs in world first surgery," *CSIRO*, September 11, 2015, csiro.au.

Steve Henn and Cindy Carpien, "3-D Printer Brings Dexterity to Children with No Fingers," *WBUR News*, June 18, 2013, wbur.org.

TJ McCue, "3D Bioprinting BioBots Wants Piece of $50 Billion Pharmaceutical Industry Research Spend," *Forbes*, March 11, 2015, forbes.com.

Tanya Lewis, "3D-Printed Material Mimics Biological Tissue," *Live Science*, April 4, 2013, livescience.com.

Bridget Butler Millsaps, "3D Printing to Make Impact in the Insurance Industry: Trials in the UK Offer Replacement of Bespoke Items," *3DPrint.com*, April 14, 2016, 3dprint.com.

Louis Columbus, "2015 Roundup of 3D Printing Market Forecasts and Estimates," *Forbes*, March 31, 2015, forbes.com.

Donna Taylor, "Move over 3D printing, self-assemblng [sic] 4D-printed materials are on the way," *New Atlas*, June 3, 2013, newatlas.com.

Randy Rieland, "Forget the 3D Printer: 4D Printing Could Change Everything," *Smithsonian.com*, May 16, 2014, smithsonianmag.com.

Tom DiChristopher, "From teeth aligners to engine parts, 3-D printing business grows," *CBNC*, August 17, 2013, cnbc.com.

Chapter Six: Medicine and Neuroscience

James Klatell, "Meet The 95-Year-Old Graduate," *CBS News*, May 11, 2007, cbsnews.com.

"Ruth Flowers aka 'Mamy Rock' dies at 82," *Thirst4Beats*, May 30, 2014, thirst4beats.com.

"Oldest tandem parachute jump (male)," *Guinness World Records*, Junes 27, 2014, guinnessworldrecords.com.

Erik Horne, "VIDEO: Johanna Quaas, 89, the world's oldest active gymnast, to be honored in Oklahoma City," *NewsOK*, May 14, 2015, newsok.com.

Neil Amdur, "Former Longtime Coach Accuses Hunter College of Age Discrimination," *The New York Times*, September 3, 2015, nytimes.com.

Karen Crouse, "100 Years Old. 5 World Records," *The New York Times*, September 21, 2015, nytimes .com.

"America's Got Talent 87-Year-Old Singer Charms Socks Off Nick Cannon," *2Paragraphs*, June 2, 2015, 2paragraphs.com.

Dan Fitzpatrick, "Rising U.S. Life Spans Spell Likely Pain for Pension Funds," *The Wall Street Journal*, October 27, 2014, wsj.com.

Elizabeth Arias, Ph.D., "National Vital Statistics Reports, Volume 54, Number 14—United States Life Tables, 2003," *Centers for Disease Control and Prevention*, March 28, 2007, cdc.gov.

"Global Health and Aging," *National Institute on Aging, National Institutes of Health, and World Health Organization*, October 2011, who.int.

"A Reimagined Research Strategy for Aging," *SENS Research Foundation*, 2016, sens.org.

"Cover Trail: The Forever Pill," *Bloomberg Businessweek*, February 12, 2015, bloomberg.com.

Bill Gifford, "Does a Real Anti-Aging Pill Already Exist?," *Bloomberg Businessweek*, February 12, 2015, bloomberg.com.

Max Roser, "Life Expectancy," *Our World In Data*, 2016, ourworldindata.org.

"Global Health and Aging—Living Longer," *National Institute on Aging*, 2016, nia.nih.gov.

"This Baby Could Live to Be 142 Years Old, *Time*, February 23, 2015, backissues.time.com.

"The Human Genome Project Completion: Frequently Asked Questions," *National Human Genome Research Institute (NHGRI)*, October 30, 2010, genome.gov.

"We sequence your whole genome to help you improve your health, longevity, and much more. Order now for $999," *Veritas Genetics*, 2016, veritasgenetics.com.

"A 26-hour system of highly sensitive whole genome sequencing for emergency management of genetic diseases," *Genome Medicine*, September 30, 2015, genomemedicine.biomedcentral.com.

"Genetic testing in minutes with gold nanoprobes," *NanoWerk*, May 29, 2014, nanowerk.com.

Mark Johnson and Kathleen Gallagher, "Sifting through the DNA haystack," *The Milwaukee Journal Sentinel*, December 21, 2010, archive.jsonline.com.

Mark Johnson and Kathleen Gallagher, "Gene insights lead to a risky treatment," *The Milwaukee Journal Sentinel*, December 25, 2010, archive.jsonline.com.

"Prof. Sia Develops Innovative Lab-on-a-Chip," *Columbia University Engineering*, July 31, 2011, engineering.columbia.edu.

"Jack Andraka Reflects on His Work in Cancer," *American Society of Clinical Oncology (ASCO)*, May 26, 2016, am.asco.org.

Brooke Borel, "The high schooler who invented a test for pancreatic cancer: A Q&A with 'teenage optimist' Jack Andraka," *TED Blog*, July 11, 2013, blog.ted.com

John Travis, "Making the cut," *American Association for the Advancement of Science (AAAS)*, December 18, 2015, science.sciencemag.org.

"10 Breakthrough Technologies 2014," *MIT Technology Review*, technologyreview.com.

Tom Simonite, "10 Breakthrough Technologies of 2015: Where Are They Now?," *MIT Technology Review*, December 26, 2015, technologyreview.com.

"10 Breakthrough Technologies 2016," *MIT Technology Review*, technologyreview.com.

Declan Butler, "Brazil asks whether Zika acts alone to cause birth defects," *Nature*, July 25, 2016, nature.com.

"First trial of CRISPR in people: Chinese team approved to test gene-edited cells in people with lung cancer," *Nature*, July 28, 2016, nature.com

Alison Abbott, "Major funder tracks impact," *Nature*, July 28, 2016, nature.com.

Angela She, "CRISPR in Neuroscience: How Precision Gene Editing May Unravel How the Brain Works (and Why It Sometimes Doesn't)," *Harvard University*, April 6, 2016, sitn.hms.harvard.edu.

Anne Trafton, "New approach to boosting biofuel production," *MIT News*, October 2, 2014, news.mit.edu.

Tim Folger, "The Next Green Revolution," *National Geographic Magazine*, 2016, nationalgeographic
.com.

"FDA concludes Arctic Apples and Innate Potatoes are safe for consumption," *U.S. Food and Drug
Administration*, March 20, 2015, fda.gov.

"Recent Trends in GE Adoption," *United States Department of Agriculture—Economic Research Service
(USDA ERS)*, November 3, 2016, ers.usda.gov.

Ariel Schwartz, "The $325,000 Lab-Grown Hamburger Now Costs Less Than $12," *Fast Company
& Inc.,* April 1, 2015, fastcoexist.com.

Adele Peters, "These Makers Are Building the Products Disaster Areas Need—in the Place Where
They're Needed," *Fast Company & Inc.,* August 29, 2016, fastcoexist.com.

David Pimentel and Marcia Pimentel, "Sustainability of meat-based and plant-based diets and the
environment 1,2,3," *The American Journal of Clinical Nutrition*, 2003, ajcn.nutrition.org.

Stacey Rosen, Karen Thome, and Birgit Meade, "Food Security of Developing Countries Expected to
Improve Through 2026 as Food Prices Fall and Incomes Rise," *United States Department of
Agriculture—Economic Research Services (USDA—ERS)*, June 30, 2016, ers.usda.gov.

Alexandra Ossola, "Genetically Modified Mosquitos Massively Reduce Dengue Fever Risk," *Popular
Science*, July 6, 2015, popsci.com.

Jennifer Kay, "Millions of genetically modified mosquitoes could be released in Florida Keys," *Sun
Sentinel*, January 25, 2015, sun-sentinel.com.

"2015 Plastic Surgery Statistics Report: Cosmetic Plastic Surgery Statistics," *American Society of
Plastic Surgeons*, 2015, plasticsurgery.org.

Daniel S. Hamermesh, "Beauty Pays: Why Attractive People Are More Successful," *Princeton
University Press*, April 21, 2013, press.princeton.edu.

Sumathi Reddy, "Fertility Clinics Let You Select Your Baby's Sex," *The Wall Street Journal*, August 17,
2015, wsj.com.

Elizabeth Arias, Ph.D., "United States Life Tables, 2003," *National Vital Statistics Reports*, March 28,
2007, cdc.gov.

Alice Park, "A New Technique That Lets Scientists Edit DNA Is Transforming Science—and
Raising Difficult Questions," *Time*, June 23, 2016, time.com.

"Jack Andraka Reflects on His Work in Cancer," *ASCO*, May 26, 2016, am.asco.org.

John Travis, "Making the cut: CRISPR genome-editing technology shows its power," *Science*,
December 24, 2015, science.sciencemag.org.

David Cyranoski, "Chinese scientists to pioneer first human CRISPR trial," *Nature*, July 21, 2016,
nature.com.

Shirley S. Wang, "Scientists Cook Up Lab-Grown Beef," *The Wall Street Journal*, August 5, 2013, wsj
.com.

"The Hottest Tech in Silicon Valley Made This Meatball," *Fortune*, May 1, 2016, fortune.com.

"Biotechnology allows growing very low nicotine tobacco," *Farm Journal's AGPRO*, January 26, 2016,
agprofessional.com.

Chapter Seven: Energy and Environmental Systems

"Smog Free Project," *Studio Roosegaarde*, 2016, studioroosegaarde.net.

Elisabeth Braw, "World's first smog filtering tower goes on tour," *The Guardian*, September 19, 2015, theguardian.com.

John Cairns, "NIMBY, BANANA, CAVE and other acronyms," *News-Optimist*, October 3, 2012, newsoptimist.ca.

Robert Walton, "Washington Post: Utility industry is 'waging a campaign' against rooftop solar," *Utility Dive*, March 10, 2015, utilitydive.com.

Luke Edwards, "Future batteries, coming soon: charge in seconds, last months and power over the air," *Pocket-lint*, May 24, 2016, pocket-lint.com.

David L. Chandler, "An 'Almost Perfect' Battery," *MIT Technology Review*, October 20, 2015, technologyreview.com.

Andy Boxall, "Graphene batteries may slash your phone recharge time to 15 minutes," *Digital Trends*, July 11, 2016, digitaltrends.com.

Mike Williams, "Carbon's new champion," *RICE University News & Media*, October 9, 2013, news.rice.edu.

Louise Donovan, "Your computer is about to achieve transcendence," *Lifeboat Foundation*, April 28, 2014, lifeboat.com.

Grégoire Molle, "How Blockchain Helps Brooklyn Dwellers Use Neighbors' Solar Energy," *NPR*, July 4, 2016, npr.org.

Samuel Taylor Coleridge, "The Rime of the Ancient Mariner (text of 1834)," *Poetry Foundation*, poetryfoundation.org.

"United Nations Global Issues: Water," *United Nations*, 2016, un.org.

"Global Diarrhea Burden," *Centers for Disease Control and Prevention*, 2016, cdc.gov.

"Facts About Children, Women & The Safe Water Crisis," *Water.org*, 2016, water.org.

Céline Nauges and Jon Strand, "Water Hauling and Girls' School Attendance: Some New Evidence from Ghana," *Springer Link*, Jul 9, 2015, link.springer.com.

"Facts about Water: Statistics of the Water Crisis," *The Water Project*, August 31, 2016, thewaterproject.org.

"Indoor air quality guidelines: household fuel combustion," *World Health Organization*, 2016, who.int.

"Household air pollution and health," *World Health Organization*, February 2016, who.int.

Eleanor Chute, "For clean water, take a page from Carnegie Mellon researcher's book," *Pittsburgh Post-Gazette*, August 22, 2015, post-gazette.com.

"Reinvent the Toilet Challenge," *Bill & Melinda Gates Foundation*, 2016, gatesfoundation.org.

Ariel Schwartz, "Take a Seat on This Gates-Funded Future Toilet That Will Change How We Think About Poop," *Fast Company & Inc.*, February 20, 2014, fastcoexist.com.

"Facts and trends. Water. Version 2," *The World Business Council for Sustainable Development*, 2009, sswm.info.

Marissa Brassfield, "USDA: Global Food Insecurity Will Drop in Next Decade," *Abundance Insider*, July 15, 2016, diamandis.com.

"USDA predicts global food insecurity will drop to 6% of world population from 17% today," *Next Big Future*, July 7, 2016, nextbigfuture.com.

Lucy Wang, "World's largest smog-sucking vacuum cleaner could rid cities of pollution," *Inhabitat*, January 16, 2016, inhabitat.com.

Pallava Bagla, "Scientists Make Sea Water Drinkable, Produce 6.3 Million Litres a Day," *NDTV*, May 6, 2016, ndtv.com.

Natalie Myhalnytska, "Norwegian Startup Created Solution That Turns Desert Soil into Fertile Soil," *Magazine MN*, Mar 21, 2016.

Lulu Chang, "Wind turbines now produce enough power to energize 19 million U.S. homes," *Digital Trends*, December 29, 2015, digitaltrends.com.

"About TAHMO," *TAHMO*, 2016, tahmo.org.

Hal Hodson, "Sensors to give early storm warnings to people near deadly lake," *New Scientist*, December 15, 2015, newscientist.com.

Doug Woodring and Steve Russell, "How Plastics-to-Fuel Can Become the Next Green Machine (Op-Ed)," *LiveScience*, September 21, 2015, livescience.com.

Leanna Garfield, "The world's largest vertical farm will produce 2 million pounds of lettuce every year," *Business Insider*, April 7, 2016, businessinsider.com.

"Sorek Desalination Plant, Israel," *Water Technology*, 2016, water-technology.net.

David Talbot, "The world's largest and cheapest reverse-osmosis desalination plant is up and running in Israel," *MIT Technology Review*, 2015, technologyreview.com.

"Irrigation & Water Use: Overview," *United States Department of Agriculture Economic Research Service*, 2016, ers.usda.gov.

"U.S. could feed 800 million people with grain that livestock eat, Cornell ecologist advises animal scientists," *Cornell University—Cornell Chronicle*, August 7, 1997, news.cornell.edu.

John Pohly, "How Much Water???," *Colorado State University*, 2016, colostate.edu.

Cynthia Nickerson and Allison Borchers, "How Is Land in the United States Used? A Focus on Agricultural Land," *United States Department of Agriculture Economic Research Service*, March 1, 2012, ers.usda.gov.

"Major Land Uses," *United States Department of Agriculture Economic Research Service*, October 11, 2016, ers.usda.gov.

"Our complete line of Aeroponic Systems," *Aeroponics.com*, 2016, aeroponics.com.

Sarah DeWeerdt, "Can Cities FeedUs?," *University of Washington*, August 27, 2010, conservationmagazine.org.

"Revolutionary ultrasonic nozzle that will change the way water cleans," *University of Southampton*, November 10, 2011, southampton.ac.uk.

"Newark steel mill becoming world's largest vertical farm," *myCentralJersey.com*, August 19, 2016, mycentraljersey.com.

"Trends in Higher Education: Tuition and Fees and Room and Board over Time, 1976-77 to 2016–17, Selected Years," *CollegeBoard*, 2016, trends.collegeboard.org.

"$100 in 1980 → $287.64 in 2015," *The Bureau of Labor Statistics*, 2016, in2013dollars.com.

James B. Steele and Lance Williams, "Who got rich off the student debt crisis," *Reveal*, June 28, 2016, revealnews.org.

Julia Glum, "Student Debt Crisis 2016: New Graduates Owe a Record-Breaking Average $37,000 In Loans," *International Business*, May 6, 2016, ibtimes.com.

Dave Rathmanner, "2016 College Students and Personal Finance Study," *LendEDU*, May 26, 2016, lendedu.com.

"More Than Eighty Percent of Americans with Student Loans Make Sacrifices to Meet Monthly Payment," *American Institute of CPAs*, May 12, 2016, aicpa.org.

Emil Venere, "New environmental cleanup technology rids oil from water," *Purdue University*, April 4, 2016, purdue.edu.

"Solution Found—Technology Available to Clean Up EPA Contamination Disaster of the Animas River in Colorado," *PR Newswire*, August 13, 2015, prnewswire.com.

Pam Frost Gorder, "Scientists develop mesh that captures oil—but lets water through," *The Ohio State University*, April 15, 2015, news.osu.edu.

Sean Yeaton, "Robotic sailboats built to clean up oil spills," *CNN*, October 20, 2011, cnn.com.

Darren Quick, "MIT researchers devise technique to clean up oil spills using magnets," *New Atlas*, September 13, 2012, newatlas.com.

"Milkweed guzzles litres of oil," *Science Illustrated*, June 1, 2016, pressreader.com.

Troy Turner, "Sea Cleaning Drones," *Yanko Design*, May 21, 2012, yankodesign.com.

Carol Rasmussen, "NASA/Forest Service Maps Aid Fire Recovery," *NASA Jet Propulsion Laboratory, California Institute of Technology*, April 9, 2015, jpl.nasa.gov.

"The New Generation Fire Shelter," *National Wildfire Coordinating Group*, March 2003, nwcg.gov.

Leslie Reed, "Aerial 'fire drone' passes Homestead test," *University of Nebraska–Lincoln*, April 22, 2016, news.unl.edu.

Jason Reagan, "Korean Firefighting Drone Takes the Heat," *DroneLife.com*, January 27, 2016, dronelife.com.

Mark Prigg, "Could 'hover homes' protect California from the big one? Firm reveals plans to raise houses on giant magnets in event of quake," *Daily Mail*, June 10, 2015, dailymail.co.uk.

Janet Lathrop, "New Radar System Helped Dallas Area in Christmas Tornado Outbreak," *University of Massachusetts at Amherst*, January 25, 2016, umass.edu.

Avery Thompson, "India Is Building a $60 Million Monsoon-Predicting Supercomputer," *Popular Mechanics*, June 12, 2016, popularmechanics.com.

Narendra Shrestha, "Our new anti-earthquake technology could protect cities from destruction," *The Conversation*, July 2, 2015, theconversation.com.

Joni Blecher, "A Photovoltaic Balloon Could Bring Electricity to Disaster Zones," *Smithsonian.com*, December 19, 2014, smithsonianmag.com.

James Maynard, "Flirtey Drone Delivers Drugs from Ship to Shore," *Tech Times*, June 24, 2016, techtimes.com.

"Military Portable Aluminium Roadways, Temporary Runways and Helipads," *army-technology.com*, 2016, army-technology.com.

Chapter Eight: Innovations in Education

Andrew Woo, "Is Student Debt Stopping Millennials from Homeownership?," *Apartment List*, May 19, 2016, apartmentlist.com.

"Trends in Higher Education: Types of Loans," *CollegeBoard*, 2016, trends.collegeboard.org.

Dave Rathmanner, "January 2016 Student Loan Borrower Survey," *LendEDU*, January 22, 2016, lendedu.com.

Josh Mitchell, "School-Loan Reckoning: 7 Million Are in Default," *The Wall Street Journal*, August 21, 2015, wsj.com.

Josh Mitchell, "155,000 Americans Had Social Security Benefits Cut in 2013 Because of Student Debt," *The Wall Street Journal*, September 10, 2014, wsj.com.

"Parents Save for Kids' College Despite Carrying Student Debt," *College Savings Foundation*, 2015, collegesavingsfoundation.org.

"High School Students and Their Parents Save for a Broad Range of Higher Education Paths," *College Savings Foundation*, September 20, 2016, collegesavingsfoundation.org.

"Consumer Reports Partners with Reveal to Investigate the Nation's $1.3 Trillion Student Debt Crisis—What Caused It and What People Can Do About It," *Consumer Reports*, June 28, 2016, consumerreports.org.

Drew, "18 Insane Things Graduates Would Do to Get Rid of Their Student Loan Debt," *Student Loan Report*, June 21, 2016, studentloans.net.

A Stronger Nation 2016, *Lumina Foundation*, 2016, luminafoundation.org.

"Status Dropout Rates," Institute of Education Sciences, *National Center for Education Statistics*, May 2016, nces.ed.gov.

Donna Rosato, "Having the College Money Talk: 10 key questions every family should discuss," *Consumer Reports*, June 28, 2016, consumerreports.org.

Victoria Simons and Anna Helhoski, "2 Extra Years in College Could Cost You Nearly $300,000," *NerdWallet*, June 21, 2016, nerdwallet.com.

"Review nationwide student transfer behavior," *The Successful Registrar*, 2012, studentclearinghouse .org.

Yuritzy Ramos, "College students tend to change majors when they find the one they really love," *Borderzine*, March 15, 2013, borderzine.com.

Jeffrey J. Selingo, "College (Un)bound: The Future of Higher Education and What It Means for Students," *Jeff Selingo*, April 28, 2015, jeffselingo.com.

Nick Anderson and Danielle Douglas-Gabriel, "Nation's prominent public universities are shifting to out-of-state students," *The Washington Post*, January 30, 2016, washingtonpost.com.

"Traditional residence hall, Elkin, closed for 2015–16," *The Penn*, August 24, 2015, thepenn.org.

"Drexel to Open Newest Market Street Landmark a Recreation Center Complex," *Drexel Now*, February 5, 2010, drexel.edu.

Lawrence Biemiller, "Campus Architecture Database: University Center," *The Chronicle of Higher Education*, June 16, 2010, chronicle.com.

Georgia Tech Athletic Association, Financial Statements, *Georgia Tech Athletic Association*, June 30, 2015 and 2014, fin-services.gatech.edu.

Jaison R. Abel, Richard Deitz, and Yaqin Su, "Are Recent College Graduates Finding Good Jobs?," *Federal Reserve Bank of New York*, 2014, newyorkfed.org.

Jeffrey J. Selingo, "College Isn't Always the Answer," *The Wall Street Journal*, May 26, 2016, wsj.com.

Jaison R. Abel and Richard Deitz, "Do the Benefits of College Still Outweigh the Costs?," *Federal Reserve Bank of New York*, 2014, newyorkfed.org.

Douglas Belkin, "Big Perks for College Presidents," *The Wall Street Journal*, June 16, 2016, wsj.com.

Mary Beth Marklein, "College major analysis: Engineers get highest salaries," *USA TODAY*, May 24, 2011, usatoday.com.

Richard Arum and Josipa Roksa, "Academically Adrift: Limited Learning on College Campuses," *University of Chicago Press*, 2010, press.uchicago.edu.

Brad Plumer, "Only 27 percent of college grads have a job related to their major," *The Washington Post*, May 20, 2013, washingtonpost.com.

"Marking 10-year partnership, UNICEF and Gucci celebrate education successes across Africa and Asia," *United Nations News Centre*, June 3, 2015, un.org.

"Filling classrooms with poorly trained teachers undercuts education gains, warns UN," *United Nations News Centre*, October 2, 2014, un.org.

"Sustainable Development Goal for Education Cannot Advance Without More Teachers," *United Nations Educational, Scientific and Cultural Organization*, October 2015, uis.unesco.org.

"UN News—Nearly 69 million new teachers needed to achieve global education goals, UNESCO reports," *UN News Centre*, October 5, 2016, un.org.

Julie Petersen and Shauntel Poulson, "To Drive Innovation in Education, Foundations Are Starting to Act Like Venture Capitalists," *Impact Alpha*, April 6, 2016, impactalpha.com.

"2015 Global Edtech Investment Spikes to Record $6.5 Billion," *The Business Journals*, January 4, 2016, bizjournals.com.

"Higher Education Retail Market Facts & Figures," *National Association of College Stores*, 2016, nacs .org.

"Achieving the Dream Launches Major National Initiative to Help 38 Community Colleges in 13 States Develop New Degree Programs Using Open Educational Resources," *Achieving the Dream*, June 14, 2016, achievingthedream.org.

Danielle Douglas-Gabriel, "College courses without textbooks? These schools are giving it a shot," *The Washington Post*, June 15, 2016, washingtonpost.com.

Bob Ludwig, "WOW! UMUC Wins National Award for Eliminating Textbooks in All Undergraduate Courses," *University of Maryland University College*, November 20, 2015, globalmedia.umuc.edu.

Krystal Steinmetz, "This Simple Idea Could Cut Costs for College Students Across the US," *Money Talks News*, March 2, 2015, moneytalksnews.com.

Paul Sawers, "Udacity turns 5: Sebastian Thrun talks A.I. and plans for a nanodegree in self-driving cars," *VentureBeat*, July 4, 2016, venturebeat.com.

Tamar Lewin, "Instruction for Masses Knocks Down Campus Walls," *The New York Times*, March 4, 2012, nytimes.com.

Dhawal Shah, "By the Numbers: MOOCS in 2015," *Class Central*, December 21, 2015, class-central.com.

"Online Master of Science in Computer Science," *Georgia Tech College of Computing*, 2016, omscs.gatech.edu.

"2016–2017 Tuition and Fee Rates per Semester," *Georgia Institute of Technology*, 2016, omscs.gatech.edu.

"Our mission is to provide a free, world-class education for anyone, anywhere," *Khan Academy*, 2016, khanacademy.org.

"Khan Academy Resources: A Postsecondary Mathematics Research Project," *WestEd*, 2016, wested.org.

Mike Snider, "Cutting the Cord: The Great Courses' new streaming service," *USA TODAY*, August 9, 2015, usatoday.com.

Arthur Scheuer, "Xavier Niel explains 42: the coding university without teachers, books or tuition," *VentureBeat*, June 16, 2016, venturebeat.com.

Fremont, "42: Revolutionary Coding University Free, Non-Profit and Open to All," *42*, May 17, 2016, 42.us.org.

"Lighting the spark of learning," *Hole-in-the-wall*, 2016, Hole-in-the-wall.com.

"Starbucks partners with Arizona State University, offers online college program to workers," *NY Daily News*, June 16, 2014, nydailynews.com.

Mikhail Zinshteyn, "A For-Profit College Initiative That Just Might Work," *The Atlantic*, November 24, 2015, theatlantic.com.

Lindsay Gellman, "What Happened When a Business School Made Tuition Free," *The Wall Street Journal*, April 6, 2016, wsj.com.

"Endowment," *Harvard University*, 2016, harvard.edu.

"The Yale Investments Office," *Yale Investments Office*, 2016, investments.yale.edu.

"About UoPeople," *University of the People*, 2016, UoPeople.edu.

"2016 Retention/Completion Summary Tables," *ACT*, 2016, act.org.

"College Is Not Affordable," *Pew Research Center*, 2016, pewresearch.org.

"New Educational Goal but Chronic Shortages of Teachers," *UNESCO Institute of Statistics*, October 2015, uis.unesco.org.

"Infographic: Course Materials—Student Spending and Preferences," *The National Association of College Stores*, 2016, nacs.org.

Ben Popken, "College Textbook Prices Have Risen 1,041 Percent Since 1977," *NBC News*, August 6, 2015, nbcnews.com.

"Helping More Community College Students Succeed," *Achieving the Dream*, 2016, achievingthedream.org.

Tamar Lewin, "Instruction for Masses Knocks Down Campus Walls," *The New York Times*, March 4, 2012, nytimes.com.

Kevin Carey, "The End of College: Creating the Future of Learning and the University of Everywhere," *Penguin Random House*, March 3, 2015, penguinrandomhouse.com.

"Courses and Specializations," *Coursera*, 2016, courser.org.

"Leadership," *Coursera*, 2016, courser.org.

"Online Master of Science in Computer Science," *Georgia Tech—College of Computing*, 2016, omscs .gatech.edu.

"2016–2017 Tuition and Fee Rates per Semester—Fall 2016," *Georgia Institute of Technology*, 2016, bursar.gatech.edu.

"A personalized learning resource for all ages," *Khan Academy*, 2016, khanacademy.org.

"Our Supporters," *Khan Academy*, 2016, khanacademy.org.

"A free, world-class education for anyone, anywhere," *Khan Academy*, 2016, khanacademy.org.

Mike Snider, "Cutting the Cord: The Great Courses' new streaming service," *USA TODAY*, August 9, 2015, usatoday.com.

"Aaron Sorkin Teaches Screenwriting," *MasterClass*, 2016, masterclass.com.

"Starbucks partners with Arizona State University, offers online college program to workers," *NY Daily News*, June 16, 2014, nydailynews.com.

Mikhail Zinshteyn, "A For-Profit College Initiative That Just Might Work," *The Atlantic*, November 24, 2015, theatlantic.com.

"Harvard Congressional Report," *Harvard University*, March 31, 2016, harvard.edu.

"The Yale Investments Office," *Yale Investments Office*, 2016, investments.yale.edu.

"Combating Zika Virus through Education: New Tuition-Free Health Studies Degree Launched," *University of the People*, May 3, 2016, uopeople.edu.

"Trends in Student Aid 2015," *College Board*, 2016, trends.collegeboard.org.

Chapter Nine: The Future of Leisure and Recreation

Brian Sigafoos, "Estimated Sport Participants, 2000 Based on BRPS Survey," *Quora*, November 5, 2014, quora.com.

Jeffrey M. Jones, "As Industry Grows, Percentage of U.S. Sports Fans Steady," *Gallup*, June 17, 2015, Gallup.com.

"In Case You Missed It: A Lake Tahoe Resort Gets a 'Snow Factor,'" A 1,000-Passenger Cruise Navigates the Northwest Passage—and More!," *Scientific American*, August 1, 2016, scientific american.com.

Megan Michelson, "U.S. Ski Areas Can Now Make Snow in the Summer," *Outside Online*, May 26, 2016, outsideonline.com.

Josh Dean, "Kelly Slater Built the Perfect Wave. Can He Sell It to the World? The Surfing legend's top-secret machine could change the sport forever," *Bloomberg Businessweek*, May 24, 2016, bloomberg.com.

"Fantasy Sports Services in the US: Market Research Report," *IBIS World*, 2016, ibisworld.com.

"Fantasy Sports Services in the US: Market Research Report," *IBIS World*, May 2015, ibisworld.com.

Darren Heitner, "The Hyper Growth of Daily Fantasy Sports Is Going to Change Our Culture and Our Laws," *Forbes*, September 16, 2015, forbes.com.

"So Many Apps, So Much More Time for Entertainment," *The Nielsen Company*, June 11, 2015, nielsen.com.

Anne Freier, "Mobile devices generate more emotional ad engagement than TVs," *mobyaffliates*, January 8, 2016, mobyaffiliates.com.

Jane McGonigal, "Video Games: An Hour a Day Is Key to Success in Life," *The Huffington Post*, February 15, 2011, huffingtonpost.com.

"KeyArena History," *KeyArena at Seattle Center*, 2016, keyarena.com.

"Prize Pool," *The International DOTA 2 Championships*, 2016, dota2.com.

"Fantex, Inc.," *U.S Securities and Exchange Commission*, January 13, 2016, sec.gov.

Jeffrey M. Jones, "As Industry Grows, Percentage of U.S. Sports Fans Steady," *Gallup*, June 17, 2015, gallup.com.

Darren Heitner, "The Hyper Growth of Daily Fantasy Sports Is Going to Change Our Culture and Our Laws," *Forbes*, September 16, 2015, forbes.com.

"Industry Demographics: Actionable Insights & Insightful Data," *Fantasy Sports Trade Association*, 2016, fsta.org.

"The International DOTA 2 Championships," *DOTA 2*, 2016, dota2.com.

"KeyArena History," *Key Arena at Seattle Center*, 2016, keyarena.com.

Chapter Ten: Financial Services Innovation

Shira Ovide, "Silicon Valley's Soft Landing," *Bloomberg*, January 8, 2016, bloomberg.com.

Juro Osawa, "China Mobile-Payment Battle Becomes a Free-for-All," *The Wall Street Journal*, May 22, 2016, wsj.com.

"China's economy grew by around 7 percent in 2015, services made up half of GDP—Premier," *Reuters*, January 16, 2016, reuters.com.

"National Income and Product Accounts Gross Domestic Product: Fourth Quarter and Annual 2015 (Third Estimate) Corporate Profits: Fourth Quarter and Annual 2015," *BEA—Bureau of Economic Analysis*, March 25, 2016, bea.gov.

Prachi Salve, "Not 264 Million, Middle Class Is 24 Million: Report," *IndiaSpend*, October 29, 2015, indiaspend.com.

Bob Pisani, "Here's where fintech is heading next," *CNBC*, June 6, 2016, cnbc.com.

Deirdre Kelly, "Massive money-transfer industry disrupted by startups," *The Globe and Mail*, May 30, 2016, theglobeandmail.com.

T.S., "Why does Kenya lead the world in mobile money?," *The Economist*, May 27, 2013, economist.com.

"Overcome Cash Flow Gaps. Get Paid Instantly," *Fundbox*, 2016, fundbox.com.

"LoyaltyCapital empowers local businesses to do more for you and the community," *Zipcap*, 2016, zipcap.com.

Ruth Simon, "The Coffee-Break Loan: Business Owners Promised Money in Five Minutes," *The Wall Street Journal*, March 12, 2016, wsj.com.

"Personal Loans," *Lending Club*, 2016, lendingclub.com.

PTI, "Consumer, SME loan market to reach $3 trillion in 10 years: Report," *The Economic Times*, July 13, 2016, economictimes.indiatimes.com.

Peter Diamandis, "Pebble Time Crowdfunding > $20 million," *Peter Diamandis*, 2016, diamandis.com.

"Our mission," *Kickstarter*, 2016, kickstarter.com.

"Top 10 Best Rated Crowdfunding Sites," *Consumer Affairs*, 2016, consumeraffairs.com.

"Raise Money for Charity," *GoFundMe*, 2016, gofundme.com.

Debbie Strong, "High School Senior with Two Jobs and Scholarships STILL Can't Afford College—So She Does Something Crazy," *Woman's World*, April 19, 2016, womansworld.com.

"7 Year-Old Virginia Boy Raises $10,000 for Elementary Schools in Flint, Michigan," *Sunny Skyz*, February 22, 2016, sunnyskyz.com.

"President Obama To Sign Jumpstart Our Business Startups (JOBS) Act," *The White House*, April 05, 2012, whitehouse.gov.

"Crowdfunding Industry Statistics 2015 2016," *CrowdExpert.com*, 2016, crowdexpert.com.

"Ultrasound Nerve Segmentation," *Kaggle*, 2016, Kaggle.com

Alexander Hatcher, "Crowdsourcing Your Drug Dealer," *Word Press*, April 30, 2014, hatcheralexander.wordpress.com.

Alicia H. Munnell, "'Alternative work arrangements' now 16% of workforce," *MarketWatch*, April 28, 2016, marketwatch.com.

"Ready to declutter your wardrobe?," *Vinted*, 2016, vinted.com.

"Welcome to your dream closet," *Le Tote*, 2016, letote.com.

Kate Silver, "Finally, You Can Rent a Farm Animal," *Bloomberg*, August 17, 2016, bloomberg.com.

Ellen Huet, "What Really Killed Homejoy? It Couldn't Hold On to Its Customers," *Forbes*, July 23, 2015, forbes.com.

"Earn money hiring your stuff. Find rentals at neighborly prices," *Open Shed*, 2016, openshed.com.au.

"Find your perfect parking space," *JustPark*, 2016, justpark.com.

"On-Demand, 24/7: The best of your city delivered in minutes," *Postmates*, 2016, postmates.com.

"Shipping made easy," *Shyp*, 2016, shyp.com.

"BorrowMyDoggy connects dog owners with local dog lovers across the UK and Ireland for walks, sitting, and happy holidays," *BorrowMyDoggy*, 2016, borrowmydoggy.com.

"We Do Chores. You Live Life," *TaskRabbit*, 2016, taskrabbit.com.

"Find the Best Wineries & Wine Tasting," *CorkSharing*, 2016, corksharing.com.

"The future of dining is here: Join us at a communal table with hosts in over 200+ cities," *EatWith*, 2016, eatwith.com.

"What do you need done? Find it on Fiverr. Browse. Buy. Done," *Fiverr*, 2016, fiverr.com.

"Find a New Experience: Discover and book unique experiences offered by local insiders," *Vayable*, 2016, vayable.com.

"How can I earn money on Skillshare?," *Skills Share*, 2016, help.skillshare.com.

"Business experts on your terms," *Hourly Nerd*, 2016, hourlynerd.com.

"Quirky: The Invention Platform," *Quirky*, 2016, quirky.com.

"TechShop is a vibrant, creative community that provides access to instruction, tools, software and space. You can make virtually anything at TechShop. Come and build your dreams!," *TechShop*, 2016, techshop.ws.

"Welcome to the world of trips. Homes, experiences, and places—all in one app," *Airbnb*, 2016, airbnb.com.

"The Crowdshipping Community," *PiggyBee*, 2016, piggybee.com.

Erin Carson, "10 rideshare apps to crowdsource your commute," *TechRepublic*, April 10, 2014, techrepublic.com.

"Your cars for every occasion," *DriveNow*, 2016, de.drive-now.com.

"RENT THE CAR: Own the adventure," *Turo*, 2016, turo.com.

Douglas Macmillan, "GM Invests $500 Million in Lyft, Plans System for Self-Driving Cars," *The Wall Street Journal*, January 4, 2016, wsj.com.

"Free to List Your Desk or Office Space," *Desks Near Me*, 2016, desksnear.me.

"Sharing Marketplace for Business Equipment and Services," *Floow2*, 2016, floow2.com.

"Be the Founder Of Your Life," *WeWork*, 2016, wework.com.

Eliot Brown, "WeWork Targets Asia as Valuation Hits $16 Billion," *The Wall Street Journal*, March 10, 2016, wsj.com.

Randyl Drummer, "WeWork and Other Shared-Office Providers Aiming to Reinvent How Office Leasing Works," *Costar*, March 24, 2016, costar.com.

"Introducing the YouEconomy," *Success*, June 10, 2016, success.com.

Abha Bhattarai, "After shoppers return items, some buyers try selling them again," *The Washington Post*, July 1, 2016, washingtonpost.com.

"The sharing economy—sizing the revenue opportunity," *PWC*, 2016, pwc.co.uk.

Drew Desilver, "More older Americans are working, and working more, than they used to," *Pew Research Center*, June 20, 2016, pewresearch.org.

"Defeat Malaria," *International SOS*, April 11, 2016, internationalsos.com.

"A child dies every minute from malaria in Africa," *World Health Organization*, 2016, afro.who.int.

"About MalariaSpot," *Malaria Spot*, 2016, malariaspot.org.

Gunther Eysenbach, "Crowdsourcing Malaria Parasite Quantification: An Online Game for Analyzing Images of Infected Thick Blood Smears," *National Center for Biotechnology Information*, November 29, 2012, ncbi.nlm.nih.gov.

"The Science Behind Foldit," *Foldit*, 2016, fold.it.

"Global Fintech Investment Growth Continues in 2016 Driven by Europe and Asia, Accenture Study Finds," *Accenture*, April 13, 2016, newsroom.accenture.com.

"Sea Hero Quest," *Sea Hero Quest*, 2016, seaheroquest.com.

"Play Sea Hero Quest and #gameforgood," *Alzheimer's Research UK*, 2016, alzheimersresearchuk.org.

Sarah Kaplan, "Two minutes playing this video game could help scientists fight Alzheimer's," *The Washington Post*, May 7, 2016, washingtonpost.com.

Charlie Sorrel, "Use It Or Lose It-How Brain Exercise Fights Alzheimer's," *Fast Company & Inc.*, August 19, 2016, fastcoexist.com.

"Raymond Orteig—$25,000 prize," *Charles Lindbergh*, 2016, charleslindbergh.com.

Alan Boyle, "SpaceShipOne wins $10 million X Prize," *NBC News*, October 5, 2004, nbcnews.com.

Brian Caulfield, "Rocket Man," *Forbes*, February 1, 2012, forbes.com.

"This privately built, piloted craft reached space and returned safely, expanding opportunities for commercial spaceflight," *SpaceShipOne*, 2016, Airandspace.si.edu.

"Identify Organisms from a Stream of DNA Sequences," *InnoCentive Challenge*, 2016, innocentive .com.

Gail Porter, "NFL, Under Armour, GE & National Institute of Standards and Technology (NIST) Announce Five Winners of Head Health Challenge III," *NIST*, December 15, 2015, nist.gov.

Tomas Kellner, "Failing Better: $2 Million Innovation Challenge Seeks Advanced Materials to Protect Football Players from Brain Injury," *GE Reports*, January 30, 2015, gereports.com.

"Carbon Monoxide Poster Contest Winners," *United States Consumer Product Safety Commission*, 2016, cpsc.gov.

"NIDA Issues Challenge to Create App for Addiction Research," *National Institute on Drug Abuse*, November 3, 2015, drugabuse.gov.

Dr. Ellen Gilinsky, "A Summit to Remember," *The EPA Blog*, May 18, 2016, blog.epa.gov.

Jon Greenberg, "47% say they lack ready cash to pay a surprise $400 bill," *Punditfact*, June 9, 2015, Politifact.com.

SOURCES

"UFA2020 Overview: Universal Financial Access by 2020," *The World Bank*, August 18, 2016, worldbank.org.

Mary Wisniewski, "Campaign to Legalize Lottery-Like Savings Awards Gains Momentum," *American Banker*, September 30, 2014, americanbanker.com.

Richard Eisenberg, "Will Prizes Get More Low-Income People to Save?," *Forbes*, July 17, 2015, forbes.com.

Ben Steverman, "Put in $25, Get $10,000 Back. Your Bank Becomes a Casino," *Bloomberg*, September 23, 2014, bloomberg.com.

Bill Fay, "How Credit Unions And Banks Are 'Gamifying' Savings," *Debt.org*, July 2, 2015, debt.org.

Christina Lavingia, "How Lottery Savings Accounts Fool You into Saving More," *Go Banking Rates*, April 29, 2014, gobankingrates.com.

Melissa Schettini Kearney, Peter Tufano, Jonathan Guryan and Erik Hurst, "Making Savers Winners: An Overview of Prize-Linked Savings Products," *The National Bureau of Economic Research*, October 2010, nber.org.

"World Bank Group and a Coalition of Partners Make Commitments to Accelerate Universal Financial Access," *The World Bank*, April 17, 2015, worldbank.org.

"Standard of living in India," *Wikipedia*, 2016, Wikipedia.org.

"Uncertainty in the Aftermath of the U.K. Referendum," *International Monetary Fund*, July 19, 2016, imf.org.

James Manyika, Sree Ramaswarny, Somesh Khanna, Hugo Sarrazin, Gary Pinkus, Guru Sethupathy and Andrew Yaffe, "Digital America: A tale of the haves and have-mores," *McKinsey & Company*, December 2015, mckinsey.com.

James Manyika, "Are you part of the digital haves or the have-mores?," *McKinsey & Company*, December 17, 2015, mckinsey.com.

Christopher Mims, "31% of Kenya's GDP is spent through mobile phones," *Quartz*, February 27, 2013, qz.com.

Syed Zain Al-Mahmood, "Mobile Banking Provides Lifeline for Bangladeshis," *The Wall Street Journal*, June 23, 2015, wsj.com.

"Digital Pathways to Financial Inclusion: Findings from the First FII Tracker Survey in Kenya?," *InterMedia*, July 2014, finclusion.org.

Kalyeena Makortoff, "Kenya launches first mobile-only bond," *CNBC*, October 1, 2015, cnbc.com.

"5 billion people to go online by 2020: Google," *The Times of India*, November 20, 2015, timesofindia.indiatimes.com.

Robert D. Boroujerdi and Christopher Wolf, "Themes, Dreams and Flying Machines," *The Goldman Sachs Group,* December 2, 2015, goldmansachs.com.

Melody Petersen, "Google may invest in SpaceX to back Elon Musk's satellite project," *Los Angeles Times*, January 19, 2015, latimes.com.

Robert Wall, "OneWeb Plans Further Microsatellite Funding Round," *The Wall Street Journal*, June 25, 2015, wsj.com.

Cara McGoogan, "Facebook's solar-powered internet drone takes maiden flight," *The Telegraph*, July 22, 2016, telegraph.co.uk.

"Project Loon," *X*, 2016, x.company.

"Li-fi 100 times faster than wi-fi," *BBC News*, November 27, 2015, bbc.com.

Peter Diamandis, "Mobile is eating the world," *Peter Diamandis*, 2016, diamandis.com.

Dominic Frisby, "Zimbabwe's trillion-dollar note: from worthless paper to hot investment," *The Guardian*, May 14, 2016, theguardian.com.

Steve H. Hanke, "R.I.P. Zimbabwe Dollar," *CATO Institute*, 2016, cato.org.

Gertrude Chevez-Dreyfuss and Nikhil Subba, "U.S. tech company files bitcoin ETF application with SEC," *Reuters*, July 12, 2016, reuters.com.

"Bitcoin ATMs in United States," *Coin ATM Radar*, 2016, coinatmradar.com.

Michael J. Casey and Paul Vigna, "BitBeat: Payments Industry Rep Weighs in on a 'Revolutionary Time,'" *The Wall Street Journal*, June 24, 2014, wsj.com.

Emanuel Derman, "'The Age of Cryptocurrency,' by Paul Vigna and Michael J. Casey," *The New York Times*, March 18, 2015, nytimes.com.

Stan Higgins, "Central Bank Digital Currencies Could Boost GDP, Bank of England Says," *CoinDesk*, July 18, 2016, coindesk.com.

Sophia Yan, "China wants to launch its own digital currency," *CNN*, January 22, 2016, money.cnn.com.

"Justice Department Convenes Summit on Digital Currency and the Blockchain," *United States Department of Justice*, November 9, 2015, justice.gov.

Justin OConnell, "More US Colleges & Universities Offering Bitcoin Courses in the Fall," *Cryptocoins News*, August 27, 2015, cryptocoinsnews.com.

"IRS Virtual Currency Guidance: Virtual Currency Is Treated as Property for U.S. Federal Tax Purposes; General Rules for Property Transactions Apply," *Internal Revenue Service*, March 25, 2014, irs.gov.

Pete Rizzo, "CFTC Ruling Defines Bitcoin and Digital Currencies as Commodities," *CoinDesk*, September 17, 2015, coindesk.com.

Rachel Emma Silverman, "Charities Seek Donations in Bitcoin," *The Wall Street Journal*, April 12, 2015, wsj.com.

Anna Irrera, "UBS Building Virtual Coin for Mainstream Banking," *The Wall Street Journal*, September 3, 2015, wsj.com.

Matthew Finnegan, "Bitcoin and beyond: Which banks are investing in the blockchain?," *Techworld*, April 08, 2016, techworld.com.

John Biggs, "Citibank Is Working On Its Own Digital Currency, Citicoin," *TechCrunch*, July 7, 2015, techcrunch.com.

"Citi Crosses $1 Trillion Transaction Value Milestone in Institutional Mobile Banking," *Business Wire*, February 23, 2016, businesswire.com.

Anthony Cuthbertson, "Bitcoin now accepted by 100,000 merchants worldwide," *International Business Times*, February 4, 2015, ibtimes.co.uk.

Darren Rovell, "Sacramento Kings to accept Bitcoin," *ESPN*, January 16, 2014, espn.com.

Kate Gibson, "Report: Nearly 5 million Bitcoin users by 2019," *CBS News*, March 17, 2015, cbsnews.com.

Sydney Ember, "Data Security Is Becoming the Sparkle in Bitcoin," *The New York Times*, March 1, 2015, nytimes.com.

Maria Aspan, "Why Fintech Is One of the Most Promising Industries of 2015," *INC. Magazine*, September 2015, inc.com.

Liz Alderman, "In Sweden, a Cash-Free Future Nears," *The New York Times*, December 26, 2015, nytimes.com.

Greg Garneau, "The Blockchain, the Wheel, Airplane and the Internet Are the Four Greatest Inventions," *IHB*, February 9, 2014, ihb.io.

Erin Sullivan, "World's first Bitcoin marriage to take place at Walt Disney World," *Orlando Weekly*, October 1, 2014, orlandoweekly.com.

Minouche Shafik, "A New Heart for a Changing Payments System," *Bank of England*, January 27, 2016, bankofengland.co.uk.

Gideon Gottfried, "Blockchain Platform Colu Partners With Revelator in Push to Fix Music's Data," *Billboard*, August 18, 2015, billboard.com.

Nathaniel Popper, "Bitcoin Technology Piques Interest on Wall St.," *The New York Times*, August 28, 2015, nytimes.com.

"US Congress cites for a national policy for blockchain technology," *The Paypers*, July 22, 2016, thepaypers.com.

Cory Dawson, "Vt. eager for blockchain, but agencies slow to change," *Burlington Free Press*, July 26, 2016, burlingtonfreepress.com.

"IBM to Open Blockchain Innovation Center in Singapore to Accelerate Blockchain Adoption for Finance and Trade," *IBM*, July 11, 2016, ibm.com.

Oscar Williams-Grut, "Santander is experimenting with bitcoin and close to investing in a blockchain startup," *Business Insider*, June 17, 2015, businessinsider.com.

"Blockchain, Mobile and the Internet of Things," *Insights*, Mar 17, 2016, insights.samsung.com.

Olivia Cain, "Counterfeit aircraft parts in the USA," *NetNames*, March 11, 2014, netnames.com.

Luke Parker, "LenderBot by Deloitte and Stratumn to bring insurance to the sharing economy using bitcoin's blockchain," *Brave New Coin*, July 14, 2016, bravenewcoin.com.

B. Holmes, "Jetcoin Gears up to Disrupt the Sporting Industry," *Brave New Coin*, April 22, 2015, bravenewcoin.com.

Gertrude Chavez-Dreyfuss, "Overstock to issue stock to be traded on blockchain platform," *Reuters*, March 16, 2016, reuters.com.

"Profiles in Innovation—Blockchain Putting Theory into Practice," *The Goldman Sachs Group, Inc.*, May 24, 2016, scribd.com.

Jigmey Bhutia, "Robots will destroy 15 million jobs warns Bank of England," *International Business Times*, November 13, 2015, ibtimes.co.uk.

"Support Blue Angel Jeff Kuss Family," *GoFundMe*, 2016, gofundme.com.

"Can computer vision spot distracted drivers?," *Kaggle*, August 1, 2016, kaggle.com.

"Maximize sales and minimize returns of bakery goods," *Kaggle*, June 8, 2016, kaggle.com.

"Can you detect duplicitous duplicate ads?," *Kaggle*, July 11, 2016, kaggle.com.

"Help improve outcomes for shelter animals," *Kaggle*, March 21, 2016, kaggle.com.

"Annual Nominal Fish Catches," *Kaggle*, 2016, kaggle.com.

"Welcome to Eleven James," *Eleven James*, 2016, elevenjames.com.

"M-PESA Timeline," *Safaricom*, 2016, safaricom.co.ke.

"Why does Kenya lead the world in mobile money?," *The Economist*, May 27, 2013, economist.com.

"Overcome Cash Flow Gaps. Get Paid Right Away," *Fundbox*, 2016, fundbox.com.

Ruth Simon, "The Coffee-Break Loan: Business Owners Promised Money in Five Minutes," *The Wall Street Journal*, March 12, 2016, wsj.com.

"Mary Kay Inc. has tapped one of its own, Julia A. Simon, to serve as Chief Legal Officer and Corporate Secretary," *Direct Selling News*, December 7, 2016, directsellingnews.com.

Abha Bhattarai, "After shoppers return items, some buyers try selling them again," *The Washington Post*, July 1, 2016, washingtonpost.com.

"Global capital markets: Entering a new era," *McKinsey & Company—McKinsey Global Institute*, September 2009, mckinsey.com.

"GDP (current US$)," *The World Bank*, 2015, data.worldbank.org.

"World Economic Outlook October 2016," *International Monetary Fund*, 2016, imf.org.

"Digital Pathways to Financial Inclusion. Findings from the First FII Tracker Survey in Kenya," *DocPlayer*, July 2014, docplayer.net.

Kalyeena Makortoff, "Kenya launches first mobile-only bond," *CNBC*, October 1, 2015, cnbc.com.

Property Trading Game from Parker Brothers: Monopoly Electronic Banking Edition," *Hasbro*, 2016, hasbro.com.

"Digital Currencies," *Bank of England*, 2016, bankofengland.co.uk.

"2015 Gift Card Sales to Reach New Peak of $130 Billion," *PR Newswire*, December 8, 2015, prnewswire.com.

Chapter Eleven: Safety and Security

Monica Davey, "Chicago Police Try to Predict Who May Shoot or Be Shot," *The New York Times*, May 23, 2016, nytimes.com.

"Vancouver police arrest more than 100 in riot," *CBC News*, June 16, 2011, cbc.ca.

Bill Mann, "Social Media "Vigilantes" I.D. Vancouver Rioters—And Then Some," *The Huffington Post*, July 2, 2011, huffingtonpost.ca.

Chapter Twelve: The Dark Side

Elizabeth Weise, "Robocalls are worse than annoying—they're likely scams," *USA TODAY*, July 28, 2016, usatoday.com.

"27M Americans Lost an Average of $274 in Phone Scams Last Year, According to New Report from Truecaller," *WebWire*, January 25, 2016, webwire.com.

Michael Sainato, "Stephen Hawking, Elon Musk, and Bill Gates Warn About Artificial Intelligence," *Observer*, August 19, 2015, observer.com.

"Hyatt Hotels Current Valuation," *Macroaxis*, November 30, 2016, macroaxis.com.

Grace Caffyn, "Bitcoin Pizza Day: Celebrating the Pizzas Bought for 10,000 BTC," *CoinDesk*, May 22, 2014, coindesk.com.

"7,500 Online Shoppers Unknowingly Sold Their Souls," *FOX News,* April 15, 2010, foxnews.com.

David Boroff, "Creator of website hitmanforhire.net took on clients, committed extortion, authorities say," *NY Daily News*, February 29, 2012, nydailynews.com.

Nick Bilton, "Girls Around Me: An App Takes Creepy to a New Level," *The New York Times*, March 30, 2012, bits.blogs.nytimes.com.

Toivo Tanavsuu, "From file-sharing to prison: A Megaupload programmer tells his story," *Arstechnica*, June 24, 2016, arstechnica.com.

Herb Weisbaum, "Warning: Burglars read the obituaries, too," *NBC News*, June 27, 2012, business .nbcnews.com.

Eric Mack, "Twitter, Facebook, Foursquare: Tools of the modern burglar?," *CNET*, April 5, 2012, cnet.com.

Jennifer Levitz, "Online Daters Are Falling Prey to Scams," *The Wall Street Journal*, 2016, wsj.com.

Ramanujam Venkatesan, Arvind Choudhary and Satyendra Kuntal, "Kidnap and Ransom Insurance: at an Inflection Point," *Cognizant*, 2016, cognizant.com.

Edward C. Baig, "Mattel unveils rebooted ThingMaker as 3D printer," *USA TODAY*, February 13, 2016, usatoday.com.

Devlin Barrett, "Threat of Plastic Guns Rises," *The Wall Street Journal*, November 13, 2013, wsj.com.

Brittany Vonow, "KING OF THIEVES Incredible criminal career of Hatton Garden heist mastermind Brian Reader exposed in new book," *The Sun*, September 3, 2016, thesun.co.uk.

Matt Levine, "Guy Trading at Home Caused the Flash Crash," *Bloomberg View*, April 21, 2015, bloomberg.com.

Olga Kharif, "Mobile Payment Fraud Is Becoming a Pricey Problem," *Bloomberg Businessweek*, February 12, 2015, bloomberg.com.

Chris P., "Mobile malware getting out of control? Study claims 614% increase on year, Android accounts for 92% of total infections," *Phone Arena*, June 28, 2013, phonearena.com.

Marc Tracy, "A Body of Data, Exposed," *The New York Times*, September 11, 2016, nytimes.com.

Mark Newgent, "Baltimore Examiner going out of business," *The Red Maryland Network*, January 29, 2009, redmaryland.com.

"Cincinnati Post stops the press after 126 years," *NBC News*, December 31, 2007, nbcnews.com.

Nick Madigan, "An Abrupt End to the Tampa Tribune After a Blow Delivered by Its Rival," *The New York Times*, May 20, 2016, nytimes.com.

Jeffrey Pfeffer, "The case against the 'gig economy,'" *Fortune*, July 30, 2015, fortune.com.

Sarah Knapton, "Robot mother builds 'cube babies' then watches them take first steps," *The Telegraph*, August 12, 2015, telegraph.co.uk.

"Current Report Filing (8-k)," *ADVFN*, 2016, advfn.com.

"Cincinnati Financial Chairman to Retire from Active Company Employment," *PR Newswire*, August 12, 2016, prnewswire.com.

Becky Yerak, "Allstate: Driverless cars could threaten our business," *Chicago Tribune*, February 22, 2016, chicagotribune.com.

Leslie Scism, "Driverless Cars Threaten to Crash Insurers' Earnings," *The Wall Street Journal*, July 26, 2016, wsj.com.

Danni Santana, "Allstate's Tech Company Reveals New View of Telematics Value," *Insurance Networking News*, August 11, 2016, insurancenetworking.com.

Theo Francis, "The Driverless Car, Officially, Is a Risk," *The Wall Street Journal*, March 3, 2015, wsj.com.

Caitlin Bronson, "Self-driving cars will be bad for insurance, Buffet says," *Insurance Business*, May 3, 2016, ibamag.com.

Mayo Clinic Staff, "Spinal cord injury—causes," *Mayo Clinic*, October 8, 2014, mayoclinic.org.

Christopher Langner, "Commodities' $3.6 Trillion Black Hole," *Bloomberg*, February 18, 2016, bloomberg.com.

Alfred Ng, "Florida woman's hit-and-run escape foiled after her own car calls police on her," *NY Daily News*, December 6, 2015, nydailynews.com.

Thomas Claburn, "Google Automated Car Accidents: Not Our Fault," *Information Week*, May 12, 2015, informationweek.com.

Andrea Peterson and Matt McFarland, "You may be powerless to stop a drone from hovering over your own yard," *The Washington Post*, January 13, 2016, washingtonpost.com.

Laura Wagner, "North Dakota Legalizes Armed Police Drones," *NPR*, August 27, 2015, npr.org.

"Gartner Says Uses of 3D Printing Will Ignite Major Debate on Ethics and Regulation," *Gartner*, January 29, 2014, gartner.com.

David Daw, "Criminals Find New Uses for 3D Printing," *PCWorld*, October 10, 2011, pcworld.com.

James Legge, "US government orders Cody Wilson and Defense Distributed to remove blueprint for 3D-printed handgun from the web," *Independent*, May 10, 2013, independent.co.uk.

Andy Greenberg, "$25 Gun Created With Cheap 3D Printer Fires Nine Shot," *Forbes*, May 19, 2013, forbes.com.

Bridget Butler Millsaps, "Australia's Gold Coast: Loaded 3D Printed Gun Found in Raid of Sophisticated Meth Lab," *3D Print*, December 10, 2015, 3dprint.com.

Dan Bilefsky, "The Graying Thieves Who Nearly Got Away With a Record Heist in London," *The New York Times*, December 12, 2015, nytimes.com.

"Hatton Garden: Who were the jewellery heist raiders?," *BBC News*, January 14, 2016, bbc.com.

Carol Matlack, "Instead of Playing Golf, the World's Elderly Are Staging Heists and Robbing Banks," *Bloomberg*, May 28, 2015, bloomberg.com.

"HGP Write FAQ," *The Center of Excellence for Engineering Biology*, 2016, engineerinbiologycenter .org.

Curt DellaValle, "Monsanto's GMO Weed Killer Damages DNA," *AgMag*, July 17, 2015, ewg.org.

Oscar Williams-Grut, "After Firing Its CEO, Lending Club Is Facing a Crisis," *Inc.*, May 17, 2016, inc.com.

"Flash Robs," *Crime Museum*, 2016, crimemuseum.org.

"Flash Rob," *Wikipedia*, 2016, wikipedia.com.

Julie Jargon and Ilan Brat, "Chicago Police Brace for 'Flash Mob' Attacks," *The Wall Street Journal*, June 9, 2011, wsj.com.

Sonia Azad, "Flash Mob Robbery Caught on Camera at Galleria Area Store," *ABC 13 Eyewitness News*, December 9, 2011, abc13.com.

Dan Scanlan, "Saturday night flash mob takes over Jacksonville Walmart," *The Florida Times Union*, July 17, 2012, jacksonville.com.

Renae Merle, "Wells Fargo fires 5,300 people for opening millions of phony accounts; company fined $185M," *Chicago Tribune*, September 9, 2016, chicagotribune.com.

Chris Isidore and David Goldman, "Volkswagen agrees to record $14.7 billion settlement over emissions cheating," *CNN Money*, June 28, 2016, money.cnn.com.

Mark Calvey, "Printer giant HP thinks it oughta be in pictures," *San Francisco Business Times*, September 28, 1997, bizjournals.com.

Mike Spector, Dana Mattioli and Peg Brickley, "Can Bankruptcy Filing Saving Kodak?," *The Wall Street Journal*, January 20, 2012, wsj.com.

Tim Worstall, "Jaron Lanier's 'Who Owns The Future?' What On Earth Is This Guy Talking About?," *Forbes*, May 15, 2013, forbes.com.

"David S. Rose," *David Rose Photography*, 2016, davidrose.com.

Giovanni Rodriguez, "The Exponential Enterprise: Your Most Feared Competitor Now Has a Name," *Forbes*, October 31, 2014, forbes.com

Brian Stelter, "News Corporation Sells MySpace for $35 Million," *The New York Times*, June 29, 2011, mediadecoder.blogs.nytimes.com.

Bill Tancer, "MySpace Moves Into #1 Position for all Internet Sites," *Experian Marketing Services*, July 11, 2006, experian.com.

"NewsCorp, which paid $580 million for MySpace has sold it for $35 million," *The Oregonian*, June 29, 2011, oregonlive.com.

Pete Cashmore, "MySpace, America's Number One," *Mashable*, July 11, 2006, mashable.com.

"Company Overview of Hyatt Hotels Corporation," *Bloomberg*, September 27, 2016, bloomberg.com.

Sam Matthews, "The Investor's Introduction to Hyatt Hotels," *Market Realist*, December 30, 2015, marketrealist.com.

"Our Company," *Hyatt*, September 27, 2016, investors.hyatt.com.

"Hyatt Hotels Corporation," *Google*, 2016, google.com.

Rolfe Winkler, "The Secret Math of Airbnb's $24 Billion Valuation," *The Wall Street Journal*, June 17, 2015, wsj.com.

"Quicken Loans Fast Facts," *Quicken Loans*, 2016, quickenloans.com.

"CEO Interview: Bill Emerson," *PwC*, 2016, pwc.com.

Jerry Hirsch, "Elon Musk: Model S not a car but a 'sophisticated computer on wheels,'" *Los Angeles Times*, March 19, 2015, latimes.com.

Richard N. Foster and Sarah Kaplan, "Creative destruction," *McKinsey & Company*, September 2001, mckinsey.com.

Kim Gittleson, "Can a company live forever?," *BBC News*, January 19, 2012, bbc.com.

Fortune Editors, "The results of the 2015 Fortune 500 CEO survey are in . . . ," *Fortune*, June 4, 2015, fortune.com.

"LIMRA Survey: More Than Half of Financial Executives Surveyed Predict Outside Disruption in Life Insurance Market," *LIMRA*, January 13, 2015, limra.com.

Joseph Steinberg, "These Devices May Be Spying on You (Even in Your Own Home)," *Forbes*, January 26, 2014, forbes.com.

"French taxi drivers destroy livery cabs in violent anti-Uber protest," *New York Post*, June 25, 2015, nypost.com.

Robert Schmidt, "The Pitched Battle Over Mutual Fund Reports You Probably Don't Even Read," *Bloomberg*, August 23, 2016, bloomberg.com.

"Senior Citizens Depend On Paper Social Security Checks," *Consumers for Paper Options*, 2016, paperoptions.org.

"Paper Savings Bonds: Bring Back an Important American Tradition," *Consumers for Paper Options*, 2016, paperoptions.org.

"SEC Filings, 10-Q," *Cincinnati Financial Corporation*, September 30, 2015, phx.corporate-ir.net.

"Section 1: 10-K (10-K): The Travelers Companies, Inc.," *United States Securities and Exchange Commission*, December 31, 2015, investor.travelers.com.

Henry Fountain and Michael S. Schmidt, "'Bomb Robot' Takes Down Dallas Gunman, but Raises Enforcement Questions," *The New York Times*, July 8, 2016, nytimes.com.

"Your Full-Service Life Insurance Brokerage," *Pinney Insurance*, 2016, pinneyinsurance.com.

Andrew Hessel, Marc Goodman and Steven Kotler, "Hacking the President's DNA," *The Atlantic*, November 2012, theatlantic.com.

Alice Park, "U.K. Approves First Studies of New Gene Editing Technique CRISPR on Human Embryos," *Time*, February 1, 2016, time.com.

Nicholas Wade, "Scientists Seek Moratorium on Edits to Human Genome That Could Be Inherited," *The New York Times*, December 3, 2015, nytimes.com.

"Our Mission: To Understand the Blueprint of Life. Home of GP-write and HGP-write," *The Center of Excellence for Engineering Biology*, 2016, engineeringbiologycenter.org.

Neil Gough, "Online Lender Ezubao Took $7.6 Billion in Ponzi Scheme, China Says," *The New York Times*, February 1, 2016, nytimes.com.

Ruth Simon, "Crowdfunding Sites Like GoFundMe and YouCaring Raise Money—and Concerns," *The Wall Street Journal*, February 29, 2016, wsj.com.

Peter Moskowitz, "Crowdfunding for the Public Good Is Evil," *Wired*, March 16, 2016, wired.com.

Erik Ortiz, "Chicago clothing store loses $3,000 worth of jeans in flash robbery," *NY Daily News*, July 30, 2012, nydailynews.com.

Jeff Bennett, "Thieves Go High-Tech to Steal Cars," *The Wall Street Journal*, July 5, 2016, wsj.com.

"How We See It: Autonomy and Self-Driving Cars," *Car and Driver*, June 17, 2016, blog.carand driver.com.

Joel Achenbach, "107 Nobel laureates sign letter blasting Greenpeace over GMOs," *The Washington Post*, June 30, 2016, washingtonpost.com.

"And the 2016 World Food Prize goes to . . . Biofortified Sweet Potatoes," *Golden Rice Project*, 2016, goldenrice.org.

"Targeting Aging with Metformin," *American Federation for Aging Research*, 2016, afar.org.

"Robotic surgery technique to treat previously inoperable head and neck cancer tumors," *University of California, Los Angeles, Health Sciences*, December 20, 2014, sciencedaily.com.

Part Two: What Exponential Technologies Mean for Personal Finance

Chapter Thirteen: The Financial Plan You Need Now for the Future You're Going to Have

"Life Expectancy for Social Security," *Social Security Administration*, 2016, ssa.gov.

Dan Fitzpatrick, "Rising U.S. Life Spans Spell Likely Pain for Pension Funds," *The Wall Street Journal*, October 27, 2014, wsj.com.

Sarah Knapton, "World's first anti-ageing drug could see humans live to 120," *The Telegraph*, November 29, 2015, telegraph.co.uk.

Johannes Koettl, "Boundless life expectancy: The future of aging populations," *Brookings*, March 23, 2016, brookings.edu.

Peter Diamandis, "Demonetized Cost of Living," *Peter Diamandis*, 2016, diamandis.com.

Peter H. Diamandis and Steven Kotler, "Bold: How to Go Big, Create Wealth and Impact the World," *Diamandis*, February 2015, diamandis.com.

Joanna Stern, "This $50 Smartphone May Be All You Need," *The Wall Street Journal*, July 19, 2016, wsj.com.

Javed Anwer, "Ringing Bells Freedom 251 review: A miracle that it exists and works like a phone," *India Today*, August 12, 2016, indiatoday.intoday.in.

Sascha Segan, "Hands On with the $20 Indian Android Tablet," *PC Magazine*, November 29, 2012, pcmag.com.

"The shirt you can't get dirty: Researchers create ultralight coating that can repel alcohol, coffee, oil and even petrol," *Daily Mail*, January 17, 2013, dailymail.co.uk.

Tom McKay, "Nobody is Buying a PC Anymore—Here's Why," *News.Mic*, December 3, 2013, mic.com.

Franklin B. Tucker, "With Full Slate, Planning Punts Possible Airbnb Regs to Summer Review," *Belmontonian*, January 7, 2016, belmontonian.com.

Matthew Wilde, "Food inflation: Rising transportation costs increase grocery bills," *Cedar Valley Business Monthly*, April 15, 2012, wcfcourier.com.

Chapter Fourteen: Career Planning

Robert E. Scott, "The Manufacturing Footprint and the Importance of U.S. Manufacturing Jobs," *Economic Policy Institute*, January 22, 2015, epi.org.

Carl Benedikt Frey and Michael A. Osborne, "The Future of Employment: How susceptible are jobs to computerisation?," *Oxford Martin School, University of Oxford*, September 17, 2013, oxfordmartin.ox.ac.uk.

"Databases, Tables & Calculators by Subject," *Bureau of Labor Statistics Data*, November 23, 2016, data.bls.gov.

Isabelle Fraser, "How you will buy your house in 2025: drones, virtual reality and big data," *The Telegraph*, March 8, 2016, telegraph.co.uk.

Ira Monko, "Artificial Intelligence in Real Estate: Today, Tomorrow and the Future," *OnBlog*, June 9, 2016, onboardinformatics.com.

Craig Guillot, "Your smartphone: A great tool for a better remodeling project?," *Bankrate*, November 3, 2015, bankrate.com.

Matt Burns, "This Could Be the Mortgage Industry's iPhone Moment," *TechCrunch*, November 24, 2015, techcrunch.com.

Michele Lerner, "How Do Real Estate Agents Get Paid?," *Realtor.com*, December 3, 2013, realtor.com.

Karen Turner, "Meet 'Ross,' the newly hired legal robot," *The Washington Post*, May 16, 2016, washingtonpost.com.

Stacy Liberatore, "Your AI lawyer will see you now: IBM's ROSS becomes world's first artificially intelligent attorney," *Daily Mail*, May 13, 2016, dailymail.co.uk.

Melissa Korn, "Imagine Discovering That Your Teaching Assistant Really Is a Robot," *The Wall Street Journal*, May 6, 2016, wsj.com.

Mark Lelinwalla, "Drone-Guided Robot Bulldozers Being Used in Japan to Combat Construction Labor Shortage," *Tech Times*, October 14, 2015, techtimes.com.

Patricia A. Daly, "Agricultural employment: has the decline ended?," *Bureau of Labor Statistics*, 2016, bls.gov.

"Data: National Agricultural Statistics Service (NASS)," *USDA Office of the Chief Economist*, 2016, usda.gov.

"History & Background," *United States Department of Agriculture Economic Research Service*, 2016, ers.usda.gov.

Ian D. Wyatt and Daniel E. Hecker, "Occupational changes during the 20th century," *Bureau of Labor Statistics*, March 2006, bls.gov.

"Agriculture 1950: Changes in Agriculture, 1900 To 1950," *Bureau of Census*, 2016, census.gov.

"Population profile of the United States, 1976," *Bureau of Census*, 2016, census.gov.

"Top 20 Facts About Manufacturing," *National Association of Manufacturers*, 2016, nam.org.

Lauren Csorny, "Careers in the growing field of information technology services," *Bureau of Labor Statistics*, April 2013, bls.gov.

"U.S. Tech Industry Employment Surpasses 6.7 Million Workers," *CompTIA*, February 29, 2016, comptia.org.

"Occupational Employments Statistics—Occupational Employment and Wages, May 2015," *Bureau of Labor Statistics*, 2016, bls.gov.

"Occupation Outlook Handbook—Travel Agents," *Bureau of Labor Statistics*, 2016, bls.gov.

"Occupation Outlook Handbook—Software Developers," *Bureau of Labor Statistics*, 2016, bls.gov.

Eckehart Rotter, "Facts and Figures," *German Association of the Automotive Industry*, 2016, vda.de.

"World Robotics 2015 Industrial Robots," *International Federation of Robotics*, 2016, ifr.org.

Chris Weller, "Law firms of the future will be filled with robot lawyers," *Tech Inside*, July 7, 2016, techinsider.com.

Karen Turner, "Meet 'Ross,' the newly hired legal robot," *The Washington Post*, May 16, 2016, washingtonpost.com.

James Bessen, "How Computer Automation Affects Occupations: Technology, Jobs, and Skills." *Boston University School of Law*, November 13, 2015, bu.edu.

Katie Allen, "Technology has created more jobs than it has destroyed, says 140 years of data," *The Guardian*, August 18, 2015, theguardian.com.

"Automation and anxiety," *The Economist*, June 25, 2016, economist.com.

"World-Class Finance Orgs Drive Higher Value, Great Agility Than Peers While Spending More Than 40 Percent Less," *The Hackett Group*, August 27, 2015, thehackettgroup.com.

Frank Tobe, "Huge employer in China makes big step toward robots," *The Christian Science Monitor*, November 17, 2011, csmonitor.com.

"Digital American: A Tale of the Have and Have-Mores," *McKinsey & Company*, December 2015, mckinsey.com.

Steven Johnson, "The Creative Apocalypse That Wasn't," *The New York Times Magazine*, August 19, 2015, nytimes.com.

"The Data Journalism That Wasn't," *Future of Music Coalition*, 2016, futureofmusic.org.

Chapter Fifteen: College Planning

Harriet Edleson, "Older Students Learn for the Sake of Learning," *The New York Times*, January 1, 2016, nytimes.com.

Kerry Hannon, "Over 50 and Back in College, Preparing for a New Career," *The New York Times*, April 3, 2015, nytimes.com.

Chapter Sixteen: Protecting Your Privacy

"Be in the know with TransUnion®: Get your Credit Score & Report," *TransUnion*, 2016, transunion.com.

"Your Credit, Your Identity," *Equifax*, 2016, equifax.com.

"What's your FICO® Credit Score?," *Experian*, 2016, experian.com.

"About the United States Postal Service," *United States Postal Service*, 2016, usps.com.

"Give your mailbox a makeover," *DMAchoice.org*, 2016, dmachoice.thedma.org.

"HTTPS and HTTP Difference," *Instant SSL by Comodo*, 2016, instantssl.com.

"Publications: Identity Theft and Your Social Security Number," *Social Security*, 2016, ssa.gov.

"Deceased Taxpayers—Protecting the Deceased's Identity from ID Theft," *Internal Revenue Service*, 2016, irs.gov.

Jason Cipriani, "Two-factor authentication: What you need to know (FAQ)," *CNET*, June 15, 2015, cnet.com.

"A 12-point checklist for victims of identity theft," *Bankrate*, 2016, bankrate.com.

"TeleCheck: Who is TeleCheck?," *First Data*, 2016, firstdata.com.

"Why is Certegy® involved in my transaction?," *Certegy*, 2016, askcertegy.com.

"Welcome to the Federal Financial Institutions Examination Council's (FFIEC) Web Site," *FFIEC—Federal Financial Institutions Examination Council*, 2016, ffiec.gov.

Chapter Seventeen: The Investment Strategy You Need for the Future

"Tax Rules on Early Withdrawals from Retirement Plans," *Internal Revenue Service*, March 18, 2013, irs.gov.

"CPI Inflation Calculator," *Bureau of Labor Statistics*, 2016, bls.gov.

David, "Duration of Stock Holding Periods Continue to Fall Globally," *Top Foreign Stocks*, September 6, 2010, topforeignstocks.com.

"Compare highest CD rates," *Bankrate*, 2016, bankrate.com.

Tim McMahon, "Annual Inflation," *Inflation data*, 2016, inflationdata.com.

Michael W. Roberge, Joseph C. Flaherty, Jr., Robert M. Almeida, Jr., and Andrew C. Boyd, "Lengthening the Investment Time Horizon," *MFS*, July 2016, mfs.com.

Warren Fiske, "Mark Warner says average holding time for stocks has fallen to four months," *PolitiFact*, July 6, 2016, politifact.com.

Michael Rawson and Ben Johnson, "2015 Fee Study: Investors Are Driving Expense Ratios Down," *Morningstar*, 2016, news.morningstar.com.

Rob Silverblatt, "How Mutual Fund Trading Costs Hurt Your Bottom Line," *US News*, March 4, 2013, money.usnews.com.

John C. Bogle, "Arithmetic of 'All-In' Investment Expenses," *Financial Analysts Journal*, January/February 2014, cfapubs.org.

Landon Thomas Jr., "At BlackRock, a Wall Street Rock Star's $5 Trillion Comeback," *The New York Times*, September 15, 2016, nytimes.com.

Jeff Schlegel, "BlackRock, Morningstar and Ric Edelman Team Up for New ETF," *Financial Advisor Magazine*, March 26, 2015, fa-mag.com.

"BlackRock Launches iShares Exponential Technologies ETF," *Business Wire*, March 24, 2015, businesswire.com.

Todd Shriber, "Edelman, iShares Launch Exponential Technologies ETF," *ETF Trends*, March 24, 2015, etftrends.com.

"Morningstar Exponential Technologies Index," *Morningstar*, 2016, morningstar.com.

"iShares Exponential Technologies ETF," *iShares*, 2016, ishares.com.

"XT iShares Exponential Technologies ETF XT Quote Price News," *Morningstar*, 2016, etfs.morningstar.com.

"iShares Plans an Exponential Technology ETF," *Zacks*, January 6, 2015, zacks.com.

Aaron Levitt, "The 10 Technology ETFs You Should Consider," *ETFdb*, June 2, 2016, etfdb.com.

David Sterman, "5 Unique ETFs to Diversify Your Portfolio," *Street Authority*, July 9, 2015, streetauthority.com.

Chapter Eighteen: Where You'll Live in the Future

"Public Policy," *Naturally Occurring Retirement Communities*, 2016, norcs.org.

"Working With NORC Programs and Villages," *Irving Levin Associates*, 2011, levinassociates.com.

"Community-Centered Solutions for Aging at Home," *U.S. Department of Housing and Urban Development*, Fall 2013, huduser.gov.

Susan Luxenberg, "For Boomers & Their Aging Parents," *HomeSmart*, February 19, 2011, homesmart.org.

"Newest Communities," *Fellowship for Intentional Community*, 2016, ic.org.

"Communities by Country," *Fellowship for Intentional Community*, 2016, ic.org.

"Welcome to the Fellowship for Intentional Community," *Fellowship for Intentional Community*, 2016, ic.org.

"About the Fellowship for Intentional Community," *Fellowship for Intentional Community*, 2016, icorg.

"Cohousing in the United States: An Innovative Model of Sustainable Neighborhoods," *The Cohousing Association of the United States,* April 22, 2016, cohousing.org.

Keith Wardrip, "Fact Sheet: Cohousing for Older Adults," *AARP,* March 2010, aarp.org.

"Senior Cohousing: Completed and In-Process Communities," *The Cohousing Association of the United States,* July 15, 2016, cohousing.org.

"Roommate Agreement," *The Big Bang Theory,* 2016, the-big-bang-theory.com.

"What Is an Ecovillage," *Red Iberia de Ecoaldeas,* 2016, rie.ecovillage.org.

Kim Velsey, "Celebrity Rejects," *Observer,* May 11, 2016, observer.com.

"About United States of America," *Co-operative Housing International,* 2016, housinginternational .coop.

"A Look at Student Housing Cooperatives," *Fellowship for Intentional Community,* 2016, ic.org.

Andrew Scharlach, Carrie Graham and Amanda Lehning, "The 'Village' Model: A Consumer-Driven Approach for Aging in Place," *Oxford Journals,* March 30, 2011, gerontologist.oxfordjournals .org.

"Village to Village Network helps communities establish and manage their own Villages," *Village to Village Network,* 2016, vtvnetwork.org.

Sherri Snelling, "The Village Movement: Redefining Aging in Place," *Next Avenue,* June 4, 2012, nextavenue.org.

"What percentage of the American population lives near the coast?," *National Oceanic and Atmospheric Administration,* 2016, oceanservice.noaa.gov.

Christopher Mims, "Driverless Cars to Fuel Suburban Sprawl," *The Wall Street Journal,* June 20, 2016, wsj.com.

Chapter Nineteen: A Second Home

Adam Desanctis, "Vacation Home Sales Retreat, Investment Sales Leap in 2015," *National Association of Realtors,* April 6, 2016, nar.realtor.com.

"Where's Your Next Hideaway," *The Hideaways Club,* 2016, thehideawaysclub.com.

"Celebrate Your Love for Travel . . . Year After Year," *Banyan Tree Private Collection*, 2016, bt privatecollection.com.

"Timeshares and Vacation Plans," *Federal Trade Commission,* 2016, consumer.ftc.gov.

"Travel Well. Live Inspired," *Inspirato,* 2016, inspirato.com.

"Your Home. Away From Home," *Destination M,* 2016, destination-m.com.

"It's Your World. Enjoy it!," *Quintess Collection,* 2016, quintess.com.

"Timeshares and Vacation Plans," *Federal Trade Commission,* 2016, consumer.ftc.gov.

Chapter Twenty: Long-Term Care in the Future

Loraine A. West, Samantha Cole, Daniel Goodkind and Wan He, "65+ in the United States: 2010," *United States Census Bureau,* June 2014, census.gov.

"A Profile of Older Americans: 2015," *Administration on Aging,* 2016, aoa.acl.gov.

"Cost of Care," *Genworth Financial,* June 22, 2016, genworth.com.

"Who Needs Care?," *Administration on Aging,* 2016, longtermcare.gov.

Barbara Feder Ostrov, "Why Long-term Care Insurance Is Becoming a Tougher Call," *Time,* March 8, 2016, time.com.

Chapter Twenty-one: Estate Planning for the Family of the Future

Peter Diamandis, "Are We Moving Closer to Having Designer Babies?," *The Huffington Post,* October 2, 2016, huffingtonpost.com.

Michael J. Rosenfeld, "Marriage, Choice, and Couplehood in the Age of the Internet," *Stanford University,* April 20, 2016, web.stanford.edu.

Kimberly Leonard, "Moms Are Older Than They Used to Be," *U.S. News,* January 14, 2016, usnews.com.

Wendy Wang and Kim Parker, "Record Share of Americans Have Never Married," *Pew Research Center,* September 24, 2014, pewsocialtrends.org.

"17 Percent Have Said 'I Do' More Than Once, Census Bureau Reports," *United States Census Bureau,* March 10, 2015, census.gov.

Belinda Luscombe, "How Shacking Up Before Marriage Affects a Relationship's Success," *Time,* March 12, 2014, time.com.

Amanda Gardner, "More U.S. Couples Living Together Instead of Marrying, CDC Finds," *U.S. News,* April 4, 2013, health.usnews.com.

Glenn Stanton, "What Is the Actual US Divorce Rate and Risk?," *The Witherspoon Institute,* December 16, 2015, thepublicdiscourse.com.

Jennifer Newton, "Over 50s fuel U.S. divorce revolution: Record number of older couples break up with a quarter now splitting later in life," *Daily Mail,* November 3, 2015, dailymail.co.uk.

Sam Roberts, "Divorce After 50 Grows More Common," *The New York Times,* September 20, 2013, nytimes.com.

D'Vera Cohn, "How many same-sex married couples in the U.S.? Maybe 170,000," *Pew Research Center,* June 24, 2015, pewresearch.org.

Warner Todd Huston, "Interracial Marriages on the Rise in the US," *Breitbart,* January 4, 2015, breitbart.com.

Ron L. Deal, "Marriage, Family & Stepfamily Statistics," *Smart Stepfamilies,* April 2014, smartstepfamilies.com.

"10 Percent of Grandparents Live with a Grandchild, Census Bureau Reports," *United States Census Bureau,* October 22, 2014, census.gov.

Dawn, "Single Mother Statistics," *Single Mother Guide,* September 17, 2016, singlemotherguide.com.

"Surprising facts about birth in the United States," *Baby Center,* April 2015, babycenter.com.

"Marriage and Divorce," *Centers for Disease Control and Prevention,* 2016, cdc.gov.

"Marriages and Divorces," *Divorce Statistics,* 2016, divorcestatistics.org.

"32 Shocking Divorce Statistics," *McKinley Irvin Family Law,* October 30, 2012, mckinleyirvin.com.

"Why Marriage Matters: Facts and Figures," *For Your Marriage,* 2016, foryourmarriage.org.

"Unmarried Childbearing," *Centers for Disease Control and Prevention,* 2016, cdc.gov.

Rae Ellen Bichell, "Average Age of First-Time Moms Keeps Climbing in the U.S.," *NPR,* January 14, 2016, npr.org.

"How Many Children Were Adopted in 2007 and 2008," *Child Welfare Information Gateway,* September 2011, childwelfare.com.

Karen Valby, "The Realities of Raising a Kid of a Different Race," *Time,* 2016, time.com.

Jennifer J. Wioncek and Michael D. Melrose, "Florida Passes Fiduciary Access to Digital Assets Act," *Wealth Management,* June 27, 2016, wealthmanagement.com.

Erik Sherman, "State lets heirs access dead person's online accounts," *CBS News,* August 19, 2014, cbsnews.com.

"What is a legacy contact on Facebook?," *Facebook,* 2016, facebook.com.

"About Inactive Account Manager," *Google,* 2016, support.google.com.

"Beyond the bucket list: Experience leisure in a whole new way," *Merrill Lynch,* 2016, ml.com.

Epilogue: Welcome to the Greatest Time of Your Life

Alyssa Brown and Lindsey Sharpe, "Americans' Financial Well-Being Is Lowest, Social Highest," *Gallup,* July 7, 2014, gallup.com.

Index

About the Author

Acclaimed Financial Advisor

Ric is one of the nation's most recognized financial advisors. He was named the no.1 Independent Financial Advisor by *Barron's* three times,[1] and in 2016 was named among the country's Top Ten Wealth Advisors by *Forbes* magazine.[2] RIABiz named Ric one of the "10 most influential figures" in the investment advisory field,[3] and *InvestmentNews* named him among the "15 most transformative people in the industry"[4]. Ric was also voted by readers of *Wealth Management* as one of the "four most influential people in the financial services field."[5]

Bestselling Author, Radio and TV Host and Educator

Ric is a no.1 *New York Times* best-selling author. With more than 1 million copies collectively in print, his books on personal finance have been translated into several languages and educated countless people worldwide. Ric's radio show has been on the air for more than 25 years and is heard throughout the country. For three years in a row, Ric was named among the top 100 talk radio hosts by *TALKERS* magazine,[6] which in 2012 named his program the no. 2 most important weekend-only talk show in the nation.[7] Ric's television series, *The Truth About Money*, airs on public television stations across the United States and in Asia and is available on Amazon Prime.

Ric also offers an award-winning 16-page monthly newsletter and free online personal finance advice, information and education at RicEdelman.com, and he is a popular speaker.

Philanthropic Activities

Ric and Jean Edelman support numerous charities and philanthropic organizations. They are benefactors of the Jean and Ric Edelman Fossil Park and the Edelman Planetarium, both at Rowan University, and the Inova Edelman Center for Nursing at Inova Health Foundation, as well as the Inova Center for Advanced Medical Simulation and the Northern Virginia Therapeutic Riding Program. They also support the STEM Learning Program at the Wolf Trap Foundation for the Performing Arts, HEROES, Make-A-Wish Foundation, the Leukemia & Lymphoma Society and many others.

[1]According to *Barron's*, "The formula [used] to rank advisors has three major components: assets managed, revenue produced and quality of the advisor's practice. Investment returns are not a component of the rankings because an advisor's returns are dictated largely by each client's risk tolerance. The quality-of-practice component includes an evaluation of each advisor's regulatory record." The rankings are based on the universe of applications submitted to *Barron's*. The selection process begins with a nomination and application provided to *Barron's*. Principals of Edelman Financial Services LLC self-nominated the firm and submitted quantitative and qualitative information to *Barron's* as requested. *Barron's* reviewed and considered this information, which resulted in the rankings on Aug. 27, 2012/Aug. 28, 2010/Aug. 31, 2009.

[2]*Forbes* rankings are the opinion of SHOOK Research and are based on advisor interviews, client retention, industry experience, compliance record, assets under management and revenue generated for the firm. Investment performance is not considered. Advisors do not pay to be in the ranking.

[3]The RIABiz listing of the 10 most influential figures in the Registered Investment Advisor industry is in recognition of notable, driven and influential executives who are advancing their firms and are considered to be influential in the RIA business. Investor experience/returns were not considered as part of this ranking.

[4]*InvestmentNews* 15th Anniversary Issue. June 23, 2013.

[5]Wealthmanagement.com/WealthManagement Madness, March 2014.

[6]*Talkers* Magazine "Heavy Hundred" ranking is based on a number of both quantitative and qualitative criteria and is determined by collective analysis of the TALKERS editorial board with input from a wide variety of industry leaders. Investor experience/returns were not considered as part of this ranking.

[7]*Talkers* Magazine "250 Most Important Radio Talk Show Hosts in America" ranking (April 2012) is based on courage, effort, impact, longevity, potential, ratings, recognition, revenue, service, talent and uniqueness of the talk show host.

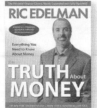

The Truth About Money

The 4th Edition is a comprehensive, practical, "how-to" manual on financial planning, and is one of the most highly acclaimed books in the personal finance field. You'll discover everything you need to know about investments, insurance, long-term care, planning for retirement, buying and selling your home, getting out of debt, how to pay for college, weddings and cars — and much more.

🏆 *New York Times* Bestseller
🏆 Book of the Year Award for Excellence in Financial Literacy Education — Institute for Financial Literacy[8]

🏆 Gold Medal Axiom Award[9]
🏆 Apex Award[10]
🏆 Book of the Year — *Small Press* magazine[11]

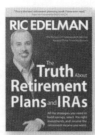

The Truth About Retirement Plans and IRAs

The #1 national bestseller[12] from the #1 independent financial advisor in America, ranked three times by *Barron's*[1] is a guide to making the most of your retirement plans and assuring long-term financial security.

🏆 #1 *Washington Post* Bestseller[12]

🏆 *Publishers Weekly* Bestseller[13]

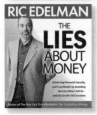

The Lies About Money

Ric shares his most valuable lessons gained through two decades of working directly with individuals and families. He reveals the lies that have infiltrated your retail mutual funds and retirement accounts, and teaches you how to invest your money in your employer retirement plan, how to save for college, and for those who are retired, how to generate more income without sacrificing security.

🏆 Axiom Personal Finance Book of the Year[14]

🏆 Book of the Year Award for Excellence in Financial Literacy Education — Institute for Financial Literacy[15]

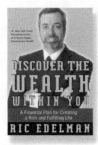

Discover the Wealth Within You

Everyone knows that financial planning is all about goals. But most people incorrectly think that financial goals consist of paying for a child's college education, covering major medical expenses and preparing for retirement. Ric points out in *Discover The Wealth Within You*, those aren't goals, they're obligations. And that's why most people rarely get excited about financial planning. He shows that paying attention to the pursuit of happiness can turn financial planning—a task many people find boring and even downright onerous—into an exciting adventure.

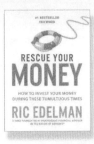

Rescue Your Money

In this updated edition of his 2009 bestseller,[16] Ric offers no-nonsense, practical advice for how to keep your investments safe in any economic climate.

Everyone knows that the ideal investment strategy is to buy low and sell high. But how do you know what stocks will pay off? And how do you know when it's the right time to sell? No matter what you hear, there's no such thing as a sure bet: following fads, listening to the media, and even taking the advice of an investment manager on a roll won't guarantee a payout. To help you understand how to do it correctly, Edelman shows you the one major goal you should have as you seek investment success; the two major obstacles you'll encounter; the one big question you'll have to face; and two basic "truths" that confront—and confound—every investor.

🏆 #1 *Washington Post* Bestseller[16]

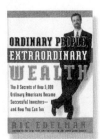

Ordinary People, Extraordinary Wealth

How did a secretary, a firefighter, a retired naval officer, a housewife, a construction worker, a schoolteacher, and a pharmacist become wealthy? Ric studied the wealth-making habits of these and 5,000 other ordinary Americans and reveals his findings in this extraordinary book that outlines in eight easy, practical steps and secrets to achieving and maintaining wealth.

🏆 #1 *New York Times* Bestseller

The New Rules of Money

In *The New Rules of Money*, Ric puts you on the right financial course. His 88 strategies are fun to read and easy to follow, and he shows you how to maximize your personal finances in today's economic climate. He tells you the best strategies for paying for college, buying a home, saving on taxes, and choosing the right investments. He changes your thinking on insurance, retirement, and estate planning.

What You Need to Do Now

In troubled times, it's only natural to worry about financial security. Ric provides a back-to-basics plan for getting started on the road to financial freedom.

The time to act is now — to preserve your financial well-being, secure your family's future, and ensure your peace of mind.

Ric gives you an eight-point action plan to secure your financial independence.

*Available at booksellers everywhere

[8]In 2011 *The Truth About Money* 4th Edition received the Book of the Year Award from the Institute for Financial Literacy for Excellence in Financial Literacy Education. Each year, the Institute for Financial Literacy presents EIFLE Awards to individuals and organizations that have shown exceptional innovation, dedication and commitment to the field of financial literacy education.

[9]In March 2012 *The Truth About Money* 4th Edition was named Book of the Year by the Axiom Business Book Awards for earning the Gold Medal in the category of Personal Finance/Retirement Planning/Investing. This award was presented by Jenkins Group Inc., operators of IndependentPublisher.com.

[10]In 2011 the Award for Excellence as a Book/eBook, from the APEX Awards for Publication Excellence, was issued to *The Truth About Money* 4th Edition. The Annual APEX Awards for Publication Excellence is an annual competition for Communications Professionals. Awards are based on excellence in graphic design, editorial content and the ability to achieve overall communications excellence. APEX Grand Awards honor the outstanding works in each main category, while APEX Awards of Excellence recognize exceptional entries in each of the individual categories.

[11]In 1997 *The Truth About Money* 1st Edition was named Business Book of the Year by *Small Press* magazine for earning the Gold Medal in the category of Business. The books were judged on content, originality, design and production quality. With that in mind, the award would honor the many people who worked to publish the book: author, editor, designer and publisher. This award was presented by Jenkins Group Inc., operators of IndependentPublisher.com.

[12]*The Washington Post*, Washington Bestsellers Paperback Nonfiction General. April 20, 2014.

[13]*Publishers Weekly*, Publisher's Weekly Trade Paperback. Week ending April 13, 2014, powered by Nielsen Bookscan.

[14]In March 2008 *The Lies About Money* was named Personal Finance Book of the Year by the Axiom Business Book Awards for earning the Gold Medal in the category of Personal Finance. This award was presented by Jenkins Group Inc., operators of IndependentPublisher.com.

[15]In 2009 *The Lies About Money* received the Retail Book of the Year Award from the Institute for Financial Literacy for Excellence in Financial Literacy Education. Each year, the Institute for Financial Literacy presents EIFLE Awards to individuals and organizations that have shown exceptional innovation, dedication and commitment to the field of financial literacy education.

[16]*The Washington Post*, Washington Bestsellers Paperback Nonfiction/General. March 29, 2009.

[17]As of January 5, 2017